WOMAN'S
CREATION

WOMAN'S CREATION

Sexual Evolution and the Shaping of Society

Elizabeth Fisher

McGraw-Hill Book Company

New York   St. Louis   San Francisco   Bogotá   Düsseldorf   Madrid
Mexico   Montreal   Panama   Paris   São Paulo   Tokyo   Toronto

An earlier abbreviated version of "Mother and Child: The First Couple" was published in APHRA, Spring-Summer 1976, Vol. VI, Nos. 3 and 4, under the title "In the Beginning Was the Dyad."

Grateful acknowledgment is made for the following quotations: "Because I Know So Little" by Jane Mayhall, © 1972 by The New York Times Company, reprinted by permission of the author and the New York Times; The Mountain Gorilla by George B. Schaller, pp. 283–84, The University of Chicago Press, 1963, © 1963 by George B. Schaller, permission granted by the publisher; The Masks of God: Occidental Mythology by Joseph Campbell, pp. 82–83, Viking Compass Edition, © 1963 by Joseph Campbell, reprinted by permission of the publisher, Viking Penguin Inc.

Reprinted by Arrangement with Doubleday & Company
First McGraw-Hill Paperback edition, 1980
1 2 3 4 5 6 7 8 9   FGFG   8 7 6 5 4 3 2 1 0

Library of Congress Cataloging in Publication Data

   Fisher, Elizabeth.
     Woman's creation.

   Reprint of the ed. published by Doubleday, New York.
   Bibliography: p.
   Includes index.
   1. Sex role. 2. Social evolution. I. Title.
  [GN479.65.F57 1980]   301.41'2   79-26916
ISBN: 0-07-021105-1

Because I Know So Little

Because I know so little, I grope for more.
If I knew as much as you, I'd be afraid to
try my luck. I'd be stuck on the sticks of
reason, information that comes to naught.
You, who tell me life is useless rubbish,
and you can prove it with a twirl of diagrams,
heavy numbers. I can't concentrate on that,
I search through my dumb old feelings. And
trust and plough into what I'd like to be
true, mysteries, dark, unending, and all the
black night of search and dreaming, always
open, unanswered, shining through.

Jane Mayhall

To my parents and to *APHRA*

Acknowledgments

There were many who helped me along the way. This book would not have been possible without the revival of feminism, in the Women's Liberation Movement beginning about 1967, and the innumerable women whose thinking contributed to my own ideas.

I want to thank all those who wrote for and edited APHRA; it was in our discussions about the magazine and the movement that my ideas took form. In the early years particularly, from 1969 to 1973, method and feeling were united and the creative process of the group endeavor—the very real lift of women helping women—was carried over into the initial stages of this work also. There were fruitful interchanges with Ellen Harold, Margaret Lamb, Vivien Leone, and Leah Zahler, all of whom contributed ideas, intellectual stimulus, and research leads.

In the academic world many new acquaintances gave time and critical thought. Sally Binford read an early draft of Part I; Ruby Rohrlich-Leavitt read a draft of Parts I to III; while Eleanor Leacock read the next to last draft of Parts I to IV. They were generous with comment, corrections, and reference sources.

Two three-month fellowships at the MacDowell Colony and one three-month stay at the Virginia Center for the Creative Arts supported me in parlous times. Libraries became my dearest haunts; the several libraries of New York University provided the major sources from which I worked. There were also the University of Virginia Library with its open stacks, the State Library of New Hampshire through the patience of the Peterborough Town Library, the library of the Wenner-Gren

Foundation, and a fruitful month at the Frederick Lewis Allen Room of the New York Public Library. To all of them I owe thanks and apologies, for books borrowed and kept overlong.

Alix Shulman encouraged and advised. Gloria Dialectic read and criticized and discussed. My agent Ellen Levine maintained belief in the book during the long waiting.

After I had already handed in a draft of the book, Rosemary Poulos suggested a missing piece of the puzzle, in conversation, enabling me to revise Part IV so as to make a more cohesive theory.

Mary Nelson and Lillian Shelton helped with typing and research for the earlier versions. Evelyn Patterson typed the final draft, fitting my needs into her very limited time, deciphering my chicken tracks to produce accurate typescript, and enjoying the work besides. Nina Masonson helped track down recalcitrant sources and read and corrected notes and bibliography. Candace Watt proofread galleys.

Dolores Walker provided counsel over the years. Vera Schneider helped me to clarify and organize the book into its present form and prepared the bibliography. At a crucial moment she restored my confidence in myself and in the work, enabling me to bring it to a conclusion. Savelli stayed with me in a rocky period and helped me by advice and example. During the seven years it took me to write this book, I could always count on my long-time friend and sister Gerry Sachs for encouragement and support. In a world where even one friend is a miracle, I found I had several.

Contents

Introduction

This book began to write itself in 1971. It grew out of an essay I wrote that spring for Volume 2, Number 2, of *APHRA*, which we called The Whore Issue, for it was devoted to prostitution. Partly by default, partly by desire, I was elected to write an article that would tie together the magazine's contents. With ten days before deadline, I found myself in the Reference Room of the New York Public Library on Fifth Avenue and Forty-second Street, looking at two drawers of cards listing their material on prostitution. The enormity of the subject and the small amount of time available made it clear that research was impossible at the moment so I sat down and did a speculation about the meaning of prostitution in a patriarchal society, titling it "Hustlers All."

Afterward, dissatisfied and provoked, I had a halcyon week of intense cerebration in which the plan and themes of the book were born. After one visionary night, I said to myself, "I've just rewritten Engels' *Origin of the Family, Private Property, and the State*," which was patently untrue since at that moment I had written nothing, though later on it would be true and untrue. I had no concept of how far afield the research would take me, of how many byways I would traverse or disciplines enter upon, of what an extraordinary self-education would be involved.

There was one time around 1973 and 1974 when, dissatisfied with the extant translations of Sumerian and Akkadian, I contemplated applying for a grant to learn cuneiform—the wedge-shaped signs on clay that are believed to have been the first written language. I slogged on instead, comparing one translation with another and trusting also to my judgment as a translator—though I had worked only from Italian and French—and as a researcher. In the process of digging one finds information to prove many points. In the long run one scholar's version is chosen over another's on the basis of past experience and past reading and of what seems logical and valid; obviously emotional response plays a critical role in the decision.

Once embarked upon the project I realized that the book had been many years, most of my adult life, in the shaping, though the immediate impetus came from the thinking engendered by those early years of the Women's Liberation Movement. It did not begin as a women's liberation book per se. I had been struggling over these problems from my first introduction to political ideas in early adolescence. It was, however, an attempt to look with a female perspective at what till now had been seen largely through the male eye. The stimulus and excitement born of the movement, of shared ideas and of women talking and writing to and for each other, gave me courage to see my disadvantages as assets and to dare such an ambitious undertaking. In the idealism of those first years, we had had a vision that the whole sickness of civilization could be seen in miniature in the power nexus between the sexes and that in attacking the latter we could also come out with a kinder, more just, and loving world. Things have not turned out to be that simple, but it should be remembered that the movement's origins were political and idealistic, a search for understanding which would change thinking and doing.

In my years of editing *APHRA* I saw much of the work that came out of the movement: the underground newspapers, the manifestoes, the pamphlets, the articles, the books. Within the mass were brilliantly provocative ideas and facts, and much, much testimony. Ideas fed on each other, going back and forth; new intellectual possibilities arose. For thousands of years, men's experiences had been considered objective reality, women's labeled narcissism. We realized we must develop a new methodology. Carol Hanisch formulated the statement, the personal is political, a concept not new to art or artists, and we decided that our thinking could and should be shaped by our own and other women's personal experiences. At the same time we had to go back and to re-examine everything we had been taught, testing it in the light of our new awareness about the upper-class male framework in which history had been written as well as the sexual bias inherent in the English language. Later I was to hear academic women complain that perhaps the worst crime perpetrated on women was the internalization of male thinking. Whatever the defects of my education, I was spared much of that approach. I had not had to write for the grades and approval of a male-oriented academic establishment, permitting me fresh insights and an unconventional approach.

In a recent television interview Simone de Beauvoir said that all her intellectual influences were male. Though I was introduced early on to certain beacons—Marx-Engels, Wilhelm Reich, Kropotkin, in that order and widely separated in time—many of my influences were female. As it happened, women, not men, encouraged me to write, and read and discussed my work. When I began to write seriously, women writers treated me as a colleague and provided intellectual stimulus. In the late nineteen fifties and early sixties I met several women whose dedication to art and ideas provided examples I could follow.

Two feminist classics taught me to question received authority. I came across Virginia Woolf's *A Room of One's Own* one summer when I was seventeen and never saw the world—and male dignity—in the same light again. A few years later Ruth Herschberger's *Adam's Rib* confirmed for me what I was learning in life about the slanted vision and particularity of the experts. At the time I was earning my living with skills centered around writing and editing. From finding mistakes in the Encyclopaedia Britannica to watching the process of arbitrary judgment and borrowing involved in producing a new dictionary, lessons in skepticism were not wanting.

As the work progressed, many of my hunches would be verified by material published after I had formulated my own ideas so that I could go back and rewrite with more confidence. I had already questioned the received tenets of ethology in the first section of the book when David Pilbeam's article attacking naked apery came my way. And I had written the first version of the Sumerian chapters before Thorkild Jacobsen published *The Treasures of Darkness,* confirming and adding substance to my vision of Sumerian religion as a political expression of support for hierarchical authority.

In our time the myth of neutrality, impartial intellectual objectivity, has finally been demolished. There is no intelligence without feeling. In order to think you need to care. One may feel in negative, destructive ways, but hostile or positive, you cannot think without wanting to think, and that's desire.

Numbers are not without association, as in the probably apocryphal tale about the now-extinct Tasmanians' counting system—one, two, plenty—or our own special feelings about the holy three and cabbalistic magic in numbers. Words are all the more replete with associations and with their specific historical uses in each language.

Observers bring their own experiences with them: women and men have a different reality. Several articles and books have been written to point up how the limitations of English, where the male form is the prototype and the female the variation, force a certain amount of sexism on the most recalcitrant writer, womanfully though we struggle against it.

The usage of the generic term *man* and of male pronouns to cover both sexes effectively excludes women from conscious thought much of the time. With one word to cover two meanings—the abstract generic for humanity, humans, or humankind that in Latin is *homo,* and the specific gendered individual of the male sex known as *vir* in Latin—writers switch back and forth between both meanings or use them interchangeably with resultant confusion. For this reason, I avoid the male pronoun unless I am specifically referring to male individuals, and I use *man* or *men* in the limited sense only, choosing derivatives of *homo* for the generic usage. In quotations from other writers, I italicize *man* or *he* when it is used in the general sense, not for sarcasm or irony, but to point up what I consider intellectually questionable usage, a confusion which serves to misdirect thinking and keep women invisible. Similarly, unless otherwise indicated, italicized emphasis in quotations is mine, not the authors', to call attention to the cultural bias we have inherited from the past.

A related decision concerned the use of dates. In the first four parts of the book, the archaeologists' term B.P. (before the present) refers to actual years past rather than the supposed beginning of the Christian or Common Era. In Part V, when I take up the beginnings of historical civilization with the invention of writing, I have adopted the dates used in most sources, so as not to place an extra burden on reader and author. From Chapter 29 to the end of the book, I use B.C.E. and C.E. Thus first millennium refers to the thousand years between the presumed birth of Jesus Christ and 1000 B.C.E., second millennium to the previous thousand years, and so forth.

In the Hebrew calendar, by coincidence, I would find myself with a dating scheme rather closer to the initiation of writing since it begins 5,738 years before this current year of 1978; in the Chinese I would be using the date 4738. Though custom forces a Western, white, European date scheme on one who is writing within our time and context, we can, and we must, remind ourselves of the limitations and artificial conventions within which we are constricted even as we strive after closer approximations to understanding.

Finally, in the words of Herodotus, I will not apologize for digression: digression is part of the plan.

ELIZABETH FISHER

Part I

MOTHER
AND CHILD:
THE FIRST COUPLE

Men have had every advantage of us in telling their own story. Education has been theirs in so much higher degree, the pen has been in their hands. I will not allow books to prove anything.

—Jane Austen, *Persuasion*

1

Science Imitates Society

How did woman come to be the prototype possession? Almost universally, she has been treated as property to be traded, sold, or otherwise disposed of. In Western culture it is the father who gives the bride away, in the Trobriand Islands the mother's brother, among the African Hadza it is the mother who receives strings of beads as bride price for her daughter, but the girl herself is still being bestowed on a man.

In some societies women are measured in cattle—so many head to acquire a bride; in others the groom and his kinsmen baldly describe marriage, "We pay for her genitals."[1]

Long before Descartes shaped his proof of existence by way of the mind, the first principle of man's dawning consciousness would seem to have been "I own, therefore I am." And shaped by human preconceptions, behavioral scientists—psychologists and ethologists—have looked at animals and tried to interpret their actions by the same theorem. They have seen possession as the first aim of man and animal, and interpreted nature as a scheme of conquest and arrogation, with sex as the first battleground, the female the first conquered territory.

Moreover, since maleness has been associated with aggression for so long, the scientists have tended toward certain value judgments and confusions. There has been a basic assumption that male sexual activity and positions are admirable, the female's humiliating, and a second assumption that, maleness and aggression being almost synonymous, aggression is more to be admired than peacefulness, which latter is humiliating as well as female.

How did civilized man come to be dominant over woman? How did it get to be the way it is between the sexes?

The traditional answer is that it is a fact of nature, the result of the male animal's superior strength. Our whole civilization has taken it for granted, and language and culture are shot through with particulars sustaining and re-enforcing this position. Pyramidal hierarchy is seen as the basic order of nature, of all organic and often inorganic phenomena. Philosophy, science, and religion have based their premises on the female's natural inferiority to the male; in recent years ethologists, behavioral scientists who study animals, have charted animal life in terms of dominance-submission relationships with the female seen as universally submissive to the male. Aristotle, Hobbes, Rousseau, Darwin, Freud . . . most of the world's great thinkers have accepted women's inferiority as a first principle or an unexamined substratum when they presented their contributions to human understanding. Men and women, we have been exposed to it all our lives in almost every form of human intellectual or artistic striving and we are all, often unconsciously, deeply indoctrinated with this belief.

A more recent theory has it that in its origins the human species was socially organized as a matriarchy before the present patriarchal system was instituted. Nineteenth-century thinkers saw matriarchy as a lower order. Women, the reproducers, are closer to nature. In due time this lower social order gave way to the higher order of patriarchy, for intelligence is possessed in greater degree by the male; some thinkers saw it as a male attribute. And the patriarchy under which we now live was a necessary development for progress and civilization, though the more tolerant thinkers looked forward to a future when it would give way to a less cruel society. Forms of this theory were presented by the nineteenth-century scholar Bachofen and sustained by Marx and Engels. Discredited by late nineteenth- and early twentieth-century science, it was taken up by students of the human psyche and by artists.[2] In recent years some women have also seen in primitive matriarchy a partial redemption from the overwhelming blackness of the picture presented by the world of actuality and imagination as we know it. They have shaped the theory to say that matriarchy was not only the first but also the better order of human life and have traced our troubles—the actual position of women and the general ills of civilization—to the aggressiveness and misguided intelligence of the male dominators.[3]

A third theory, which has only very slowly gained ground among scientists, both ethologists and physical and social anthropologists, has it that humanity, being based on co-operation, has its origins in primitive egalitarianism and that this egalitarianism may even apply to the sexes, that the earliest humans shared tasks and that dominance is inherent neither in the animal world nor in humanity. That, in the last analysis, we have been misled by comparatively recent patterns of human history into misinterpreting what we see around us in nature and what we dig up to interpret the past.

One problem in studying our origins and the world around us is that language itself assumes that all life is constructed on the principles of the human patriarchy of Western civilization.

Biology as a science is very new—Darwin's *Origin of Species* was published in 1859, *The Descent of Man* in 1871. In the even newer sciences of psychology, anthropology, and ethology, historical preconceptions of the female's role have shaped the formulation and presentation of information. Scientists projected Western customs—where woman is treated as man's possession and the father gives his daughter to a son-in-law of his choice—onto unrelated fields and treated us to a view of animal and human behavior with the female as the universal possession. Thus ethologists tell of a male monkey "taking" or "possessing" a female, though their own descriptions make it clear that it was the female monkey who took the initiative, choosing time, place, and partner. They discuss sexual relations and "presenting"—an animal's act of offering or showing its hindquarters to another animal. Though this might be considered a sexual gesture with a connotation of genital pleasure, it has been made into an indication of both female behavior and submission. As Wolfgang Wickler says, "In the social context, male sexual actions imply dominance and female sexual actions submissiveness. . . . if a male rhesus monkey mounts another male, it is the more dominant individual that plays the masculine role."[4]

According to many ethologists, the subordinate male presents to the dominant male as a conciliation-humiliation technique, and he is described as "cringing," "crouching," etc., words also frequently used to refer to the female animal. If it were viewed as distraction behavior—some animals don't feel like fighting, as some humans don't feel like fighting—we would have less emotional response. And the fact of the matter is that it is not a clear-cut distinction, except in the minds of the observers and the possibly artificial categories invented by the ethologists. Sometimes it is the "subordinate" who mounts, rather than presenting, and sometimes the "dominant male" presents his rear. Infant langur monkeys have a syndrome at about age two of "mounting": they jump up on adult males and hug them around the waist. Clearly the words are far from adequate to describe what really goes on.[5]

As long as the masculine role is aggrandized and the female role derogated, as long, that is, as nature is seen from a male-supremacist view, human sexual encounters will be tainted. We are imprisoned in a conquest vocabulary which places females in the "submissive position." Convention equates the female's role in sex with surrender rather than admitting that, animal or human, surrender-aggression is involved for each sex, a reciprocal relationship in which sometimes the female approaches the male and the male refuses or accepts and vice versa; reciprocity exists among animals as among people, though on different and more shallow levels, and both sexes participate. Among mammals, rape does not normally occur, and it is the female who calls the tune, whereas among humans, with the invention of sexual coercion, it is more often the male who leads.

Anthropologists' reports on human groups which took shape outside the enslaving and colonizing traditions of the West are also distorted by subjectivity. Claude Lévi-Strauss based a whole theory of human relatedness on the premise that in human society a man must obtain a woman from another man, who gives him a daughter or a sister.[6] In *The Elementary Structures of Kinship* he described all human relations in terms of men, with women as the medium of exchange connecting them. He used Radcliffe-Brown's reports on Australian Aborigines, gathering and hunting peoples who had never developed agriculture, to formulate universal rules about marriage and kinship systems, whereby marriage and family were forms of communication for men, based on reciprocal exchanges of women. It was a typical male cosmology; how or whether women communicated or what existence they had beyond serving the purpose of their male relatives was none of his concern.

Fortunately for human knowledge, some other anthropologists did field work among these bands and discovered that the elegant symmetry of Lévi-Strauss's theory had no relation to the Australians' reality. The complicated exchanges across group subdivisions described by Radcliffe-Brown were not those the Aborigines themselves observed. However, though the later anthropologists negated the Lévi-Strauss concept, they themselves decided that women were still being exchanged by men, not as communication, but because they belonged to different clans with gathering and hunting rights on specific land areas. Accordingly men enlarged their economic possibilities by marrying women of different clans, thus gaining hunting rights over additional pieces of land. Women were still being seen as the primordial possession, whether used for economic advantage or for communication.[7]

The truth of the matter is that none of these anthropologists really told us how the Australians themselves regarded women, for they interpreted the Aborigines' actions in light of their own assumptions. The tribes under discussion did not recognize paternity. For them a woman was a being who produced children regularly thoughout the period between puberty and menopause. In the Aborigines' eyes the man with whom she was living had no connection with these biological facts. Although it was recognized that biological paternity did not exist for these Australians, man-woman relationships were still described in a projection from Western mores: "A woman passes through the possession of quite a number of different men in her lifetime."[8] It was as though a man possessed a woman just by the act of going to bed with her, when the simple fact was that a woman could expect to have several husbands during her life.

Actually the relationship of the Australian Aborigine woman and man is a reciprocal economic one: she gathers and does some hunting, supplying 70 to 80 per cent of the food, he hunts for the remaining 30 or 20. She cooks the food she has found, and he prepares that which he has obtained. Marriages are arranged by older men and women, but after adolescence the participants usually manage to assert their own desires. This information has become available only in the past decade or so, partly because of the increased participation of women anthropologists and the revival of hitherto buried material, partly through the application of new ecological perspectives.[9]

Modern science developed out of a civilization based on war and slavery, and it has produced the threat of planetary destruction, along with numerous benefits. In consequence, there is a new respect for those long-surviving peoples who used to be called primitive, ignorant, and incompetent, as well as interest in other forms of life that can enlighten us about the destructive elements now threatening our own society.

2

The Idea of Dominance

Civilization is stratified, and in consequence when scientists looked at nature they tended to see it in terms of pyramidal hierarchy rather than interlocking vectors. The twentieth-century science of ethology was no exception. It was founded on principles of dominance-submission and the charting of animal hierarchies. Like Lévi-Strauss's kinship theory, these would seem to be elegant constructs bearing a limited relation to reality. Dominance is, after all, a laboratory concept. It simply means that when a piece of food is thrown before two animals, one of them often defers to the other, seeming to acknowledge the other's prior right rather than risk a fight. It was first noted in relation to chickens, and it does not extend in ramifications to the liege-lord fealty value human psychologists have assigned it. Once accepted, it was used in laboratory experiments to prove all kinds of things: that males dominate females, elders youngers, largers smallers, but mostly on the basis of projections already in the minds of the experimenters. Small wonder that it was ill-fitting and uncomfortable when applied to observations in the wild. And small wonder also that male and female observers often came up with different results, with males being more likely to discern sharp dominance-submission relations than females.

Phyllis Jay's studies of langur monkeys in India found them unaggressive and unhierarchical, the females strongly oriented to maternal behavior. She noted that when a langur was born, it was often passed around from female to female and touched and caressed.[1] When a team of Japanese and Indian men studied langurs, their description of langur troop organization and aggressive behavior was significantly different from Jay's. One of the most startling discrepancies was that where she had only seen baby langurs passed from monkey to monkey and returned to their mothers, they also saw infants "kidnaped" by females from other troops and observed that "when a newborn infant was taken by a female from a neighboring troop, it was usually difficult for the mother to get her infant back."[2]*

Another example of what might well be a subjective view is the description by Kinji Imanishi of male dominants monopolizing female Japanese macaques at Takasakiyama: "It is observed that some estrous females *escape* from the central part and make a *secret* consort relation with one of the males in the peripheral part."[3]

In recent years, both the concept of dominance and the related hypothesis that the highest-ranking males produce the most offspring have been questioned by female and male investigators. It was found that the various measures of dominance were not consistent one with another: a monkey who ranked high on the dominance scale by one criterion—say, mounting— did not necessarily achieve a high rank if measured by aggressive encounters. Thelma Rowell studied forest baboons in Uganda, and it is her opinion that dominance hierarchies are often a product of artificial laboratory situations. Observers make monkeys compete for a reward and then chart the ranks they themselves have produced.[4]

Within the diversity of nature isolated examples to prove almost any thesis can often be located, not to mention that a

---

* In partial explanation, the langurs studied by Jay lived in forested sections of India, while some of those studied by the Indian and Japanese observers lived in closer proximity to humans and to each other, factors believed to encourage aggressive and aberrant behavior. In recent years Sarah Blaffer Hrdy has studied langurs in southern India and observed infants kidnaped and murdered by males who were not initially troop members but who then joined the troops to which the murdered infants had belonged.

lively imagination can twist the supposed evidence of observation into proof of a subjective preconception. The notion of the female as passive and the male as active is a time-honored one, and many scientists of the last century took it for granted in their work. However, it is not so in nature, and the evidence has been as close as any country cat or dog.

Darwin's chivalrous notion of sexual selection—that the males fight for the possession of the female, who stands by and then accepts the winner ("the female, though comparatively passive, generally exerts some choice and *accepts* one male in preference to the others"), thereby ensuring the amelioration of the species—was a projection of Arthurian legends, the knight jousting for the favors of the fair lady.[5] In fact, Konrad Lorenz gives the latter as an example of sexual selection in humans, though surely medieval knights represented an infinitesimally tiny proportion of the human population at the time, the age of chivalry being more a literary phenomenon than an actual one.[6]

In any case, the notion that the male animal possesses a passive female is hogwash. No one possesses anyone. Animals meet, mate, and part, sometimes immediately, sometimes after the rearing of the young, even, as is presumed in the case of gibbons, wolves, and Canada geese, after a lifetime. There is no notion of possession in the limited mind of a male animal. Possession is a figment of human imagination. Perhaps it is human bravado in front of the universe, a way of asserting oneself against its immeasurable force. Still, the puny man who thinks he possesses land, or almost any commodity, is clearly illuding himself. Sometimes possessions possess us, but we are all possessed by time's sweep: even when we consume our possessions, it is only temporary; we are ourselves eventually consumed.

Mice are impervious to the labels attached to their behavior by human observers as well as to the philosophical implications out of which our language has grown. The female wild mouse is about as passive as Mae West. She marks her burrow with her own brand of perfume—her urine—a sign which says, in effect, "Hey, fellows, come up and see me. I want you." Or possibly "it," because what she wants is sex—or, in the language of the biologists, "relief of genital tension." She certainly doesn't want impregnation, though that is probably what will occur as the result of her actions. Male mice are attracted by the odor of the estrous female's urine. They mark the area with their own urine in response, rolling on her marking. If two males happen on her trademark at the same time, they may fight, but not if she's around. If she's there she begins sex relations, though whether she takes her choice or the one closest to her is not a question human observers can yet answer, Darwin's theory of sexual selection to the contrary. The female mouse copulates with numerous males in succession. Once copulation has begun, males do not fight or interfere.[7] The other mice wait patiently until the female is ready for them: they also service who only stand and wait. This is what occurs also among humankind's closest animal relatives, the chimpanzees, and there is certainly a long tradition of promiscuity or free sex in human life, whether in the recent custom of sexual swinging or in various sanctioned and unsanctioned forms throughout our existence.

Animal behaviorists often attempt to explain the order in which females copulate with males in terms of hierarchy, but actual observations are inconsistent with rigid theories about brute strength and bullying power being the directive behind sexual relations—at least where animals are concerned.[8]

The vocabulary of humankind gives us many semantical absurdities as it is applied to animals. Among the simians, for instance, in species where there is no sexual swelling—a visible indicator to mark the female primate's sexual desire—it is the female monkey who initiates sex. Thus, in one description of howler monkeys, "When a howler female's endocrines make her *receptive*, she *approaches* the male."[9] Primate observers constantly talk of the male or series of males "possessing" the female, though how anyone can know who possesses whom is beyond me. True, it is the male who is perched behind and over the female, but he cannot copulate without her aid and cooperation. Harry Harlow, famous psychologist at the University of Wisconsin, demonstrated this fact on rhesus monkeys, by rearing them in isolation so that they had no chance to learn about sexual behavior. (Afterward, being left with a batch of virgin monkeys, civilized humans introduced rape into the monkey cosmos. In order to breed the unco-operative females, the psychologists invented "a restraining device to hold the female in proper position . . . we call it the rape rack."[10])

"Mounting" is the male-oriented but not always accurate term of biology. The male chimpanzee sometimes stands behind the female, clasping her round the waist; other times he squats, with his buttocks barely clearing the ground. Gorillas have been observed to sit with the female before them, a position which George Schaller describes as seated in his lap, though to a woman observer the female gorilla might well appear to be on top, with her partner underneath.

When the male primate approaches the female with sex in mind, zoologists usually describe him in some admiring term of force or activity; when the female does likewise she is "soliciting" him—the same word used to describe a human prostitute. If a male ape or monkey looks at a female for purposes of sexual invitation it is a glare; if the female looks fixedly at the male for the same reason it is only a look or at best a stare. Lionel Tiger and Robin Fox speak of the female's estrous period as "a kind of sexual mania," though she is only doing what comes naturally and there is nothing maniacal about it for her, while K. R. L. Hall describes the female patas monkey's sexual approach as "a *cringing* half-run with short quick steps toward the adult male."[11] One wonders what adjective a male approach would have elicited.

Jane Goodall's articles on chimpanzees written for the academic communities use the conventional zoologists' phrase "period of sexual receptivity" to describe a chimpanzee in heat, but when she writes for the general public she speaks of sexual attractiveness. In *My Friends the Wild Chimpanzees* she describes ugly old Flo, the most aged female of the fifty-odd animals she had come to know individually during the years of her study: "Despite her decrepit appearance, she had more suitors than any other female," and she adds that while the female chimpanzee is normally attractive for ten days or so, one time Flo's period of sexual attractiveness lasted almost five weeks.[12]

The prospect does indeed rouse admiration in humans, taught that sexual attractiveness is chiefly a property of youth and beauty. Still, why not call it Flo's "period of sexual desire"? According to Goodall, she was followed constantly by a crowd of eager chimpanzees, so it must have been she who decided when, though whether copulations were indiscriminate or chosen does not come out in the report—only that there were seven in succession one time, twenty another. Nor was there any fighting or restiveness on the part of the waiting males, any particular dominance order observable.

Desire and sexual satisfaction as related to the female have been hard for the biologists to swallow. People thought that a scream emitted by female cats during the sex act was a scream of pain because the male cat's member is spiny. Still, we do not know what goes on in the mind of an animal when it screams, and animals are not the only creatures who have been known to scream with pleasure. An experiment with a smooth glass rod used in place of the male cat produced exactly the same sort of scream from the female cat—and the scientists were forced to admit that perhaps females, at least among the felines, do it because they want to, not because they are overpowered by a masterful male.[13]

In *The Naked Ape* Desmond Morris acknowledges satisfaction and orgasm in the human female but explains the woman's orgasm as "a borrowed male pattern" stemming from our upright posture. By his reasoning it is useful for the woman to lie still after sex, giving the sperm enough time to reach the egg. He claims there is no equivalent among the nonhuman primates. "The female monkey shows little sign of emotional upheaval and usually wanders off as if nothing had happened."[14] Recent researches contradict him. Animals are difficult to observe in the wild, and there are no primatologist equivalents of Masters and Johnson wiring apes and monkeys to meters and sensors in an effort to penetrate their physical and emotional responses. In 1971 Suzanne Chevalier-Skolnikoff conducted a year-long study at the Primates Laboratory of the Department of Psychiatry, Stanford University School of Medicine. She chose to observe stumptail macaques, monkeys whose sexual behavior has several characteristics that make them easier to observe than other monkeys. She produced incontrovertible evidence of orgasms in the females—"the first observations of orgasms in any nonhuman female mammal." She recorded both heterosexual and homosexual behavior among her subjects, reporting that homosexuality occurred in the rather high proportion of one to every four heterosexual encounters. Female homosexual behavior was observed more frequently than male homosexual activity—twenty-three female-female encounters, several of which led to orgasm, as opposed to thirteen male-male ones. "All normal animals probably have the capacity for both male and female sex roles throughout their lives," she concluded. Primatologists now acknowledge that female primates are capable of taking active roles in coitus and their capacity for orgasm is more similar to that of males than was previously thought.[15]

In Goodall's field observations the female chimps "remained still, moved away calmly, or rushed off screaming." Active participation by female as well as male is indicated by field studies, with varied reactions by each at the conclusion of each copulation. If anything, observations of the female primate's sexual activity corroborate Masters and Johnson's findings that women were capable of multiple orgasms, though one should be cautious in drawing analogies between animal and human behavior. On a purely physiological basis, female primates demonstrate, at certain given moments, a more intense sex drive and greater capacity for coitus than the male—behavior human males tend to characterize as "insatiable" or the afore-cited "sexual mania."

As far back as 1948, Ruth Herschberger had looked with a critical eye at the pronouncements of the supposedly objective scientists. In *Adam's Rib* she questioned the findings of the Yerkes Laboratory, where studies of chimpanzees were supposed to shed new light on the behavior of humans. She questioned the assumptions of experiments which purported to demonstrate that males were "naturally dominant" over females and to reveal a "biological basis of prostitution . . . the mature and sexually experienced female trades upon her ability to satisfy the sexual urge of the male." She pointed out that

Yerkes had manipulated his material. He had thrown out all observations "for Lia and Patti (two females) because they are highly dominant."[16] In other words, when females show dominance over males, their actions are disregarded in the statistical analysis because they might disprove the thesis already in the mind of the scientist.

In 1971, Naomi Weisstein commented on the limitations of psychology as a science. She describes the self-fulfilling prophecy built into experiments—how subjects perform to bear out the expectations of the experimenters: "If one group of experimenters has one hypothesis about what they expect to find, and another group of experimenters has the opposite hypothesis, both groups will obtain results in accord with their hypothesis. The results obtained are not due to mishandling of data by biased experimenters; rather the bias of the experimenter somehow creates a changed environment in which subjects act differently . . . students become intelligent because their teachers expect them to be intelligent, and rats run mazes better because experimenters are told rats are brighter [than the testers thought they were]."[17]

In other words, experiments generate their own answers according to what is in the experimenters' minds. Possibly the experimenters choose a form which prefigures results consistent with their prejudices or preconceptions.

One doesn't know how much effect the earlier book of Herschberger or the later paper of Weisstein has had. Yerkes is still revered as the father of a whole new area of science, and from its modest beginnings his laboratory has grown into a network of primate laboratories across the United States, while the study of apes and monkeys has mushroomed and spread all over the world. Laboratory science has been useful in medical research, testing drugs, discovering the pathology of cells, even for rough observation, say, on the growth cycle of animals. But when it comes to describing the behavior of animals, let alone predicting that of humans, its validity is questionable.

3

Our Primate Relatives

Still humans are primates—if we are going to speculate on the road to humanity, a look at the other members of our order should be useful. So it had seemed to the scientists, though they started with a strong anthropomorphic bias. Yet, they, too, began to feel that captive conditions and a human environment might well have considerable distorting effect on the behavior of animals. If one looks at domesticated cats and dogs and sees how they take on the characteristics of the people with whom they live, or at prison populations, it seems fairly obvious that we cannot learn much about the "natural" behavior of animals without seeing them in their usual environment.

In 1931 Clarence Carpenter was a psychologist at Pennsylvania State University who had been influenced by *Mutual Aid*, the book in which the anarchist Peter Kropotkin took exception to the extremes of Darwin's followers. Where they argue that evolution and survival of the fittest meant constant aggression, exemplified by a competitive pyramid, Kropotkin theorized that animal and human societies were based on sharing and co-operation, one individual helping another. Carpenter was the first scientist to go out and spend a lengthy period of time observing primates in their natural habitat—fifteen months in the jungle blinds watching howler monkeys on Barro Colorado Island in Central America—and to report in detail on what he found. The results supported Kropotkin rather than

the social Darwinists. Howler monkeys live in troops: they are
not aggressive, they do not have sharp dominance hierarchies,
and they do not compete for females; each female mates with
many males—in general they are a co-operative society which
operates for the defense and protection of all its members.

Since then, but above all in the sixties and seventies, more
than fifteen species have been studied in the wild. Not only
were laboratory studies incorrect, but later field studies often
contradict the generalizations drawn from earlier ones. Every
variety of behavior has been found and every combination of
sexual grouping: monogamy (among gibbons); mixed male-
female groups, all-male groups, all-female-and-young groups,
one male and several females (under hardship conditions); aggressive females among the patas monkeys, aggressive males
among the baboons, aggressive males and females among the
macaques, pacific males and females among the langurs; fairly
rigid hierarchies and loose open groups; small groups and large
ones. The only consistent relationship is the one between
mother and child.

Jane Goodall's study of chimpanzees in the Gombe Stream
Reserve in Tanzania, which began in 1960 when she was
twenty-six years old and is to be continued at least until 1980,
did the most to revolutionize scientists' thinking about primate
and early-human societies.[1] A young woman with a passion for
animals and no formal training, she had worked as secretary to
the physical anthropologist Louis Leakey. He encouraged and
enabled Goodall to go out alone and watch chimpanzees. He
was interested in comparing them with the earliest humans,
and the fact that she had no academic background, not even an
undergraduate degree, was in her favor: he felt she would have
a freer mind in consequence. It was in the early years that she
made her great discoveries about tool use, meat eating, open
groups, and free sex among chimpanzees. She found that, although highly social, chimpanzees were little interested in dominance and aggression per se and that they had no stable
groupings at all, let alone the male-dominated families or
harems postulated by earlier scientists. They moved in small
temporary groups, which might consist of any combination of

age/sex classes. Lone males and, occasionally, lone females were also encountered. The only group that was stable over a period of months was a mother with her infant and older offspring. During those first years also she found few dominance interactions.[2]

A year-long study of chimpanzees in the Budongo Forest, in Uganda, by a husband-wife team, Vernon and Frances Reynolds, confirmed Goodall's report. They concluded that dominance interactions formed a minute fraction of observed chimpanzee behavior. No evidence of a linear hierarchy of dominance among males or females was found, nor were any permanent leaders of groups discernible.[3] Both study projects reported that in the wild the apes mate most frequently during moments of social excitement—on arrival at a particularly rich feeding place or at a meeting of two large groups—and that, as mentioned before, they are sexual swingers, though it is in the nature of the primate physiology that the female gets to swing more than the male.

Evolutionary theory used to be based on the fact that humans were thought to be the only primates who ate meat as well as vegetables. The hunting syndrome was used to explain the human condition. War, aggression, divergence of sex roles, and male dominance were the results of group hunting activities in which males alone participated to provide the principal sustenance for our prehuman forebears. Goodall's work with chimpanzees was the first of many studies which resulted in the overturn of such simplistic ideas about human evolution. To begin with, we are not the only omnivorous primate; the amiable, noncompetitive, nonhierarchical chimpanzees of the Gombe Stream Reserve were discovered to eat meat in addition to vegetables. Baboons and vervets had previously been observed to eat insects, small rodents, and birds' eggs; Goodall saw the forest-savanna chimpanzees catch and eat baby monkeys, bushbuck, and bush pig. She also watched as they shared their prey with other chimpanzees who held out a hand to beg for meat—the only primate besides humankind known to share food. Moreover, the chimpanzees engaged in what looked like the beginnings of group hunts: they deployed themselves at the base of several trees so as to trap an animal within a given area.

Today, aggression is being discarded as a prime mover. It makes little evolutionary sense to consider that it is the function of maleness to be overbearingly aggressive, to fight constantly, and to be dominant.[4] A 1975 newspaper article headed "Study Links Aggression in Rats to Prenatal Zinc Deficiency" indicates the current direction: aggression viewed as aberrational rather than normal behavior.[5]

Prepared or manufactured tools were long considered a human invention and were associated with the killing of animals. Goodall discovered that chimpanzees also used prepared tools, though not for hunting. A chimp will pick up a blade of coarse savanna grass and trim off the edges to taper it, or take a twig and strip it of its leaves, then carry the tool until she or he finds a termite hill, often as far as a hundred feet, once for almost half a mile. They use these instruments as probes and, when the insects bite, draw them out covered with termites, which they then eat.

This is a technique chimpanzee infants learn by observing their mothers and are able to perform at the age of about three. Before Goodall's report, a standard definition of humankind had been "the toolmaker." After it, she pointed out that social scientists must accept chimps as man, by definition; they must redefine man; or they must redefine tools.[6]

Till recently, archaeologists have based their accounts of the development of humankind on stones and bones, on tools and fossils. Tools of the kind Goodall's chimpanzees use would not, of course, survive in the archaeological record, nor, it has been observed from recent ethnographic work in Africa, would vegetable debris; hence the great overvaluing of hunting as the significant behavior pattern of prehistoric humans, rather than one complex of behavior among many others.

Goodall found among chimpanzees many syndromes and gestures shared by humans. Most of the primates are both highly social and highly tactile. Among the lower monkeys, grooming—a kind of picking over of the skin and finger-combing of the fur—takes up hours of each day's time. Chimpanzees not only groom each other; they communicate by calls and gestures and touch. They greet or reassure by touching; they embrace, they pat, they kiss, they reach out a hand to beg. She theorizes that either these gestures in humans and chimps have evolved along parallel lines or they have a common origin in a remote ancestor of both species.[7] Today's encounter groups, "please touch" therapies, etc., testify to the felt need when this kind of nonverbal emotional communication dwindled among humans.

Vernon Reynolds goes even further in finding parallels between humans and chimpanzees. He sees a paradigm for the flexibility and growth of human societies in the open, shifting groups of the chimps—as opposed to the tight bands and rigid hierarchies of, say, the baboons and the rhesus monkeys.[8]

Another exception to the male-aggression competitive-pyramid theory of existence came from George Schaller, who spent a year in 1959–60 studying the mountain gorilla of Africa. Schaller's gorillas were remarkably pacific, a far cry from the would-be rapist and murderer depicted in the original *King Kong*. His description of gorilla relations between the sexes contradicts the projection of unwilling females pursued by ravening males. Engels, for instance, assumed that monogamy was an advance desired by the females so that they would be spared the necessity of "surrendering" to many males.[9] And as late as 1927 anthropologist Robert Briffault could write:

> The congress of the sexes is assimilated by the impulse to hurt, to shed blood, to kill, to the encounter of a beast of prey and its victims, and all distinction between the two is not infrequently lost. It would be more accurate to speak of the sexual impulse as pervading nature with a yell of cruelty than a hymn of love. The circumspection which is exhibited by animal females in yielding to the male, the haste which is shown by most to separate as soon as impregnation has taken place would appear to be due in a large measure to the danger attending such relation rather than to "coyness."[10]

Compare this sadistic fantasy with Schaller's observations:

The group rests scattered over a steep hillside. A peripheral male stands looking down the slope. A female appears behind him, clasps him around the waist and mounts him, thrusting about 20 times. The male at first pays no attention, but after about 10 seconds turns his head and looks at her. Suddenly he swivels around and sits. With his right hand he reaches over, grabs the female by the hip and pulls her to him. She sits in his lap, facing away from him, her body supported by stiff arms propped on the ground, as the male thrusts about 10 times.

The dominant male, who has been resting 15 feet away, slowly rises and walks toward the pair. The copulating male immediately desists and ambles 10 feet uphill. The dominant male sits behind the female one minute, then moves and rests 15 feet away. The other male reoccupies his former spot, and the female approaches him. He reaches out with both hands, swivels her around and again pulls her into his lap. He thrusts rapidly, about two times per second. After about seventy thrusts he begins the copulatory sound —the rapid o-o-o noted in the previous copulation. The female waves her head slowly back and forth, and, at about the hundredth thrust, suddenly twists sideways and sits beside the male, who then rolls over and rests on his abdomen for 10 minutes. . . .

After a prolonged rest, the female rises and stands by the rump of the male. He glances up and they stare at each other. The process of pulling her into a sitting position and thrusting is repeated. At about 75 thrusts he begins his copulatory sound. His eyes are closed, and the thrusts rock her back and forth, a motion not only aided with his hands on her hips but also by her body. His lips are pursed and the sounds grow more rapid, become slurred; her lips are also pursed and her mouth slightly parted. At about 120

thrusts the male suddenly opens his mouth with a
loud sighing "ahh," and the female opens her mouth
at the same time. He relaxes but she rises and leaves.[11]

Schaller's gorillas sound almost tender in their "love-making," though it is still a fairly rudimentary business. In Goodall's
reports, chimpanzees come somewhat closer to certain human
stereotypes: females sometimes approach the males, but more
often the male initiates activity, sometimes with persistent, almost bullying displays of branch shaking and foot stamping. In
other observations, of free-ranging chimpanzees not fed by humans, as often as not a female or male would quietly approach
the other, and females were more likely than males to initiate
mating.[12]

Rape is nonexistent among chimpanzees. If the female persists in ignoring a male chimpanzee's courtship displays, he
eventually wanders off. But chimpanzee females have a bright
pink sexual swelling which advertises their readiness to engage
in sexual activity during estrus; Goodall describes it as looking,
from a far distance, like a pink flower among the trees. Neither
gorilla nor human females have a visible indication of their sexual desire; hence, among gorillas it is the female who approaches the male. Since the upright posture would preclude a
visible indication of desire among early hominid females, during our earliest evolution it must also have been the human female who approached the human male. The implications of
this will be far-reaching when we come to look at later myths
and restrictions—the ambivalence of human male attitudes toward the human female's sexual role.

There are no gorilla families, in the human sense, no more-
or-less permanent mating relations, though they move in fairly
stable groups. Dian Fossey spent several years in the late sixties
and early seventies studying gorillas. She has found more flexible groupings than the one silver-backed (mature) male, several
young males, and several females composing the groups
Schaller charted. In the wild, groupings comprised of gorilla females and their young are common, while adult male gorillas
are frequently solitary.[13]

The original theories of dominance and male possession of
the female as the rule among apes and monkeys were based on
Solly Zuckerman's observations of a colony of hamadryas baboons in the London zoo. "Every ape or monkey enjoys a position within a social group that is determined by the interrela-
tion of its own dominant characteristics and those of its
fellows. The degree of its dominance determines how far its
bodily appetites will be satisfied. *Dominance determines the
number of females that a male may possess,* and except on occasions where there is a superfluity of food, it also determines
the amount a monkey eats," he wrote.[14]

Till ethologists went out into the wild and disproved Zuckerman's theses, the so-called "harem organization"—groups
consisting of one adult male, several females, and their young—
was believed to be the characteristic primate family. Dian
Fossey demonstrated that this is not necessarily the case among
gorillas. Like chimpanzees, male gorillas have a fierce-appearing
threat display, but it is just that, noise and motion unaccom-
panied by actual fighting. Schaller's final conclusion was that
gorillas are unaggressive and undersexed, presumably by human
standards.

Still there was always the baboon to fall back on. This ill-
tempered and ugly monkey was a favorite point of departure
for the neo-Darwinists. Those who used the baboon as a model
for human evolution saw our earliest groupings as fascist states.
Wherever the baboon analogy was cited, one could expect a
denigratory view of women coupled with talk of man's innate
aggressiveness—as though human males were composed of electric circuits with little aggression condensers wired in forever.
The popularizers Konrad Lorenz, Robert Ardrey, Desmond
Morris, Robin Fox and Lionel Tiger, and even some of the academics who had studied baboons in the field—K. R. L. Hall,
Hans Kummer, Sherwood Washburn, and Irven DeVore—were
very fond of basing their speculations about prehistoric and
present-day humankind on these creatures. It was argued that
baboons, like early hominids, lived on the ground, in a savanna
environment, and that both baboons and hominids evolved
with strict controls, in large troops organized for aggressive-

defensive tactics against predatory animals. Baboon organization was thus taken as a model for early human organization.

The analogy between baboons and humans, popular as it was, is extraordinarily far-fetched. Baboons are four-footed monkeys with tails; they belong to the catarrhine family—the Old World monkeys—which parted company with us some thirty to forty million years ago. Gorillas and chimpanzees are much closer to us physiologically and phylogenetically; they belong to the same family, the hominoids, though they are pongids and we are hominids; they stayed in our line for some twenty to thirty-six million more years. Recent blood analyses indicate that the pongids may have branched off from our line as recently as five million years ago. Chimpanzees and gorillas approach erect posture; in fact, it is probable that their knuckle walking and brachiation developed after humans diverged from the anthropoid apes. They have no tails, and they have larger brains than other monkeys, though smaller ones than humans, and, as noted before, many more gestures and syndromes in common with humans than do the lower monkeys.

Baboons further differ from us in that they have a considerable degree of sharp physical differentiation between the sexes. The male baboon is twice the size of the female baboon and has built-in weapons, large protruding teeth, which are lacking in the female. Human males, on the other hand, are only slightly larger, on the average, than females, a difference roughly proportionate to that between male and female chimpanzees, and their teeth are not specialized for aggression. Almost the only point of comparison between baboons and early humans is the fact that both are largely ground-living, though four out of five baboon species sleep in trees at night.

The first troops of baboons to be studied, in the nineteen fifties, consisted of groups of forty to eighty or more baboons, depending on the locality, who lived in moderate harmony among themselves, and even with neighboring troops, despite a great show of bullying and threats. They were also relatively promiscuous: female baboons copulated with the younger and less dominant baboons during the beginning of their period of sexual desire; toward the middle or the end of the estrous period, when "they were most fertile," they formed "consort relationships"—"a spatial relationship lasting for *an hour*, a day, or several days" with the most dominant male of the group, thus facilitating impregnation by a stronger male, and, *q.e.d.*, sexual selection.[15] However, not taking into consideration the difficulties of observation, it was also found that one could not always chart the linear gradations of dominance, for a lower-ranking male would sometimes combine with the most dominant male of the group—or even the second in the hierarchy—and arrogate rights to which he was not entitled, according to the human theories about rank which then prevailed.[16]

In the field it developed that, unlike all other species of baboons, the hamadryas do have the harem family organization observed by Zuckerman in the London zoo. Hamadryas baboons live in deserts, and, wherever researchers studied monkey species in hardship conditions, they found it not unusual for the ecological problem of survival to be facilitated by several females clustered around one male. The first formulation was that where the male is twice as large as the female, as among the hamadryas, one male consumes twice as much food as two females, hence it is economical to cut down on the number of males. This is the common teleological fallacy. As varying species turn up with the same organization, the scientists finally acknowledged the obvious: one male can impregnate a number of females, and before the species disappears, the emergency pattern concentrates on reproduction—something like flowers going to seed in a drought. Eventually, when conditions are too severe, as has been observed in specific instances among vervets and baboons, the animals do not copulate or reproduce themselves at all.

Humans have never had any hesitation about adopting this hardship principle with regard to domestic animals. Except for one or two males kept as studs, male animals are slaughtered for food while females are kept for breeding. The zoologists' reluctance to admit the secondary, though essential, nature of the role in reproduction played by males points up one source of male hostility to women and the need to derogate female functions: the overcompensation which stems from the fear of superfluity so deeply ingrained in male consciousness.

The macaque is another largely ground-living, social, and highly aggressive monkey who has been much studied and who seemed to fit the dominance-hierarchy approach fairly well. However, in order to study troops of macaques, humans have often instituted artificial feeding stations. When the monkeys gather at an artificial source of food, there is a plethora of aggressive incidents, as well as ample opportunity to chart the dominance pyramid.

In a colony of Japanese macaques at a primate research center in Oregon, the animals are already crowded into artificial conditions—230 animals in two acres—so that ethologists can observe "dominance hierarchies." When the monkeys were jammed into a fifty-foot-square pen, "group attacks greatly increased in frequency." This research is funded by the National Institutes of Health—i.e., taxpayers' money.[17]

In the same way, Goodall installed banana feeding stations so as to study the chimpanzees at close range. With an almost unlimited source of bananas in one place, instead of food scattered through the trees, she found an increase of "dominance interactions" and aggressive behavior among the chimpanzees, the males in particular. There are fewer such incidents when the chimpanzees feed on their own or even when they catch wild animals. Dominant males do not force the possessor of a dead animal to drop his prey; they are more likely to wait and beg for a share, though there were instances where one animal distracted another one so as to grab a choice morsel.

What, then, is "natural behavior"? In recent years the Gombe Stream Research Center has been supported by Stanford University. Though Goodall had begun as an independent researcher, it was only through accreditation in the male-dominated academic world that she could continue her investigations and avail herself of the facilities—money and people—necessary to extend them. She took her doctorate under Robert Hinde at Cambridge University and is presently working with David Hamburg of Stanford University, who helped her to obtain generous grants for her center. Students from all over the world pursue their studies there. With a population of research students almost as large as the indigenous population of chimpanzees wandering through the forest, both human and ape species enter on a new form of coexistence, in which the chimpanzee is in neither a wild state nor a domesticated one. Humans introduce alien elements, e.g., the current dominant male is described as having acquired his position by clattering some large gasoline tins downhill in a noisy display. Studies increasingly emphasize male aggression and dominance hierarchies, since those are the questions with which ethology concerns itself in large part.

Moreover, almost at the same time the students recorded vicious behavior among chimps—males attacking males—they themselves were under threat from outside political elements in Tanzania. The first chimpanzee attack was recorded in 1974. In 1975 a student was kidnaped by local terrorists and the center was subsequently closed for two and a half years. Nonetheless, in 1978 Goodall announced that she had evidence of war among the Gombe Stream chimpanzees, citing five attacks and six male deaths. Some animal behaviorists applaud the finds as evidence of innate aggression and beastliness among the chimps. Others feel that intruding humans changed the ecology and introduced alien and life-threatening elements into the original habitat, thus provoking the chimpanzees to behave like civilized humans.[18]

As to the baboon-human analogists, they had long rejected the comparison of chimpanzees or gorillas with humans on the grounds that the first two are "unsuccessful species"—there are few of them left—while baboons and humans are numerous and have adapted to a wide variety of environments. On this reasoning, the brown rat and the German cockroach would be the most successful of all—like humans they are spread throughout all the continents, rather than the single continent where baboons are found.

But "success" is one of those subjective words whose meaning constantly changes. Humans, who in Darwinian terms are successful because they leave the most progeny, have found that the leaving of children reaches a point of no return. The old Darwinian concepts, revolutionary in their day, are only a partial explanation of the complexities existing between life and environment, hence the twentieth-century emphasis on ecology. And once the human brain entered the picture, physical development was only one factor. Kropotkin pointed out back in 1891 that "thousands of weak-bodied and infirm poets, scientists, inventors and reformers, together with other thousands of so-called 'fools and weak-minded enthusiasts,' have been the most precious weapons produced by humanity."[19]

The baboon explanation for *Homo sapiens* was that once humans left the trees, they were more vulnerable to predators, hence the development of aggression, hunting, and weapons, as well as physical and role differences between the sexes. Still, baboons do not use tools, and they have not been notably effective in advancing themselves culturally over the forty million or so years they have been evolving. Chimpanzees do use sophisticated tools—and their tool use is more efficient than their weapon use. Though they pick up stones and branches to throw, it is unaimed throwing, for display rather than directed aggression. They play with objects, as humans do, and some groups live in a more or less savanna environment.

One feels that an antidemocratic attitude is implicit in the claim that humans are like baboons. The statement made by Irven DeVore on a CBS television program that "each individual has its own rank and knows its own place . . . only in this way could baboons and man have beaten the odds" is a typical example of this need to exalt aggression, rigid closed societies, and dominance far above their true position in the constellation of human characteristics.[20] It is a position which can be used to justify the military-corporate state, unequal opportunity, and current forms of world dominance, just as Darwinism was often used to support exploitative capitalism and imperialism in the nineteenth century.

Moreover, even baboons are not like baboons—at least not like those cited in the baboon-human analogy. The popularizers had drawn their examples from abnormal groups. The initial studies were of animals who live in game parks—open country where predators, especially humans, are abundantly present—and the animals are under considerable tension. When the same species is studied in different environments, in open country and in forest, away from human contact, the results are quite different.

Forest baboon groups are fluid; they are not tightly closed but change composition regularly. The core of the stable group is formed by adult females and their offspring. Food and cover are scattered, and there is little fighting over the one or the other. Aggression is infrequent, and it is difficult if not impossible to discern dominance hierarchies. Intertroop meetings are rare, and when they occur they are friendly. If the troop is frightened, it flees. The males do not form a rear guard; on the contrary, since they are the biggest and strongest, they are often the first up the trees, leaving the females, encumbered as they are with infants, to fend for themselves. The adult females determine when the troop will move, and where, and adult males are not always found in protective positions, in front and at the rear.[21]

The argument for evolution based on male aggression among ground-living primates was also thrown off when K. R. L. Hall did a study of an even more terrestrial monkey than the baboon. The patas monkey is faced with problems not unlike those of the baboon and incipient humans, but the adaptation was a very different one. The patas live in a plains environment even more treeless than that of most baboon species. And they have evolved with marked sexual dimorphism—the male patas is twice as large as the female, just as the male baboon is twice as large as the female baboon. However, the solution to survival in a hostile environment was to develop silence, caution, and speed—patas monkeys can sustain a fifty-mile-an-hour pace over long distances and look somewhat like greyhounds. They rarely fight—the male acts as a watchman and decoy while the females flee. Although quite unaggressive, within this context, it is the female who displays fighting behavior more than the male. They are organized in small groups, like those of the hamadryas baboons, with one male to several females, as well as their young, but the male displays none of the dominance observed among the game-park baboons, and, as has been noted before, it is the female who initiates sex, though her ap-proach is not the usual presenting of the hindquarters; she runs toward the male to signify desire.[22]

Other land-living monkeys who are neither aggressive nor hierarchical are the vervets, also known as the thicket or sa-vanna monkey. Since they are relatively unspecialized in their physical development, and since they represent a transition be-tween arboreal and terrestrial existence, they, too, are being studied for analogies with early human evolution.[23]

The most salient observation to come out of primate studies is the fact of varying adaptations within individual species. Every kind of "family" organization can be found. As noted earlier the only consistent relationship in all the primate group-ings is the one between mother and child. Just as human groups have developed diversely, the result not only of differing environments but also of the quirks of isolation and genetic drift, so animal populations vary according to their ambiance. To a certain degree, this variation depends on how the observer interprets what is seen.

Is there anything positive we can take from ethology for our speculation on the origins of human sexual behavior? Even al-lowing for observer bias and special interest, the evidence for change and individuality among nonhuman primates stands and will certainly apply in even greater measure to humans. We can suppose that there is no one way in which we evolved and no one position for the human female, save when certain societies became so strong that they tried to impose their ways on other societies, as happened in the past four hundred years with the expansion of Western European culture.

4

Aggression and Maleness

Another question to consider is the equation of aggression with the male hormone testosterone, resulting in the generalization that males are more aggressive than females.

In animals, this is often but not always true. Ethologists have not found male wolves to be more aggressive than female wolves, though the females are probably shyer of observation, as are, for example, the Gombe Stream chimpanzees. Elephant females dominate the elephant herd, chasing out males as they grow up; female lions and tigers are reported to be more aggressive than the males; while among the simians not only patas but also gibbon females are described as more aggressive than the males. A corollary to this is that when primatologists find a species with aggressive females we are normally informed that the male is "undersexed." But in studying aggression among female animals, while they may be normally unaggressive, presumably because they are occupied with pursuits other than dominance, per se, when it is a threat that concerns them, as to their young, it is a byword that the female fights like hell. Male rats rarely attack female rats, but if an unknown male enters the nesting area where a female is nursing she attacks and always succeeds in driving him away. While female rats are seen to fight less often than males, when they do, they attack viciously, without the preliminary threat postures and aggressive grooming displayed by male rats.[1]

Among zebras, the stallion protects his group from hyena at-tackers, who follow in a semicircle behind. If one zebra is in poorer condition than the others or is slowed down by hyena bites and falls back, the whole pack immediately surrounds it. At that point the stallion does not try to defend the individual, though a mother will defend her foal.[2]

In terms of being less aggressive than the male, primate fe-males carry their infants with them, so that much of the time they are held down, literally, by an infant clinging to their stomachs, cradled temporarily in one limb, or riding on their backs. Carnivore females leave their infants in the den while they go out to hunt, which gives them considerably more mo-bility than primate, including early hominid, females.

In nature—a nonexistent abstraction invented by humans to describe everything that is—there are no value judgments. What works, even if somewhat inefficiently, survives; what doesn't, disappears. Females, who are more necessary over the long run for the survival of the species, must also be more shy and cautious—which is not to be equated with lack of aggres-sion. Males are expendable, and among many species, including the social primates, they are often described as serving as shock troops or advance guard; even isolates, who are commonly male, may have some scouting function: the ultimate existence of the species rests on a less exposed position for females and infants. In the wild, primatologists have reported an almost universal inhibition of aggression against infants; they enjoy tolerance from both males and females within their own spe-cies. This is an attitude common among humans, too, though far from universal, as witness Mylai, Dachau and Auschwitz, etc. The atypical behavior of zoo and captive animals is also worth noting in this context: they may unpredictably attack and kill their own or strange infants.

The linkage of male sexuality to aggression, almost axiomatic in our history, has led to hideous brutality among humans, not least of which is the justification of rape. Scientists have had a tendency to project recent human history onto physiology in their conclusion that testosterone is a cause of aggression. The study of hormones—a word which dates back only to 1904—is still in its infancy. What is clear is that sex is energizing, be it testosterone or estrogen. When that energy finds no outlet, it gets displaced into irritability and, on occasion and in some species, into fighting behavior. Yet the relationship is not at all clear-cut, and there are hints that, operating on the basis of human preconceptions, scientists have jumped to conclusions. The castrated animal loses its spirit—but this applies also to females when they are spayed. We are told that injecting testosterone makes a female more aggressive; we are not usually told that injecting estrogen is also likely to make her more aggressive. Estrogen increases mounting and fighting behavior in female and male rats. And large doses of testosterone injected into animals of both sexes make them so passive that they neither feed nor fight.[3]

Environmental and social factors influence the secretion of hormones, so that behavior is a two-way street. Perhaps a simpler statement with regard to humans is that behavior often originates in the head, and the body follows the brain: e.g., people who "fall in love" secrete more sex hormones. The question of hormones is far more complex than was first realized; new hormones and hormone relationships are still being discovered. David E. Davis wrote in 1962 about the finding that LH, a hormone produced by the pituitary gland, also increased aggression: "At the moment we cannot say whether LH, testosterone, or some other hormone was the first to be associated with aggressive behavior. A speculation may be made, and perhaps it will be tested some day. Since one function of LH is to stimulate production of testosterone through the Leydig cells of the testis, it would seem that LH is more basic and the connection of testosterone with aggression is secondary."[4]

Studies of rhesus monkeys at the Yerkes Primate Center in Atlanta, Georgia, probed for proof of a relationship between dominance rank, as measured by aggressive behavior, and the quantity of offspring given males produced. Biochemical tests revealed no correlation between high rank and reproductive success; in fact, low-ranking and even adolescent males fathered as many infants as did the highest-ranking males.[5]

In the Japanese-macaque colony in Oregon where aggressive

behavior patterns were produced by confined conditions and provisioning, no correlation was observed between dominance position and testosterone level. High-ranking males did not mate more frequently than low-ranking males, and the mating appeared to be random on the part of the females, who were making the choices. The researchers concluded that testosterone was less important than social stimuli in eliciting masculine patterns of aggressive behavior. They also concluded that rank was not highly correlated with aggressiveness; the dominant males were not at the top of the hierarchy because of fighting ability or physical characteristics such as size. These data, published in 1976, contradict many earlier reports.[6]

Male bias in the early part of the twentieth century led researchers into many false assumptions—semantic and cultural—about aggression and active sexuality. They were believed to be dictated by hormones possessed chiefly or solely by males. As of 1978 hormone research indicates that current terminology is incomplete and inadequate. Testosterone is an androgen, a family of hormones produced in large part by the testes but also found in the adrenal glands of both sexes and in the ovaries. Estrogens are a family of sex hormones produced in largest quantities by the ovaries, but also found in the testes and adrenal glands. Moreover, androgens are normally converted by cells in many parts of the body, including the brain, into estrogen, in both sexes![7]

5

Maternal Sexuality

In order to probe the origins of the myth of male supremacy and the reality of male power over women, we must consider the nature of human sexuality. One of Freud's great contributions to human understanding was his delineation of infant sexuality—gratification from the oral pleasures of nursing. However, he paid little attention to the physical responses of the other half of the couple—the mother's sensual joy. I believe that female primates, including humans, have two kinds of sexuality, maternal and genital. Because of our history, this area—the sexual pleasure that comes after childbearing—has been largely ignored. Many male scientists and male doctors—and there are very few women in these fields as yet—think in terms of the "race of man" and see the female as existing for male use and male gratification, so nursing, like motherhood, is a noble and giving function. The female is the font of life, but it is rarely acknowledged, at least in modern Western society, that she might just nurse because she enjoys it.

According to Niles and Michael Newton, long before the concept of "duty" evolved, the survival of the human race depended on the satisfactions gained from the two voluntary acts of reproduction—breast feeding and coitus. They had to be pleasurable enough to ensure that they would occur frequently.[1] One has only to look at the beatific expression on the face of a Nambikwara woman photographed by Lévi-Strauss as she lay on the ground nursing her baby to see an exemplification of these pleasures. Why do primitive women go on having and rearing babies? Many of them have access to forms of birth control—from abstinence to abortion to plant potions to infanticide—which are used when need dictates. There are nonliterate societies where moral strictures like those of the Judeo-Christian religion are lacking, where there is no great idealization of the mother, and where children are welcomed and fed equally by the whole group.

In such a situation, mothers enjoy having babies not because they are sacrificing and noble, not necessarily for the prestige, but because it is a pleasurable experience. Even parturition may not always be painful, as is usual among us; Niles Newton argues that in societies where sexual attitudes are not puritanical, it is less arduous, and she finds parallels between uterine contractions of orgasm and those of childbirth. But whether one accepts this theory or not, and it would certainly be difficult of investigation, there is no doubt that the sensual contact between mother and child after birth is relatively undiscussed and unexplored, except from the point of view of its utility for the physical and emotional development of the child.

In peasant and primitive societies babies are nursed not for the six months usual with us, but for periods of from two to four years. This is done not only as a birth-control measure but also because it is a sensually pleasing experience for mother and child, else there would surely have been a rising of women long before this century.

A contemporary of mine who had nursed her two babies was mildly shocked when I asked her about nursing as sexual pleasure. "Not sexual," she said, "but irresistibly moving. I felt it deep inside, in my belly, in my womb." She spoke of the intense, almost indescribable sensation when the baby begins to suck and the milk flows—milk letdown—and of the need to caress the baby, to touch her or his head, arm, or foot, making clear that it is a reciprocal and active happening "but not sexual, oh, no."

"Do you know," I asked her, "that in many societies it is normal for the mother to caress her baby's genitals during nurs-

ing?" Alice Rossi writes of non-Western societies which show
an easy natural pattern of maternalism and finds them characterized by an indulgence and acceptance of the sexual component of maternalism that is denied by Western societies. Even
a slight exposure to ethnographic literature points up the contrast with Western mother-child relations, where sexuality is
culturally repressed. We can hardly imagine an American
mother engaging in labial, clitoral, or penis stimulation of her
infant without guilt or social condemnation, yet this is an accepted and expected pattern in many societies where mothering and sexuality are closely linked.[2]

As Western taboos have begun to loosen, more and more
women acknowledge the eroticism of the mother-infant relationship. The sensation of nursing is another kind of orgasm.[3]
In their discussions of the sensual gratification for the mother
in nursing, both Rossi and the Newtons tend to talk in terms
of its usefulness—how it will stimulate milk flow, provide better
nutrition and psychological health for the child, etc. Well, useful it may be, as coitus is useful; but both are pleasurable, and
looking at mammals, I would think that for the female—cat,
monkey, ape, or human—there are two areas of sexual pleasure,
the one being coitus, the other lactation.

In our culture, where civilization and brain have begun to
control physical and purely emotional responses and where the
patriarchy has ruled these thousands of years, there is rejection
and fear of maternal sexuality. Psychoanalysis is afraid that the
baby may be swallowed by the mother's sensual needs. Rossi
discusses Western analysts' argument that the woman's need to
mother is often greater than the optimum required by the infant. In many primitive societies women satisfy both sexual and
caretaking desires by nursing their young. The male-dominant
family and political systems of the West, in combination with
Christian theology, make a sharp distinction between motherhood and female sexuality. Maternity is culturally defined and
differentiated from sexuality, so that women are asked to deny
the evidence of their senses by repressing the sexual component
of infant care. She suspects that the more male dominance
characterizes a Western society, the greater the separation be-

tween sexuality and maternalism. It is to men's advantage to restrict women's sexual gratification to adult heterosexual intercourse, though women and children may pay the price of a less rewarding relationship, physically and psychologically.[4] Until very recently our culture insisted that the breast could be displayed publicly only in a sexual connotation, but not when nursing, with the result that women refused to try nursing their babies or stopped when they discovered that it involved a psychological blend of the sexual and the maternal.[5]

But of course, while maternal sexuality may have been repressed, it has also been transmuted and transformed and translated into the heterosexual experience. The breast is an erotic area, and the whole elaboration of sexual enjoyment between humans, in which foreplay—kissing and caressing, nibbling, nuzzling, and sucking, including stimulation of the breast— produces vaginal lubrication and clitoral sensation, just as nursing does, shows that it has been brought over into the meeting between men and women. Masters and Johnson spoke of women who could achieve orgasm through stimulation of the nipple. And Goodall suggests that some forms of kissing may come from the sucking response—as chimpanzee infants reach for or hold their mothers' nipples in their mouths when they are frightened or hurt.[6] Like so many parts of our animal nature, the sexuality is there if unacknowledged. And looking at maternal sexuality, one realizes that this, too, is what the female has brought to the human sexual experience—not only prolongation, but enrichment and elaboration.

If humans are the only animals who make love face to face, the personalizing of the act comes not from the genital meeting alone but from the ornamentation and affection around it, a personalizing which does not exist among the animals nor often enough among humans. In the emphasis on genital orgasm of, say, Wilhelm Reich, we detect a curious anti-female and anti-art component, a denial of the aesthetic variations, the enormous extension and adornment of sex which can occur among humans at their best.

Having absorbed certain facets of the mother-infant sexual relationship into the meeting between woman and man, male

thought then rejected the sensual side of childbearing. Characteristic of male resentment of the female body is the etherealiz-
ing of motherhood. We like to think of virgin birth, of motherhood as the one selfless, pure act, and today, in the final
exaggeration, mothers are attacked for being anything less than
all-giving and undemanding. Since so much depends on them,
they are always being judged. They are supposed to give birth,
give food and tender care and let go without asking for anything in return and with little help from society. But there has
always been interaction—among animals and among early and
later societies.

Robert Briffault's three-volume *The Mothers* is on the surface a great glorification of women, in actuality a not-so-subtle
put-down. He speaks of sex as a nasty business made beautiful
by the tenderness and love transferred from the maternal relationship, and "maternal love is sacrifice."[7] From this premise
comes the sadomasochistic foundation of male-dominated sex:
one person is the tender, sacrificing giver, another the receiver;
one the instrument, the other the player, and so forth. To see it
as a linked, reciprocally enjoyable experience takes enormous
cultural reconditioning. Tenderness and love, yes, but also sensual exploration that incorporates the physical side of motherhood as a fructification of the sexual act. It is common among
male writers to denigrate woman by calling the clitoris an imitation of the penis, her orgasm an imitation of a male syndrome. One is much more likely to hear psychoanalysts discussing the breast as penis symbol than the penis as breast symbol,
but fellatio, in which the penis becomes the breast, is an imitation of nursing. Extensions, inversions, and variations of the
theme of our sexual patterns are usually imitations of maternal
functions. And it is through love-making only that the mature
male can return to earlier sensations or, on a now-different
level, partake of a universality of experience so that in the most
playful and fanciful way, man becomes woman and woman becomes man, exchanging and recapturing roles, in the caressing,
say, of his nipples, vestigial organs which are biologically useless
but not sensually so.

Since sexuality was defined in the narrow Western patriarchal sense, when the ethologists looked at the primate world some of them marveled at how small a part sex played in the female monkey's life: "During most of life a female is not involved in sexual activity. Most of the time, she is either juvenile, out of estrous, pregnant, or lactating."[8] Clearly they were under a misapprehension. Copulation may be infrequent, but sex in the broad sense ("the whole sphere of behavior related even indirectly to the sexual functions and embracing all affectionate and pleasure-seeking conduct"—Webster's New International Dictionary) is more present in her life than in that of the male. As a baby she participates in the mother-infant relationship, she copulates, then she gives birth and participates again in the nursing relationship. For the male, on the contrary, sex is represented by the months or years of infancy, after which he is limited to the brief acts of coitus permitted by diverse estrual females. The frequency of these matings is not dependent on dominance hierarchies or male aggression as had been postulated by the ethologists, but on the female's choice.[9] Among one troop of forest baboons, it was an old male with broken canines who most frequently completed successful matings, even though he was less aggressive than and frequently lost fights with younger and more vigorous adult males.[10]

As far back as 1926 it was suggested that, among humans, the sexual gratification inherent in childbirth and nursing might well account for a difference in focus between the sexes.[11] The male looks for gratification only in the sex act, whereas the woman has prolonged periods of sexual pleasure available with each childbirth. With this deprivation, male animals crowd around a female in estrus, waiting and at the ready. Can we infer from this the later emphasis in human males on any possible sexual encounter? Yes, from our general animal inheritance; no, for our specifically human endowment. For both women and men, the biological inheritance of our status as mammals—the breast-feeding animal—is at variance with our human capacities. This is what humanity and its concomitant social elaborations have meant, that we spend our energies not so much on primary gratifications of the senses as on the more complex and controlled pleasures and satisfactions which have grown out of these elemental needs. But the substitution of quantity for quality is culturally imposed, the result of a perversion of sexual expression into the comparatively recent human invention of winning and losing, not to say counting, with the male as the winner, the female the loser, and the keeping score thereof.

Now that humans have translated maternal sexuality into adult sex, most modern women are willing to forgo the basic pleasures of mother-child sensuality for the greater part of their adult lives. Men, too, have begun to realize the price of vertical relationship. As Jean Baker Miller points out, "Civilizations developed inequalities enforced by power and made most people spend their lives doing work without pleasure, at the same time evolving all manner of ways to separate and isolate people from pleasurable interaction with one another."[12] As women have fewer children and patriarchal pressures relax, people are beginning to insist on the affective sensory satisfactions that have so often been missing from bare-boned heterosexual relationships. On one level there is struggle to unloose women and men from the distortions imposed by sex as conquest, puritanical contempt for sex, and male emotional rigidity, which are the heritage of the past. On another there is wide experimentation with formerly forbidden unions—woman-woman, man-man—as well as a search for variations in the one-to-one bonds of traditional monogamy.

In the past, homosexuality, particularly between males, has often caricatured the more ugly aspects of heterosexual relationships defined as male dominant, female submissive. Today women and men may refuse imposed standards, as in the past a few individuals undoubtedly have rejected descriptive labels imposed by society and acted intuitionally. There have been sexual meetings on an equal basis, despite the heavy socializing to which we are and have been subjected by our dichotomizing tradition. More and more women and men seek relationships combining passive and active roles. Homosexuality is also more open and more tolerantly viewed by society and is probably on the increase. Lesbianism would seem to make more sense than male homosexuality, however, given the female's broad range of sexual possibility, our animal inheritance, combined with the human brain which elaborates on this heritage. We all loved our mothers first.

The theory of evolution by aggression grew out of our cultural ideas comprising possessive monogamy, the warlike nature of man, though not woman, and the view of nature as a constant state of hostilities, an unending battle in progress. Though Darwin's theory of survival of the fittest was its implicit base, for the social Darwinists, if not for Darwin himself, these are concepts which go back before Tennyson's "nature red in tooth and claw" of the nineteenth century, to Thomas Hobbes, with his "warre, as if every manne against every manne," and to earlier philosophical formulations. Today as more women participate actively in scientific research, new understandings and new information enable us to achieve a more holistic view of human origins.

Part II

WOMAN EVOLVING

Eons long, those low-browed creatures
Lived without the help of teachers.
  —Nineteen-thirties summer-camp song

6

From Man the Hunter to Woman the Gatherer

Just as the study of animal sexual behavior was colored by cultural projections, so were early researches into human origins. One school presented a dogma of human evolution shaped by tools and killing because our forerunners on the dry savannas of Africa took to meat eating. It stressed the role of headmen and their access to more women than ordinary mortals, with the result that they left more progeny, on the model of the now disproven animal-behavior thesis that dominant males are more successful in reproducing themselves than low-ranking ones. It successfully mingled the two meanings of the word *man:* generic, to refer both to women and to men, and specific, to refer to males only, further contributing to the invisibility of women. A somewhat more sophisticated phrasing explains the rise and spread of humanity and our conversion to civilization thus: "Hunting is the master behavioral pattern for the human species. It is the organizing activity which integrated the morphological, physiological, genetic and intellectual aspects of the individual human organism. . . . Man evolved as a hunter; he spent over 99 percent of his species' history as a hunter; and he spread over the entire habitable area of the world as a hunter."[1] There is little room for women in this theory, which is based on the education of male children for hunting and on the belief that man made tools in order to hunt.*

On the basis of artifacts dating back several million years and on the progression of fossil bones, particularly the ever-enlarging skulls found by the paleontologists, textbooks were wont to ascribe the use of tools to the fact that prehumans stood on two legs and had their upper limbs free to manipulate objects. They developed brains because they used the tools to take meat. They had begun to eat meat because they lived in a savanna where game was plentiful and fruit sparser than it had been in the forests where their ancestors lived. They developed the nuclear family because human infants were slower in developing than those of other animals, and women therefore took care of children while men became food suppliers and protectors—a particularly pat and inaccurate oversimplification.

In recent years it has been pointed out that too much attention was focused on hunting and too little on gathering and on the mother's role in child raising. Women anthropologists have outlined our development in terms of Woman the Gatherer rather than Man the Hunter, based on the fact that in climates of the sort in which prehumans first emerged from the ancestral ape population, among the gatherer-hunters who are the sole remaining representatives of the way of life practiced by our ancestors for more than 99.5 per cent of human existence, women supply most of the food, often as much as 80 per cent, with men bringing in the minor portion.[2]

Human development was not a question of first standing up, second developing tools, third evolving group hunting, even food sharing, and fourth developing brain and humanity. All the processes were occurring simultaneously. We stood up at

---

* The new and quickly popular school of sociobiology is the most recent expression of this kind of blatant sexism in the treatment of evolution. The approach and the name were originated by Edward O. Wilson of Harvard University. A glance at the chapter on sexuality in his book *On Human Nature* (Harvard University Press, 1978) reveals his bias and his reluctance to acquaint himself with the recent labors of physical anthropologists, archaeologists, primatologists, physiologists, and others outside his chosen field of laboratory entomology.

the same time our brains were in process of becoming human, though we do not yet know just how and when this took place.[3] The first prehumans must have had the beginnings of self-awareness and human responsiveness buried within their flattened skulls. Along with human relatedness there were the beginnings of human—that is, reasoning and malicious rather than thoughtless and passing—aggressiveness.

To use hunting as an explanation for humanity, including human aggression, begs the whole question of evolution. By itself, hunting explains neither its own development nor the other components of human behavior.

It was the work of Raymond Dart, a professor of anatomy at the University of Witwatersrand in South Africa, which presented the initial evidence for the step-by-step male-aggressive theory of evolution, whereby *man* first stood up, leaving his arms free to manipulate tools, then developed a "striding walk" to cover great distances on the desiccated savanna, made tools, and became a hunter. It focuses on "the violent nature of man"—not humanity—and sees sex as part of his "innately violent instinct," with woman surfacing only occasionally as prey, victim, tool, or masochist. The theory was first given wide circulation in the books of Robert Ardrey, amiably but firmly amplified by Konrad Lorenz, and has since been widely disseminated in film and fiction.

In 1925 Dart discovered the first skeletal remains of a creature presented as the precursor of humankind. Ever since Darwin's theory of evolution was accepted by the scientific community, paleontologists and physical anthropologists have been searching for the "missing link," a fossil that would provide the connection between humans and the animal world, the ape from which our species had ascended. Dart's find, a child's skull at first dated to some half a million years ago, provided a solution which was accepted by many theoreticians. After that first fossil, which Dart named the Taung baby, other skeletal remains were dug up in South Africa, by Dart himself and by a colleague, Robert Broom. Their dates were pushed back to about a million years before our time. Dart and Broom did not find stone tools in the immediate vicinity, but there were animal bones with or near the disparate portions of hominid skeletons. Though it was not clear whether the prehumans were the eaters or the eaten, Dart thought he could distinguish signs of wear on some of the million-year-old bones. He concluded that the earliest tools and weapons used by our ancestors had been shaped from the bones of their kill, and he extrapolated this lurid hypothesis:

> The blood-bespattered, slaughter-gutted archives of human history from the earliest Egyptian and Sumerian record to the most recent atrocities of the Second World War accord with early human universal cannibalism, with animal and human sacrificial practices or their substitutes in formalized religions and with the world-wide scalping, head-hunting, body-mutilating and necrophiliac practices of *mankind* in proclaiming this common bloodlust differentiator, this predaceous habit, the mark of Cain that separates *man* dietetically from *his* anthropoidal relatives and allies *him* rather with the deadliest of carnivora.[4]

Popularizers like Robert Ardrey went even further, calling the animal bones weapons pure and simple, claiming that "*man* is a predator whose natural instinct is to kill with a weapon" and that when archaeologists discuss "tools" they really mean weapons. He described our predecessors as killer apes and gave a more extreme version of the aggression theory of evolution. His ideas are graphically enacted in the Clarke-Kubrick film 2001: A *Space Odyssey*, which opens on an arid desert with piles of bones here and there and several hairy creatures crouch-hopping about. Suddenly one of the apelike individuals picks up a bone hesitantly, swings it idly, and, in a flash of genius, brings it down on a fellow creature's head. From this first scene of unmotivated violence, the film leaps to others depicting group hunts and skirmishes against neighboring bands. In four scenes with a total of twenty-odd males, only one female appears: a nighttime shot shows a group huddled on the ground sleeping as one member holds a baby to her breast.

Theories of evolution in which only men evolve are still widely circulated and widely taught in both popular and semi-scientific media, though they relate much more to the ethos of historical civilizations than to that of primitive peoples or to the animal world.[5]

In the past, creation myths commonly attacked, blamed, or punished women for the human condition. The almost total disappearance of woman in 2001 typified the high misogyny which characterized the nineteen fifties and sixties. If the ratio of females to males presented above—the section in the film titled "Dawn of *Man* Four Million B.C."—had actually obtained, there would have been no proliferation, no evolutionary success, and no human race. Taken to its extremes, the devaluing of women, highly illogical but not at all uncommon in many cultures, accomplishes just this—witness the example of the King William Island Netsilik Eskimos, who were described by Rasmussen in 1931 as a tribe on the way to extinction because of their high rate of female infanticide.[6]

Physical-anthropology textbooks used to focus on hunting as the chief occupation of our ancestors:

> Let us consider an early human hominid hunting group as it rests after the day's activities. The males are planning the next day's hunt. They ask for the support of supernatural entities; they decide which animals to hunt and how to divide the carcasses among the hunters and their families; and they conclude the planning session by talking about the females *who are not present. Of course we dare not speculate about what the females were doing.* After this human condition was achieved, nothing could stop the evolutionary success and progress of this fortunate primate except *man* himself.[7]

Thus Buettner-Janusch in 1966.

Much was made of the males' superior strength and intelligence and it was assumed that one of their functions was to defend females and children against predators in the open savanna. In 1970 David Pilbeam described our hominid forebears more evenhandedly, speculating that the females would have provided most of the food by foraging for plant food and small game, but he still saw the males as responsible for planning and protection, a position he later abjured.[8]

Recently, voices have been raised to point out that there is little substantiation for the view that there are more predators on the savanna than in the forest. Louis Leakey decided in 1972 that predators were not that much of a danger to our first ancestors,[9] while Clifford Jolly feels that there is little evidence for the "catastrophic desiccation" depicted in the desert scene from 2001 as well as in other male-aggression evolution theories.

Jolly is one of the younger anthropologists who would set aside "the current obsession with hunting and carnivorousness" and look for a different kind of behavior in early hominids associated with open-country grassland alternating with patches of woodland and forest edges. His paper "The Seed-Eaters" offers an interpretation of human evolution based on an analogy with gelada baboons and would have had us sitting on our haunches chewing grass and weed seed for some ten million years while we were becoming prehumans. During this time, he feels, we developed fatty buttock pads and such sexual differentiations as beards and breasts. It's a somewhat deterministic theory which claims that our grinding molars and the manipulative tongues that were later so useful in speech developed out of a diet of hard, round pellets. He sees a fairly early division of sex roles in which males, who had been used as scouts against danger, became mammal hunters, while females and young, in continuing to gather vegetable produce, invented cultural devices, such as bags and digging sticks, enabling them to bring back enough for the males to eat. Jolly's theory would have had one species of hominid continuing to be chiefly vegetarian and coexisting with an omnivorous line that developed into humanity.[10]

It is a projection of Western civilization's imperialist values to perceive hunting as conquest, as an extension of aggression, and to admire or dislike it as such. The reports of anthropologists who have studied extant gatherer-hunters—African

Pygmies, the Hadza, the Kalahari San (the people who used to be known as Bushmen), and Australian Aborigines—provide some sharp contrasts between the stereotype of hunting as aggressive male adventure and actuality. Colin Turnbull's studies of African Pygmies overturned many of our preconceptions about size, dominance, and subject-master relations. In the two Pygmy groups he studied he found very little aggression, emotional or physical, citing as proof the absence of warfare, feuding, witchcraft, and sorcery. Moreover, their hunting was not in itself an aggressive activity. Knowing that they were depleting natural resources, there was regret at destroying life, even an element of compassion for the animals killed. His belief that the Pygmies were very gentle people is an opinion shared by many others who have worked with hunters.[11]

Since the nineteen twenties and thirties, when Dart and Broom were making their discoveries, other very early prehuman skeletal parts have been unearthed, in Kenya, Tanzania, and Ethiopia, often in association with crude stones that have been shaped by other than natural agencies and can be identified as tools. Many of these predate the remains discussed by Dart and Broom, carrying the story of human evolution back four or five million years, and most scientists no longer believe that the first implements our ancestors used were the bones from their kill. In the caves in the Transvaal where Dart and Broom had worked, all the bones—of hyenas, baboons, and prehumans among others—were in varying states of preservation. It could not really be demonstrated that the wear on those claimed as tools had not been caused by time, weather, and accidents of displacement, similar to the elements affecting the remains of the presumed tool users.[12] It was not clear which were the eaters and which the eaten.

Moreover, few anthropologists today give credence to the killer-ape theory, and some previous exponents of the baboon-human analogy have recanted in favor of the chimpanzee. At the moment, a rare species of pygmy chimpanzee, *Pan paniscus*, which lives in the forest regions of Zaire, is under scrutiny as our closest animal relative.

That the notion of instinct aggression still lingers on in the popular mythology is not surprising. If, over millions of years, male humans hunted and developed tools primarily as weapons and butchery instruments, then there is little hope for change since these "behavior patterns" are biologically inherent, genes for aggression having been selected for successful evolution over the eons. Books and films that glorify male violence and possession take the onus of moral responsibility and change off the public. Kubrick and Lorenz reciting their "new litany of 'innate depravity'" are only the latest version of the Calvinist notion of original sin, and Ardrey's claim for a territorial imperative is a reworking of the earlier argument for property rights versus human rights, which grew out of the nineteenth century's "instinct of property," used as a justification for capitalism and imperialist expansion.[13] Both arguments have had a wide popularity through the ages; they have always been useful for defending the status quo against demands for more equitable treatment by the underclasses, and they save the bother of thinking. Even a thinker as great as Freud in certain areas fudged the social implications of carrying his thoughts to their logical conclusions by accepting ideas already exploded in his own time with regard to instinct, evolution, and anthropology.

The vision of man as an angry beast with an instinct for destruction does not apply to the beasts themselves. It is human brain power, with its capacity for cruelty and kindness, which projected the former onto the beasts. An animal who hunts is not aggressive, she or he is hungry, while the cat playing with a mouse is unaware of the mouse's suffering (a suffering which is certainly made less acute than a human's would be by the relative simplicity of the mouse's brain and nervous system).

On the basis of the animal studies discussed in Part I, as well as newly discovered fossils and new approaches to social anthropology, evolutionists are changing their minds. They are coming to realize that co-operation, mutual aid, and kindness have been more conducive to survival than the nineteenth-century battle mentality projected onto nature.

The male bias in anthropology led to systematic undervaluation of the role of women. The price of having a civilization largely recorded by men has been the glorification of what men are, do, or have, the denigration of women's occupations, faculties, and physiology. Only child care, which involved the upbringing of males, was spared, to a certain extent.

Today the androcentric nature of science has come under scrutiny, and the theories of Dart, Broom, and their popularizers are seen as a reflection of our recent culture rather than that of our past, theories which arose in a society that glorifies competitiveness, out of a civilization distinguished by the brutality with which it has attacked less fortunate people.[14]

7

The Carrier Bag
Theory of Evolution

Since hunting is of less importance than was earlier
thought . . . it might then be equally profitable to
consider *Man* the Gatherer or *Man* the Potter.
                    —D. W. Deetz, *Man the Hunter*

Without trying to grasp all of the fortuitous combination of accidents and purposes which created a larger brain and human evolution, something which may be beyond the scope of the most sophisticated minds and computers, let us take a glance at our past in the light of new discoveries and with a feminist consciousness. The previous explanation for human evolution gave hunting as the master behavior pattern for the human species, claiming this activity provided a school of learning wherein children—boys, of course—were informed about animal behavior and anatomy, men learned to co-operate, and thus the human nervous system developed.[1] Perhaps there is an alternative: I submit woman's invention of the carrier bag as the take-off point for the quantum advance which created the multiplier effect that led to humanity.

Humans developed from hominids who lived in tropical and semitropical zones, in Africa it is now believed. For the first several million years our history was made in frost-free zones. There is good reason to believe that during this time we were eating mostly vegetable food and that it was women who supplied the major portion of what we ate.

Present-day anthropologists look at opposite ends of the spectrum when they seek to divine the nature of our predecessors four to five million years ago. In the older part of the spectrum, they make analogies with close animal relatives like the chimpanzee, as we saw in Part I. At the same time, however, they study extant Stone Age foragers for subsistence clues, always realizing that there must be an enormous gap between the first prehumans and any present-day humans, no matter how limited their technology. In the second area, and with tools several million years more advanced than those of our ancestors, the scientists were astonished to discover that among the few remaining people in the world who do not (or did not in the near past) practice agriculture but live (or lived) in a way reminiscent of our Stone-Age origins, food gathered by women supplied the bulk of the daily diet. In temperate and tropical zones, plant and vegetable food, sometimes shellfish, supplied 65 to 80 per cent of the diet, and women did the gathering, though men might satisfy their own individual needs by gathering food when out alone. According to Richard B. Lee, hunting is the dominant mode of subsistence only in the highest latitudes (60 or more degrees from the equator). In cool to cold temperate latitudes, 40 to 59 degrees from the equator, fishing dominates. In warm temperate, subtropical, and tropical latitudes, gathering is by far the most important means of subsistence.[2] Only among the tiny segment of Central Arctic Eskimos does hunting (including seal hunting and fishing) provide the entire food supply. And Eskimos, who until quite recently lived farther south than they now do, prove nothing except the extreme hardship conditions to which the human species is able to adapt, though probably only temporarily since Eskimos as Eskimos in a primitive habitat were a dying people ten years ago; today there are probably more anthropologists studying them than extant tribespeople.

While humans are and always have been omnivorous, during the major part of our evolution, as in most parts of the earth even today, vegetables provided most of our sustenance, a fact

which is reflected in our eight-yard-long gut, the shape and surface of our teeth, possibly in the fact that animal fats seem to
contribute to hardening of the arteries and that most of the
known long-lived peoples—the Hunzas, the Abkhasians, and
the Ecuadorians—eat very little meat.

Our early ancestors did more rather than less gathering, for
they did not have weapons like those of recent Stone Age peoples, let alone the ones present-day humans use.[3] The savanna
mosaic with its varied terrain was rich in fruits, nuts, seeds, and
other plant foods. Judging by recent fossil finds, the earliest
prehuman groups lived near water sources with forest cover adjacent; later they moved out into the patchy savanna with its
many different kinds of vegetation: high grass, bushes, and
trees along river courses.[4]

Plant food leaves little trace in the archaeological record,
while animal bones remain. Laboratory analysis of human coprolites—fossilized feces—can provide more exact information
on what our ancestors ate. Developed only in the last ten years,
few studies have been completed. The results are often ambiguous, but they tend to confirm the proposition that vegetables
were predominant and that in most places protein sources were
infrequently supplied by big-game hunting. We have no studies
going back to our African antecedents, but coprolites from a
seaside camp at Terra Amata on the French Riviera dated to
about two hundred thousand years ago—a time when most
textbooks claim big-game hunting was the predominant human
activity—have been analyzed. They showed flecks of charcoal,
indicating the use of fire, and portions of undigested seafood in
the form of mollusk shell. The seaside campers may have been
enjoying roast oysters. Twelve-thousand-year-old coprolites
from Mexico indicated a diet based largely on millet seed,
while comparatively recent remains, from archaic Indians in
Southwest Texas about 3000 B.P., showed a diet consisting of
plant food—flowers, grasses, seeds, and fruit—with grasshoppers
as the major source of animal protein and lizards, rodents, and
fish as minor sources.[5]

Essential to the procuring of all these foods is the container.
The first cultural device was probably a recipient. Jane Goodall

commented that when she provided an unlimited source of bananas at her camp, the chimpanzees were particularly frustrated at being unable to take away more fruit than they could hold in their arms. Though chimpanzees share some food, mothers in particular sharing with infants, one distinction that scientists make between animals and humans is that the latter universally share food, given the delayed development of the human child, born with a large head and brain and a weak, small body.

Chimpanzees catch small animals without weapons, and several scientists have demonstrated that early hominids could have captured small animals like rabbits and baby gazelles by hand and scavenged the uneaten portions of cheetah and lion kills. Where male evolutionists used to believe that *men* first stood up in order to use tools for hunting, today women scientists suggest that women and men stood up in order to have their hands free for gathering and carrying.[6]

Meat, which would have been a rare and welcome treat, can be dragged back to camp in one piece; small animals, taken by the hand, can be torn up and shared out at the spot, but gathered food needs something to hold it. The first container could have been adapted from nature—a large leaf for folding, a piece of bark, a broken ostrich egg, like those still used for carrying water by the Kalahari Desert San. If the early hominids made nests for sleeping, as chimpanzees and gorillas do, they could have applied their knowledge of nest making for contriving a basketlike device, or adapted a netlike sling or an animal skin, similar to those used for carrying babies.

Many theorizers feel that the earliest cultural inventions must have been a container to hold gathered products and some kind of sling or net carrier.[7] The baby carrier was particularly important, given the increasing immaturity of infants, as demonstrated by the ages of tooth eruption on fossil jaws.[8] Moreover, five million years ago our ancestors had already evolved the flat foot for standing upright, running, and walking much as we do, in contrast to the grasping foot which characterizes chimpanzees, gorillas, and other primates less close to us, and the evolutionary process which resulted in the comparative hairlessness of humans must also have been in course; so infants could not cling with their feet and had less and less to which to cling. As a result of the long period during which offspring had to be carried, females had to develop a method of portage for their infants. Plenty of material was available— vines, hides, human hair. In Sally Slocum's theory, the technique was extended from carrying babies to carrying food and was followed by other cultural inventions—choppers and grinders for food preparation, and eventually weapons.

Women, then, would have been the first to devise containers: they themselves were containers of children, and they were used to carrying small children on their backs or their hips, or in their arms. Much later, they are associated with the earliest traditions of basketry and pottery, and even now they frequently serve as bearers or porters in non-Western societies.

Human mothers did not stay home with babies until very recently. The earliest evidence for settled living shows up in the archaeological record only some twelve thousand years ago. Most humans on earth were nomadic long after that, staying in one spot for only brief periods, in some places for a short season. People on the move carry their babies with them. Both baby carrier and food carrier are universal among gatherers and hunters, even those with the sparest range of material equipment.

The invention of the container can be seen as fundamental in the evolution of a large-brained, two-legged human being. It freed the hands for gathering and provided temporary storage for food such as nuts and fruits. Moreover, the concept of the container was essential in the development of an infant sling. In the civilized West, this last disappeared for centuries, not to say millennia. In the nineteenth century C.E., it was replaced, for the affluent, by the expensive and cumbersome baby carriage, which had to be wheeled with two hands. Most women had to carry their babies in their arms or in a shawl, to stay indoors with them, or to find someone else to stay with them.

The infant carrier bag was not reinvented until after World War II, when the first canvas sling seats were introduced. I remember being stared at on the subway when I carried my six-months-old daughter on my hip so that I could make my way down from exile in the Bronx to my former home in Greenwich Village. Now many forms are on the market—back packs similar to those in which Indian papooses were carried, shoulder slings, and hip carriers—but they are still not all that common. The baby carrier enables a woman to get around and to have her arms free—for gathering fruit or for digging into her purse for change. But our Western image is of an immobile woman, seated indoors, holding a babe in arms or rocking a stationary cradle.

Is it devolution in Western civilization that we lost this cultural device after the invention of village life and agriculture, though peoples like the American Indian kept it all the time?

8

Woman the Potter: Household Equipment as the Key

When the Indian potter collects clay, she asks the consent of the riverbed and sings its praises for having made something as beautiful as clay. When she fashions the clay into a form, she does so by evoking the shapes of sacred things in which the power moves and the life dwells. When she fires her pottery, to this day, she still offers prayers so the fire will not discolor or burst her wares. And, finally, when she paints her pottery, she imprints it with the images which give it life and power—because for an Indian, pottery is something significant, not just a utility but a "being" for which there is as much of a natural order as there is for persons or foxes or trees.
—Jamake Highwater[1]

The carrier bag and women's gathering activities could have been the master pattern in human evolution. An extension of this idea involves the invention of many kinds of household equipment, from containers to baskets and pottery, from digging sticks to stone pounding tools and scrapers and cutters, all used primarily by women in the recent past.

The use of the carrier bag facilitated the accumulation of botanical information. Hominid females would communicate the whereabouts of a rich stand of fruiting bushes, when seeds or nuts could be picked from grass or trees and where they grew, so that a whole store of knowledge of different kinds of plants enlarged the human brain, which in turn enabled the developing hominids to classify and investigate the natural world about them, in the classic model of the feedback mechanisms that shaped the evolution of humanity.* Experimentation with the materials necessary for containers and carriers led to the exploration of the raw materials in the world around so that the developing hominids came to penetrate the resources of their environment and to develop technology.

Food was shared first with infants but also with older siblings and with compatible females who went out to gather, thus increasing both socializing and planning capacities of the new species. Divining different uses for materials exercised the brain, which in turn allowed the hominids to improve their inventive utilization of natural resources in the immediate vicinity. Most of these resources—both containers and foods—would not survive in the fossil record, of course.

We can imagine the great discovery when a mother was able to carry water back to a sick child in a temporary camp or resting place, by using a natural container—an empty ostrich shell or a hollowed-out gourd, perhaps the bole of a tree, or even an animal-hide pouch or natural sponge. Chimpanzees use leaves as sponges to sop up water from the hollow of a tree trunk, say, an example of animal tool use, but they have never reached the evolutionary level which would permit them to give their infants or other chimpanzees water.

Materials which do show up in the archaeological record are stone tools. The earliest remaining tools—natural stones, called manuports by the archaeologists, and very simple flaked stones —are two to five million years old. As recently as ten years ago, their use was credited to men, and they were interpreted as

---

* "There is of course a constant feedback so that tool use contributes to the patterning of the brain, thus becoming both subject and object in both a neurological and philosophical sense."—William S. Laughlin[2]

weapons or implements for big-game hunting. Today they are being re-examined in the light of the greater importance now assigned to women, as well as to plants, in human evolution, and they look more like household equipment. Tools which used to be called choppers were probably used for pointing digging sticks (today used chiefly by the women of foraging as well as of horticultural peoples), and for cutting by means of a sawing action. Others of heavier stone were used for hammering and bashing, for example, breaking open nuts and preparing parts of plants inedible in their natural state but palatable and digestible after pounding. They would also have served for breaking open animal bones and for dealing with tough parts of animal hide, eaten even today by foraging peoples.[3]

The digging stick was probably the second hominid invention, after the container. This universal tool of present-day women foragers and horticulturalists could have been developed by combining two techniques, known to be used by chimpanzees, in a conception imagined several million years ago by the larger and more complex brain of our forebears. Jane Goodall has described (see Chapter 3) the process by which young chimpanzees learned from their mothers how to prepare leafy branches as probes with which they extracted juicy white grubs from termite hills. In laboratory studies, chimpanzees have been observed to use sticks as levers to open doors as well as to draw fruit within their reach. With more brain and manual dexterity, our ancestors would have been more inventive, combining the principle of the lever and the probe to produce the digging stick.

These tools would have been used for collecting plants and eggs and for extracting honey, termites and other insects, and small burrowing animals. Implements included sticks for digging and knocking down, rocks to crack open nuts or fruits with tough outer coverings, and several kinds of containers. Sharp-edged rocks may also have been used for cutting some of the savanna roots and tubers in the hominids' new environment, foods that were tough and fibrous but large enough to be divided.[4]

The temporary windbreak or shelter made from branches

was another invention that would grow almost naturally out of the primate's nest-making ability. Even today it is women who are responsible for building windbreaks or branch huts among such foraging groups as the Mbuti Pygmies and the Kalahari San, as well as among many groups, both foraging and horticultural, with much more advanced techniques.

With the passage of time, tool use and manufacturing ability improved. Roughly round stones of about a million years ago, formerly described as missiles, proved on close examination to have been shaped by battering and bashing. Under the old aggression-evolution theories they had been viewed as leather-thonged bolas like those used by South American tribes for throwing. Now it is believed that they were used primarily for pounding vegetable food and for breaking and splitting open animal bones to reach the marrow within. Large cutting tools of the same period—one million years ago—also evidence growing technical command. They appear to be only incidentally associated with meat eating and were probably connected with the collection of vegetable foods more than with animal-food preparation.[5] Although archaeologists used to claim that all the stone tools of these early periods were used for killing animals and cutting meat, it is now thought that only the light-duty tools of a million years ago—flake knives, small scrapers, and chopping tools—may have had some connection with butchery practices.[6] Scrapers are used in connection with the tanning of hides, a technique performed only by women among such northerly peoples as the Eskimos, the Montagnais Naskapi, and the Cree, and both women and men among, for example, the Kalahari San.

By this time the pounding stones may have been used not only for tenderizing roots and tubers to make them more palatable and more digestible but for making meal out of seeds, and for removing the husks of nuts, fruits, and seeds.

A few million years after the invention of the container, the digging stick, the pounding stone, and cutting and chopping or pointing tools, women may have come upon a discovery which was to revolutionize the world for the species we now know as humanity. This was fire, which is presently thought to have come into use about a million years ago.

Most of us have read Charles Lamb's story of roast pig, in which the accidental burning of their house produced the world's first gourmet dish for the male protagonist and his son. Archaeology tells us that fire was invented long before both the keeping of animals and the building of permanent houses. Despite Lamb's own tenderhearted care of and collaboration with his sister Mary, it is unsurprising in the context of the times that he saw only men involved with the first use of fire. In my own fantasy I can picture an accidental discovery of fire. After millions of years of hominid existence in Africa, a severe electrical storm ignited a dry stretch of savanna grassland. The fire blazed, destroying miles of terrain, forest and plain. The sparse inhabitants of the valley—scattered bands of ten or more people—fled as did the animals, those which were not caught and consumed by flames. Many perished. It was weeks before one band ventured back to their old round, the fields and clumps of bushes where they were wont to pick fruits and dig tubers. One woman idly probed the scorched ground with her digging stick and a blackened tuber came to light. She picked it up and her daughter began to play with it. Charred on one side, baked dark on the other, it still retained some of the fire's heat, and as the child held it, tossing it from one hand to the other, the vegetable broke open. Experimentally, she put it to her mouth, then excitedly offered the roast yam to her mother. It was delicious—mealy, tender, and fluffy—and tasted far better than the raw or even pounded product they were accustomed to eat.

More realistically, did the process of chipping away at a piece of wood with a particularly hard stone or flint while sharpening a digging stick produce a spark which ignited the wood? Or possibly, in making a stone tool, using one implement as shaper, the other as shaped, a woman produced a spark which ignited her grass basket of seeds or roots, and the same fortunate experimental probing led to further developments. Whatever the sequence of events which produced the fire and the brain power to use it—whether brilliant flash or long-term experiment—women's connection with vegetable and animal food must be placed at the pivot of the plot; they were early and initially involved in the utilization of fire.

Fire proved to be one of the most effective instruments known to humans. Historically it has been used by women and men, on individual and group scales. It seems to me more likely that from its use in cooking came its other uses, not proof but evidence for its invention by women. Fire made available foods which in their raw state were poisonous or barely edible. It tenderized meat, making meat protein more accessible; it made starches more digestible. It also enhanced aesthetic appreciation by improving flavors and offering opportunities for creative combinations of foods. It enabled humans to store meat and fish through smoking and, eventually, made possible a wide variety of prepared dishes. It offered the possibility of cleanliness, another aesthetic improvement and an aid to health, through the heating of water, in containers or by placing hot stones in natural rock basins.

In hunting it serves, in small, to smoke out animals from their burrows, a technique currently used by the South-West African G'wi women as well as by the women of the Pitjandjara and other Australian Aborigine peoples. In large, fire drives which forced herd animals into prepared traps—over precipices, into pits or runways—required the co-operation of groups of women and men. Before farming, fire was used to change the ecology of the landscape, to produce desired plants, to increase grass cover, and to attract grazing animals for easier hunting. One example is given where burns were set primarily to encourage certain much-prized plants; as a secondary result, fleeing animals were intercepted by lines of hunters.[7] Once people began to farm, clearing by fire was the most energy-saving method of cultivation known to preindustrial humans, as it still is.[8]

Women are still the keepers of the flame among nomadic foragers; they cherish a lighted coal in their carriers as they go from camping ground to camping ground; they nurse the fire and they may also start one with the most primitive of fire-producing devices.

Later in history they will be associated with the hearth as goddess of warmth and fire. Sculptured female figures found buried by or in the hearth in paleolithic mammoth-hunting cultures have present-day counterparts in the goddess who appears under various names in Siberian and Aleut tribal folklore.[9] The Cherokee Indian town of Chota was supposed to be the home of the "mother fire" and was therefore considered the leader and most important of the seven Cherokee towns. There is a double association, with maternal warmth, the mother's body heat, and the maternal nursing function, which was extended to the preparation of food.

After the initial use of fire for cooking and nighttime warmth in the species' African homeland, it was, of course, used for heat, in fact made possible our perdurance in the chillier climates to which we spread. The knowledge of fire enabled us to sojourn in cooler places and in Europe, to survive the ice ages, which came so much later in the unfolding story.

The container invented by woman had increased in complexity—a varied range of forms and materials would have been in use—by the time fire was utilized. The baked clay pot was far in the future, but the first cooking utensil could have been an animal-hide sack into which hot stones were dropped to make broth, mush, or cooked fruits and vegetables, with or without meat and fish ingredients. Tubers, roots, and meats could be roasted in the coals; the techniques involved were rudimentary and immediately available to the less imaginative. Building a fire utilizes principles of convection and heat radiation; it is a process of energy conversion whose principles were only later articulated in the science of physics. Cooking is chemistry. The initial experiments for the production of fire and kitchen equipment and an inductive range of food production and cooking methods involved considerable imaginative projection and ingenuity. By the time they occurred, woman's large brain was ready for the challenge that the material and the ingredients presented. In the recent past, women did the scraping and tanning of hides in many foraging societies. In her field work among the Montagnais Naskapi Indians, Eleanor Leacock observed a Montagnais woman who was busy tanning an animal hide while her husband sat beside her rocking their sick baby. Either of them could comfort the ailing child but only the woman knew how to tan leather.[10] A half million years ago we can see women using their stone scrapers to produce the first cooking pot.

The experiments in science and technology that produced cooking also, much later, produced the first pottery, initially made of unbaked clay, later fire-hardened. Leather bags and pottery for carrying water made it possible to sleep for a few days away from a water source. Women carrying water are universal images, whether in Africa and Australia, or in the biblical tale of Rebecca bringing the water jar from the well.

Women, then, would have been the primary inventors and users of a whole complex of devices and techniques around which group activities and subsistence were organized, leading to the creation of culture and, eventually, civilization.

9

Woman the Hunter

There was probably little differentiation by sex, both in size and in occupation, among human ancestors of some millions of years ago.[1] Even today, in societies where men hunt animals and women gather plants, as among the African San, the division of labor is not hard and fast: men will stop to gather vegetable food for themselves; if—as often happens—the hunting is unproductive they may bring back gathered food rather than return empty-handed; in season, they help the women collect a particularly plentiful resource, such as mongongo nuts.[2] The division of labor that exists is related to mobility: women with infants to protect and carry cannot move fast enough and far enough to hunt efficiently.[3]

In group hunting, particularly in net hunting and fire drives, women have always participated, whether among the fairly egalitarian African Pygmies or the horse-riding, male-dominant North American Sioux. Prairie tribes like the Shoshone, the Paiute, and the Ute organize community rabbit hunts in which young and old take part.

Women frequently scout and set nets. Australian Aborigine women are trackers and they hunt small game; on occasion they also bring down a kangaroo with their trained dingoes, while in certain tribes women supply the major portion of animal and fish food, as well as the preponderant plant food. Foods hunted by Tiwi women in northern Australia include

opossums, iguanas, bandicoots, several kinds of snakes and lizards and rats, as well as shellfish and vegetables. They provide
most of the protein and all of the plant food, with equipment
consisting of a trained dog, an ax, fire, and a bark container.[4]

There are many other specific examples of women participating in hunting despite the fairly general sex differentiation
which prevailed in the recent historical past. Occupational
differences between women and men are quite sharp among the
Ojibwa and Greenland Eskimos, yet both are such individ-
ualistic societies that women have often hunted with weapons,
taught by their fathers or by necessity when no man was available, or even because they wanted to.[5]

Women have been the bearers and nurturers; they have also
worked alongside men and made major innovations, something
observers of the human scene could easily have verified. Everywhere one looks, except for a few technologically advanced cultures, women turn out to be the base on which first life, then
society are built.

Three to five million years ago the activity which supplied
the modest proportion of meat eaten by our hominid forebears
was probably closer to scavenging than to hunting in the modern sense. Small animals and vulnerable young would have
been captured by hand or brought down with a stick or a
stone, and large animals that were ill or caught off guard would
also have been captured. Even in the recent past, San and
Hadza were not above following vultures to the lair of a sick or
wounded animal, or otherwise competing with animal scav-
engers.

Males could have been more far-ranging than females, since
the latter would have carried their infants with them, on the
hip or the shoulders, and would often have been accompanied
by half-grown children while they collected plant food. But not
always. Though most of the females would have been occupied
looking after infants and young children, foraging for plant
food not too far from the base, females without offspring and
males would have engaged in hunting and carrying back the
food obtained from the chase.[6] Female chimpanzees have recently been observed to participate in the hunt. In a year-long

study project Geza Teleki recorded ten kills by male chimpanzees and two by females.[7]

Nancy Tanner and Adrienne Zihlman point out that early hominids hunted by day, as primates—baboons and chimpanzees—do now, thus avoiding competition with and danger from the larger animal predators, who hunt at night and sleep during the day. They suggest that the females used their digging sticks to unearth burrowing animals—hares, porcupines, gophers, moles, etc.—and that in the process of exchanging information about animal holes, as earlier about plant locations, they stretched their brain power and communicating ability, thus furthering human development. If defense against predators was needed the hominid females and males would jump up and down and wave their arms and make noises to frighten away the larger animals, methods still used by present-day gatherer-hunters.[8]

That the idea of women hunters was not unknown to later authors is clear from Classical accounts and Greek vase paintings. The tradition of women participating in these activities lingered on long after the actuality seems to have disappeared. It must have been based on some memories of the past. Indo-European women hunting on horse and on foot are frequently depicted and evidence of their activities will be discussed in a later chapter. Though the late stages of pregnancy and the nursing of infants would interfere with the pursuit, young women and nonmothers evidently joined the young men in the hunt, as Cherokee and Iroquois Indian women often did.[9] The concept of the woman hunter is known to Greek mythology and must have been based on some experience. The goddesses of the hunt prove that exceptional women did hunt, as exceptional women have done everything males do.

There are two reasons why we have had so many fulsome descriptions of Man the Hunter. As noted earlier, Western men have seen hunting as conquest activity and chosen to focus on it. They wrote extensively about the glories of the chase and paid little attention to women's food-gathering activities. One much quoted description of the Australian Aborigines devoted five times more space to the former than to the latter, though the women provided the bulk of the tribes' daily diet, about 70 per cent by weight.[10]

Moreover, we think in terms of man the hunter, instead of women and men the hunters, because men had time to invent the myth. Among modern hunter-gatherers, where both women and men have more leisure time than people in technologically advanced societies, women put in time regularly for gathering—every day or several days a week—else the people would not eat. While men may, infrequently, go out on a hunt which lasts for long hours, overnight, even days, they also rest for days, weeks, or sometimes months after the fatigues of hunting. The kind of hunting which developed in our species' maturity was a young person's game, requiring magnificent eyesight, co-ordination, and endurance. The G'wi, the Hadza (who spent more time gambling their arrows than shooting them), the Ainu, all tended to retire from long-distance spear or arrow hunting—both of which developed long after the earliest hominid period—by their middle or late thirties, though they continued to participate in the kind of hunting done by women with children.[11] In after years there was plenty of time to sit around and tell of past exploits, to create a mythology, as, in the past five thousand years, surviving older men talked and wrote about the exciting battles in which so many younger men had lost their lives.

If one factor could be offered to explain why man has played a greater part than woman in taking credit for civilization, if not in creating it, the concept Man the Idler is illuminating. E. H. Gombrich tells of an isolated tribe in Africa, close to the center of the Sudan, where the young men spend most of their time decorating their own and each other's bodies with colored earth, modifying or repainting the elaborate designs as soon as they become smeared. He comments that here, as elsewhere, it is the women who do most of the work.[12] Back in 1623, when the Englishman Richard Jobson anchored in the mouth of the Gambia, he noted that among the Mandingo the women did most of the work and that the men were occupied for only two months of the year. His observations were substantiated in a book published a hundred years later, *Travels into the Inland*

Parts of Africa by Francis Moore. The men worked without respite at seed time and harvest, but for the rest of the year they lay on the *bentang* in the shade, smoking, gossiping, and playing a game which resembled chess. Although game abounded in the forest and the river swarmed with fish, they hardly even bothered to hunt or fish.[13]

After all, is it not idle speculation which is at the bottom of so much human knowledge and art? Humans are the only animals that ask why, and men have been freer than women both to seek the answers and to take credit for answers found by women and men.

10

The First Teachers

There was nothing resembling the nineteenth- or twentieth-century family among early hominids. They would have had even longer and closer mother-child relations than have been described for chimpanzee and gorilla groups. Social groupings would have been the rule, but there may have been occasional male solitaries, as there are among great apes, and in line with the recently documented cases of two World War II Japanese soldiers who managed alone for decades in the South Pacific. Human behavior has always been subject to flexibility and change, and it is likely that even the very earliest societies took different forms in different environments.[1]

With the understanding gained from studying our primate relatives we can see the flexible human group (or band) as an advance over other primate groupings. Let us not be fooled by the seeming anarchy of forest chimpanzees and baboons at one end of the evolutionary scale or of foraging humans at the other. A flexible structure is still a structure. Randomness does not prevail; in fact it is a more complex organizational form than the comparatively inflexible ordering of, say, a game-park baboon troop.[2] Evolutionists note that the most permanent tie among chimpanzees is that between mothers, infants, and half-grown young—the human family without a father. Adult male chimpanzees are attracted to the group by the mother-child relationship and not for sexual reasons. In the same wise it is speculated that early hominid bands would have consisted of two or three compatible families of mothers and offspring, to which three or four adult males might attach themselves.[3] The basic human organization centers also around the mother, and in times of crisis society breaks down to this form. Elaborations on this unit are the product of our social evolution.

On the surface rigidity looks easier and more efficient than an open structure, but it doesn't advance the group. Authoritarianism is a specious efficiency: you have one leader and when that leader goes the group falls apart, not having learned to share or to devise peaceful transitional ways of adapting to change. In the long run, authoritarianism and rigidity are counterproductive. Flexibility is the only way we've survived, for conditions are always changing and living organisms must change, too. This is even more true in the case of humans who change their environment and then have to adapt to the new environment. The more radically they change the environment, the more radical the necessary adaptations.

Since promiscuity has remained a constant in human society throughout history, despite the strongest societal controls at times, and since it is a relatively universal characteristic among the primates, it would have been more rather than less prevalent in our remote past. Out of the family of mother and infant and older children would develop close relations between brothers and sisters—words that evoke the strongest connotations of loyalty for most human groups. We shall not look for a father as father until millions of years later—perhaps nine or eight thousand years ago. This does not mean that a male was not associated with an adult female for a period of time or that he would not have taken a playful, tolerant, and protective interest in her children or in all the children of the group.

In the savanna-fringe life of early hominids, mothers were —as they still are—the first teachers. They showed their children how and where to gather food. They taught, by example and precept, the principle of food sharing. Chimpanzees do not teach their children directly; females are accompanied by their offspring, who learn by watching their mothers termite.

With the larger hominid brain and some means of communication, hominid mothers would have instructed their infants directly, a basic difference between animal and human capacities. Early lessons would have been in the use of a digging stick to locate tubers, roots, and burrowing animals.[4]

The food-sharing adaptation was necessitated by the delayed development of the human child. Till the last decades, an artificial relationship was postulated, based on the modern Western industrial family, which assumed that women stayed in the home, or at the home base, taking care of babies while men brought home the bacon, going out to hunt and providing food and protection.

Any observation of non-Western societies would have disproved this projection immediately. Before industrialization, women usually had their babies with them, whether they went out to work or gathered close to shelter. Sometimes, as among the San and the Mbuti Pygmies today, women went away to gather or hunt, and young children or elderly adults were left in charge of infants, a practice also common among agricultural peoples. Male protection of females is not characteristic of foraging societies; it is a phenomenon that seems to have grown with the conquest syndrome, myth and reality, and with the invention of war, which will not be seen in human society until millions of years later—about 5000 B.P.

Sometimes women's contributions to subsistence were used as evidence of the brutalization of our non-Western fellows, but certain obvious deductions were not drawn. The fact is that, with mothers supplying most of the food for small children, increased co-operation was taught on all levels. Mothers gathering together, with and for children, increased communicating abilities, enlarging the brain, and further facilitating human intercourse and sociability. The institution of meat sharing was also affected by the set toward group activities encompassing plant and animal food.

Within the last ten or twenty years studies at both ends of the evolutionary time scale have controverted the past teachings about males going out to hunt while females stayed at the home bases. At the beginning of the time scale males would seem to have played a peripheral role. At our end, when we speak of contemporary gatherer-hunters, we must remember that *Homo sapiens* is another species, albeit related to our ancestors who lived some four million years ago. Moreover, even though present-day foragers may seem to be using technologies as primitive as those used by members of our own species as recently as ten to twenty thousand years ago they—we—have been evolving constantly in the relatively brief period during which our own species has existed, let alone the several million years that separate us from our antenators.

Two elements of distortion creep into reports on foragers written by members of our own Western culture. One is the already mentioned projection of our society's values and preconceptions. The other is the often unrecognized fact of Western influence: there is no society on earth today that has not been touched to a greater or lesser degree by the dominant West. Sometimes this influence has been at work for centuries; in other instances it is more recent; in either case, present-day communications make it omnipresent.

Comparisons with hominids of four million B.P. have bearing, then, not so much in terms of brain and consciousness as on the basis of ecological circumstances; they are always a rough approximation.

Hominids' language abilities would have been inferior to those of the later human species though superior to chimpanzee and gorilla capacities for communication. In the field, chimpanzees are known to employ more than twenty-three different calls or vocalizations, each with its own specific message, and they also use a number of gestures, facial expressions, and body postures to signal information. At a minimum, toolmaking hominids would have had a much larger range of sounds and gestures on tap.[5] However, the early hominid brain would hardly have encompassed the abstract idea of possession, which comes much later in evolution, nor would any hominid male conceive of copulation as meaning male possession of females.

The development of humanity centers around the first couple, mother and child. The children remain close to their mother. Other males are brought in as her temporary or long-term mate, but daughters, sons, even grandchildren, remain in close association with the mother figure over a period of years, stretching out into decades. The mother is the first teacher and out of her teaching came the communicative and socializing abilities which characterize human beings. For the spark that set off the chain of events leading to the later development of our species, in trying to pinpoint the place where a difference in degree becomes a difference in kind, it is necessary to look at the fossils which document human development and change.

11

Early Stages of Evolution

Archaeology and paleontology developed in an age of expanding technology, and the initial explorations of our past tended to focus on tools more than on people, particularly since the former were more commonly unearthed than the latter. In line with the thinking that had defined our species as *man* the toolmaker, the stages of human evolution were originally classified not so much by the physical or human attributes of the changing fossils as by the European place names where different kinds of tools made by our ancestors had first been found.

But the material culture remaining is only the tip of the iceberg. Some years ago Lewis Mumford complained that it wasn't the tools, or the bricks, or the labor which created the Pyramids, it was the human imagination. In that instance human imagination took shape in an exploitative and power-oriented conspicuous display. The songs and stories of the workers, male and female, have not come down to us, though they, too, were products of the human imagination. When it comes to our earliest ancestors, we do not know what degree of imagination they possessed, just where in time the phenomenon we think of as human consciousness began to take form.

Today, the more we learn from scientific advances, the more we are able to face the limitations of our knowledge till now. The resultant enlargement of thought allows us to contemplate, emotionally if not intellectually, the concatenation of forces, understood and undreamed of, which must have been responsible for the world and people of today. New methods and new disciplines are being utilized and old disciplines are adapted to new uses: radiocarbon dating for periods as far back as fifty or sixty thousand years ago; potassium argon dating for long-range calculations, from the millions to several hundred thousand years ago; geology; geography; climatology; paleobotany to analyze pollens; demography; statistics; chemistry and physics; ethnography and social anthropology; to name just a few. Specialists in all these fields have joined hands with the diggers and explorers—the archaeologists and paleontologists—though unfortunately investigations based on technology all too often overvalue the mechanical at the cost of the creative.

Parallel systems of classification of tools and fossils have been devised and are used in combination in attempts to fathom our beginnings. The fossils were originally named after the places where they had been found, and a family tree of human origins was constructed, synchronizing with the millions of years which had been labeled in terms of the kinds of tools our ancestors made. Eventually Louis Leakey coined a name for the creature he considered to be our first forebear: *Homo habilis,* translated by him as able or handy *man,* representing a group of fossils he defined as toolmaking hominids. Other physical anthropologists preferred to see these fossils as a subgroup of one species of advanced ape they had previously classified as *Australopithecus,* the southern ape.

Because one has to start somewhere, let us begin, more or less arbitrarily, with this creature, the ape person so inaccurately depicted by Ardrey, Kubrick, Dart, Broom, etc. An earlier ape, *Ramapithecus,* dated to some fourteen million years ago and known only from jaws and teeth, may or may not have been on the direct line of humanity and may or may not have made stone tools, depending on which paleontologist's theory one accepts.

Until the last few years, however, few scientists questioned both the toolmaking abilities and the close relationship to humanity of the fossils classified under the names *Australopithecus africanus* and *Homo habilis*. No stone tools had been found near the remains described by Broom and Dart, so that the two primate species identified by them as *Paranthropus* were only dubiously assigned to the hominid line. In 1959, however, at Olduvai Gorge, a Tanzanian section of East Africa's Great Rift Valley, where Mary and Louis Leakey had been excavating for twenty-five years and had already found numbers of stone tools and other signs of hominid activity, Mary Leakey came upon a 1.75-million-year-old skull which has been equated with the line of *Paranthropus*, or, as it was eventually denominated, *Australopithecus robustus*.

On the basis of Broom and Dart's South African findings, it had been thought that *Australopithecus* dated back less than a million years. After Mary Leakey's discovery, several more fossil remains were found at Olduvai, giving a fairly complete chronology going back some two million years.

Since 1959 more and more specimens and more varied parts of prehuman lines have been located. To the onlooker it seems as if the story is revised every time the paleontologists find a new fossil—heel, jaw, tooth, or skull as the case may be. Fortunately the slowness of academic publication and scientific caution, debate, and study provide some braking action.

The few stone and bone relics of the remote past which do remain are preserved only under very special conditions of climate and geology: limestone caves, volcanic ash, and dryness.

What is found is not, of course, a true random selection; it is governed by the limiting conditions which permit fossilization, particularly when we go back into the millions of years. Africa's Rift Valley is a lode which has produced a long and fairly consecutive record; in the rain forests not too far away all indications of human habitation would be destroyed by forest rot and humidity. Excavation proceeds apace, and all too often the odd bits and pieces which do emerge are put together and looked at as a linear record of the past, with modifications each time a new piece of "hard evidence" is found. Serious scholars realize that at the moment we have only discrete pages, not a complete book.

Richard Leakey made a spectacular announcement of a new discovery in 1972; in the six years since then, the story of human evolution has once again been rewritten, on the evidence of subsequent discoveries, and it is in constant process.

Two species of *Australopithecus* are presently traced. The first specimen found by Mary Leakey would have belonged to a physically larger line which is thought to have died out because it used natural tools (manuports) but did not manufacture them. Other specimens with a more delicate skeleton were found in coexistence with the larger *robustus* line, but they occurred also at earlier strata. They were initially classified as *Australopithecus*, though some of them were later dubbed *Homo habilis* by Louis Leakey. It is from this species that most paleontologists considered the human race to have descended—or perhaps ascended would be more accurate.

In early books on the subject Mary Leakey was not mentioned. We were told that Louis Leakey discovered that famous first specimen in East Africa, though his wife had actually discovered the skull in situ. Some accounts say that Louis Leakey was indisposed that day and that when Mary sent word he came rushing from his tent to examine the prize of twenty-five years' searching. Louis, however, spoke at the scientific conference where he announced the discovery and presented the skull, strikingly displayed in a black-velvet-lined case.

It is part of the general invisibility of women that husbands have long taken credit for the combined work of husband-and-wife teams, often with more or less generous acknowledgments to their wives. Evidently, Mary Leakey, who recently published a two-volume report on her diggings at Olduvai Gorge, is the diligent and painstaking worker while Louis was the organizer and administrator, as well as the showman. It was he who met the press and the public, who rounded up grant money for support and handled all the other components which are so essential in our present society to back up and make possible scientific research. He was the one who originally staked out the Rift Valley as a place to dig because of its geological components and would seem to have had great enthusiasm and organizing ability.*

The Leakeys' son Richard continues the tradition of his parents. Fossil discoveries in South and East Africa have pushed hominid ages back as far as three to five million years. Digging at one of the sites where australopithecine and habiline fossils had been located, Lake Turkana (formerly Lake Rudolf) in the Omo Basin, Leakey produced, in 1972, a skull of far larger capacity than had been thought possible for the 2.6-million-year-old stratum in which it was located. "The skull had been crushed to hundreds of fragments that were found, eroding on a slope, *and have been pieced together by Dr. Meave Leakey, Richard Leakey's wife*," the *New York Times* reported.[1] If the discovery holds up, it means that the next accepted date of human evolutionary change—the species nominated *Homo erectus*—would have to be pushed backward from one million years ago to almost three million, contemporaneous with *Australopithecus* and *habilis*.

Perhaps the most amusing case of the wife's work being absorbed by and credited to the husband occurred in 1961 when, according to François Bordes, "M. Yves Coppens discovered in Chad, 600 kilometers northeast of Fort-Lamy, a cranium and facial bone fragments of a being similar both to the *Australopithecus* and to *Pithecanthropus*, which was provisionally christened *Tchadanthropus uxoris* ('the Tchad man of the wife,' for it was in fact discovered by Madame Coppens)."[2]

One is reminded of the debate about whether Edmund Hillary or Tenzing Norgay should be called the conqueror of Everest. The need to credit one individual with conquest or discovery is part of our Western individualist way of thinking, the aggressive, hierarchical, and pyramidal context and language in which we shape and express our ideas. We talk about low man on a totem pole, but there can be no high man without the low man, just as, in the circus pyramid, the man or woman who stands on top of other shoulders is certainly not more impor-

---

* As noted in Chapter 3, he also played a role in primate research, steering several young women into the neighboring aspect of human evolution constituted by animal behavior studies.

tant than those who form the base of the pyramid. Most discoveries are co-operative feats which could not take place without the combining of several intelligences: ideas belong to everybody, and new ideas and discoveries come from the synthesis of those of the past.

As recognition for women began to penetrate the popular consciousness, Mary Leakey was introduced into the texts more often, though Louis still held the main spotlight. At the time of his death, in 1972, they were separated, and since then she has emerged from the shadows. Three years later, she took a leaf from his book and held a press conference in Washington to announce a spectacular new discovery, thus reaching the front pages of the *New York Times*.

She had located 3.75-million-year-old jaws and teeth "from at least eleven specimens," leading her to the conclusion that "true *man* had evolved and lived in East Africa" at the same time the physical anthropologists were claiming the human precursors—*Australopithecus* and *habilis*—existed in Tanzania, in Kenya, and in Ethiopia.[3] In the light, then, of recent finds, the debate over *Australopithecus* may be beside the point: both delicate and robust forms may have become extinct, and we would be descended from a separate line represented by the recent, independent finds of Mary Leakey and her son Richard.

The latter has now augmented the controversial skull fragments announced in 1972 and labeled East Rudolf Skull 1470 with other finds. There are similar large-brained skulls as well as two thighbones "of remarkably human proportions."[4] Skull 1470 had a cranial capacity of 800 cubic centimeters, within the parameters of the species known as *Homo erectus* and one third larger than the 1.9-million-year-old skull that Louis Leakey found at Olduvai Gorge in 1963, together with a variety of stone tools, and that provided the basis for his *Homo habilis* classification. Mary Leakey also found fossil footprints showing that hominids walked upright, much as we do, almost four million years ago, and she and her son feel that true humans had already evolved by then. An American, C. Donald Johanson, dug up three-million-year-old fossils in Ethiopia, which he

places in the same species as Mary Leakey's specimens, though
he disagrees with the Leakeys' interpretation.[5]

This would mean that humans must have diverged from
other apes at least five or six million years ago, probably earlier.
The British anatomist C. E. Oxnard suggests that the two species of *Australopithecus* are species unrelated to humans, closer
to orangutans, and that they became extinct about a million
years ago.[6]

Going along with the Leakeys' theory of human origins,
what do we know about how our ancestors, *habilis* or *erectus* as
the case may be, lived? They walked upright, judging from the
footprints and from the shape of their hip- and thighbones and
the position of the foramen magnum, the hole in the skull
through which the spinal cord joins the brain. Richard Leakey
feels, on the basis of the thighbones and of an anklebone from
Lake Turkana, that his *erectus* discovery had a walk more erect
than that of the australopithecine specimens. Both species had
small human-like teeth, not the large tearing canines of, say,
the male baboon or the relatively large canines of both female
and male chimpanzees.

The assumption that both must have had a more complex
organization of the brain, prefiguring the brains of later prehumans and eventually humans, has been given substantiation by
studies of extant fossil skulls. Close comparison with the skulls
of gorillas and chimpanzees shows that there was more space
and height within the *habilis* skull for forward and middle
lobes of the brain, where thought and speech are supposed to
originate, somewhat less for visual areas. Moreover, the cerebel-
lar lobes—the areas controlling balance, motion, and manipulation—were located under the cerebrum (the roof brain), as in
humans, rather than behind it, as in great apes, giving the skull
a more humanlike shape.[7]

Habilis brains were about the size of the present-day gorilla's,
one third larger than that of today's chimpanzee; if Richard
Leakey's *erectus* discoveries hold up, an even larger brain is indicated. Since the habilines were considerably smaller than
both chimpanzees and gorillas, the hominid's brain-size ratio

indicates far more intellectual capacity than is possessed by our ape cousins.

The *Homo erectus* stage in human evolution was formerly dated to a million years ago in Africa, perhaps 600,000 years ago in China, to which it was believed the new species had spread in the intervening 400,000 years. The African estimate may be pushed back two million or more years by the findings of the Leakeys, mother and son, in Tanzania and Kenya respectively, and by C. Donald Johanson's Ethiopian discoveries, while Chinese reports now place their *erectus* species (formerly known as *Homo pekinensis*—Peking *man*) as far back as a million years ago. *Homo erectus* is the least studied stage in our prehistory. Brains were larger and more human, skeletons taller and more erect, though one must still imagine a creature far removed from our present condition, both in physique and in brain power. Since the original discovery in Choukoutien in 1927, fragments of *erectus* skeletons and artifactual evidence of their occupations have been discovered in wide-ranging areas—Africa, Spain, Hungary, and Indonesia. In some areas *erectus* made handaxes, in others they did not, but the tools found in conjunction with their living sites are identified as the Acheulian tool culture and span a range of almost a million years. They are more complex and better worked than previous tools, and an increasing number of large animal bones are found nearby, while charcoal fragments indicating the use of fire also appear for the first time.

Formerly these stones and bones were taken to mean that hunting shaped humanity, but with our more sophisticated knowledge, as well as the evidence from studies of recently existing foraging groups like the African San and the Australian Aborigines, who leave similar quantities of preservable debris at their campsites though plants are their major food source, we can take these surviving relics as indicating increasing acculturation in all areas. There is, however, no evidence of artifacts of adornment until, possibly, about 300,000 years ago, nor of art or religious ceremony, not even ritual burials, one of the earliest signs of awareness of mortality—i.e., human consciousness—among our forebears.

With *erectus*, however, hunting becomes a more organized,

less fortuitous activity. Wooden spears may have been in use toward the end of this period: a fifteen-inch tip found in Clacton, England, is dated to about 250,000 years ago, and fragments of what may have been wooden spears are found in Germany and Spain for about the same date. At Torralba, Spain, stone and bone tools and the remains of large mammals were found together; at Ambrona, Spain, the bones of some twenty elephants, along with butchery tools. These animals could hardly have been killed by individuals or with the weapons then available. Group hunts in which both sexes participated, using fire drives, could have enabled hominids to trap large animals in swamps or pits.

Tools of this period are more varied and require more complex abilities than those of the previous epochs. Though what many of them were used for is not exactly known, we have seen that their functions are presently being reinterpreted. They would have been used by males and females, though males would have been freer to participate in group and individual hunts and, possibly, to develop skill with wooden spears.

It seems likely, however, that the hunting activities of *Homo erectus* have been overrated. The first unquestionable wooden spears are dated to about a hundred thousand years ago. In excavations outside Europe, in Southeast Asia, in Syria, in the Near East, and in East Africa, animal bones are scarce or absent, so scientists hypothesize that these early humans lived largely on plants, insects, and small animals. Moreover, the wear on stone tools found in England and dated to several hundred thousand years ago shows that they were used for woodworking, for scraping hides, for cutting plant material, and for boring wood or bone, as well as for cutting meat.

Though fruits and vegetables must have been the major source of nourishment for almost all hominids, the first evidence of plant food is found in the most northerly area to which *erectus* has been traced. These were hackberry seeds from Choukoutien, in China, a dig now placed at one half to a million years before our time. In that cold-temperate climate one can imagine that the berries would have provided a welcome sweet taste sensation in the comparatively short season during which they fruited. Evidence of gathering does not usually survive. From the tool kit, with its broader variety of better-worked tools, we surmise that an augmented range of foods was used and that knowledge and methods had increased in sophistication. Some plant products—roots, nuts, pith, etc.—need preparation like soaking and cooking to make them edible or palatable; from the evidence, women would have invented cooking by this time (see Chapter 3).

While we can only speculate on *erectus'* sexual and cognitive life, we must imagine an increased capacity for both cruelty and kindness. The discovery of bashed-in brain cases at Choukoutien led earlier writers to accuse *Homo erectus* of beastly crimes like murder and cannibalism. The actual beasts do not normally kill and eat other members of their own species. It is humans who invented the purposeful killing of their own kind. However, the Choukoutien evidence is ambiguous.

Charcoal remains in the North China caves show that fire was used by their inhabitants, permitting Robert Ardrey to describe *erectus* as dining on "roast brother," instead of marveling at the female experiments in physics and chemistry which produced heat and cooked food for early humans.

On the other hand, myth-oriented writers like Joseph Campbell presume that the open brain cases were evidence of sympathetic magic practices. He compares *erectus* customs with present-day human beliefs whereby eating the brain, heart, liver, body, or blood (symbolically in the form of the Catholic host) of one human gives another human some of the attributes of the person consumed. In certain cultures it is a mark of love and respect to eat parts of one's dead in a mourning ceremony. In New Guinea among the Fore, the brains of relatives recently dead were consumed at ritual feasts, while in parts of northern South America mothers customarily ate their dead children at funeral observances, in token of deepest affection.[8]

Bone marrow and brain from whatever sources seem to be cherished delicacies among our animal cousins and our forebears. Observers have described the care with which chimpanzees open the skulls of their kill—baby baboons and small monkeys—and scoop out the brain with the aid of leaf sponges and fingers. The elephant skulls at Torralba were opened at the base for extraction of the brain by *erectus*. One can imagine brain and marrow as rare natural sources of rich, tender fatty food.

Cannibalism as a last resort against starvation is—and has been—engaged in many times in human existence. The Eskimos, the Ojibwa, many Siberian tribes and other far northern peoples have often been forced to eat their fellows. They do it reluctantly—the Ojibwa have developed cultural defenses like the Windigo syndrome with which to handle their repugnance. Sumerian and Egyptian writings document the bitter times of war and famine "when the mother ate her child," while, in the year 1973, a young woman and man in the Canadian Arctic and a group of South American athletes in the high Andes all survived plane crashes by eating their fellow victims.

The stimulus to our human storytelling propensities is there; the actualities are still unknown.

12

Sex and Consciousness

When I'm playing the piano, I make love. It's the
same thing.

—Arthur Rubinstein

What were the sexual meetings of the first prehumans like?
Did the females have numerous quickies, like chimpanzees, or
slow, ponderous encounters like the gorilla? Judging by the
brain cases, one can assume a wider range—more possibilities,
more individual variations, more factors to be combined resulting in more diversity and more choices. Here the studies of
Jane Goodall and her comments on the differing personalities,
sexual and otherwise, of her chimpanzee subjects come to
mind. Anyone who has kept pets knows how much animal personalities differ, as gardeners know that each plant, even each
rose, is unique, but it is hard to keep that tremendous scale in
mind, from the minimal to the major variations. Three million
years ago our forebears probably had long, dreamy and short,
intense encounters, and more besides.

Did the females have estral cycles like every other primate
but the human one? That is, did they have periods of up to ten
days every month (except during nursing and pregnancy) when
they mated with every male available? And if they were loosely
promiscuous, like the majority of primates, when did estrus,
with its intense sexual activity followed by a period of disin-
terest on the part of the female, disappear and the human con-

dition, in which sexual desire occurs at any time, make itself felt?

There are those who say that estrus never did disappear in the human female, that it is merely masked by culture. Lionel Tiger and Robin Fox make this claim in *The Imperial Animal*, and Mary Jane Sherfey, a psychoanalyst, also has a long discussion about cornification, the second half of the menstrual cycle in the human female, in which she makes a fairly ambiguous implication for the same claim.[1] She cites Kinsey's report on sexuality in the human female as supportive evidence. This report consisted of circumstantial and uncontrolled subjective evidence from a relatively small group of women, but it was the only evidence we had had, up to that time, on many of the subjects Kinsey asked about. I have heard it used to make a case for the opposite, i.e., that women had more sexual desire just previous to and around the time of menstruation, which was put forward as a natural form of birth control.[2] Tiger and Fox's evidence for estrus in the human female is similarly scant and unconvincing. I myself have never met any female who felt that she became more passionate at ovulation time: if they know when it is, they are likely to become dispassionate—for obvious reasons.

It used to be assumed that sex was the glue which kept primate societies together, a premise known as Zuckerman's theory of sociology in primates, after its originator, the English primatologist who had based so many theories of human and monkey social organization on his London zoo studies of the hamadryas baboon. Of course, in the nineteen thirties when this theory was elucidated, when scientists said "sex" they meant male activity and female receptivity. Artists never had any doubt about the active status of female sexual desire, from the anonymous author who wrote about Potiphar's wife through Aristophanes in *Lysistrata*, Chaucer's Wife of Bath, Racine's Phèdre, and so on.

But knowledge of female physiology is still in its infancy. In the last two or three decades, science has emerged from its Victorian fairy-tale world and acknowledged that female animals, including primates and humans, have assertive sexual drives, though the underlying attitude still considers active sexuality a male characteristic. There is a hangover of the old terms. "What does it matter whether you call it receptivity or desire?" said a leading physical anthropologist. "It's all behavior." Which is like saying, What does it matter whether you call it murder or self-defense, it's all behavior. This kind of semantic confusion exerts considerable influence on human thought. We often think what we say instead of saying what we think. The peculiar scientific illogic which nominates admired qualities as male so that when a female has them she is described as having male components, is still all too prevalent. Freud's outdated explanation of libido as a male attribute[3] is echoed by endocrinologist John Money's description of androgen as the hormone causing sexual desire in males and females.[4] Since androgen is produced in large amounts in the male testes, and in smaller amounts in the female adrenals, this would seem to be a new version of the Freudian statement making desire a male characteristic which is present in females to a minimal degree, so that an active female can be derogated as a "masculine" woman. Mary Jane Sherfey's The Nature and Evolution of Female Sexuality is a peculiarly contradictory effort to reconcile Freudian theory with newer biomedical information. Discussing the effects of estrogen and androgen on women's and men's desire and performance, she notes that new discoveries about hormones necessitate a complete revision of currently held opinions with regard to their control of sexual activity.[5] (The inadequacy of earlier assumptions about male and female hormones was discussed in Chapter 4, and reference was made to the enormous new body of knowledge about the complexities of hormone interaction that has been and is still being accumulated.)

In both sexes orgasms are caused by muscular contractions against the body chambers which fill with blood to produce erection. Male and female orgasms are biologically identical. The body chambers which produce erection in the male are located externally in the penis; in the female they are in the vestibular bulbs within the surface tissue alongside the opening of the vagina. On the basis of Sherfey's review of Masters and

Johnson's anatomical and physiological findings, with clarification from other sources, there is today no doubt about the human female's activity in sex.

There has been a tendency to attribute passivity to the female because the male organ must be inserted into the vagina. However, the act of penetrating is only one part of a much more complex sexual sequence. The female genital is extremely active in the sex act; it is not just a passive receptacle for sperm. The clitoris has a greater concentration of sensitive nerve endings than the penis or any other organ in the body. The clitoris is like a submerged iceberg; its functioning cannot be understood if it is seen merely as a small penis. The clitoral shaft extends to the mouth of the vagina and is connected to the vestibular bulbs, which encircle the vaginal opening. Circumvaginal muscles connect both structures so that the movement of one pulls on and is felt by the other. Wider areas of sensitivity are encompassed in erotic stimulation in the female than in the male, and she has a more extensive network of blood vessels which become engorged with blood—the process of vasomotor congestion that causes the penile erection and produces enlargement of the clitoris and swelling within the female genital.[6]

After Zuckerman voiced his theory that primate societies are glued together by continuous male sexual activity with diverse periodically receptive females, the field primatologists came back with incontrovertible evidence that females initiate sexual activity, but they also discovered something else. The famous year-round male sexual activity seemed to be limited in the wild. Monkeys, too, had mating seasons, like many of the lower mammals, as witness the fact that babies were born at given periods of the year. Among the monkeys which have birth seasons are langurs, macaques, savanna, hamadryas, and gelada baboons. Rhesus monkeys who breed all year round in laboratory and zoo conditions also have breeding seasons in the wild, alternating with periods of several months when the females do not come into estrus.[7]

So, to balance the acknowledgment of female sexual desire, the scientists happily pronounced that while a she-baboon or rhesus was definitely active in estrus, she was fortunately not in estrus much of the time. According to Phyllis Jay, "The majority of a female monkey's time is spent either pregnant or lactating, she is able to engage in sexual activities only for a small portion of her life, and yet the troops still stay together."[8]

One feels that the day was saved for male sexuality since the troops stayed together in spite of rather than because of aggressive female sex. In fact, one ethologist, Wolfgang Wickler, registered a grand protest against his confreres' happy conclusion that it was not sex—in the female—which kept the troops together. Yes, he said, it is true that the females are not engaged in sexual activity with the males during the major part of the year, but this does not mean that the males are not sexually potent—a fine distinction, since if they are not copulating, how can one tell about the state of their desires? But Wickler insisted that spermatogenesis went on all year round, though how he knew this and what kind of desire it indicated I cannot say, nor did he bring forth evidence of male masturbation or homosexuality in the wild to support his claim. (Alison Jolly contradicts his assertion about year-round spermatogenesis, at least where the squirrel monkey is concerned. In this New World species, the males grow fat around the shoulders during breeding season in connection with seasonal spermatogenesis.[9]) If male monkeys of other species do have year-round potency, one wonders whether they, unlike human males, are able to control themselves, since rape, homosexuality, and masturbation to orgasm are not seen in the wild. In nature it is the male who is "responsive" to the female's active desire for intercourse.

When we take maternal sexuality into account, the fact that nursing females are also gratifying a broad sexual drive, so that female sexual opportunity is more constant than males', the whole brouhaha may tell us more about the human male ego and how it is tied up with the notion of "continual potency" than it tells us about the state of a male monkey's putative potency when he is not utilizing it.

It is a male assumption—and an extremely harmful myth—that human males are "sexually potent" at all times. This is far from the case, just as it is not true that human females are "sexually receptive" all the time. (The possibility may exist, but in fact sexual desire in both sexes is controlled by many conscious and unconscious factors—liking, deprivation, habit, social expectation, fatigue, to name a few.) This great oversimplification, which is still common usage in the literature, just about eliminates from consideration everything that makes us human: art, beauty, choice, affection, imagination, etc. Still, it has been a myth of long standing and is behind the use of rape as a reward for soldiers and the hideous entanglement of sex and conquest which is so basic to our social ills.

In animal sex we do not know the extent to which choice enters. Hierarchy had been postulated as the controlling element in primate sexual encounters, in demonstration of Darwin's principle of sexual selection and evolutionary logic. As was pointed out, recent field studies have cast doubt on the cardinal tenets of animal behaviorists, and dominance theory is falling into disrepute among scientists today. Where charted in the wild, dominance hierarchies were unstable and contradictory.[10] Results were largely anthropomorphic projections, except where caused by stress conditions, many of which could be related to human contact. Sexual encounters never did fit neatly into the predictions of human observers, despite considerable rationalization and bending of evidence. All that could be said was that, to the extent to which choice entered, it was the female who made the decision, though not with Darwinian logic.[11]

The way in which sexual selection applies to human relations is clear: "Let's face it, the man with the most money and the biggest Cadillac still gets the prettiest chicks," said a film star on television. The dominance factor with us is not size or strength or intelligence but money, which might well be quite deleterious from an evolutionary point of view, vide Tommy Manville, the much-married playboy of the nineteen thirties and forties.

For our ancestors in a prematerialist world in which it is ecology rather than economics which describes their life-support system, the choice made by the female would have been determined by the male's attractive qualities. Tanner and Zihlman have postulated sociability as the determining factor.[12] They feel that hominid females chose the more amiable males as mates, thus encouraging our evolution toward cooperation and food sharing.

With the acknowledgment that female primates exercised an active role in sex relations and frequently became more aggressive in estrus, primatologists (and other writers on human evolution) often explain human females' loss of estrus in terms of the dangers of aggression—in the female. As Wolfgang Wickler tells it:

> In general females in heat appear to become more aggressive. . . . In the rhesus monkey, oestrous females often cross group boundaries, according to Carpenter: "Estrus only makes it possible for the female to penetrate and to be tolerated within a foreign group." Washburn and DeVore (1962) state that oestrous in baboons disrupts all other social relations; the female leaves her preference group and child (if present).
>
> Most authors agree that the rank of the female is altered for the heat period . . . *The female in oestrus even takes food morsels from the hands of the male.*
>
> That females in oestrus leave their preference group and follow the highest-ranking male is an *indication that they are very "self-confident" during this phase.* In some cases, this has been more closely investigated: rhesus monkey females in oestrus are particularly aggressive (Carpenter, 1942); they become aggressive toward other females and at the same time begin to approach males (Rowell, 1963), *they even threaten their prospective male consorts* (Chance, 1956). The same applies to the chimpanzee (Reynolds and Reynolds, 1965). *Receptive female chimpanzees present without any sign of fear;* at other times they present in a timid manner, and this at least indicates that fear is compensated when the female is in heat.[13]

Clearly such behavior in a human female would never do; estrus had to go. What there is in the world scheme which pronounces male aggression useful and female aggression harmful, this writer cannot say, but so it would appear to many of the primatologists. Phyllis Jay finds that "there are apt to be striking changes in a female's behavior during estrous periods. She is more active and aggressive, and seeks the attentions of adult males, often including the ones she may have avoided when she was not sexually active. Not only are some social relationships at least temporarily altered by the stresses of increased activity, but when many adult females in a group are receptive at the same time, there may also be substantial changes in the behavior of the group as a whole."[14] For John Pfeiffer, it goes beyond primate activity. "The typical pattern among mammals involves regular bursts of *sexual frenzy* which take precedence over all other activities. At every ovulation or immediately after, all nonhuman females including occasional nursing females come into estrus, or 'heat.' Sexual activity is so concentrated during such periods that it tends to interrupt the care of the young and all other forms of behavior. . . . If all the females in a primate troop were subject to three days of *sexual mania* every month or so, it would probably be to the detriment of their slow-maturing infants.[15]

The general consensus in the academic community, then, is that estrus disappeared among human females because it was useful for developing a monogamous family life, the usual teleological fallacy.

In fact, Jane Goodall, in a burst of human self-congratulation, compassionates her chimpanzee friends: "It is obviously fruitless to speculate as to the sorts of heterosexual relationships that might develop if chimpanzee physiology were different: if, for example, *Flo had been able to offer Rodolf continuing sexual satisfaction,* if the female reproductive cycle of the chimp were the same as the human cycle."[16]

On the other hand, the aforementioned claim by Mary Jane Sherfey, a practicing psychoanalyst, not a prehistorian or an ethologist, that estrus—"the ungovernable sexual drive of women"—never did disappear was advanced to justify the *status quo ante.* "The forcible suppression of women's inordinate sexual demands was a prerequisite to the dawn of every modern civilization and almost every living culture. Primitive woman's sexual drive was too strong, too susceptible to the fluctuating extremes of an impelling aggressive erotism to withstand the disciplined demands of a settled family life." Sherfey's work was presented first to her Freudian colleagues, just as the women ethologists had to be accredited by their male superiors in the academic hierarchy. So female sexual desire—"the intense insatiable erotism in women," she terms it—calls down upon itself the fiercest of reprisals; once again the victim is blamed for the crime.[17]

Having been forced to acknowledge the existence of active female sexuality some millennia after the artists, the scientific mind still finds it a threatening concept. Therefore, periodic active sexual desire, in animals, is countered by a formulation which declares that human females have permanent sexual receptivity—passive—else we could not have had, first, humanity and, second, civilization. While most historic civilizations have involved forcible sexual repression of the female, this is not necessarily the case in nonliterate cultures. We have paid a high price for female sexual repression: the thinking which says because it happened that way, that was the way it had to happen, ignores the lesson of science. There are and there can be myriad forms in nature and myriad solutions to given situations: one can get to Mars by a planet collision as well as with a space ship, though neither event may happen in our lifetime.

My own thinking on the disappearance of estrus and birth seasons involves looking not at why it happened but at how it happened. To look for a cause and tell us that estrus disappeared because it would interfere with the human family is circular reasoning which tells us nothing. It sees the human family—an extremely varied and far from immutable phenomenon—as a given and sees it usually in the current nuclear form, despite the many contradictions from ethnography and history.

The problem is that most of the discussants talk about sex and reproduction as discrete entities, as though the higher centers of the brain were not involved. The physiology of the present-day human brain—described as the most intricate piece of matter in the known universe—has still not been thoroughly studied and is most imperfectly understood. The workings of imagination, cognition, creativity, as well as the involvement of the brain in sex, are mysterious but not unconnected. The deeper nerve centers, where emotion is commonly located, are also involved in every action, be it intellectual or physical. "There is no behavior without emotion," was the way Piaget put it. Emotions drive our intellect. The mind controls the body; the emotions control the mind; sometimes the emotions bypass the mind.

Common sense, art, and certain deductions from the effects of lobotomy and from the functioning of brain-damaged people tell us that the creative and imaginative faculties are linked with sexual energies; they are the wellspring. Creative artists often comment on the similarity between the sex act at its best and the creative act—the passion, the sweating, the sense of being outside oneself, of communion with the universe, the exhaustion and, usually, pleasant draining that ensue. Both involve a successful mingling of conscious and unconscious control not often or easily achieved, though sex can be and usually is practiced on partial and rudimentary levels that come nowhere near its larger possibilities. The reconciliations of tenderness and force, thought and spontaneity, the infinite variations and balances possible in human sex are, of course, nonexistent among animals.

Much has been learned about the brain and the body in the last two decades. Molecular biology has discovered the secret of life, but human consciousness is almost as much of a mystery as ever. We have no equations to explain imagination. There are hints of how the process takes place: evidence of electric activity along with indications that it is the deeper emotion centers which set the level of activity involved in memory fixation. According to C. U. M. Smith, a constant rearrangement, reordering, and turning around of the representations of the perceptual world seem to occur.[18] But the brain works as a whole, which is why damage to any one part affects the personality, a gestalt of all the individual parts and functionings that constitute a human essence.

One cannot localize areas of the brain by experimental means, as has been attempted, and say this area controls speech, this area controls vision, this area controls sexuality. Motivation, drive, is said to be located in the hypothalamus, with the emotions; memory is placed in the amygdala; but it is not known whether these are ultimate locations or only way stations on the road to the cerebrum. Cerebration, logic, is by definition a function of the higher centers, the cerebrum, yet this ascription was made before biophysicists and biochemists began their examinations of molecular psychobiology, the latest approach to brain physiology. The ascription is not wrong; it is incomplete. The large cortex of the human cerebrum, with its many uncommitted areas, is seen not only as the differentiation between humans and all other animals but also as a source, roughly, of our human thinking, reasoning, feeling, conscious powers. An intricate network of associative connections throughout the brain is activated whenever we exercise these powers. There is far more evidence that the "buck" stops in the cerebral cortex than that it starts in the hypothalamus.[19]

Sex takes place in the head. Negative evidence from the use, or perhaps one should say the misuse, of lobotomy confirms that the brain works as a whole, as well as that there is a relationship between sexual energies and creativity. The excision of the frontal lobes, by cutting connections with the thalamus, is a butchery technique which invariably results in personality deterioration. Any psychosurgery—of necessity a relatively blind amputation—mutilates the brain and destroys or injures personality.[20] Lobotomized patients can perform routine work, but, lacking neural connection with the centers for creativity and imagination, they cannot perform executive or inventive work. Lobotomy has been more frequently performed on female than on male patients: in Canada it was recommended as a technique enabling hospitalized housewives to return home and fulfill their household tasks; partial lobotomy has also been used to "cure" female patients diagnosed as suffering from "nymphomania"—uncontrollable eroticism as the doctors called it. It was recently used on youths to subvert homosexuality. The basic effect of lobotomy is to eliminate or cut down on fantasy and imagination, thereby damping down sexual expression.[21]

The hypothalamus was usually given as the controlling factor in sexual behavior when discussion was not limited to androgen and estrogen. Sometimes we were told that estrogen or androgen, released, operates on the neural pathways to the hypothalamus. But recent studies by John Money and Anke Ehrhardt indicate that cultural and social training are far more influential than hormone action in shaping the sexual orientation and behavior of boys and girls after birth. Interpreted, this means that the higher centers of the brain are the ultimate factors in sexual, as in other conscious, and self-conscious, human behavior. Emotional elements, from the deeper centers, are also called into play, while the endocrines are probably the most malleable elements—in contradistinction to animals. In this connection, common scientific parlance, which equates feminine, passive, and neuter, is responsible for much confusion. For example, patients are given cortisone to counteract masculine behavior and secondary sex characteristics ascribed to androgen. This is called feminizing them, though what is actually accomplished is neuterizing, since cortisone has a negative effect on sexual expression of any kind, male or female.

In modern Western society, a sexually incomplete person of either sex is directed toward femaleness, since the long tradition of equating femininity with passiveness makes it more socially acceptable to be a partial female human being. A tragic example was the instance of a male baby accidentally injured and castrated as the result of a circumcision operation. According to the *New York Times*,[22] specialists advised changing the baby's sex to female. While operations can be performed to approximate a vagina, neither clitoral nerves, ovaries, nor uterus can be inserted in this unfortunate individual, whose sexuality has been irreparably damaged and who will never be able to produce a child.

In early hominid society there were no sophisticated medical techniques to implement such artificial "advanced concepts." Fortunately for us, the ecology of survival demanded that all its members be actively and integrally related to nature. And survive and thrive it did, or we would not be here to project ourselves backward attempting to describe it.

The role of sex as a source of energy and creative imagination has been given much more weight by artists, theologians, and psychoanalysts than by the scientific community. Sex is, after all, not only the source of love poetry but an indirect force in all religion and art. The meshing of sexual drive with emotion and with the higher centers, in all its complexity and pervasiveness, may be little understood but it is not in doubt. Whether the sexual energy is tapped by sublimation, as Freud felt, or by direct involvement, on the model of Wilhelm Reich, is far from clear. I would guess that they are both right in part; that it can work either way and both ways. According to Reich, the relation between sexual gratification and sublimation is not mechanical, i.e., the more suppression of sex, the more achievement in other areas; it is functional. Sexual energy can be sublimated to some degree, but if the diversion goes too far, sublimation changes into the opposite, an interference with the capacity to work.

Hormone information has been much misused. Laboratory researchers report that testosterone injected in female mice will make them mount and otherwise display male behavior, yet there are women who cannot enjoy sex unless they are on top of the male instead of in the more usual supine position. Surely this is not testosterone but cultural consciousness, an association of the inferiority assigned to women in our culture along with the internalization of male values. Being on top is identified with the whole hierarchical structure which assigns superiority to the superior position. It is therefore a refusal to be trapped or victimized by social values, rather than a physiological response. In the same wise one could cite women of the past who rejected sex because of the inferiority assigned to the woman's role in our culture. Virginia Woolf and Harriet Taylor Mill, wife of John Stuart Mill, both seem to have suffered from sexual inhibition not as a lack of hormone secretion but from an abundance of mental ability which made them reject the patriarchal tradition, where sexuality is defined in terms of submission-domination, with femininity and submission used interchangeably. In such a society, free sexual expression with the person you love might well be a threat to an intelligent woman. As long as sex is defined as man possessing woman,

woman will be threatened, though the actualities of the situation would seem to be the opposite: man enters woman and woman possesses man, at least that part of his body which is inside her. Perhaps the emphasis on male possession of females stems from the male fear of being twice possessed by woman—once inside her womb and a second time, partially, inside her vagina. Since he is the more vulnerable one, it is he who has felt the necessity to assert and enforce the opposite: that she is weak, vulnerable, and possessed by him.

We apprehend our senses through our brain. Therefore, the growth of the brain gave us a more acute awareness of sensation, and the consequent feedback encouraged the development of sensual areas. We cannot know what *Homo habilis* and *Homo erectus* looked like—whether they had all-over hair or how their fleshy features were shaped. Desmond Morris has described humans as "the sexy ape," citing the male's large penis, the female's enlarged breasts, the increased tactility of human skin, our many erogenous zones, and the year-round potential for sexual intercourse, none of which can be deduced from fossil evidence.[23] These human features cannot be unrelated to the growth of the brain, i.e. the degree of conscious control over sexuality and the greater range of bodily and mental possibility for elaboration, as against the capabilities of animals. In addition there is the continuance of sexual drive after reproductive powers wane, not only in the female after menopause, but also in the male despite a falling off of sperm production. We can look at this human sexuality not in terms of its function for the human family, since the extremely varied human family has as often required sexual inhibition as it has sexual expression, but as a result of brain enlargement and complication. It is human range which distinguishes us from animals, the multiplying of input factors which go to make up our behavior, the enormous enlargement of possibilities and possible combinations.

All of this rich sexuality with its embroidery and complications is adaptive not so much in the sense of its limited, defined-after-the-fact practical usefulness as in the added possibilities it gave us as humans. The richness and ornamentation of life are made possible by the human brain with its power of naming and visualizing, the mysterious imagination. What I take to be the magic mingling of body and mind, sexual and emotional drive with the capacity for memory and combining that begin to add up to creativity bring pleasure and enjoyment, which certainly need no excuse in nature. The orchid's beauty may, to some extent, be a functional adaptation, but the human's is a development of self-awareness. The orchid's beauty exists in the human's eye, but the orchid does not know whether it is beautiful or ugly nor does the chimpanzee— though the latter may just begin to have glimmers of aesthetic appreciation for a bright color or an interesting object. As long as aesthetic quality doesn't interfere with survival, it will endure, and to the extent to which it facilitates survival by adding pleasure, it will be encouraged to increase.

The increase and refinement of sexuality is an increase in humanity; it accompanies and cannot be dissociated from all our other human qualities, nor from human culture. Humanity's self-awareness added a premium to brain and consciousness and sexual elaboration. The more they are enjoyed, the more they are facilitated and encouraged by the feedback relationship which is a tenet of Darwinian natural selection. Thus we may owe culture to the fact, also, that we have more sexual energy and more diffusion of sexual energy into other pursuits. This is a more positive view than the negative Freudian claim that repression and sublimation were necessary for humanity; not so much repression as diversion and diversity were the human qualities.

The loss of estrus is vaguely recognized by both ethologists and physical anthropologists as a crucial marker on the road to humanity. It is significant particularly to those attached to the idea of the "pair-bond" and to the notion of a male-female-child grouping as an inherent characteristic of humanity. They see it as useful for maintaining the nuclear family, for attaching a father to the basic mother-child pattern of the primate world. So, in their descriptions, all too often, the loss of estrus seems to be tantamount to a loss of active sexuality in the female, making possible her "permanent receptivity" to one male, as opposed to the promiscuity of, say, the female chimpanzee "swinger."

The rare primates whose groups consist of male-female-infant are often described as undersexed.[24] The teleological explanation of the loss of estrus in human females would make her undersexed also. We know that this is far from the case, despite valiant efforts throughout patriarchal history to impose or support this concept. To me the loss of estrus relates to the human development of consciousness and conscious control of and participation in the basic acts of life, reproduction being the primary one, with nourishment and survival to reproductive age as corollaries. We lost estrus because we were human, as a concomitant of humanity: we didn't become human by losing estrus.

The more brain the more sex; primates have more than other animals, and humans have more than primates. And because human sex is so much more than mere brief copulation, there is an enlarged component of sex in other behaviors. Sex is vitalizing and pervasive. Thus the loss of estrus was not a loss but a gain.

For a clue as to how it might have happened, a sentence in Jane Goodall's article on chimpanzee communication stirs the imagination: "In the field I once observed a slight swelling in the sex skin of an anoestrous female in response to prolonged inspection by a male."[25] What we have here is a phenomenon related to human responsiveness, a personal relation rather than a glandular one. This is the process that would have been taking place in our own evolution. The popularized version of science says the brain enlarged in order to facilitate culture. I say as it enlarged it was more efficient, but also just more in every sense.

Hominid females lost estrus because people—even hominid people—liked making choices. And there was, as I have said, no visual estral signal among hominid females once they stood upright. There may never have been a visual signal, as there is not among certain monkeys. In the same way, we do not know human canine teeth were reduced, either because weapons were used or because hominids ate seeds some fourteen million years ago: maybe there never were large canines among our lemur ancestors. Judging by the wide range of human behaviors to be found today, and judging also by the individuality displayed among such animals as the chimpanzee, among early hominids sexual behavior would already have been quite varied. It is likely, however, that sex and affection need not yet have been related, as they are not in many human cultures—from classical Greece to Victorian England to the Mae Enga of New Guinea.

In the upright position there was no possibility of a visual genital indication of estrus in the female, though the male's erection was more visible than that of his chimpanzee or gorilla cousin's. To the extent to which verbal relating was unestablished, it would have been the female who selected the male for mating, rather than vice versa, as is conventionally felt to happen among humans. The enlarging brain was the human specialization. Since sex in humans is regulated by the brain more than by the glands, there was no pressure to develop a specialization like the female chimpanzee's unwieldly genital swelling. The invisibility of the female organ might have contributed to the loss of estrus, the visibility of the male's erection to human male vulnerability and the imposition of forcible male dominance in later human history.

Choice was another human specialization resulting from the enlarging human brain. Males and females who have been deprived of sexual outlet for a considerable length of time may be excited by any member of the opposite sex of reasonable appearance by culturally imposed standards of aesthetics. Normally, however, the sexual approach is selective, rather than generalized as in the case of apes and monkeys. What motivates the choice is enormously variable and at times quite mysterious, recognized in such popular phrases as "love at first sight," "a chemical attraction," etc.

If we think of the female hominid approaching the male, we can see the periods of sexual license which have existed in many human cultures as atavistic relics of prehuman society. Dionysian festivals of Greece, medieval weddings in Germany and Sweden, the *katayausa* of the Trobriand Islanders described by Malinowski, various celebrations among the Australian Aborigines and the Ojibwa permitted and encouraged public mating with the woman making the advances, or general promiscuity. And if we think of *habilis* and *erectus* as being on

the way to human status, though with few of the material possessive complexities of our own times, we might envision a
rather more amiable choice and coming together, by mutual
agreement, of male and female—with more coming together,
relatively less choice.

However, the idea that a male would have much voice in
choosing a female or would have maintained any kind of individual long-term control over her or her offspring is a modern
invention; there would have been no place for such a phenomenon in the lives of early hominids.[26]

Sexuality among human males and females is not seasonal
but it is also far from constant. In the female both pregnancy
and nursing probably interfere, psychologically and physically.
But males, too, have other interests, and their cyclicity is on a
much smaller time scale—in terms of hours, days, weeks. Constant sexual expression is not possible for them either, as many
a frustrated woman has been forced to accept under monogamous conditions. The myth of the ever-ready human male is a
cultural stereotype which oppresses the male no less than the
female.

Much is often made of the fact that humans are supposedly
the only animals to copulate face to face and its relation to the
upright position and to the forward placing of female and male
sexual organs. Many scientists think in terms of the missionary
position. Actually, human postures in coitus are extremely
varied, *vide* the *Kama Sutra,* Greek vase paintings, and other
artistic and ethnographic sources.

But standing up did make us more vulnerable, in intercourse as in other pursuits. Some primates perform their sexual acts in the middle of the group, often with youngsters running up to peer curiously, to touch or otherwise harass the
linked couple. For us sex implies surrender, hence the usual
desire for some privacy. Human positions, whether seated face
to face, as among the Trobriand Islanders, lying flat or on one's
side, kneeling on all fours, face to face or face to back, to mention only a few possibilities, all involve coming together in an
unordinary posture. Sex on the fly is not feasible; standing positions are not comfortable or easily achieved. Female animals on
all fours can escape more readily, though the male might have

somewhat more difficulty in disengaging himself. In this respect we are more like the ponderous and shy gorillas, who were thought to avoid being seen in intercourse by the ethologists. In zoos, gorillas have been observed copulating face to face.

Actually, the whole growth of humanity makes it impossible to separate normal copulation from other aspects of consciousness. As the human brain enlarged, so were sexual acts beginning to be elaborated. We can only speculate on the degree to which the plasticity of human behavior, in sex as in social organization, would have been in effect some millions of years ago. In our present state of evolution, the brain is so adaptable that societies can train both women and men to the most contradictory and seemingly unnatural sexualities, passive or active, abstaining or indulging. *Habilis* and *erectus* would have been rather closer to the animals than the angels.

Clifford Jolly and Ralph Holloway, along with Wolfgang Wickler and Desmond Morris, talk of the growth of human female breasts as a sexual signal to males, since the upright posture precluded visual genitals in the female. It is hard to believe that *habilis* and *erectus* males were so dim-sighted they couldn't tell the difference between the male and female pubic area. Moreover, the breast is not an erotic stimulus save in certain cultures. Among the Mangaians, Donald Marshall reports their surprise at Western male fixation on the breast, for "they consider this organ of interest only to the hungry baby."[27] Different societies have found the female ankle, collarbone, buttocks, hair, hips, eyelashes, whatever, sexually arousing. We have fewer reports on what it is that stimulates the human female's sexual desire. The fact that the human male's penis is both larger and better equipped sensually than the organ of any other primate is related to the increased capacity for pleasure made possible by the human brain. The relative hairlessness of humans makes our entire bodies into erogenous zones. And the development of the human female's breast, in all its variety— small and round as among the Balinese, or long and pointed as described in the *Arabian Nights*—is a part of the growth of maternal sexuality, along with the growth of other forms of sexuality which accompanied the enlarging human brain.

The search for purpose in these features is misleading, while the claim that females became more sexually interesting and interested—Holloway says that there was "an increase in epigamic features of such secondary sexual characteristics as permanent breasts, fat distribution and other possible changes toward facilitating more permanent sexual receptivity of the female"[28]—so as to facilitate male-female bonding is a ridiculous and false analogy. Humans don't bond, they relate, and not necessarily permanently or predictably. There are societies like the Nayar in India where there is no way of telling who is the father of the child, for individual women are, in effect, married to a group of men; there are societies where women live with their children in separate houses while men live together in a men's house. Many versions of the extended family in which children are communally raised exist. Sometimes all women of a certain relationship are called "mother," all men "father," though the child usually knows who is its real mother, if not necessarily its father.

For early hominids there were other complications and dangers, besides sexual vulnerability, as a result of our newly assumed upright position. It's hard to hold a brief for the efficiency of natural selection when we look at our bodies, and women may have even more reason to cavil at those who have misinterpreted the theory so as to project purpose outward. Human childbirth is a good example of the looseness with which natural selection functions. When we stood upright, the position, shape, and size of the pelvic girdle changed so as to facilitate balance and walking on two legs. In the process childbirth became more difficult, since at the same time the bony skull was enlarging and the period of gestation increasing. Neoteny, the process by which human children are born undeveloped—though not as undeveloped as, say, the kangaroo infant which continues to develop within its mother's pouch—was one result, with a consequent longer period of infant dependency. In humans, the process became circular, demanding more responsibility and interaction from mothers and more cooperation from the group, as a result of which further brain enlargement occurred.

13

The Brain Is the Human Adaptation

Struggling with the origin of consciousness, which is what I would take as the index of humanity, one notes that the growth of the human brain brought us discomforting polarities. If human nature is social in its simian origins, human consciousness is solitary. I am I, alone, separate—and the realization must have been frightening, indeed, still is, often enough. This is the cosmic loneliness which propelled humanity to project purpose outward: the conviction that there is a divinity which shapes our ends seems to embody a universal human yearning, and it is hard to shake, hence the tendency to project purpose onto nature and natural phenomena, leading to the widespread teleological fallacies.

Neither natural selection nor even the catch-all "cultural evolution" explains the poems of Sappho or Shakespeare, the novels of Tolstoy or Emily Brontë. What utilitarian function is served by lovemaking, Lucullan feasts, or so many other delightful components of human life and society? Necessity may be the mother of invention, but she can hardly be credited with art, ornaments, and most of the pleasures to which the poet invited us.

Asking the question of how the human brain evolved, Noam

Chomsky suggests that natural selection is the answer only if we realize it is no answer: "The processes by which the human mind achieved its present state of complexity and its particular form of innate organization are a total mystery. . . . It is perfectly safe to attribute this development to 'natural selection,' so long as we realize that there is no substance to this assertion, that it amounts to nothing more than a belief that there is some naturalistic explanation for these phenomena."[1] Chomsky seeks some understanding of the human mind through the study of language. He says of this uniquely human phenomenon that it is wrong to think of it solely as informative. Human language can be used to inform or to misinform, to clarify one's own thinking or to display one's cleverness, or just for fun in play. This concept seems to me to be applicable in a larger sense to humanity itself. We are both purposive and purposeless.

To the extent to which natural selection does exist, it is looser and allows for more inefficiency than was envisioned by Darwin. Genetics did not exist as a science when he was writing, and the experiments of Mendel were unknown to him, so he hypothesized about inheritance without knowing the details. Mendel's work substantiated some of Darwin's hypotheses, but it made others, like sexual selection, less tenable. Genes are not inherited along sexual lines; a male offspring receives genes from both mother and father, though some genes, like the one for hemophilia, are sex-linked, i.e., carried by the mother and transmitted to the son. Intelligence is not one of these, though theorists as diverse as Darwin, Freud, and Erich Neumann have often written on the assumption that it is.

We saw how untenable are the theses of man the toolmaker and man the hunter as explanations for the growth and development of humanity, and why women and men would have had similar manual dexterity and intelligence. Both used their heads and hands, and they collaborated and worked together, though men may have been able to do the more showy things when women took care of the necessities.

About the possibilities for malignity, motivated and motiveless, which began with humanity, and that linking of aggression and sexuality which is a human expression, not an animal one, and, in my view, a recent one, we must hypothesize and dig for connections. We can only speculate on the sexuality of early hominids and humans, through *erectus*, and on the development of conscious control over sexuality which led to the disappearance of estrus and to human groupings, in whatever forms they took in the long beginning of our species' existence. In Chapter 12, however, we saw that it was the enlarging human brain which brought about the loss of estrus, or rather the gain of increasing responsiveness, both emotional and physical, in female and male.

From the sparse evidence, we cannot know when societal controls on sexual encounters began, though conscious control and elaboration of sexual encounters and family and friendly relations are incipient in the incipient human brain.

There is considerable debate about the degree of humanity possessed by early hominids. Many physical anthropologists see them as closer to animals like the gorillas and the chimpanzees than to any humans living today or in the recent past. The difficulties of postulating theories about human origins on the actual brain organization of our presumed fossil ancestors, with only a few limestone impregnated skulls—most of them bashed, shattered, and otherwise altered by the passage of millions of years—as evidence, would seem to be astronomical. It is, however, a characteristic of the present-day human brain that it is not only undaunted but actually provoked and stimulated by intellectual and objective problems.

There is one branch of physical anthropology called paleoneurology which is attempting to do just that—to add to our knowledge of human evolution by studying casts of fossil skulls of *Australopithecus*, *Homo habilis*, and *Homo erectus*. The paleoneurologist Ralph Holloway quarrels with earlier interpretations of human development as stemming from hunting and looks to the skulls for evidence of brain power shaping behavior, rather than vice versa. He also disagrees with other physical anthropologists about the subhuman characteristics of the earliest hominids.

He argues that the early hominid skulls—*Australopithecus*,

habilis, and the presumed *erectus* skull E.R. 1470 pieced together by Meave Leakey—differ from chimpanzee and gorilla skulls not only because they have more space for brains (the usual measurement is in terms of cubic contents: the habiline brain is described as averaging 600 cc. as compared to the 400 cc. average for chimpanzee brains) but also because they have another shape. He reminds us that actual brain size has long been recognized as a very crude index of intelligence and cognition: Anatole France's brain at 1,000 cc. is said to be one of the smallest human brains on record (smaller than the brains of one-million-year-old *erectus* skulls estimated at 1,200 cc.), despite his indubitable intellectual achievements. Holloway gives an example of two Bantu brothers suffering from pathologically small brains (microcephaly), with brain measurements roughly the size of most australopithecine skull capacities, about 500 cc., who yet learned to talk and perform most other human acts.

Holloway feels that the position of the parietal and temporal lobes on the skulls he analyzed, from cleft marks showing that the cerebrum was above the cerebellum rather than behind it as in apes, is evidence of an enlarged cerebral cortex in habiline and erectine skulls. He would allow them more cerebration, i.e., more facility for communication and problem-solving ability, than other physical anthropologists admit. He also feels that Broca's area, the place in the frontal lobe most sharply associated with speech though not necessarily the only one nor even the source of origin for our language capacities, is farther forward, making language possible, if not proven, several million years ago. For Holloway the specifically human brain organization was already in force, and he agreed early on with the Leakey classification of *habilis* as a human not an ape, as presently with the newer Richard Leakey claim that *erectus* existed in Kenya as far back as 2.6 million years ago and was the precursor of modern humans.[2]

In 1969 Holloway had already claimed evidence for the humanity of australopithecine and habiline brain cases, distinguishing a capacity for speech not only in their shape and spaciousness but because their possessors had produced tools to pattern. In a lump of stone they could imagine the finished implement, he said, enabling them to create stone tools, a process which required more conceptual ability than merely trimming the leaves off a stick, as chimpanzees do. On this basis he concluded that they had the beginnings of human imagination and conceptualization.[3]

Analyses of later *erectus* skulls convinced him that human language and human cognition were already operant during the million or more years when bands of *erectus* roamed through Africa and into Asia and Europe.[4] Other students of the period disagree with him, though all acknowledge that the beginnings of speech and thought must have existed.[5]

At the present time the scientific community acknowledges only that the chief distinction between humanity and other animals is food sharing, a social co-operative process believed to have begun some four or five million years ago. The straight-line simplistic thinking of the human brain shaped and enlarged by the syndromes of hunting is all too prevalent. Popularizers still write about "the hunting hypothesis."[6] In 1972 John Pfeiffer insisted that "the increasing emphasis on big game which started perhaps 2 million years before had an enormous effect on *man*, nearly doubling the size of *his* brain and transforming an advanced form of Australopithecus into Homo erectus."[7]

Despite recent research to the contrary academics also find it difficult to surrender their cherished notions about the formative role of hunting in evolution. In 1967, Sherwood Washburn stated flatly that "our intellect, interests, emotions, and basic social life—all are evolutionary products of the hunting adaptation." A decade later his foreword to a group of studies of the gathering-hunting Kalahari San still emphasized the "fundamental role which hunting has played in human history," though he was a little less positive that the entire story could be told within its context—"*it may well be* that it was the complex of hunting-weapons-bipedalism which accounts for the evolutionary origin of *man*." His conclusion is a perfect example of the way in which the switch from the gendered to the generic meaning of the word *man* allows for ambiguity and loose thinking: "Hunting was a major factor in the adaptation of *man*. If we are to understand the origin of *man*, we must understand *man* the hunter and woman the gatherer."[8]

After all, lions, hyenas, wolves, all have hunted big game, and their brains haven't doubled in the last few million years, and omnivores galore exist—bears, boar, beaver, to name only a few—nor do their brains change considerably in the fossil record. If hunting really were (a) a male thing and (b) the one syndrome which was responsible for the evolution of hominids into humans, how is it that women are so close to men physically and intellectually, in manipulativeness and ingenuity? Why was there no specialization and how did woman, too, inherit the presumed male qualities attributed to big-game hunting?

The truth is that whatever hominids did—collected seeds, made pets, skinned animals, told stories, sang songs—as long as they did it on a human level, it would have doubled their brains. Cognition, human consciousness, is what makes the difference between us and other animals, a difference not limited to one sex. There is great variation in the size of human brains but very little known difference in the internal structure of a female or male brain.[9] And as we saw, size itself is a vague and inconclusive measure. It is the human brain organization which is significant, that famous imagination about which science knows so little and the artist so much. The enlarging brain was the human adaptation. Everything else followed.

Part III

—⚎——⚎——⚎——⚎——⚎——⚎——⚎—

SAPIENT AT LAST

Hark, Nature, hear, dear goddess hear!
  —Shakespeare, *King Lear*

14

Human Like Us

The earliest member of our own species was found at Swanscombe, England, and dated to a period some two hundred thousand years ago when the climate there was semitropical.[1] Another skull of roughly the same age was excavated in Steinheim, Germany. The tools found near Swanscombe remains do not differ greatly from the handaxes and flakes found in Africa and Southern Europe with *erectus* fossils or fragments. But the skull conformations of Steinheim and Swanscombe people bear more resemblance to ourselves than they do to the well-known species today nominated *Homo sapiens neanderthalensis*, which is supposed to have lived in Western Europe from about 75,000 to 35,000 B.P. It is this last who gave rise to the folklore of Neanderthal man, the stooped and brutal caveman dragging his wife and brandishing a club, who used to inhabit comic strips and cartoons. The first Neanderthal specimen was discovered near the river Neander in Germany in 1856, before Darwin's theory of evolution had been published.

However, it was the discovery of an almost complete skeleton at La Chapelle-aux-Saints in 1908 which gave us the legend of the lumbering individual who could not stand upright, though endowed with a brain larger than most of ours today. (Remember, however, that it is not brain size but brain organization which is the determining factor in human consciousness and cognition.) To some extent, brain organization can be de-

duced from the conformation of the skull. In the case of Swanscombe person, the hominid who lived some hundred and fifty
thousand years before *neanderthalensis*, it was possible to trace
the pattern of the artery which supplies blood to the meninges
—the membrane embracing the brain—by the impression left
on the inside of the skull bones. The meningeal artery's form
was, according to Björn Kurtén, "very advanced in comparison
with that of homo erectus . . . its complexity reflects that of
the brain. The pattern seen in Swanscombe *man* is of a type
encountered even in some modern *men*."[2]

After considerable puzzling over the contradictory fact that
fossil hip and leg bones of African finds indicated an upright
posture some millions of years earlier, new investigations of the
specimen from La Chapelle-aux-Saints were undertaken. In
1957 the skeleton was examined by two doctors, William L.
Straus of Johns Hopkins University School of Medicine and
Alex Cave of St. Bartholomew's Hospital Medical College in
London. According to them, the skeleton was that of a man between forty and fifty, which at that time would have made him
an old man, and he had been afflicted with severe, deforming
arthritis of the jaws, spine, and, possibly, lower limbs, hence
his physical peculiarities, differentiating him from his fellows
and from earlier specimens.[3] So do legends and myths become promulgated as science, until a newer and more accurate
version of the explanatory tale comes along to supersede the
earlier one, a story which may come a little closer to the realities of the past we humans seek to comprehend.

The evidence about Neanderthals' thinking processes comes
to us out of their burial practices, as well as the more sophisticated tools they left behind. While we know nothing of their
family groupings, we infer a concept of humanity from the fact
that their dead were reposed, sometimes folded into what is
still referred to by present-day ethnographers as the "death position," legs drawn up, even bound to the trunk, in shallow
graves or natural depressions with stones on or around them.
The bodies were not actually buried, in the sense of interment;
they were placed. "Earth to earth" and "dust to dust" are
much later concepts, stemming from misconceptions and mis-

analogies which arose during the Neolithic, after the appearance of agriculture and animal breeding. Different types of graves from this period have been found in France, Italy, South Germany, Eastern Europe, North Africa, and Southwest Asia.

As might be expected in dealing with a period covering tens of thousands of years and distances to be measured in the thousands of miles, the graves, the groups, and the appurtenances vary. But the fact is that they exist: in Krapina, Yugoslavia, a find of ten bodies that had been broken open and in some cases burned, like the remains of animals eaten for food, suggested the practice of cannibalism so that much is made of our people-eating ancestors.[4] Given the hardships under which they lived during the Ice Age, it may well be that some crisis came along and cannibalism was a last resort. At Monte Circeo in Italy, a Neanderthal skull surrounded by a circle of stones was found within a cave; the way in which it had been broken open has led some paleohistorians to perceive a resemblance to ritual cannibalism practiced by South Sea Islanders in recent times.

Death as a long sleep is suggested by the finding of what might have been a flint pillow under a youth buried at Le Moustier, while the placing of a flint hand ax or other personal possession near a dead body has been interpreted as evidence of a belief in immortality, with the object ready for use when its owner was reborn or arrived in a spirit land.

In other places, a body with animal skulls, horns up, ranged around it, a burial of an individual clasping the bones of a boar; and pieces of ocher and supplies found in and around the graves pique the imagination, tantalizing it with questions that may never be answered.

Joseph Campbell, who is Jungian in his orientation, feels that the flexed position of some of the bodies from this period represents the fetal position and a desire to return to the womb. One asks oneself whether these people would have known what the fetal position was, since it is only in rare instances that an infant keeps its legs drawn up, or more often one leg, for even a brief period after birth. Moreover, graves containing several bodies occur, as at Le Moustier, where one person will be extended, another folded up. Grahame Clark, who makes much of the mystique of hunting and male killing, suggests that the burial of a woman at La Férrassie with her arms folded and her legs "so tightly flexed as to suggest that the corpse may have been bound with thongs . . . may reflect a desire on the part of the living to keep the dead securely away."[5] A more literal-minded reporter says that the reason primitive people often bury their dead with legs folded up is because the more compact shape requires less digging.

In the beginning was the word, says the Bible, just as the Egyptian Ptah created Shu and Tefnut by pronouncing them. Words are symbols; they are also magic. Through words we can create equivalences for mysterious or little understood processes, substitute art for reality, and counter the physical limitations of the natural world. Actually, for most of us and in many very early creation myths, in the beginning was the mother.

> Pukwi made the country the first time. The sea was all fresh water. She made the land, sea and islands. She came out of the sky in daytime. She was as big as Karslake Island. Like an alligator she was and she was black. . . . Puriti said, "Don't kill our mother." But Iriti went ahead and killed her. He struck her on the head. Her urine made the sea salty and her spirit went into the sky.
> Now she travels by day from east to west and back along the Milky Way at night. At midday she makes camp and builds a big fire and causes great heat.[6]

So runs a Tiwi creation myth told to Jane Goodale by a nine-year-old.

Everywhere that ethnologists and historians probe, the myth of the Great Mother precedes the later tales of God the Father. Scholars have come up with much evidence of a female creation image prior to the almost universal male creator of historical times. Their investigations are supported by ethnographic research: Turnbull found the myth of a female generator ousted by a male god among the Mbuti Pygmies; Lucas

Bridges in Patagonia heard versions recounted by the Onas and the Yahgans; examples can be cited from classical sources, as in ancient Persia, to the above-told Australian folktale.

There is nothing in the evidence to tell about Neanderthal birth or Neanderthal woman's physiology. We cannot even prove that Neanderthals had language, though most paleontologists believe they did, placing speech as far back as *erectus*. Holloway, as noted in Part II, would assign language even to extinct branches of our genus like *Australopithecus*. One die-hard anatomist at Yale still holds out for the beginnings of language with the later *Homo sapiens sapiens*, on the basis of the presumed shape of Neanderthal's vocal cords, and a few other physical anthropologists are loath to grant speech to our Neanderthal ancestors.[7]

Whether they spoke or not, and I am inclined to believe they did, the awareness of death in European cave burials some fifty thousand years ago is the first concrete evidence we have of human consciousness as opposed to animal responses. We are all frail and anxious creatures at the mercy of forces over which we have little or no control, and death is the supreme demonstration of this fact. Humans are aware of their helplessness, and the instantaneous emotions of animals are reinforced in us, supported, increased, or dispelled by our reasoning powers. Magic, religion, and science have all developed to allay our fears, to explain phenomena which the insignificant individual cannot understand or change. Magic was the first of these, and for early humans, perhaps long into our history, magic, religion, and science were synonymous.* Hence the rituals and ceremony around that most traumatic of experiences, the loss through death of loved ones, and the development of myths to alleviate the pain experienced by the living, to appease the fear of death, or to keep the dead from taking us with them.

Women, however, had an inherent magic quality: from time to time they gave birth, and there must have been something both mysterious and normal about this capacity. Birth and death have always been associated in the human mind: "A time to be born and a time to die," "Man is born and man

---

* "I still believe they're one," said the noted architect Louis Kahn in 1972.[8]

must die," "The moment we are born we start to die." Birth is the primal metaphor, and death its first polarity; together they are the original thesis and antithesis of human thought.

In Part I we saw that the mother-child relationship is the one universal throughout the order of Primates. The mother is the whole world for the infant, and for the human child, as awareness shapes, it is primarily the mother who gives or denies food, attention, love, protection. Father and surrogate parents all come later, artificially, socially, humanly. Goodall tells of the traumatic, often fatal, effects on the infant chimpanzee in the case of its mother's death, even though an older sister may attempt, usually ineffectually, to replace or substitute missing maternal care.[9]

It is another index to the flexibility and advance over the animal condition that humanity has devised so many assists and alternatives to the original dyadic relationship of mother and child. Still, the archetype of the Great Mother, with her polarized capacity for good and evil, for birth and destruction, remains. A host of folk sayings bear witness to her primacy: "You only have one mother." "Fathers can be many, but mother is only one." If we need her so much, what will happen if she chooses not to fulfill our needs? And in our childish vision of her great powers, it is only choice that keeps her from aiding or assuaging us, never necessity or incapacity.

Females can identify with the mother and expect to achieve her power; males have had to reach outward and compensate for their inability to bear children. Womb envy precedes penis envy—which last has been well discussed by Shulamith Firestone as a symptom and symbol of an already existing power relationship.[10]

The Neanderthals, thirty-five to seventy-five thousand years ago, could not have been aware of the sequence of coitus, fertilization, pregnancy, and childbirth. We know from the work of ethnographers in Oceania and Australia that the knowledge of biological fatherhood is a recent arrival on the human scene, for the original settlers of Australia some twenty to twenty-five, possibly even forty, thousand years ago were unaware of the male role in procreation and remained unaware of it during the thousands of years that they were cut off from contact with the rest of the world.

Much has been written about male fear and envy of women's generative and sexual powers, and it is often given as a major reason for the widespread oppression of the female that confronts us today. Did womb envy originate in Neanderthal times? There is as yet no evidence to show whether or not this awareness of the female's awesome powers obtained in Neanderthal times.

Judging from present-day foraging peoples, both in the far north and under temperate weather conditions, there is no reason to believe that Neanderthal humans were as aggressive as various Freudian and Jungian projections would have them.[11] That the mother was important we may be sure; men could well have had high respect for the female without feeling it necessary to "break and control and employ" her powers, especially in conditions which put no premium on many births.[12]

Western European Neanderthals did and do capture the imagination of paleoanthropologists because it was possible—by playing fast and loose with the very sparse evidence—to fit them into the conquest-oriented, male-dominated theories which characterized prehistoric studies until the last decade, theories in large part a projection from the cultural values of the people doing the studying. They have been more studied than any group of the period, out of all proportion to their numerical representation. This is partly because of the accident of preservation in limestone caves, but also because they were found in Europe, which is where most of the people who did the studying came from.

It distorts the story of human evolution to believe, as we used to be taught, that humanity was shaped from the "cavemen" of Western Europe. David Pilbeam suggests that during mild-weather epochs there would have been anywhere from five to ten humans living in Africa for every single individual who lived in Europe. When the arctic temperatures of glacial times prevailed, the proportion would have been twenty Africans for every European.[13]

Coexistent with Western European Neanderthals were many

groups of humans in Asia and Africa who, it is now thought, were less specialized physically. Most paleoanthropologists believe that the classic Neanderthals of Western Europe constituted a genetically isolated pocket whose physical characteristics differed from those of other humans of the period. They existed for many thousands of years in the rigid conditions of the last Ice Age and in milder interglacial periods. What they do demonstrate is the new species' ability to adapt to the most extreme weather conditions, and with an extraordinarily limited range of cultural devices. Analyses of fossils and burial practices suggest extremely high mortality rates.[14] When one considers that they had no snowshoes, that the needle for sewing weatherproof clothes like those of the modern Eskimos was not invented until some fifteen thousand years ago, twenty thousand years after they disappeared, that the dog had not been domesticated, and that their hunting tools consisted of wooden spears with a simple flint or bone tip, their survival is indeed wondrous. But these "mighty hunters" either died out or were absorbed by the more modern-appearing Neanderthaloids of the Near East.

We do not know whether there was a sharp division of sex roles among the classic Neanderthals, though recent studies of their tools show many scrapers and knives which must have been used in the preparation of hides. As noted earlier, the curing of skins was traditionally woman's work in the animal-dependent cultures of modern northerly peoples like the Eskimo and the Montagnais.[15]

It makes sense to believe that the division of labor was functional: in glacial climates women had more need of shelter when they were nursing infants; they also could not travel as far or as fast as men. When they were in the late stages of pregnancy or encumbered with small children, they would have done less hunting and more preparation of hides; in a northerly climate there was little plant food to depend on.

In other parts of the inhabited world the division of labor would have been closer to that of the few remaining foragers left on earth today. However, Neanderthal humans had far more limited tools with which to encounter their environment.

Even the handax, which has been found in Western Europe and southern Africa, was not in use in southern Asia. There would have been less specialization in the mild-climate areas, with women still doing more of the gathering than men, and men doing more of the hunting than women, but with both participating according to necessity.

In the past it was thought that humans and prehumans lived mostly by hunting, but with the recent investigations of foraging diets and the new vision of tool use it is today believed that then as now plants would have provided the major portion of sustenance in mild and temperate climates, where most humans lived during the past two hundred thousand or so years. Group hunting using fire drives and traps would have been the means by which Neanderthals procured most of their meat; fire-hardened wooden spears with or without flint tips were also used by individuals.

Family arrangements cannot be demonstrated until quite late in the archaeological record. Humans, even very early humans, have the largest input of variability, a result of the many combinations made possible by their large brains. As the species with the most diverse physical endowment—with the possible exception of our earliest domesticated animal, the dog—and the widest range of behavior, we would have begun to diverge early on.

The traditional idea that there was a sharp distinction, even a clean break, between our own species and the Neanderthals is still held by some physical anthropologists. Others feel that there is not very much difference between us and our forebears of up to one or two hundred thousand years ago. Even though we were evolving, the brain was essentially the same.[16] Therefore examples from recently existing foraging peoples, in particular those who used only stone tools, may have more bearing on how our Neanderthal ancestors lived than on the lives of the previous species, *Homo erectus* and *habilis*.

It used to be taught that the nuclear family was the basic human organization, with the father providing the food and the mother and children staying at home. Later it was propounded that the basic organization of foragers—the people who used to be called hunters—consisted of bands of related men who took wives from the men of neighboring bands, giving their sisters or nieces in exchange. By this reasoning, relationships were traced through the male line and women left their own bands to live with those of their husbands. This arrangement makes for a weak position for the woman, who is among strangers, unprotected by long-term affection relationships with her own female and male relatives, as was the case in agricultural China.

Recent field work among existing foragers has provided a different picture. Wives and husbands are not anchored by property arrangements, and bands themselves split and re-form. Often a husband will stay with his wife's family for a year or two, but in the long run the determining factor is likely to be the presence of a sister or brother, of either the wife or the husband.[17] Among some groups, like the San of Africa, it is customary for husbands to join their wives' groups, where they are without influence based on blood relationships. Marriages may be planned by parents; they are made by children and unmade with comparative ease.[18]

Chastity and lifelong monogamy are rare among small-scale foraging societies today and sexual experience is allowed for in most nonliterate cultures. "There are no virgins in the villages —for every female child begins her sexual life very early," said Malinowski of the Trobriand Islanders, a statement which applies among African San, Australian Aborigines, Samoans, Arctic Eskimos, Amerindian Utes, and many other nonliterate cultures with both complex and simple material attributes.[19] Childish sexual play merges gradually into full intercourse.

In Neanderthal times, without the understanding of physical fatherhood and with much sexual freedom, the work of women and men was necessary and recognized as such. In the hardship of the European Ice Age, even in periods of mild climate, aggression against women would have been counterproductive. Judging by later developments there would have been admiration for their reproductive powers, though we cannot demonstrate it. With possessions kept to a minimum by nomadism, there would have been a certain rough equality among our forebears.

The very minimal tool kit left by our Neanderthal ancestors does not, however, preclude a rich imaginative life. In recent years a less Western-white-oriented point of view has permitted us to see that the level of technological development does not necessarily tell us much about the mental and artistic gifts of a people. The Australian Aborigines, who have a very sparse material culture and whose passing on the land leaves few marks behind, have a very complex spiritual heritage. They have a network of myths and lore connected with each hill, each rock, each pool in their horde country; they have a pantheon of heroic creatures peopling their dream time; they have dances and rituals. During twenty to forty thousand years of isolation their cultural development focused on the spiritual and the imaginative rather than the technological, which is why today they have so much appeal to poets and the other advocates of the new consciousness, rebels against the Western materialist ethos.

Moreover, the tales associated with each physical marker—soaks, springs, lakes, water holes, rocks, mounds, distinctive groups of trees—also have a functional use. They serve as geographic references so that the literary anchoring of the landscape becomes an annotated, personalized map. One water hole was formed when the turkey Gerangalgu entered the ground; at Lake Baragu the star Gigi fell down; at another lake the great Rainbow Snake emerged; he ended his travels at the rock hole which is named after him. Here the Great Mother Gadjeri sat down and rested; there she disappeared and at another point on the landscape emerged again. This knowledge is essential in the wandering of the tribes, for it tells them how long they should walk before obtaining water, where certain plants grow, or where animals are likely to come and drink. The social and economic worlds are integrated in a framework which provides a comprehensive world view. Theirs is a universe peopled by spiritual creatures of the before and after time, shape-changing and eternal, who imbued the sites through which they passed with a spiritual aura. The living people share in this essence, for they are kin to the creatures of the timeless, imaginative world whose abstract presence is grasped through an actual relationship to the land and the adventures associated with its every physical feature.[20]

Taletelling, whether it is called connecting (Forster), time-factoring (Marshack), or classifying (Chomsky), is probably as old as our species, and it is more than likely that our Neanderthal forebears had a spiritual and mythological way of integrating themselves with their natural world, though they have left little evidence for interpretation.

At three caves in the Alps remains of cave-bear skulls and bones seem to be placed ceremonially. It has been suggested that these animals played a role in the religious mythology and the subsistence of Western Neanderthal humans.[21] Hibernating cave bears might have provided a ready food supply for our European forebears during the long glacial winters—a kind of living deep freeze. In other cases humans were buried with the bones and ashes of wild cattle, woolly rhinoceroses, horses, reindeer, and bison, also animals of economic utility. In more recent times animals like these inhabit the mythic worlds of diverse foraging peoples.

Whereas Neanderthal people used to be considered a dead end in human evolution, comprising the small group of cave people in Western Europe now known as Classic Neanderthalers, the denomination today has been enlarged to include fossils of that period from many places in the world.

We saw earlier that scientists classify our past with two parallel systems: by tools and by fossils. Early in the twentieth century a horde of tools along with several Neanderthal skeletons were found at Le Moustier in the Dordogne in France. Tools like those found at Le Moustier have subsequently been found in many parts of Europe, Asia, and South Africa and are dated to the period between 100,000 and 35,000 B.P. Therefore, tools and groups of tools produced during this period are called Mousterian, after the initial find spot, and all human remains found in conjunction with them are now classified as *Homo sapiens neanderthalensis*.[22]

The Classic Neanderthals are still considered to have become extinct, while other groups of fossils from Eastern Europe and the Near East, similar to them but somewhat more generalized in form, are called Persistent Neanderthals. However, two small groups of fossils discovered in the Near East have skulls and body skeletons closer to our own bodies and heads: they are called Progressive Neanderthals.

In the Judeo-Christian tradition, which has shaped much of Western civilization, the Near East plays an important role. The Garden of Eden, first home of our mythical ancestors, and Mount Ararat, on which, at a later date, Noah's ark came to rest after the other inhabitants of the world had been destroyed by flood, are both situated in the general area. It is curious, then, that twentieth-century studies of our beginnings, and possibly those of all modern humans, keep bringing us back to the same area, for the origin of *Homo sapiens sapiens* and again at later stages in our story.

A hypothesis is, after all, an educated myth, and a recent myth proposed by science would have us descended from these Progressive Neanderthals. They are represented in the record by seventeen fossil skeletons, or fragments thereof, found in Israel: ten individuals from a small cave called Skhul in the Wadi-el-Mughara near the coastal plain and seven people from a larger cave named Qafzeh, which is located near biblical Nazareth.

Sally Binford has presented some theories in support of the hypothesis, first broached by F. C. Howell, that these fossils represent a transition between *Homo sapiens neanderthalensis* and *Homo sapiens sapiens*. Her documentation is based on an analysis and comparison of *neanderthalensis* and *sapiens* burials in Western Europe and the Near East. Though one might question whether there are enough burials to provide a representative sample, she does find more similarities between Neanderthal burials in the Near East and the later *sapiens sapiens* burials of Europe than between the Neanderthal burials in Europe and those in the Near East. She also provides support for the theory of Neanderthals' disappearance in Europe with statistics showing as many children as adults buried, whereas in the Near East as in later Cro-Magnon burials

the ratio was two adults to every child, allowing her to speculate that more children survived to reproductive age. Comparing the way of life for the Progressive Neanderthals of the
Near East with that of the Paleolithic cave people of the Dordogne in France, she theorizes that both took advantage of
herd animals.[23]

The Progressive Neanderthals were discovered in the Jordan
upland areas, and the climate was not dissimilar to today's,
though at that time the region had more wooded areas and
more contrasts of rain and dryness. Annual migrations of wild
cattle and fallow deer occurred in consequence, animals following the valleys to new feeding grounds. Since the bone waste
found in conjunction with skeletons consists chiefly of these animals, she deduces that there may have been communal hunts
to take advantage of animal migrations and acquire surpluses of
food.

Large group hunts would have required the participation of
several bands of people, like those organized by American
Plains Indians of the nineteenth century. Opportunities for
mingling of tribes would have meant encounters between
women and men of different groups, giving rise to increased
gene flow and new combinations of physical characteristics,
with a new kind of human resulting.

A more general theory suggests that the Near East was the
crossroads of the three inhabited continents: Asia, Africa, and
Europe. It would therefore be the natural meeting ground for
peoples, genes, and ideas—logical sources for the greatest di-
versification as well as the most efficient use of possibilities—so
that new human species and new inventions would indeed be
most likely to arise in that area.[24]

Before Howell and Binford outlined their theory of a Near
Eastern origin for *Homo sapiens sapiens*, the usual explanation
was that *sapiens sapiens* developed more or less simultaneously
in a number of widely separated geographical areas, a supposi-
tion which leaves much to chance.[25] Another explanation has
the "advanced" *sapiens sapiens* invading Europe and destroying
the backward Neanderthals.[26] Binford feels that since we are
one species, with *neanderthalensis* and *sapiens* as subspecies, in-

termarriage between the two was not only possible but probable, and the mingling could as easily have been pacific as warlike. The Basque language is unrelated to any other known language, and the Basques are a short, stocky people living in the remote mountain fastnesses of southwestern France and northern Spain. They still preserve a fiercely independent sense of self, and it has been suggested, not altogether in jest, that they might be descendants of the original Western European Neanderthals.

Neanderthalensis may have survived in isolated pockets while the Near Eastern progenitors were spreading into Europe, as well as into Asia and Africa. In some cases they would have died out, in others been absorbed into the better equipped Upper Paleolithic culture of *sapiens sapiens*.

The Classic Neanderthals of Western Europe were living in a rigidly cold area comparable, say, to the present-day Arctic, in climate though not in light. The first discoveries of *sapiens sapiens* remains are dated to a warm period, one of several temporary warmings during the Ice Age. This then might have been a propitious time for expansion.

It is Binford's theory that rapid population increases would have occurred during periods of relative sedentism, times when the populations were able to settle in one upland river valley awaiting the passing of the migrating herds, instead of wandering about in search of a varied supply of animals. One of the problems inherent in obtaining an almost all-meat diet in a cold climate is that meat is hard to catch, in particular with the extremely primitive weapons which are all we know for Western European Neanderthals. If for some reason the herds fail, starvation follows—whole bands and peoples may be wiped out, as happened quite recently with a band of Eskimos, the Sadlermuits, in the Central Arctic. A temperate climate allowing dependence on varied resources of plant and animal food is obviously more secure. Thus the theory of the rapid expansion and material advance of *sapiens sapiens* during the Würm Interglacial some thirty-odd thousand years ago.

Originally studied above all in France, fossils and relics are now known from a varied area across Europe and into Asia and North Africa. But the French niveau is the most thoroughly explored, partly because of the accidental discovery there of fossils, tools, and cave art during the latter half of the nineteenth century. Much of our information is still based on the long record of finds there and in adjacent areas of northern Spain, Germany, and Italy. The periods and places have been well charted; the nomenclature for various Upper Paleolithic stages now recognized in many parts of Europe and Asia is based on the early French finds, so that French place names are used for classification.

The brains and bodies of these people are loosely indistinguishable from our own. Moreover, we have clearer evidence of a common humanity in terms of bodily physique and attitudes toward procreation because, in addition to far more copious archaeological evidence—fossils, tools, even habitations—they also left visual evidence behind in the form of painting and sculpture.

15

Paleolithic Art:
What It Tells Us

Most history has been written as if women did not exist, save as passive spectators, and accounts of the Eurasian Upper Paleolithic are no exception. Everything we read assumes a male origin and male interests. Hunting magic—sympathetic and fertility—is widely accepted as the underlying motivation, with an occasional speculation about male initiation rites thrown in. Many of the facts are still unknown, and what we do know has often been presented in highly distorted fashion. Only a few faint voices have been raised to question the confident myths which often masquerade as science or history.

There is no reason to attribute Paleolithic art exclusively to male painters and sculptors, yet scholars have been doing so for generations. A vague mark at the bottom of a drawing is variously described as a spear thrower, a throwing stick, or a broken spear. Those who perceive human evolution in terms of Man the Hunter see weapons, hunting, killing.[1] Writers interested in archetype and spirit offer explanations based on religious ceremony and ritual, and they support themselves with analogies taken from ethnographic data.[2] Men are more sweeping, women more cautious, in their interpretations.

Striking examples of cave art—paintings, engraving, and bas-reliefs—were first discovered in southwestern France and northern Spain. Several of the initial finds were made by children roaming through the caves and passages of limestone country in the Dordogne; others by amateur archaeologists who had come upon examples of Paleolithic art on their own land, or had their attention drawn to the mysterious paintings by their daughters or sons.

Beginning with the twentieth century more and more discoveries have been made, still mostly in France and Spain, though examples are found as far to the east as Kapova in Siberia. They have given rise to much literature—that human need to tell explanatory tales, to connect, and to classify—in the fields of art and mythology as well as prehistory. Examples of cave art—usually referred to as parietal or wall art, despite the fact that it is also found on floors and ceilings—abound in the Dordogne and are also found in Spain, North Africa, and Italy. Recent discoveries in Eastern Europe and Siberia have yielded chiefly small sculptures—animal and human figures. Carved and decorated artifacts—tools and tool handles, pebbles, and seemingly ornamental or ritual objects—have been collected in both areas. It is these visualizations which give us both explicit information and suggestions about the mental capacities, the appearance, and the interests of our ancestors.

The field for speculation is enormous, the range of those who would fill it equally so.

In 1965 Grahame Clark was writing about Paleolithic sculpture in *Prehistoric Societies* (revised edition published in 1970):

> Others were modeled from clay and hardened in the fire like pottery; . . . most of those found in and around a hearth at Pavlov might almost have been produced by a hunter squatting by the fire and idly kneading clay into the shape of his intended victims. . . . The *men* responsible for cave art were subject to all the tensions of the hunter's life under conditions which evidently allowed a certain leisure without rendering the winning of food in any sense

easy or secure. The content of the art itself leaves us in
no doubt that it was conceived in and intimately
bound up with the *hopes and desires of hunters;* and
its essentially masculine character is emphasized by
the *extreme rarity of plant forms.* By the same token there is no essential conflict between the esthetic
and magical aspects of cave art; it is precisely as a
means of gaining some control over the wild animals on which they depended that the cave artists set
out to delineate them with so much passion; and
their ability to achieve authentic representations was
based on a lifetime's experience watching the attitudes and behavior of their victims in the course of
hunting.[3]

The "revised and enlarged edition" of John Pfeiffer's *The
Emergence of Man* informed us in 1972:

The world's first great art "movement" lasted more
than 20,000 years, from Aurignacian to Magdalenian
times. Some of its most spectacular products are
found in underground galleries, away from natural
light in the passages and chambers and niches of limestone caves, and indicate in a most vivid fashion
how completely *hunting dominated the attention and
imagination of prehistoric man. He rarely drew people*
and *never anything* that would be recognized *as a
landscape,* although there are a wide variety of signs
which have no obvious meaning to us. *His* overwhelming concern was with game animals seen as individuals, clearly defined and detached, and isolated from
their natural settings. . . .

An important clue [to cave art] involved Cro-Magnon *man's* concern with his effectiveness as a pro-
vider. Half the battle in hunting and fighting is confidence; and if he was anything like modern *man*, he
used ritual on numerous occasions to help replenish
and increase his power. Perhaps he cast spells on his
prey. Certain places in the depths of the cave area are

covered with superimposed figures, figures drawn one
on top of the other and overlapping as if the artists
paid little attention to the work of their predecessors
but considerable attention to where the art was located. They also represented some animals with darts
or spears sticking into their sides, for example, the
bison in the Shaft of the Dead Man [at Lascaux, in
the Dordogne], which may have been killed ritually in
revenge for the death of the hunter.[4]

In 1967 Peter Ucko and Andrée Rosenfeld had published *Paleolithic Cave Art*, an exhaustive and detailed study analyzing
both art and the literature thereon, which presented convincing
evidence to contradict almost every statement in the passages
quoted above, as well as most other generalizations and one-
note, single-theory explanations for cave art.

It is not surprising that Pfeiffer, who had earlier attributed
the growth of the human brain to big-game hunting, should
overlook most other evidence to continue his focus on male
"exploits." But even the skeptical Ucko and Rosenfeld assumed
a male origin: "There may as well be one hundred reasons why
paleolithic *men* decorated caves." And, contradicting one M.
Astre who felt "from the similarity in style of all Paleolithic art
that painting and engraving must have been a specialist activity
of the sorcerers, passing from father to son," they say, "In Australia and Africa, the available evidence suggests that anyone
(at least any male) can be an artist."[5]

In 1939 Phyllis Kaberry published an account of an old
woman who participated in increase ceremonies and performed
the annual rite of repainting Kaleru, the sacred Rainbow Serpent of the Northwestern Australian Aborigines.[6] Shamanism
has always been practiced by women and men of Siberia, the
Arctic, and, in northern North America, the Ojibwa on both
sides of the Canada-United States border. In Australia it is age,
not sex, which determines the religious officiants. The more ancient the culture, the more likely we are to find shamanism, sorcery, magic, or priesthood practiced by members of both sexes,
though customs vary widely. In modern cultures ancient or

popular religions appeal to the underclasses, principally women; they also frequently involve women officiants. Spiritual yearnings and needs have never been restricted to one sex.

The picture in the Shaft of the Dead Man at Lascaux (Figure 4) is an example of the broad range of interpretations offered. Ucko and Rosenfeld describe it as "including a disembowelled bison, a 'phallic' man, a rhinoceros, and several other objects."[7]

In the passage quoted on page 137, John Pfeiffer saw it as a hunter's revenge. Grahame Clark ignores the rhinoceros to see the bison "with its entrails falling out of its side and a great single-barbed spear lying across its hind quarters and almost touching what must be either a spearthrower or the broken head of another spear; before the beast and fronted by it lies the prostrate body of a man with arms outstretched and a birdlike head."[8] The Abbé Breuil, who devoted himself to copying, studying, and interpreting cave art from the age of fourteen until his death in 1961, aged eighty-four, for a long time exercised a virtual monopoly over the field. He saw a dead hunter lying between the bison he had wounded and the rhinoceros which had subsequently killed him.[9]

Joseph Campbell approaches the painting in a more imaginative fashion, as befits the interpreter of Joyce's *Finnegans Wake*:

> The man wears a bird mask and has birdlike instead of human hands. He is certainly a shaman . . . [Australian rites provide] a plausible symbolic context for the pointing of the penis of the prostrate shaman of Lascaux—as well as for the defecation of the passing rhino, who may well be the shaman's animal familiar. The position of the lance, furthermore, piercing the anus of the bull and emerging at the penis, spills the bowels from the area between—which is precisely the region effected by the "pointing bone" of the Australians.[10]

Two female interpreters of the scene also lean toward a religious significance. G. Rachel Levy, in 1948, suggested: "The man with outstretched arms and stiff legs at Lascaux may be no corpse gored by the bison who faces him on the cave wall. His birdlike mask and his attitude may be related to the bird on the pole (if such it is) which is placed beside him. If one could imagine a hunting scene depicted in the depths of a cave, it would surely represent success and not defeat. The disembowelled bison as a separate figure would follow a fairly common precedent."[11] According to Jacquetta Hawkes, "the man appears to be birdheaded while planted beside him is a wand with a bird on its top; it is possible that this picture has totemic significance showing the human member and his totemic emblem."[12]

Actually, to interpret the myth or meaning behind this and many other cave paintings is an exercise in sheer human ingenuity. Imagine placing visitors from Mars, or even the Kalahari Desert, in front of paintings dealing with different myths in our own past, Moses and the burning bush, Christ at the wedding in Cana, or Hercules killing the lion of Nemea, and asking for an explanation. Cultural perspective and personal predilection shape the responses. We are in a better position to interpret the interpreters than the scenes interpreted.

There is no reason to insist on a male origin, as there is no reason to insist on a female origin, for Paleolithic art. Chances are that both participated, though the men may have had more leisure. Women the nourishers are more generally associated with food preparation than men. Cooking the rice and beans, getting the meal on the table—though in European Paleolithic days it was more likely to have been venison, mushrooms, and salmon—interferes with talk and thought and can be distracting. Still, in the Australian Kimberleys the men roast their catch of kangaroo, while the women attend to the food they have procured. In parts of Africa, also, hunters traditionally cook the food they have caught. As we have seen, women hunt; they also participate and sometimes officiate in religious ceremony.

Among the Vedda in Ceylon (Sri Lanka) it is the women who do the rock paintings.[13] The town of Mithila in India has a centuries-old tradition of women painters, who produce highly sophisticated work. Among the Caduveo Indians of South America women also paint, intricate decorations on ceramics and hides, as well as on the human body, while men are sculptors. There may well have been Paleolithic counterparts of our Grandma Moses, who began to paint late in life, or of Rosa Bonheur or Artemisia Gentileschi, who dedicated themselves to art from an early age. To say that only the hunter who knew the beast from the rigors of the hunt could have drawn them is foolish. It isn't the warrior who paints the battle scene, but an artist who has observed from a safe distance. Some of the peculiarities of Paleolithic animal portraits have been attributed to the fact that they may have been drawn from dead animals. Imaginary scenes based on dimly remembered reality have also been a wellspring of art.

What is true about the Paleolithic paintings and sculpture of the High Magdalenian—Lascaux is generally dated to 17,000 B.P.—is that we recognize them as art, whatever purpose or purposes they may have served at the time. It's not realism or knowledge of the wild animals' muscles and movements that the Paleolithic artists had but feeling, and a feeling which transcends the millennia, a feeling we can share. They communicate to us on a level quite different from the wonders of nature, the nest of the bowerbird, say. Even though we do not know exactly what the artists were saying, human consciousness animates their work. Though time and ruin may have added to the aesthetic force of the painting and sculpture—compare, for example, the Greek statues of the Classical period, which appeal to us for their chasteness and simplicity, but were actually painted at the time in gaudy primary colors a modern consciousness might have found off-putting—the fact that we can respond to them does tell us something about the common humanity we share with their creators.

The Upper Paleolithic period spans twenty thousand years and diverse cultures stretching from Spain to Siberia. All too often it has been treated as one unity, and the few striking pictures deep in the caves, many of which date to later periods, are usually described as typical and rule-making and are taken to represent the whole period.

Ucko and Rosenfeld have divided cave art into three categories: the first is that which is almost outdoors, in living areas at the mouths of caves and in rock shelters; the second is art which is found in corridors linked with or leading off from the above, i.e., adjacent to living areas; while the third category refers to art seemingly hidden within the recesses of enormous caves, apart from the places normally frequented by the people who made it.

The first kind, found in rock shelters and cave entrances, is analogous to art which might have existed on the walls of now destroyed houses or huts. It is art which is seen by direct light, and what remains after these thousands of years are mainly basrelief sculptures and some engravings. This was probably the most common kind of art during the period but was the least likely to endure; destruction, weather, and subsequent diverse uses of these places made it unlikely that any trace would have come down to us. Ucko and Rosenfeld point out that the apparent scarcity of this kind of painting is undoubtedly due to conditions of corrosion. Traces of ocher on bas-reliefs, engravings, and painted blocks buried in deposits show that paintings were executed at rock shelters and cave entrances.[14]

The earliest cave art known dates back to the Aurignacian period, about thirty thousand years ago, when there had been a mild interglacial period and, presumably, the new subspecies had recently spread from the Near East and colonized Europe. Some of the oldest works known, from Aurignacian levels at the cave of La Férrassie, belong to the first category, art which is almost outside. Simple outlines of animals and "vulvas"— signs which are usually interpreted as female organs—were engraved in a single continuous deep and wide groove. As in almost all other Paleolithic stone work the limestone is too corroded to be examined for actual traces of working technique.[15]

It has always been taken for granted that these vulvas were engraved by men. And yet Lorna Marshall reports that among the San of Africa young girls draw sexual symbols, including diagrammatic representations of their genital aprons, on the smooth gray bark of trees.[16]

Phyllis Kaberry reports on women's ceremonies among the

Kimberleys and records many songs and dances which refer to sexual organs, for erotic purposes as well as in childbirth and menstruation rites. Colin Turnbull writes of the *elima* of the Mbuti Pygmies, the month-long festival during which young girls learn about love-making and take the initiative with young boys. In the last few decades—with the entry of more women into anthropology and with the spread of sexual enlightenment —we have discovered that there is far less sexual repression among women of nonliterate and noncontact societies than had been assumed by earlier Victorian-conditioned reporters. It is quite as likely that the sexual representations of Paleolithic caves were made by women as by men.

What we can be sure of is that the vulva and the sexuality and childbearing capacities of women were of the highest importance. Women's genitals have a double association, with pleasure and with birth. Many of the representations may have had to do with birth ceremonies, to ease the pains of childbirth and ensure safe delivery. The vulva is the point of origin for all of us, women and men, save those rare individuals who, like Macduff, boast of being "from his mother's womb untimely ripped." (Neither Caesar's nor Macduff's entry into the world was a likely occurrence in Paleolithic times.)

According to a woman archaeologist, there are far more representations of women's thighs and vulvas in Paleolithic cave art than has been reported in the literature.[17] Not only Abbé Breuil, who played so important a role in publishing this art, but several other early researchers in the field were members of the Catholic clergy, and they tended to ignore these disquieting reminders of the dangerous female.

One of the most striking finds in cave art belongs also to the category of exposed art and is even more directly related to the human female, as well as to the human male. At Laussel several limestone blocks which contain realistic bas-reliefs of human bodies are dated to a comparatively early period; they were executed about 23,000 B.P., during the Périgordian period. As Ucko and Rosenfeld point out human beings are represented more often than is sometimes claimed.[18] Laussel has given us five representations, of which three are female, one

male, and one, a double figure of which the upper definitely
has breasts, has been called either a birth scene or a depiction
of intercourse. If the second, it would have to be seen as a flat-
tened-out stylized version of the face-to-face squatting position
Malinowski describes for the Trobriand Islanders. If a birth
scene, even taking into account the possibilities for stylistic
distortion, mother and child are of equal size, a rather unlikely
proportion. Two other possibilities exist: badly preserved and
hard to make out, Levy suggests it is a figure of a woman whose
legs come together; and Ucko and Rosenfeld think it may have
been an unfinished sculpture which was worked also from the
opposite direction.

The Venus of Laussel is one of the best known of the many
Paleolithic Venus figures (see Figure 3). She has an ample
figure with a small head; one delicate hand rests on a full but
not necessarily pregnant belly; the other arm holds an incised,
single-pointed crescent, usually interpreted as a horn, above her
shoulder. The hips and thighs and great pendulous breasts are
all burgeoning; the legs taper away without showing the feet.
Though the figure is clearly distorted in the opposite direction
from a Modigliani, she is rather more to the average taste than
other Paleolithic Venuses, Willendorf or Lespugue for example. (Picasso kept a copy of the latter in a special place in his
studio.[19]) More fleshy even than a late Renoir or Rubens, perhaps it is the desiccation of time, which has left only traces of
her original red ocher paint, that produces a general sense of
awe rather than voluptuousness.

Apropos of the drooping, usually huge, breasts which characterize many Paleolithic female images, one is reminded of
Turnbull's remark that the Mbuti Pygmies do not think a
woman's breasts attractive until they have "descended" after
childbirth, nursing, and full maturity. Compare also the Egyptian goddess Nut, apostrophized in the Pyramid Texts as "she
of the hanging breasts," "the great protectress" whose body
overarched the earth. Let us not confuse the Western attitude
toward the breast as an erotic symbol dissociated from nutrition with that of other times and places. Whether or not the
breast was a sexual symbol, the connection of the female with

maternity, all-givingness, and plenty in these representations is obvious—and it is not an exclusively male image. We have all been children, and presumably all Paleolithic children would have had a recollection of the warmth, security, and sensuality of the mother's breast and body. Nor need there have been any diffidence about acknowledging the sensual components. Children would have been nursed far longer than is today customary and carried more frequently in much closer contact with their mother's bodies, given the cold weather.

The male figure, on the contrary, is smaller, shown in three-quarter profile rather than full on, neither thin nor fat, with no indicated sexual organ, and far less striking.

Art of the second category, in cave passages adjoining or leading off from the living area, may be far more extensive than had previously been thought. Ucko and Rosenfeld point out that drafts, temperature changes, and earth movements which cause passages to be blocked might often destroy the art close to the atmosphere and the open so that the deeply hidden art discovered after thousands of years may at one time have been a continuation of now-destroyed art. Most cave systems have been inadequately explored so that often we do not know the original entrances and original habitation areas of caves where "sanctuary" or hidden art has been found. Out of the hundred or so known and explored caves with Paleolithic art, Ucko and Rosenfeld document twelve which belong to this second category. They suggest that most of the caves which have usually been ascribed to category three—the hidden art which has captured the fancy of art historians and archaeologists—may originally have been connected with inhabited areas. The Paleolithic occupants would have wandered deeper into the caves to paint and sculpt and, perhaps, use the natural chambers for theatrical ceremonies.

There is a very simple reason why our Paleolithic ancestors may have chosen the deepest caverns for their most ambitious decorations and ceremonies. During the long glacial winters these would provide most protection against the cold, with an unvarying temperature. On the hottest summer days as well as the coldest winter ones, deep inside limestone caves like Lost

River Caverns of Pennsylvania the temperature stays at close to 50 degrees. Moreover, with the current energy crisis, old limestone mines and caverns are currently being put to use or proposed as fuel-saving offices and storage facilities. Two hundred feet below the earth's surface the headquarters of the Consolidated Meat Distribution Center near Kansas City, Kansas, remain at a constant 58 degrees throughout the year.[20]

The long winters may have been a leisure and ceremonial time during which Paleolithic people subsisted on meat killed earlier and kept in natural deep freeze, in the outer passages of the limestone cave networks. The inmost chambers would have served as habitations and meeting places, providing maximum protection against the severities of the Ice Age.

There is no doubt that some of the art does lie in passages and chambers difficult of access, if not necessarily completely secret. It is hard to date these representations unless organic relics—carbonized rope or other artifacts connected with daily life that can be tested by radiocarbon analysis—are found in indisputable association with them, and even then proof is not always certain. Some caves are securely dated; many are not.

One researcher has assumed that "hidden" art works are of later date than the external representations, charting a linear chronological development for the whole phenomenon of cave art. This theory is effectively criticized by Ucko and Rosenfeld, who point out that in a period covering twenty thousand years, and with several sharp climate changes, cultures must have come and gone, risen and decayed, and similarly with schools and traditions of art. They demonstrate the enormous diversities of styles, giving examples with reproductions of horses' heads in varying modes, and tear apart the attempts to sex animals by size—smaller female, larger male; delicate figures female, heavier ones male—or to see as pregnant any animal with a protruding belly. By this reasoning, and it is a reasoning much expounded in the reams that have been written about cave art, all horses by Rosa Bonheur and Paolo Uccello would be male while those of Piero della Francesca and Marino Marini would be female and pregnant.

Much of the better known cave art—animals, imaginary creatures, and, in a very few cases, scenes—is believed to have emerged from the Magdalenian period, roughly 17,000 to 10,500 years B.P. This is the period when artifacts of bone, as well as flint tools, show an increasing richness of ornamentation, and many new inventions appear. The eyed bone needle, for sewing waterproof clothing, was discovered in the late Solutrean, some two thousand years earlier, but seems to have disappeared with that culture and been rediscovered about 15,000 B.P. A wide variety of tools which would have been used by women and men, or possibly only women, begins to be developed. Harpoons and spear throwers, which we think of as used more exclusively by men, come later in the chronology of invention, after 13,000 B.P.

In the time sequence of the Upper Paleolithic epochs in Europe and Asia, Châtelperronian is the earliest; then come the Perigordian and the Aurignacian, now thought to be two parallel cultures, overlapping if not coexistent in time. The Solutrean was a relatively brief (3,000 years) and locally limited very advanced culture. The greatest quantity of evidence—art and artifact—is, not unsurprisingly, from the final period, the Magdalenian. Climatological researches show that new cultures seem to coincide with the mild-temperature periods known as interglacials. Perhaps the earlier cultures declined under the severities of harsh glacial temperatures or of shifting ecological conditions, whereas mitigating temperatures—over thousands of years—permitted resurgence and new inventions.

The Magdalenian is known best from its middle and late stages, and in western France. It is supposed to have been a period of extremely rich resources, which began during a relatively mild phase, became quite cold, and then disappeared as the Ice Age ended and woodland forests replaced the tundra over which vast herds of reindeer had roamed. During its height, climate and geography produced cool, moist conditions not all that different from the present-day habitat of the Pacific coast of northwestern North America. The Magdalenians may have lived all year round in caves as well as, on occasion, in temporary summer camps. From their food debris, we know they lived chiefly on reindeer, on migrating salmon, occasional seals, birds, hare, etc., as well as, presumably, berries, roots, tubers, nuts, mushrooms, and honey. It is a well-balanced diet, rich in protein, though not necessarily in starch, sugar, and fat. Honey and berries, with their rare sweetness of taste—and in nature sweetness is associated with much needed vitamins— would have been obtainable only in brief seasons. They would have been much prized, as indeed they were by the Indians of the Pacific Northwest coast.

One of the many misconceptions in the interpretation of Paleolithic cave art, then, regards the myth of the dangerous and difficult hunt, practiced only by males. "They weren't hunting; they were harvesting!" said Sally Binford. If the paintings of the animals were for purposes of "sympathetic" magic—to insure success in the face of danger—why are fearsome animals like cave bear and cave lion, difficult and dangerous to catch and known to have abounded during the period, so infrequently represented? And if for the purposes of fertility magic, similar to the Australian Aborigines' increase ceremonies, why are there so few paintings of reindeer, which was the staple food of the time?

It is typical of our culture's emphasis on weapons and aggression that feathered arrows, darts, and spears were so frequently perceived in the wall paintings and engravings. Featherlike signs engraved or painted on the bodies of animals are often thought to represent arrows. However, real Paleolithic bone projectile points were either not barbed or were mounted to produce only a single barb. Fully biserial barbed harpoons only appeared in the final Magdalenian—long after most of the works had been executed.[21] The interpreters of Paleolithic art works thought they were seeing weapons not yet invented at the time the works had been executed.

Ucko and Rosenfeld also find it "strange that Paleolithic *men* who lived by hunting and gathering wild fruit and berries had no interest in the increase of vegetation," another reason for considering that cave art could not have been analogous to Australian increase rites, which are performed for vegetation as well as for animals. Noting that many of the stick and line forms which have been seen as weapons fly through the air or miss their targets, they wonder why Paleolithic humans would have wanted to depict so many hunting failures.[22]

Alexander Marshack, whose book *The Roots of Civilization* speculates on the storytelling capacities of early humans, finds a simple answer. Many objects which had previously been seen as weapons look to him like plants, trees, branches, and flowers, and he deduces stories about the changing of the seasons from them and their conjunction with animals and people. Once the suggestion has been made, they do indeed resemble bare limbs, reeds, trees, leaves, and flowering plants far more than the destructive elements for which they had previously been taken.

Marshack describes a bone object, usually called a *bâton de commandement*, on which were engraved forms that resembled barbed harpoons. He examined it under the microscope, and it was clear that the engravings were impossible harpoons: the barbs were turned the wrong way and the points of the long shafts were at the wrong end. The figures were perfect plants or branches, growing at the proper angle and in the proper way at the top of a long stem.[23] He concludes that vegetation was clearly represented on the small objects and that many of the so-called "barbed signs" and "masculine objects" in the caves probably represented plant forms.[24]

The "masculine objects" to which Marshack referred come from André Leroi-Gourhan's explanation of cave art as grounded in sadomasochistic sexual symbolism. Leroi-Gourhan has spent many years charting, counting, and doing statistical analyses of the representations in the caves. He dichotomizes every image into one of the two sexes: bison, male; horse, female; weapons or barbed signs, male; holes, rounds, wounds, etc., female. It is a wild fantasy on the already fantastic perversion which is late Freudian psychology, i.e., that human sexuality consists of male sadism and female masochism. Leroi-Gourhan's theory is based on mistaken identifications, projections of our own cultural preoccupations and preconceptions onto images which are still unexplained, though it is now clear that many represent vegetation. Looking at slides and photographs of the Magdalenian animals with overpaintings of twigged branches or leaves, it is indeed startling to realize that for half a century or more these innocent figures, often feathery and delicate in outline, were seen as deadly objects.

Awareness of the Paleolithic existence of humans and human artifacts had begun in the middle of the nineteenth century in Western Europe. Explorations of Paleolithic caves, with their spectacular wall paintings, engravings, and reliefs, commenced before the end of the century. As knowledge accumulated, research was extended to surface exploration and digs. In the eastern part of the Eurasian continent, Siberian construction workers had uncovered Paleolithic bones and carved mammoth ivory as early as 1871. Though Paleolithic art works were found in European Russia and Siberia before the Russian revolution, it was not till later, in 1923, that the first entire Paleolithic sculpture was found, a mammoth-ivory Venus figure unearthed at Kostenki, on the Don River.

In the Soviet, archaeologists work within a Marx-Engels ideology based on the assumption that matriarchy preceded patriarchy, and their attitudes are somewhat different from those common in the West. Since the early discoveries much work has been done on what was essentially a mammoth-hunting culture across the frozen tundras, in contrast to the Franco-Cantabrian area, where reindeer were a chief resource. There were no limestone caverns in the Eurasian plain, and many of the settlements have been charted from the remains of hearths, huge mammoth bones, graves, and other evidence of living sites. These northern foragers who wandered across the frozen tundras during the great Ice Age lived in skin huts or other tentlike structures erected on mammoth bones. In all the Paleolithic art found in European Russia and Siberia, not a single indubitably male figure was identified, though many small statues of females and a number of animal representations exist.[25]

There were burgeoning Venus figures with the characteristic huge, hanging breasts, bulging stomachs, and enormous buttocks, small or missing hands and feet, on the order of the Venuses of Lespugue, Grimaldi, Willendorf, and Laussel. But slender figures, long, stylized, and understated, were also found. There were even five female figures from Mal'ta and Buret in eastern Siberia, which had been worked in bone or ivory to suggest sewn clothing, not dissimilar to the hide and fur trousers and parkas worn by Lapps and Eskimos of recent times.

Fewer animal figures were found and less detail was lavished on them. In the West, cave walls had lent themselves to two-dimensional art which survived by the accident of the surface on which it had been placed; so far only two or three examples of Paleolithic cave art have been found in the East.

Whatever the reason for the frequent sculpture of female figures, it is clear that the male figure is of lesser importance in the consciousness of early *Homo sapiens*. In all the Eastern representations—animal, female, and some figures which are not necessarily female or male—there are no representations of male sexual organs as such or of coitus. As in the West there were puzzling objects. For example, some stylized ivory figurines found at Mezin in the Ukraine have been variously classified: as female nudes by Abbé Breuil, as the heads of long-beaked birds by V. A. Gorodcov, while F. K. Volkov saw them as male phalli.[26] Apart from these small ivory carvings there is no suggestion of the male organ to be found in Soviet art.

In the West an occasional figure showed an erected penis in a mysterious scene with animals, as in the much debated Lascaux crypt scene—the Shaft of the Dead Man—and a few barely decipherable small drawings may have included male genitalia. As Ucko and Rosenfeld have pointed out, there are no scenes of animal copulation, very few representations of animal sex organs, and, with the dubious exception of the unfinished double sculpture from Laussel, none of human copulation. Certain isolated signs which used to be interpreted as male and female sex symbols cannot be verified as such. The ubiquity of the female genital image and the rarity of the phallus tell us something about the biological knowledge of the people who made Paleolithic art. The phallus is not important to reproduction unless it is known that the male contributes to the making of the baby. Women were still the necessary sex. Analyses of the sculpture and paintings of Eastern and Western areas show that copulation and procreation were not yet linked in the human mind.

On the basis of the evidence, then, neither in the East nor in the West is there any demonstration that Paleolithic humans connected coitus with reproduction, placed any functional value on the male sexual organ, or saw reason to emphasize it in their art. The focus was on the female—breasts, belly, thighs, and vulva.

Women's functions may also have been studied; Marshack identified bone objects with line markings as lunar calendars. It is not unlikely that these were menstrual records, with or without reference to the astronomical phenomena which are often roughly parallel to women's monthly cycles. The Venus of Laussel holds in her hand a broken crescent. Sometimes identified as an animal horn, the crescent has lines engraved on it, and it might well be a representation of the crescent moon from which the upper part has eroded or broken off. The lines could be lunar markings denoting the menstrual cycle.

Cave art shows that the woman was more important than the male and that her body was connected with fullness and plenty. There are no aggressive images connected with women, and the art itself conveys awe and wonderment rather than terror or cruelty. Animals, plants, and people are depicted. Signs formerly interpreted as weapons are representations of nature and changing seasons. Though there is much that is mysterious, there is no positive evidence for male domination, nor for certain aggressive syndromes which appear later in the human story.

16

The Mana of Blood: Menstruation and Menopause

In Paleolithic times one of the earliest indications of religious awareness—a constant in human existence—was the finding of red-ocher decorations tingeing skeletons and associated with burials. The sacredness of the color red predates even our own subspecies, *Homo sapiens sapiens*, for lumps of red ocher have been found in Neanderthal and other Mousterian burials.

Like the body itself, implements and ornaments were often covered with the red ocher that recent nonliterates use to simulate the blood or life energy of which it is the symbolic counterpart. The red ocher sometimes lies around the skeletal remains in cakes, steeping everything in the vicinity with its color, presumably so that all the surrounding objects may keep their living quality in the other world.[1] When she was discovered, the Laussel Venus still bore traces of the red pigment with which she had been painted some twenty-three thousand years earlier.

Even today, or at least recently, body painting with red ocher is or was an integral part of many religious and ceremonial occasions in Oceania, Australia, Africa, and the Americas.

Kaberry describes its use by the Australian Aborigines at corroborees and other celebrations including puberty and marriage. The last is a simple rite: woman and man go alone into the bush for a few days and return painted with red ocher, signifying that they are wife and husband.[2]

A prized article of trade in Australia, it was also much in demand among American Indians at the time of white contact. When the Spaniard Núñez Cabeza de Vaca was shipwrecked off the coast of Texas in 1528, he made it to the mainland. Once there he survived among the strange Indian tribes by trading. He brought snails and mussel shells from the coast inland, and returned with much desired rarities, red ocher for body paint, skins, and special stones for arrowheads.[3]

From being a sacred color red has been translated into the color of luck, of renewal, and of change. It is used in good-luck amulets in the Mediterranean and also figures as a lucky color in Chinese New Year's celebrations. Above all, it has always been the color of revolution; the red flag is not merely an incitement to anger; it signifies the overturn of present rigidities and the arrival of a newer, presumably more life-giving scheme of existence.

Very little was known about the biology of human reproduction until recent times. Women have what was long considered a mysterious, even magic, issue of this red blood of life and renewal every month save when they are pregnant and until they are past the age of childbearing. Being a woman is defined by the onset of this periodic bleeding—menarche.

Women bleed; they bleed at menstruation; they bleed at childbirth. And blood is sacred; it is the stuff of life. We bleed only while we are alive, though bleeding may cause our death. It is women, however, who bleed regularly, as well as irregularly, and who produce life.

The Australian Aborigine men had not yet invented or discovered their connection with the actual conception of children, so they created various ceremonies of equivalence to female functions—the bloody Australian initiation rites which so horrified and fascinated Western male observers. Most of the early interpreters were so thoroughly indoctrinated by Western attitudes of disgust toward female biology and female sexuality that they failed to see the emulation of woman represented by the slitting of the penis into a symbolic vulva and the reiterated bleeding. The male organ of pleasure is changed to resemble the female organ, which is both that of pleasure and of childbirth. Initiation rites transpose the actual birth of male children into a ceremonial rebirth by way of men, and the male penis is converted into a womb with a vagina. Subincision is connected with the belief in the life-giving, strengthening power of blood. Blood is sacred, and at many totem rites and other solemn occasions Aborigine men gash their arms and genitals to produce it.[4]

Several anthropologists have reported on the complex and bloody rites of circumcision and subincision. The operation is often performed in several stages, first on the adolescent boy, then at intervals of a few years to lengthen the slit and to let blood. "Cut mine, cut mine," a white observer quoted the Australian tribesmen, demanding longer and longer cuts on their penises. The wound is sometimes referred to as a "penis-womb" or "vagina."[5]

Much has been made of the cruelty and bizarre nature of these rites, in which the man seems to be demonstrating his ability to withstand pain, as the woman withstands it in childbirth or in menstruation. The blood which is collected and used in various stages of the rites competes with the blood of menstruation and childbirth. There is a strong belief among the Aborigines that blood possesses magic power. A transfer of this power takes place between men of the Walbiri tribe in a ceremony in which rivulets of blood are dripped down over a squatting man by another stooping over him.[6]

The ceremony of mingling blood engaged in by Tom Sawyer and Huck Finn is not unrelated. They became blood brothers, as though formed in the belly of the same mother. Among the Ungarinyin in the Kimberleys, the quarry must be swung round when it is killed so that its blood spatters the ground. This will cause animals to breed more copiously, another illustration of the relationship between blood and birth.[7]

Many fanciful descriptions and interpretations of the Australian ceremonies have been given. Ashley Montagu hypothesizes that the men consider menstruation to be a periodic purge and cleansing and therefore perform similar bloodletting operations on themselves. Campbell suggests that since the blood is sometimes drunk or smeared on the backs of the initiates in various stages, it is analogous to and a substitute for mother's milk. Whatever the particular etiology of the rites, which vary from tribe to tribe, the element of male compensation for woman's primary role in nature is evident. In fact, Wogeo men simulate women's monthly function by cutting their penises with a shell and allowing some blood to flow out. This is called menstruation or male menstruation. It is considered cleansing and is performed periodically, although the blood which flows and the process make the men taboo for several weeks afterward.[8]

Different cultures have different ways of mediating womb envy. Margaret Mead pointed out the symbolic rebirth compassed by adolescent initiation ceremonies, the way in which the male arrogates female biological processes to himself. She cites the womb-envying patterns of several South Sea Island cultures she studied in which the basic theme of the initiation cult is that women hold the secrets of life by virtue of their ability to make children. Since men's role is uncertain, undefined, and perhaps unnecessary, by a great effort they have hit on a way of compensating themselves for their basic inferiority. They get the male children away from the women and brand them as incomplete until the men themselves have turned the boys into men. Women, they have to admit, make human beings, but in their belief only men can make men. The imitations of birth are more or less overt: in some the initiates are swallowed by the crocodile that represents the men's group and come out newborn at the end; they may be housed in wombs, or fed on blood, fattened, have food put into their mouth, and be tended by male "mothers." Universal to the cult is the myth that somehow these rituals were all stolen from the women, sometimes that women were killed to get it. To the Westerner who comes from a society that has exalted men's achievements and depreciated women's role, it is outlandish— all the more so when one realizes that these men who depend for their manhood on a fantasy structure of bamboo flutes, played inside leaf hedges simulating artificial wombs, are not peaceful shepherds but fiercely aggressive headhunters, tall, strong, and well built and capable of magnificent anger.[9]

Only in recent years and with the growing participation of women anthropologists have we begun to realize that the widespread customs of menstrual restrictions do not necessarily represent disgust or even a low status for women; they may be connected with the mana—the magic and fearful power of the blood itself, which by a mysterious and ununderstood mechanism might become a child.

The Hebrew dictum that women are unclean—"How can he be clean that is born of a woman?" is demanded by Job in the Old Testament—was inherited by Christians and Moslems and is associated with the inferior position of women among them. The reason Judeo-Christian religion finds menstruation disgusting, unclean, is because it is a reminder of the life of the body and the supremacy of women in giving birth. This represents what Campbell calls "patriarchal inversion," the need to belittle and demean what was formerly considered sacred and awe-inspiring. The *elima* of the Mbuti Pygmies, the ceremonies of the Australian Kimberley tribes to bring on menstruation, and other celebrations of menarche demonstrate that woman's periodic issue can be admired and respectworthy: one becomes a woman and one can reproduce. Its onset may also be synonymous with the beginning of pleasure—sexual life and accessibility thereto.

In her discussion of menstrual taboos, Alice Schlegel comments that the loss of the wife's services—in sex and perhaps in cooking and household work—may be annoying to the husband, particularly in monogamous families. Where menstruating women are seen as dangerous to men, to sacred objects, and even to crops, there is also the inconvenience of guarding against accidental mischief caused by menstruating women. While traditionally menstrual restrictions among nonliterates have been taken as a mark of the inferior status of women, men suffer as much or more from these restrictions. The menstrual hut or a restriction on housework may well be a welcome

monthly vacation to the woman.[10] In the Australian Kimberleys, menstruation is linked with being a woman. It has become associated with taboos and rites and has been identified
with certain magical properties, in so far as it is associated with
blood and the genitals. But Kaberry reported that she never de-
tected any disgust and horror of a menstruating woman in the
attitude of the men. During her period the woman camped
apart and kept unobtrusively out of the way, but unless one
were familiar with the general habits of social intercourse, her
segregation was not noticeable except at night, when she slept
on the other side of the fire some few feet away from her husband. She was not spoken of as being "dirty or unclean." She
was *gunbu*—forbidden on pain of sickness or death. The blood
would cause the men to sicken, so she avoided participating in
activities that involved men. She herself never referred to menstruation as *kambulo*—shameful—and she did not consider herself unclean.[11]

While menstruating women are considered ritually unclean
in parts of India and among Christian and Semitic peoples,
there are societies where she is particularly desirable. It was believed that a Kaska man who had intercourse with a menstruating woman would pass blood in his urine so that he would
sicken and die. Despite this, boys took advantage of the easy access to girls in seclusion, nor did the girls always resist their advances. When they became ill, the boys might confess such
offenses.[12] Evidently it was the blood and not the woman that
was dangerous, for in 1949, at the time of an ethnographer's report, modern Kaska youth had found a method of protecting
themselves: they still seized the occasion to make love to menstruating girls, but they used a modern invention, the condom,
to ward off the traditional dangers. Among the Hopi, on the
contrary, some people feel that sexual relations may be harmful
to the woman, even though she is more sexually attractive to
men at this time than when she is not menstruating.[13]

When Cabeza de Vaca made his arduous trek in southwestern
North America in the early fifteen hundreds, trading in the sacred red ocher, he was horrified and disgusted by the "savage
customs" he observed, including, of course, segregation and spe-

cial treatment of menstruating women. Schlegel finds "striking parallels, especially in American Indian practices, between restrictions placed upon menstruating women and men in a state of spiritual tension or danger, such as before warfare or the hunt, after homicide and during ceremonial periods." Practices concerning menstruation reflect a state of spiritual danger. Some cultures have used menstruation to explain and justify the inferior status of women, but if we think of the nature of menstrual taboos and of how similar they are to the restrictions many cultures apply to disruptions of normal physical or spiritual states—death, killing in warfare or the chase, ceremonial activities, and such—menstrual restrictions would seem of a like nature, differing only in that they are automatic and periodic.[14]

Menopause, the phenomenon which is limited for all practical purposes to the human species alone, probably occurred only among people located in favorable climatic conditions. Few Western European Neanderthal women might have been expected to survive past childbearing age, as few Arctic Eskimos, female and male, survived into, let alone past, their fifties.

Margaret Mead pointed out the advantage of menopause for human society, as well as for the women themselves. Those who managed to survive the rigors of childbearing—enforced in sedentary patriarchal societies, self-limited in nomadic foraging ones—were then free to give their energies in a wider range, to offer wisdom and experience to the young. In certain cultures many privileged positions become open to older women after they are no longer set apart by the mana surrounding their reproductive talents: they may become priests, shamans, village leaders (head*men*), etc.

Anthropologist Asen Balikci's film about the Canadian Arctic Netsilik Eskimos shows the old grandmother telling stories to the whole group, and one is reminded that when the Brothers Grimm assembled their monumental collection of folk tales their chief informants were certain old women. (The Balikci film depicted a remarkable tenderness and seeming mutual respect between the sexes which was very much at variance with earlier reports about the brutalities of Eskimo men toward their women.) The film also showed the division of meat according to custom. The two men who had caught a seal shared and ate the raw liver on the spot, then they dragged the animal back to the ice house where the young women reached into its innards and devoured handfuls of fresh blood, their portion, before the rest of the animal was cut up and distributed among the group.

Though much had been made in previous writings of the exclusion of women from the spiritual aspects of Australian Aborigine life, a woman ethnographer reported on the old woman who repainted the portrait of the Rainbow Serpent so that the spirit children might increase.[15] Another woman ethnographer, discussing the position of women in Northern Australia, notes that the counterpart in Tiwi language of big man, *aragulani*, is *parimarina*, menopausal woman, while the next stage for both is old age, *irula* for the old man and *intula* for the old woman.[16] In agricultural China, the pyramidal hierarchy of the extended family was arranged so that a woman endured the inferior status of daughter-in-law in her husband's home, looking forward to the time when she would become the matriarch, mother and mother-in-law, and pass over to the high side of the power relationship, tyrannizer rather than tyrannized. Reports have it that menopause depression was rare if not nonexistent in this culture, which offered actual and intangible rewards to the older woman after the oppression visited on the younger one.

Before the reaction against motherhood in this century initiated by Freudian psychology, the postmenopause woman was assured of a special devotion and loyalty from her grown children. "Who would have dreamed that a socially mature male of about eighteen years of age would still spend much time in the company of his old mother?"[17] Jane Goodall marveled at the strength of the mother-child affection relationships among the Gombe Stream chimpanzees, sentiments which used to be widely echoed on a human level.

Kaberry speaks at length about the bond between a mother and her children in the Australian Kimberleys: the sorrow when the daughter goes away to be married, the fifty-mile walk a daughter will make to see her mother, and the special loyalty and affection of both sexes for their old mothers. A *son*, too, though separated from his mother during initiation periods, cherishes a strong affection for her throughout her lifetime, giving her food and caring for her in old age. She is at great pains to present evidence counteracting the confident statements made by earlier anthropologists to the effect that there is no recognition among the Australian tribes of the physical tie between mother and child. In discussing the belief in spirit children the mother was described as merely a "domestic cow," a vessel and a medium through which the child passes. According to Ashley Montagu, "The relationship which the mother bears to the child is regarded as being, from the physical standpoint, none at all."[18]

Not so, says Kaberry. Among the tribes she studied, the child was very definitely linked physically to the mother, flesh of her flesh, blood of her blood, nursed by her milk, fed by her hands, though the father bears no such physical relationship. Thus two men with different social fathers (physical fatherhood being unknown, it is not the man with whom a woman has slept who is considered to be a child's father, but the one with whom she is living at the time the child is born, or the one who has dreamed the animal or plant or pool which will be the child's totem) and one mother will consider themselves brothers. In cases of confusing relationships resulting from "wrong marriages" under the complex Australian kinship system, tribal relatives will be named by the simple expedient of "throwing away" the father.[19]

In nonliterate foraging tribes old age is usually much respected, for old people have survived the hardships and danger of life and are, in contrast with our own attitudes, considered to have much-needed wisdom for the young. They are the walking books of Truffaut's *Fahrenheit 451*, to which the French film director thought civilization's progress might force us to return. The Kimberleys are no exception; postmenopausal and old women have much authority, in everyday affairs as well as in the religious life, where it is only they, along with old men, who can perform the increase ceremonies considered necessary to the procurement of existence.

Goodale tells in *Tiwi Wives* of the very special position of the older woman in Melville and Bathurst Islands in northern Australia. If she is a "first-wife" she wields much authority over her daughters and over co-wives' daughters, for she is their "supreme mother." Old women are treated with much respect by their sons. Not only are they looked after and cared for, their advice is often asked and often taken. In recent years, Western interference has vitiated much of the power of older women. Government and mission consider husbands the base of the domestic group, and the officials usually back up the husband's word in a family debate if some woman (usually the husband's mother-in-law or his mother) steps in to "interfere." Goodale finds it paradoxical that Western culture, the great "protector" of women's rights today, has contributed to the loss of so many of the Tiwi woman's traditional rights.[20]

In our culture, where women were valued chiefly as producers of children, they lost status once they were past childbearing age. In small-scale nonliterate societies, it was the process, not the product, which inspired respect or diffidence. Once the process had ceased, the women themselves often became important contributors in group councils, assuming official and unofficial roles.

Judging by our own recent social history, it may well be that the physiological process of menopause can be a spur to peak creativity for those women who live that long and who have managed to achieve self-expression in the arts. George Eliot, Virginia Woolf, Edith Wharton, and Kate Chopin are some of the writers who produced their greatest works from their middle forties to early fifties. The irregularities of hormone output at this time result in intense heights and surges of emotion not dissimilar to those of adolescence, but they appear at a stage in life when women artists may have acquired the wisdom and control which enable them to translate their emotions into their work.

17

━━ ━━ ━━ ━━ ━━ ━━ ━━

Early Households

Clues to the composition of Paleolithic households are lacking in the sparse evidence so far uncovered—tools and ornaments, dwelling places, fossils, and burials—though analogy with present-day foragers suggests they would have been based on loose and shifting mutuality. The earliest living sites in Africa some millions of years ago may have been occupied for a few nights or weeks; bone waste and stone tools and chips from the manufacture of the tools were the evidence that led archaeologists to conclude that early hominids had camped there. Traces of million-year-old human habitation have been uncovered in Chinese caves, while new evidence indicates that humans might have been living in Greece some 750,000 years ago, at Vértes-zöllös in Hungary perhaps 400,000. At Terra Amata, on the French Riviera, hearths and post holes and stone blocks have provided clues to human living arrangements perhaps 200,000 years ago. If the post holes are the remains of oval huts, as archaeologists infer, the space enclosed might have housed ten to twenty people in groups similar to mother-centered bands of more recent times.[1]

Among present-day gathering-hunting peoples living arrangements are fluid and changeable. When a difference of opinion or a quarrel arose among two members of a Mbuti Pygmy band, the group would often split. "When hostilities come into the open the solution is for one or the other disputant to pick up and leave."[2] Anthropologists call this process "resolution of conflict by fission." Similar looseness of association with frequent breakings-up and recombinations has been observed among divers foragers—the North American Athapaskans, the African Hadza, the Kalahari San. Richard Borshay Lee discusses the annual gatherings of !Kung San in the winter dry season. When bands become large, people have to work harder to procure food and more disputes arise. "This conflict usually results in one or both parties splitting off to seek greener pastures."[3] This method of solving disputes is projected for Paleolithic humans and considered instrumental in the widespread occupation of territory by developing species. Foragers—in contrast to agricultural and urban peoples—can easily vote with their feet. They do not wait till the food supply is exhausted to do so; they take steps much earlier—when their patience is exhausted.[4]

Mbuti Pygmy men, women, even children, often go off alone to live in the forest.[5] That questing and enlarging brain, with its omnipresent why, must also have contributed to the diffusion of the species over much of the planet. In recent times in North America the settling of Cape Cod and Plymouth by the Pilgrims and of Rhode Island by Roger Williams' group, both of whom made friends with local Indians, exemplify Turnbull's principle. On the other hand, most of the white invasion of the Americas reflects the later conquest mentality, a product of a technologically more advanced state of development.

Present-day foragers do not show strong male dominance though the interference of Western bureaucrats and the contact with settled agriculturalists often shifts the egalitarian balance between the sexes. Evidence from recent ecologically oriented studies shows that women contribute economically and are valued for their contribution; in consequence scholars today question previous assumptions of strong male dominance among Paleolithic peoples.[6] Even among northern peoples like the Eskimos, where meat played a major role in subsistence and was hunted chiefly by men, there is a rethinking of the old tradition that the women were owned and given by the men, with no voice in their own sexual experience. By the time students came upon many of the "primitive peoples" they had been subjected to exploitation, brutalization, and ill treatment by colonizers and were in a state of degradation.[7] In the north, whalers and fur traders introduced new elements which made it almost impossible to determine previous attitudes among the sexes.[8]

Male dominance as a concept may not be applicable to the interaction between the members of a band of Paleolithic humans; in severe weather conditions males and females would have had to be extremely tough and resourceful to survive; in milder climates with more abundant resources there would have been little reason or need for aggressive relations between the sexes.

As women anthropologists are now pointing out, in ethnographic studies most of the field work was done by male investigators using male informants, permitting a double element of distortion. In the male-dominated world of academia, the few women who did bring back new, unexpected, or unwelcome evidence during the past half century were liable to be contradicted, corrected, or just ignored by their male colleagues unless they phrased their material with great caution. No woman could have presented the findings of a Malinowski about active female sexuality and ignorance of blood ties to the father; she would have been ridiculed or rejected. In 1939 Kaberry's book *Aboriginal Woman* upset a good many of the previous generalizations about the degraded status of Australian women, including the pronouncement that they were excluded from the very rich spiritual life of the community. "My contention that aboriginal woman is not only profane but also sacred, may create some controversy; and some may assert that it is only in North-West Australia that the women participate to any marked extent in religion . . . they possess totems, have spiritual affiliations with the sacred past, and perform their own sacred rites from which the men are excluded."[9]

Kaberry's book had an introduction by her former professor, A. P. Elkin. Though he acknowledged the value of her work, in the very act of presenting it, he took gentle but firm exception to her statement about women's "sacred" nature and her evidence to show that they did not accept the men's superior spirituality: "Women may be independent, powerful, and spiritual, and yet be profane . . . I doubt that there is as much in another point made by Dr. Kaberry as she is inclined to think."[10] So much for the findings of women ethnographers among women subjects.

I have pointed out that chastity and lifelong monogamy are rare among small-scale societies and sexual experience is allowed for in most nonliterate cultures. Western males generally perceived this as under male control, although Malinowski himself made it clear that female repression was unknown among the Trobrianders and that sexual expression by women and men was considered normal and necessary. Reports on the Australian Aborigines as well as from Arctic ethnographers depicted the women as freely available but at the will of the male "possessor." From the work of Kaberry in the nineteen thirties and Jane Goodale in the nineteen fifties, it has become clear that Australian Aboriginal women exercise considerable sexual independence. Adultery and serial marriage are common, and when they want to sleep with a man they make it known by sending a gift of tobacco or some other message. Jealousy is a problem faced by either sex. Mutual fidelity is demanded—if not always received—and the husband's laxities are not condoned. Kaberry describes a quarrel in which the wife accused her husband of going with another woman: "Barudjil [the wife] . . . picked up her boomerang, banged him, then grabbed a tomahawk to enforce her point and pummeled him with the blunt edge on his arms and shoulders," after which the husband picked up his swag and departed, "hurling obscenities and an occasional boomerang at her which she avoided easily, but which came unpleasantly near where I was standing diligently making notes."[11]

According to Kaberry the Kimberley women had an irreverent attitude toward the supposedly sacred ceremonies of their men, regarding them chiefly as sexual objects to be admired as prospective lovers. She contrasts the male ethnographers' reports that for Australian men women were insatiable in their sexual demands with her own finding that women were all too apt to complain of the insatiability of their men.

Much of Kaberry's book is devoted to refuting, point by point, earlier generalizations about Australian Aborigine women as scarcely human, beasts of burden, helpless chattels of their husbands. The women of the Kimberleys have love corroborees, to charm new lovers or insure the faithfulness of husbands. They marry to have sexual access, not to have children. Questioned on whether she liked being married, one woman answered in pidgin English, "Me lik 'em boy; we walkabout, we *muna-muna* [have sexual intercourse]; got 'em one camp belonga twofellow; might be we catchem kangaroo, fish."[12]

After a boy's initiation festival all who have been present engage in group sex. At the conclusion of certain corroborees among the Wula and North Lunga, one woman will remain behind to have intercourse with some of the dancers. Sometimes a husband may be loath to give up his wife, and compulsion is brought to bear upon him. From their comments, the women were not unwilling. They stigmatized the reluctant husbands as "stingy," while compliant ones were praised as "proper good fellow."

Male anthropologists have reported on these customs as evidence of the degradation and subordination of women in Australian Aborigine society: "a mockery of all morals," expostulated Freudian Geza Roheim. As Kaberry points out, they can hardly be considered immoral in the Australian ethos, for they have religious sanction, and they subordinate and degrade the woman neither more nor less than the man.[13]

Among the Melanesians of Lesu extramarital dalliance is a social custom with all the force of tradition, and rape is unknown. Hortense Powdermaker reported that if a woman did not want to go with a man, she merely said no, giving an excuse or not as she pleased. It is a socially accepted custom for wife and husband to have intercourse with a number of additional partners. It would be considered abnormal if either one, when young, did not do so. A young married woman who did not have lovers would be like a young girl in our society who has no boy friends or is not invited to parties. Middle-aged women discussed their past affairs with her freely. Most of them had had so many lovers they could not remember exactly how many. One old woman asked Powdermaker rather indignantly how she could expect her to remember every man she had ever slept with. Permanent intrigues with one man were not common, for, if this occurred, the woman would divorce her husband and marry her lover.[14]

When a wedding is to take place, the women of Lesu practice their dances every night for ten days in advance. Two nights before the ceremony, they dance in a spirit of wild play, lifting their loincloths and exhibiting themselves. The dancing goes on through the night and ends with some of the women having intercourse with the men who have been watching. This is the rather promiscuous sexual intercourse which sometimes follows the wedding dances.[15] (Several extant descriptions of medieval peasant wedding festivities in Europe tell of similar scenes: wild dancing and drinking ending up in a grand free-for-all of promiscuous intercourse. Breughel's well-known painting from a later period stops just short of the conclusion.)

Polygyny, polyandry, and monogamy were practiced in Lesu. If a woman has two husbands, they are known as husband number one and husband number two. Sometimes all three sleep in the same house, three beds in a row, with the woman between the two men; other times, husband number two sleeps in the men's house, and the woman sleeps with her two husbands alternately. There seems to be no quarreling between the two men. The woman's children call both men *mum* (father). In the case of polygyny, the children of both wives call each one *nangga* (mother).[16]

The women of the African Hadza also practiced sex relatively freely, autonomously, and following their own desires. A man was married only so long as he lived regularly with his wife. Once he left her for no longer than a few weeks "his house had died"; he had no further rights over her or his children by her. She could marry as soon as she liked, and if her husband returned before she remarried she could accept or reject him as she chose.[17] The Hadza were always moving about, changing camp and the composition of the camp. Pressure was on the husband to maintain his associations with the women, not vice versa, since it was relationship to the mother, not the father, which influenced choice of residence. When a camp divided and the man's mother went one direction with a group of people and his wife's mother in another direction, he was faced with a direct and troublesome choice.

For all these people relationships correspond to the American custom of serial marriage. Ethnographers often use the words marriage and divorce somewhat loosely. Among the Eskimos and the Ojibwa marriage means a semipermanent and recognized union. Eskimo women and men switch partners frequently. People of the Ojibwa desert one another on any conceivable pretext, or on none at all. People marry where desire directs them; they remain together as long as inclination and habit dictate. One Ojibwa woman was married and divorced seven times, became a shaman at the age of fifty, and later found an eighth husband.[18]

Western observers use the conventions of our own language to phrase their descriptions of marriage in terms of male possession of women. For most foraging peoples, however, it is an economic partnership. In Western Australia, the tribespeople studied by Kaberry might come together on the basis of sexual attraction, but ultimately economic, social, and procreative needs were also involved.

The Northern Australian Tiwi are usually considered a male-dominant society, but, according to Goodale, both male and female Tiwi viewed their culture's rules governing choice of mates as providing them with considerable freedom and variety throughout their lives. Men achieve variety through acquisition of multiple wives, while women anticipate a succession of husbands; and both sexes manage a limited amount of sexual diversion outside marriage.[19] Tiwi marriage could be any one of a series of formalized contract relationships.

A round-up of marital and family arrangements from ethnographic data shows many variations. Polygyny is more common than polyandry; where the motivation is economic women desire polygyny as well as men. Among the Nayars of Southeast India, one woman is, in effect, married to a group of brothers.

A man may enter his wife's house only if she has put his san-
dals on the doorstep; otherwise he must wait and come back
another day. There is no way of knowing who is the father of
her children. Africa, known for its wide range of political
forms, also turns up such customs as woman-woman marriage
(a way of providing heirs for a woman landowner, who dele-
gates a chosen male to impregnate her wife), and tribes where a
pregnant bride is preferred, for she has given proof of her ability to breed. Men of the Mae Enga in New Guinea spend most
of their time in the men's house and encounter women with
the utmost hesitation. Arrangements where women and their
children have each their own home while men live in the men's
house, in a small house of their own, or with sisters or mothers,
are found in Africa, in Oceania, and in Southwest North
America. Hopi women are the homeowners in the pueblos, and
rooms are handed down from mother to daughter. Men build
houses, but they do not own them. A man feels that his sister's
home is his real home though, actually, he is peripheral in both
his sister's and his wife's home. Mandan, Iroquois, and Cherokee women were equally considered the owners of houses and
personal property. African matrilineal societies also have odd
family arrangements. In Ashanti villages, about an hour before
dusk, children could be seen scurrying in all directions carrying
pots of cooked food. They were bringing meals from houses
where their mothers lived to houses where their fathers lived.[20]
Residence groups comprised sisters and brothers and the sons
and daughters of the sisters.

Perspective is everything: male and female anthropologists
bring back entirely different reports. "Women see babies; men
see politics," said one male anthropologist. At a May 1973 conference on women and language, Ann Bodine, an anthropologist from Rutgers, cited a male ethnographer's report on
Bengali. "Basing his work on the language of the men, he came
to the absurd conclusion that the language gave its speakers
many ways to address men but no way to address women if
they were not related."[21] In actuality, the system was balanced
so that women had many ways to address women but no way
to address unrelated men. The male ethnographers had re-

ported a situation as it existed among the men and ignored the equivalent institution among women.

As Kaberry had discovered ceremonies and rights and expressions unreported by earlier male ethnographers, so Goodale's recent work among the Australian Tiwi was at variance with earlier studies. She told of the contracts women arranged with their future sons-in-law which provided the women with payments of game over periods of years, and of women's economic importance and sexual expression in Tiwi life.

Her example was given earlier of how Western civilization reinforces the man's position and weakens the woman's. This is a process which has occurred all over the world; it began with the first white contacts and has deeply infiltrated all nonliterate societies, the extent depending on the length of time during which they have had relations with patriarchal cultures. White influence usually means a loss of rights for women, whether it be among the loosely organized nonauthoritarian Navajos, the female-dominated Iroquois, African societies where women played important roles in agriculture and trade, or South American and Oceanic groups where abortion and infanticide were practiced autonomously by women as a method of birth control.

Sometimes Western white administrators insisted on the appointment of a male headman where there had been none before or where authority roles were delegated to a group of women; at others they forced the men who had hitherto hunted and played and politicked to take to farming and vested economic control in them, taking it away from the women. In the past both Christian missionary and colonial influence were male-enhancing pressures in forbidding any kind of birth control in the name of the sacredness of the unborn child's life in preference to that of the mother, as is received Christian dogma. Missionaries, administrators, and ethnologists viewed female sexual autonomy and expression as lewd and lascivious, with the missionaries seeking to enforce chastity and virginity, while administrators and colonizers introduced such civilized perversions as prostitution and rape. All assumed male possession of women and children, a concept not always applicable among non-Western peoples. A Jesuit missionary reproached a Montagnais Indian for not interfering when his wife slept with other men. "How will you know that her children are your own?" "Thou hast no sense," was the Indian's equable reply. "You French love only your own children, but we love all the children of our tribe."[22] Or, in the words of an African Ibo song, "The child of one is the child of all."

In the present, new farming methods introduced into economically undeveloped areas almost invariably concentrate on the men, who receive education in technology and are preferred in numerous ways so that the price of improved food production and industrialization is a loss of rights and function for the women.[23]

Just as earlier explorers saw kings and hierarchies where they did not exist, so male anthropologists saw male dominance and male supremacy everywhere they looked.[24] Alice Schlegel's study of Hopi Indian women found that those who had not accepted Christianity had more autonomy and control of property and the household than was indicated in a male anthropologist's report completed some twenty years earlier. Christianized Hopi women lost power, however, when they accepted the American kinship pattern.[25] Comparison of male and female scholars' reports on Australian Aborigines also reveals wide discrepancies of vision. Male anthropologists exaggerated the importance of political power and technology and minimized the Aborigine women's economic contribution, the importance of which was fully acknowledged by the natives themselves. Western men projected Western ideas of female uncleanliness onto the Australians and insisted, against the facts, that the Aborigines did not recognize the female generative principle. Male observers ignored or belittled the importance of women's ritual lives and proclaimed their subordinate status. Women ethnographers found women and men living together in partnership, with rights, self-respect, and dignity guaranteed for each sex. They concluded that the Aborigine women had complete control over their bodies and reproductive functions and that neither they themselves nor the Aborigine men saw women as contaminating, polluting, evil, or dangerous.[26]

As we saw earlier, the old assumptions about "patrilineal hunting bands" as the earliest form of social organization are no longer accepted. The argument that slow-developing human children would create strong pressure for a nuclear family was also projected from recent Western civilizations. Human development is slower than that of the large-brained primates who are our closest animal relatives. Puberty comes between ages eleven and fifteen in a human female, at seven or eight in a chimpanzee, though neither is completely mature at that time. But a task-free childhood is far from universal, for us today, among our own forebears, and among living peasant and tribal groups. Girls, in particular, begin taking care of brothers and sisters very young—as early as age five in Samoa—and they are often helping with child care and food gathering or household chores by the age of eight. A recent study of modern American families found that on the average girls contribute more home labor—chores, housekeeping, and other daily tasks—than their brothers. In nineteenth-century Europe, Karl Marx's servant and mistress, Helene Demuth, went into service at the age of eight and was employed by Marx's wife's family, the Von Westphalens, when she was eleven. Dickens' reports on children working in factories and mines as early as age six are echoed not only in other parts of the nineteenth-century civilized world but in reports from Asia and Africa today.

In the groups with the least material culture, Australian Aborigines, Congo (Zaire) Pygmies, and Kalahari San, there is less imposition on youngsters by their elders. These children may provide part of their own food as they accompany their mothers on gathering expeditions but they are not responsible for feeding others until maturity or, sometimes, marriage. Paleolithic children would also have had fewer tasks than the children of later times.

By about ten thousand years ago humans had peopled all six continents, spreading across land connections which have since disappeared, and down to the tip of South America and the southern deserts of Australia. They seemed to aggregate in fairly small groups, and, judging by surviving gatherer-hunters, they had loose ties, flexible and subject to division and regroupings, often in flux. Band associations were probably based above all on mother-daughter and sibling relationships traced through the mother. In "marriage" the groom was likely to become attached to the bride's parents' group, for a period of years or even permanently. In seasons of hardship—dryness or cold— groups of twenty to forty would have been the rule. In summer or the season of plenty, small dispersed groups in a fairly large territory might come together for meetings of as many as one to two hundred people. Large corroborees of Australian Aborigines and African San camps embodying 100 to 150 souls are recent examples, while the annual summer encounters of Greenland Eskimos ceased almost half a century ago. At these times there would have been opportunities for exchange, resulting in the diffusion of new ideas as well as cross-group matings, bringing new inherited traits into otherwise isolated gene pools. Populations had grown, though very slowly, over a period of several million years, and cultural relics in the form of tools, hearths, and ornaments had also augmented, indicating an increase in the sources of sustenance.

The evidence for early households is still speculative, but ecological circumstance, art, and the imperfect analogies drawn from present-day foragers tell us that Paleolithic women would have had control over their own bodies, sexual expression, and full economic participation in group life. Diverse family groupings had probably begun to develop in different parts of the planet. Mother-child relationships would be the most enduring, and brothers and sisters would often retain their affinities. Over time, the sexual pull between a given woman and man might also develop, through shared experience and emotion, into a specifically human creation, the very deep communion and friendship that can be created by long-term intimacy.[27]

Part IV

—:—:—:—:—:—:—:—:—

HOW THE SEXUAL CONNECTION BECAME A POWER CONNECTION

I am he who made heaven and earth, who knotted together the mountains and created what is thereon. I am he who made the waters, so that the Heavenly Cow might come into being. I am he who made the bull for the cow, so that sexual pleasures might come into being.

—*The God and His Unknown Name*
(Egyptian texts of 1350–1200 B.C.E.)[1]

18

Gathering to Farming

The first period of agriculture is generally treated, especially by older writers, as the great period for women since practically everyone is willing to allow that plants were originally the province of females, as they still are in many ethnological contexts. Certainly woman is responsible for several of the inventions which make their appearance about this time—say ten or eleven thousand years ago—and during the ensuing four thousand years: basketry, pottery making, spinning and weaving from the fleece of sheep and goats and from the fibers of flax, the chemical experimentations which produced bread and wine and beer. There are those who would credit her with the invention of planting and reaping and with the development of all agricultural pursuits until the appearance of the plow.

However, while the beginnings of agriculture were a time of importance and respect for women, so in most places on earth were the several million years that preceded them. Recent studies indicate that agriculture was not the revolutionary invention past writers took it for and that in many respects it brought adverse consequences despite the mythical and historical accolades heaped upon it by our cultural past.

It is a part of our tradition that nomadic foragers do not cultivate the land because they are unaware of the benefits of farming, that they are ignorant and inferior. It was also believed, until recently, that they spend their time in an unceasing quest for food and that their population is limited by its scarcity. In the last decade or two, investigators have re-examined these stereotypes and they find that, on the contrary, gatherers have a sophisticated knowledge of botany. They understand the processes by which plants grow and have considerable intelligence about when and where to find an enormous variety of growing things and how to use their products. It is not for lack of knowledge that they do not farm: in many cases they live better and with less effort than the neighboring peasantry.

There have been many theories about the origins of agriculture, but the latest evidence shows that systematic cultivation of grain—wheat and barley—and first the herding, then the domestication of sheep and goats probably did arise in the land of Western white culture's mythical origins, the Near East.[1]

Let us look at the sequence of events there, beginning perhaps twelve thousand years ago. We are back in the garden, eastward in Eden, where the Euphrates and the Tigris really do rise, where, according to the Judeo-Christian Bible and the Koran, the four rivers of earth have their source. Over the previous few thousand years the pattern of existence has been shifting, here as elsewhere in Eurasia and the lands around the Mediterranean, during the final retreat of the Würm glaciation.

In the Near East, people have been coming out of caves to live in more or less permanent settlements, in skin huts first, then in houses made of rock, of pressed mud, or of mud brick. On the Anatolian plain, in Palestine, on the steppes of Iran and Iraq, and in the mountain valleys of the Zagros and of Jordan, villages exist where they had not before.

Zawi Chemi Shanidar is one of the earliest; it was inhabited at the same time as nearby Shanidar Cave, though the latter had a history of human occupation dating back some fifty thousand years. Whether these villages were at first inhabited all year round is not known; the villagers of Zawi Chemi, for example, may have sought refuge in Shanidar Cave during the cold winter, returning to open-air dwellings in milder weather.

What had been going on in this area during this period and

for a few thousand years preceding it has been called the broad-spectrum revolution. For a variety of reasons people were eating differently. There was a new interest in products of the sea and shore. Archaeologists have found evidence of the consumption of fish, crabs, water turtles, mollusks, land snails, partridges, and migratory waterfowl added to that provided by the bones of larger mammals. One group at Tepe Asiab in western Iran must have lived for some time on lizards, toads, or frogs—such was the diet revealed by their fossilized feces.[2]

This period used to be viewed as a degeneration from the Eurasian Paleolithic hunting period. But the Ice Age hunter was limited to certain parts of the planet; most people on earth had probably lived largely on plants. Based on the indications provided by recent coprolite studies, the broad-spectrum revolution may have been limited to the areas intensively studied by European archaeologists of the first part of the twentieth century. Elsewhere on earth humans have often, if not always, taken advantage of varied resources. Root cultivation—of yams and other tubers, rhizomes, and bulbs—entails less technology and developed on other continents in tropical and semitropical areas. It may have had an even longer history and a gradual integration into sedentary life and formal agricultural techniques.

Intermediate forms of cultivation had long existed. Gatherers noted when a given food would be ripe and they planned their migrations accordingly. In parts of Australia and in the Andaman Islands women dug up yams and then replaced the tops to grow again. Even more sophisticated were the Australians who forbade the gathering of certain daylilies after they had flowered. The plants were to be left to bear and to disperse seed; they were referred to as "mothers."[3]

In the Near East the new attitudes toward food, wherein everything was viewed as edible, represented imaginative ways of dealing with a changing environment. Boats and rafts were used for fishing. New methods of food preparation and cooking had been devised, as indicated by larger numbers of grinding stones and pounders.

Before the kind of agriculture we know could appear, however, people had to stay in one place long enough to gather the fruits of seeds sowed weeks or months earlier. Till recently it was thought that, with limited exceptions like the Indians of northwestern America who lived largely on products of the sea and possibly the Paleolithic hunters of the Dordogne, the first permanent settlements were linked to farming. Current archaeological studies counter this belief. Twelve thousand years ago, the Near Eastern villagers were not farmers; they lived by mixed practices, collecting, fishing, and hunting, but in areas with stable resources so that people could settle down in one place to exploit them.

Not far from the sea people took advantage of the seasonal crop of shellfish; on the shores of rivers, they harvested eels, salmon, or other salt-water fish which come to fresh water to spawn, while hunting parties went out periodically in search of larger game higher up in the mountains. As the weather warmed, stands of pistachio and oak trees appeared in upland valleys and on mountain slopes, and protein- and fat-rich acorns and nuts were added to the diet. With the exception, perhaps, of the hunting parties, women would have been playing a major role in food procurement.

People had long lived in caves in the prime upland hunting grounds. Now earlier sites like Belt and Hotu caves in northeastern Iran, the Khorramabad caves of southwestern Iran, Anatolian Palagawra where the dog was domesticated some fourteen thousand years ago, and Kebarah in Lebanon multiplied. Bands moved to river and coastal areas to take advantage of different resources.

This may have been because there were fewer large mammals available, as well as more competition for them; it may also have been because the living was easier when more resources were used and the pressure of a gradual population increase was making itself felt. In these new areas of occupation, whether or not the larger mammals were still being taken, the bulk of the food was provided by gathering. As among the Australian Tiwi, it was probably the women who brought in the major portion of protein and calories in the diet, so that their role may well have been more important than it was in the reindeer- and mammoth-hunting cultures of Europe and Siberia during the Ice

Age; it certainly was not less so. Men might still have done more of the meat hunting, but they were bringing in a luxury food; the subsistence base was provided by gathering.

It is about this time, some twelve thousand years ago, that people began to gather the seeds of wild cereal—wheat and barley—from the upland slopes and mountain valleys where they grew in profusion. On a fine spring day during the early nineteen-sixties J. R. Harlan went out in southwestern Turkey with a flint-bladed sickle of prehistoric origin, one of many which have been dug up in Mesolithic sites in the Near East, and harvested "enough wild wheat in an hour to produce one kilo of clean grain."[4] Moreover, the wild grain had almost twice the protein content of domestic wheat. This in an arid zone where, because of alternating conditions of winter rain and summer dryness, almost pure stands of wild wheat, or wild wheat and barley mixed, appear. Harlan demonstrated that in a good year, experienced plant collectors could gather in three weeks more grain than they could possibly consume in a year. Here was an explanation for the existence of certain villages whose sites had long been puzzling archaeologists.

The old books used to tell us about the uncertainties of the hunt for food before the introduction of the wondrous benefits of agriculture—the "Neolithic Revolution" Gordon Childe termed it. "Man must eat to live at all; food is perhaps the one absolute and overriding need for man. In early primitive societies the quest for food was and is the most absorbing preoccupation for all members of the group. The enlargement of the food supply was therefore presumably the indispensable condition for human progress," Childe wrote in 1944.[5] And in 1951, "The community of food-gatherers had been restricted in size by the food supplies available."[6]

More and more, the studies of recent years have created a different picture. There were those who supposed extreme male dominance as a result of the presumed scarcity of food, to be filled by the unceasing efforts of male hunters: "In the hunting period the chief contributors to the sustenance of the tribes had been the men and the role of the women had been largely that of drudges," wrote Joseph Campbell.[7] There were the slightly more sophisticated who realized that females would still play an integral role. Either way, however, we are not far from the "nasty, brutish, and short" mentality that had shaped Western thinking from Hobbes through Darwin and Freud. It was the misnamed conference on Man the Hunter which shook up this certainty.*

Ecologically oriented reports demonstrate that foragers are not on a starvation level, that, in fact, they get all the calories they need with far less labor than peasant farmers. The San of the relatively desolate Kalahari region worked only an average of three days a week to procure 2,100 calories a day. In the sixties, when Richard Borshay Lee was studying them, several years of drought occurred and farmers of the neighboring areas came to the San to learn their ways; they became foragers for a time. It is assumed that gatherers and hunters in the rich environments of prehistoric times would have had an even easier time of it.[8]

"There is abundant data which suggests not only that hunter-gatherers have adequate supplies of food but also that they enjoy quantities of leisure time, much more in fact than do modern industrial or farm workers, or even professors of archeology,"[9] says Louis Binford, himself a professor of archaeology. Marshall Sahlins goes so far as to term certain of the surviving foraging groups "the original affluent societies," since by keeping their material needs minimal they are able to satisfy them in short order with a plethora of leisure time.

If many sources of food are used, it need not be the quest for food alone which occupies the time of humans. "Why should we plant when we have so many mongongo nuts?" the San told

---

* The conference, held in 1967 with the resultant book of the same name published in 1968, overturned previous thinking about human origins. Judging by surviving gatherer-hunters, our ancestors probably lived largely on vegetable food gathered by women, rather than on game supplied by male hunters. However, "it was generally agreed to use the term 'hunters' as a convenient shorthand, despite the fact that the majority of peoples considered subsisted primarily on sources *other than meat*—mainly wild plants and fish." Just so it is generally agreed to use the generic term "man" as shorthand for women, who are more than half the world's population, and in so doing our age-old biases and misconceptions, particularly the invisibility of women, need not be unduly shaken.

Lee.† When it was suggested to the Shoshone Indians that they leave their desolate valley for richer land, they protested, "What, and leave all these wonderful mice behind?" Australian gatherers reject the European imposition as long as they can. "You people go to all that trouble, working and planting seeds, but we don't have to do that. All these things are there for us, the Ancestral Beings left them for us. In the end you depend on the sun and the rain just the same as we do, but the difference is that we just have to go and collect the food when it is ripe. We don't have all this other trouble."[10]

People do not indeed live by bread alone—or even mongongo nuts and witchetty grubs—as we can see from the elaborate imaginative systems and arts created by all human groups, not merely by the so-called advanced civilizations, though these systems do not always take material or preservable forms among the nonliterate foraging groups who used to be derogated as primitive or backward.

What the gatherers do need, however, is space, a larger area of land per person than is permitted by the concentrations of population fostered, even demanded, by agriculture. It has been supposed that the forces which kept population down in the past were the same as those today in force among foraging nomads: plant potions, abortions, infanticide, and taboos on sexual intercourse during a prolonged nursing period. After people began to settle in villages, in a period of a few thousand years, the population must have grown, for more and more village sites appear at later dates, increasing in geometric proportions.

The first villages only practiced collecting and hunting. Wild wheat and barley were gathered and stored. Evidence of subterranean pits comes from several of the early sites: Shanidar

† A half pound of mongongo nuts—the average daily portion eaten by the San in the Dobe area where Lee did his studies—provides as many calories as two and a half pounds of cooked rice and as much protein as fourteen ounces of lean beef. The mongongo tree (sometimes known as "mangetti") is drought-resistant; it gives a constant supply of nuts which can lie on the ground for months without rotting. Other San groups depend on *tsi*, beans similar to peanuts, which grow on vines, to supply their basic protein and fat needs.

Cave and Zawi Chemi Shanidar in northern Iraq, Karim Sha-
hir nearby, and Mureybat on the Euphrates River in inland
Syria. At Ain Mallaha on the Levantine coast, plastered pits
suggest storage, while the stone-lined pits of Mureybat would
seem to have been used for roasting wild grain over hot stones
—necessary to remove the tough outer hulls characteristic of
this form of wheat. Snails, acorns, pistachio nuts, mussels,
crabs, whatever, would also have been stored in pits. At this
time and in these places, agriculture was neither necessary nor
desirable. The early villagers practiced empirically principles
of synergy exemplified by Kent Flannery's anecdote about sharing a bag of caterpillar-infested pistachio nuts with his co-
worker Frank Hole:

"I examined each pistachio carefully as I opened it, and as
a consequence had to discard about half; but I noticed that
Hole was able to eat 100% of the ones he selected, and I commented on his luck. To which he replied: 'I'm just not looking.' . . . a kilo of dried caterpillars may contain 3720 calories,
550 grams of protein, 2700 milligrams of calcium and a generous supply of thiamine, riboflavine, and iron . . . the protein
content is double that of the pistachios themselves, and a combination of the two foods probably has a synergistic effect exceeding the value of the nuts alone."[11]

In other words, the protein in the dried caterpillar would
complement the incomplete proteins in the pistachios, making
their total protein content available to the human metabolism.
In later days when people shifted to intensive concentration on
grain, they paid a heavy nutritional price.

More villages appeared in the nuclear Near East. Evidently
the population was increasing. We still do not know the customs or familial organization of these early Neolithic peoples.
There are remains of small huts and of larger ones, of round
and long buildings, depending on which village site archaeologists excavate. Family organization into extended or nuclear groups is predicated on the residence shape and size,
though present-day analogies allow for wide variations.

Maternal sexuality, the physical pleasure of child rearing,
must surely have played a role in the increase of population

which became feasible with a settled life, a hut or place of shelter for mother and child, stored food, and increasing group cooperation. Presumably, when it becomes easier to have more children, women do enjoy it. The inconveniences of carrying a tiny child are obviated, while stored food means not going out every day to forage. The decision not to abort or not to kill a newborn infant would have been the mother's, as it is now in many places where such customs exist, not that of the patriarch or the Church as it later developed. Probably nomadic peoples of the hills were still practicing measures to keep their population down. For the villagers, however, fixed homes, protection during the winter, not having to go out and collect food right after the child was born may also have decreased infant mortality.

In any event, the pleasure of nursing and caressing the child would have sufficiently outweighed the disadvantages of childbirth and child rearing so that more women permitted their infants to come to term, to be born, and to be brought up. The methods of abortion described for places in Oceania, South America, and Australia—pressure and placing hot stones on the belly—are far from comfortable, and they also involve attendant dangers. Herbal methods for inducing sterility or abortion have had some scientific investigation; they exist, but are not necessarily secure nor risk-free.

There is no reason to think that any male—the mother's maternal uncle, the mother's brother, or the man who had been living with the mother at the time of the baby's birth—would have had a say in the above decisions, especially the last since we don't know whether there was a social father, though it seems certain there was no concern with a physical father.

It used to be thought that agriculture first developed in the areas where wheat and barley grew wild. But as Harlan demonstrated, why cultivate when you can reach out and pick? In the mountain valleys of Iran and Iraq and along the slopes of the Jordanian mountains, in Syria and Palestine, people lived by collecting wild grains and legumes, fish and shellfish, and also by hunting deer, wild ass, and pig. The population increased, but the size of the settlements remained small. New groups and new villages were formed, for there was no shortage of available land.

The first steps to agriculture would not have been taken in the uplands where wheat and barley grew wild but in the outlying districts, marginal areas to which new groups had emigrated.

One such is Tepe Ali Kosh (the mound of Ali Kosh) on the Deh Luran plain of Iran, a lowland steppe near a swamp. Excavations there in the nineteen sixties have brought an intensive report on one of the first places where grain cultivation was practiced and on the sequence of events by which it became established. At first, the villagers lived chiefly by collecting and hunting, but they had also discovered farming. Analyses of seeds and bones show that cultivated wheat and barley were providing one third of their plant food while certain small wild peas, legumes no longer eaten by humans, wild grasses, pistachio nuts, and capers provided the rest. Goats and sheep were kept, but it was hunting—of wild cattle, gazelle, and wild ass—which supplied most of their meat.

With a diversified base of both collecting and agriculture and of hunting and herding, a fairly ideal food balance was reached. But this was not possible to maintain, for the introduction of agriculture and animal keeping disturbed the existing vegetation. New weeds, presumably brought down from the mountains with the seeds of wild grain, were introduced and the protein-rich peas and beans were driven out. Moreover, wild animals became fewer and farther away as their habitats were destroyed. Hunting was just as important when the site was abandoned as when it was first settled, but smaller animals were being taken, for the larger ones no longer had cover in the vicinity. It is estimated, however, that these Iranian villagers of ten thousand years ago ate more meat than present-day Iranian peasants, since they were living in a relatively unexploited environment rather than one in which intensive human occupation had disturbed, not to say destroyed, the ecological balance.

Subsequent phases of excavations at the Deh Luran site reveal that over a period of two thousand years, more and more cereals were consumed; the legumes were no longer eaten, though one of the new weeds, *shauk*, was introduced into the diet. Eventually the settlement petered out, the fertility of the land in the vicinity exhausted.

There were many and varied consequences from these first steps toward agriculture. People started depending on one or two grains and when the crop failed they were in trouble. A drought or a blight comes along, and famine results. With only a few sources of food, people are much more vulnerable to elements over which they have no control—weather failures, plant disease, and insect invasion. Alternatives are available to gatherers: certain plants will be drought resistant, and not all will succumb to sudden pest attacks or infestation by a given fungus or bacterium.

The first agricultural villages arose either in mountain valleys with high water tables or on lowland plains where there was a plentiful supply of underground water: at Tepe Ali Kosh the first planting seemed to have occurred close to the swamp margins, with little cultivation; digging sticks were all that was needed. "Dry farming" is the name for this period, before irrigation was practiced.

While the population was growing as the result of village life and the fact that women enjoyed having babies, the early cultivators were not better nourished than the food collectors before them. Though the cereal diet produces a great deal of food, by weight, on a small amount of land, the foraging diet provided a better balance. Moreover, as agricultural techniques improve, and people begin to water and fertilize their crops, the price of increased yield is decreased nutritional value, starch content is augmented while the percentage of protein is lowered.

But more important was the new element of risk that was introduced. Today, in the Deh Luran plain, the crops fail two or three years out of five when nonirrigation farming is attempted. Once the step to farming had begun, however, there was no going back to the gathering life unless the group emigrated to an unexploited area, of which there were now fewer and fewer. Though a more concentrated amount of food could be produced from a smaller area of land, farming meant more work and more risk. It called for periods of intense work countered by periods of comparative leisure, rather than the regular alternation of leisure and gathering the foragers practiced.

Moreover when people gather or hunt it feels like a game. When they farm it is seen as work—which is why so many foragers from Africa, Australia, and the Americas stubbornly resisted the change to farming imposed by colonial and other dominating powers. Since the large harvest of grain encouraged staying in one place, people settled down and became committed to property. More people living closer together produce increased tensions, and with settled living resolution of conflict by fission meant abandoning property in which they had invested labor and emotion.

Evidently human psychology was drastically changed, a process which intensified with time. Nature was personified and came to be seen as an adversary. Sometimes she was a beneficent and all-giving mother, but more often she was capricious, sending storms and blights or withholding rain. Anxiety and aggression increased, and new forms of religion arose to assuage the new insecurities. Farming people were more dependent on the vagaries of nature; with increasing fear arose also the need to dominate the elements, in order not to be in bondage to them, hence the setting up of a new order of relationships, vertical rather than horizontal.

One of the first areas to be affected was the tie between women and men. Among foragers children are loved and accepted by the group for themselves alone. With the cultivators children become useful as labor; they can watch the herds and they add needed hands for the intense moment of harvest when the food for the coming months must be gathered before it spoils or is dispersed. More population meant more labor to use but it also meant more mouths to feed, so that the process became circular. The question is when women stopped having children for their own sakes and began to produce children as tools and, eventually, as commodities.

The new risks played a significant role in the development of civilizations and in the two kinds of oppression which appear in human history after this time. One was the domination of women by men and the control of their reproductive capacities; the other resulted from the unequal distribution of food and other material goods.

During the several thousand years before written history, the population in the Near East grew more rapidly than it had in the preceding millennia.[12] If cultivation did begin because of population pressures, when did the reverse happen, and the increased labor demanded by farming create pressure for more children? Perhaps some of the answers can be gleaned by examining the phenomenon which used to be considered a precursor of farming but which is today seen as an accompaniment and a result: the keeping of animals.

19

The Discovery of Fatherhood

It has been said that the first domestication was that of woman by man, which set a pattern for later class differences.[1] On the contrary, I believe the sexual subjugation of women, as it is practiced in all the known civilizations of the world, was modeled after the domestication of animals. The domestication of women followed long after the initiation of animal keeping, and it was then that men began to control women's reproductive capacity, enforcing chastity and sexual repression. Originally, land was held in common, and individuals had rights to its use and cultivation but not exclusive ownership. Animals, on the other hand, may well have been the earliest form of private property on any considerable scale, making animal domestication the pivot also in the development of class differences.[2]

It used to be thought that animal herding had preceded agriculture, since animals can be driven or led, while fields stay in one place. The received idea was that nomadic hunters first domesticated animals, while agriculture arose second and in different areas, and that the wild Caucasian tribesmen came down like a wolf on the fold, conquering or infiltrating the peaceful agriculturalists, but were themselves absorbed by the more advanced farmers. Now, it seems that the opposite was true. Recent evidence shows that it was agriculture, or at least a settled life leading to agriculture, which appeared first and that animal keeping was a consequence of plant cultivation and exploitation, rather than its predecessor. The first villages were not farming settlements; they were villages of mixed practices —plant collecting and hunting—but with stable resources so that people could stay in one place to exploit them. There is consistent evidence for village life and the use of plant food before spotty and dubious evidence for animal herding appears in the record.[3]

When the early villagers discovered seed planting, who first had the brilliant idea of keeping sheep and goats? One theory is that cereal fields attracted grazing animals who were then captured and penned by the villagers for future use. Sheep and goats are more amenable to taming than wild cattle, and they were the earliest herd animals to be domesticated, by about two thousand years. Animal keeping is a way of storing surplus grains.[4] One can leave the sheep and goats at pasture in fields which shortage of labor and storage facilities prevent the villagers from harvesting, and then eat the fattened animals as desired.

Between nine and eleven thousand years ago villages which practiced mixed farming and collecting, hunting and animal herding, in varying proportions, developed in the Near East. Zawi Chemi Shanidar, Tepe Sarab, Çatal Hüyük, Cayonu Tepesi in Turkey, Ramad in Syria, Beidha in Jordan: these were some of the permanently occupied farming villages in existence nine thousand years ago. At this time other groups—most people on earth—still lived by collecting and hunting. The rapid expansion of population in the next four thousand years has been traced by surveys in the Middle East showing an increasing network of settlements, chiefly small villages.[5]

At the time that plant cultivation began, shortly before the keeping of animals, there would have been no reason to connect plant reproduction with humans in that pernicious analogy which resulted in the vision of the female as a passive receptacle. The Australians noted earlier saw the seed-bearing plant as a mother but made no connection between seeds and semen.[6] At Ali Kosh in the early stages goats and sheep were kept, but they would have been interfertile with the wild ones which lived in the vicinity. The observation that males were necessary for reproduction may have been loosely made during the early stages of animal keeping. It is only during the more sophisticated process of animal breeding, however, that it is essential to control the mating processes. Before that, as long as all males were not killed or castrated, it would seem natural that animals should copulate and natural that females should bring forth young, but there need be no connection between these facts as they were not connected for the Australians and the Trobrianders at the time of the first contact with Westerners.

Malinowski speaks of the distinction made between the flesh of the wild bush pigs and that of the tame village ones. Meat from the latter is considered a great delicacy while the flesh of the bush pig is taboo to people of rank in Kiriwina. Yet the female domestic pigs were allowed to wander on the outskirts of the village and in the bush, where they paired freely with male bush pigs. On the other hand, all the male pigs in the village were castrated in order to improve their condition. Thus, all the progeny were in reality descended from wild bush sires, but the natives had not the slightest inkling of this fact.[7] Malinowski also instanced "Mick's pigs," the European pigs imported by a Greek trader which were highly valued by the natives and for one of which they would gladly exchange five or ten of their own pigs. But when they had acquired it, they would not take the slightest precautions to make it breed with a male of the same superior race. They could not be made to understand, and all over the district they continued to allow their valued European pigs to misbreed.

When women were considered totally responsible for the creation of actual children, males developed alternatives to physical conception and childbirth—spiritual birth, rebirth, initiation. Through animal breeding man discovered that he played a role in creation, albeit a minor one, and his sense of superfluity was partially relieved.

On the other hand, many of the practices which developed for successful animal breeding could only sharpen his insecurities. Though his sex was necessary, the individual was competitively inessential. Only one male animal is needed to fertilize many females. A rundown of some of the practices engaged in by sophisticated animal breeders is enough to scarify any human male: a magazine article on Secretariat, a prized race horse withdrawn from the track and sold for stud, was rife with emotional overtones of competition and animal-human comparison.

"The champion thoroughbred must possess physical soundness, speed, endurance and temperament . . . not in the abstract but to a greater degree than the horses it will face on the track." Describing the mating of thoroughbreds, "There is no time for nuzzling or romancing, no exchange of neighs of passion. Whether the mare is willing or not, she is hobbled and held by three or four men while the stallion mounts. It is an ordeal that may well leave a gently bred young filly permanently unstrung . . . for stallions it's either feast or famine. For the rest of the year they are not only celibate but also fitted with a ring on the penis to prevent them from enjoying the consolation of masturbation."[8]

The insecurities of the human male in front of an incomprehensible and powerful universe were much intensified by the advances made with discoveries stemming from animal breeding. Crucial markers in the development of those most puzzling of human phenomena, sadism and seemingly motiveless malignity, can be charted therefrom.

The male desire for a harem counters the individual's fear that he will not measure up, not be good enough to be the one chosen "procreator." In practice it derives from the principles of efficient animal breeding, maximizing production of offspring. I have come across a recurrent fantasy among Western men of being the only male left on earth to fertilize all women, just as, in selective animal breeding, herd owners kill or castrate all but the one or two proven studs, slaughtering the rest for meat, or, in the case of oxen, using them for draft purposes. Females will be kept to increase the herd and for milk, but only one or a few of the males need be selected to inseminate the many breeders.

With sheep and goats, which are kept for wool and hair, more of the other sex may be spared. Wild cattle—aurochs—

were difficult to handle. In Paleolithic cave painting deer and horses are shown as friendly and unthreatening, but aurochs are perceived as frightening and awe-inspiring.[9] Until castration was practiced there was more reason to dispose of the surplus, leaving only one bull to serve.

The widespread adoption of the bull as metaphor, symbol of the potent human male, and its frequent appearance as lord and creator has led to speculation on a religious origin for this particular domesticated animal, with a utilitarian function growing out of the initial worship of a sacred bull.[10] In any event, if only one male is to be chosen to survive intact, he must be truly superior to those that are killed or castrated. The emphasis on competition and the fearfulness of the analogies are evident.

It was pointed out in Part I that modern humans introduced rape into the primate world with the so-called rape rack at the University of Wisconsin's Harlow Laboratory. Several thousand years earlier humans had begun to control animal intercourse, introducing forced coitus as animal keeping was transformed into animal breeding, perhaps before the idea of forcing females of their own species to perform the sexual act against their will occurred to them. The manipulation of sex for purpose turned the human act into an aggressive one rather than a joyous meeting. Even where the animal is larger and presumably far stronger than the female, rape does not occur in the mammal world. Because humans are sentient, human females can be bullied into submission; they can be injured and forced; they can also be killed in the act of rape, as has happened in numerous instances in human history. No observations of animal rape have been verified in the wild, though this is not necessarily true of animals kept by humans in zoos and laboratories and enclosures—the equivalent of human prisons, concentration camps, and insane asylums—or possibly even of closely confined domestic animals.[11]

It has been rightly recognized that there is some connection between dependence on animals and an inferior position for women.[12] This does not apply to a gathering and hunting society because foraging peoples do not establish dominance over anything. They live in a symbiotic relationship with the environment, in partnership with other elements of nature, as one of many.

Animal domestication involved contradictory aspects for human consciousness. Children are one lien on immortality and now men too participated in the future. To the dyad of mother and child, the father was added. The trinity emerged, later translated by man into a holy three. Still later, by that process of male inversion earlier referred to, the trinity was arrogated completely to the male, in the concept of the Father, the Son, and the Holy Ghost. The trinity of the Holy Family was metaphorized by Hegel and Marx into thesis, antithesis, and synthesis. In a later access of male arrogance, Edmund Wilson explicates the Hegelian dialectic not in terms of the basic three of reproduction, the great acquisition in human awareness, but as a symbolic rendering of the triune male genitals—testicles and penis.[13] These last, which formerly existed for pleasure, have now become utilitarian. Phallic images begin to surface in archaeology, at first debatable, later unmistakable. By historic times, the new emphasis, the new awareness, and changed worship have produced a rich harvest of mythical and visual reference. But at the time of which we speak, the first triune representation is still to come.

What had previously been for pleasure and divinity became a means of production. Comments on the historical development of animal-breeding techniques point up their effect on the human male's already shaky sense of self: "The males, either as castrates or intact animals, are killed for meat as described above since they are of *less value than females* and reach optimum value at a particular weight and time [my italics]." "The majority of the animals fall into two groups, one, predominantly of male and castrates, are killed quite young, and another group, predominantly of females, are killed in old age." "There are two ways of dealing with the problem of the male. Either the removal of the majority of males before puberty or their castration."[14] "The females would have been kept for their milk and for reproductive purposes whereas the males would have been killed while still young and only a few adults would have been kept to ensure reproduction."[15]

In gathering and hunting societies, even in some societies where animal keeping is of recent arrival, there is a sense of kinship between animals and humans. The traditional affinity with animals is reflected in totemism and in myths where animals or creatures part human and part animal give rise to the human race.

The interrelationship between the animal and human world surfaces from many mythologies and still obtains in folklore. Humans did not always make sharp distinctions between themselves and animals; they attributed to the latter qualities both human and superhuman. Shamans, as they go into their trance, tend to talk in tongues—in the language of birds and animals. In Mircea Eliade's words,

> relations of friendship and familiarity . . . are established between the shaman and the animals. . . . In one respect the animals are the bearers of a symbolism and mythology very significant for the religious life; to have contact with them, to speak their language, to become their friend and master means the possession of a spiritual life much more abundant than the simple human life of an ordinary mortal . . . animals possess considerable prestige, inasmuch as they know the secrets of life and nature and even possess the secrets of longevity and immortality. Thus in returning to the condition of the animals the shaman comes to share their secret language and enjoys the fuller life which is theirs . . . friendship with the animals and knowledge of their language represents a paradisial syndrome. *In illo tempore,* before the "fall" such friendship was an integral part of the primordial situation.[16]

Creatures who are part human and part animal and coexistence between animal and human are common in ethnographic literature. The serpent in Genesis is one of the few remaining vestiges of this kind of imagery in Judeo-Christian mythology, while the wily animals of Aesop's fables or the nineteenth-century Br'er Rabbit cycle told by African blacks transported to the American South represent folk adaptations of this tradition.

Many hunters have a sense of restraint about killing and are grateful to the animals who offer themselves for human uses. They believe that animals have a right to existence and that the relationship between animals and humans is a constant.

Among the Australian Tiwi if a baby animal pet survives overnight it is considered part of the community, given a name, and afforded burial and burial rites. Western observers were shocked to find Australian Aborigine women nursing their pet dingoes, treating them as their own babies.

Still there are manifest analogies with our own civilization, where pet cemeteries, pet food and pet clothing, antivivisection, and vegetarianism are only a few indices to deep-seated attitudes. The continuum between animals and people is felt by many. Small wonder then that the keeping and raising of animals had wide-ranging effects on the customs, art, and psyche of human society.

Whereas, in earlier times, humans had hunted and eaten animals, they now established a vertical relationship. Before that animals and humans were more or less equal. The weapons of the time—sling and stone, tipped spear, even bow and arrow—were not that deadly. Often the humans had to track for days. One way or another, hunting was a match of wits. Now humans violated animals by making them their slaves. In taking them in and feeding them, humans first made friends with animals and then killed them. To do so, they had to kill some sensitivity in themselves. When they began manipulating the reproduction of animals, they were even more personally involved in practices which led to cruelty, guilt, and subsequent numbness. The keeping of animals would seem to have set a model for the enslavement of humans, in particular the large-scale exploitation of women captives for breeding and labor, which is a salient feature of the developing civilizations.

Discussing blood and the supposed horror aroused in Western men by women's monthly courses, it has been a common

Freudian explanation that the first sight of a woman's genital aroused a castration anxiety in the small boy, an anxiety said to be reinforced by her monthly bleeding, which made him feel women were wounded and deformed. How much more sense it makes to associate man's castration anxiety with his own aggressive powers and the fear thereby engendered, the practices humans learned through animal breeding. The techniques involved were frightening enough if one imagined them turned on oneself, as one always must, given the human imagination. Later associations may have projected them onto women. The origins of selective breeding go back to prehistoric times. Castration of certain males was introduced in the late Neolithic, which meant that humans were practicing a certain selection— they selected some males for breeding and excluded others.[17]

The continents of Europe, Asia, and Africa have been in communication from prehistoric, possibly even Paleolithic times. Cranstone's descriptions of some of the animal-management techniques used by diverse peoples from this triangle tell their own story:

> The Kazak fit leather aprons to their rams in the spring [as a form of birth control], since autumn-born lambs have little chance [of survival]. The Masai practice the same method. The Tuareg divide their flocks of goats into two and arrange for the kids to be born at two seasons. . . . The prepuces of he-goats and rams which are not to be allowed to breed are bound with a cord. It seems to be rather unusual for males to be selected for breeding in order to pass on valuable characteristics. . . . The Nuer, however, choose bull-calves for breeding from the calves of the best milking cows and castrate most of the remainder, leaving one entire to about thirty or forty cows.
>
> Castration is the most usual method of controlling breeding. It has the effect, too, of rendering the animals easier to handle and affects their metabolism. The Lapps castrate most of the reindeer bucks and use them for draught and pack purposes and as bell-

reindeer which lead the herd. [In the wild, among red deer, an old female leads the herd.] The Tuareg say that castrated camels grow larger humps and fatten more quickly, and are more enduring and stronger as riding animals. They are also less dangerous, since bull-camels in rut sometimes attack people.

The method of castration in general use among cattle-keeping peoples, and applied to other animals such as camels and horses, is by opening the scrotum and removing the testicles. Some African herdsmen use a knife, others the blade of a spear. In New Guinea pigs are castrated in this way with a bamboo knife. . . .

A second group of methods involves damaging or destroying the testicles without removing them.

Sometimes the scrotum is bound with a cord beforehand so that the testicles atrophy. The Lapps wrap the scrotum in cloth and bite or chew it; the result is often a partial castration which however renders the animals docile and more easily tamed. The Sonjo of Tanzania are irrigation agriculturalists who also keep flocks of goats. They castrate all males at about six months, the only exceptions being those—apparently fairly numerous—whose testicles do not descend. The method is to strangulate the scrotum with a bow string, and then to crush the testicles with an elongated stone implement especially shaped and smoothed for the purpose. The Masai castrate rams by pounding the testicles between the two stones.[18]

One of the most surprising of understandings to emerge from the new archaeology has been the realization that there was far more trade and diffusion ten thousand years ago than had been projected. Objects traveled for hundreds and thousands of miles—cowrie shells, flint, obsidian, turquoise, carnelian, and even copper are found in areas far from their source—and must, therefore, have been obtained by trade. One is reminded of the *kula*, the trading expeditions covering hundreds of miles of island journeying, as described by Malinowski for the Trobrianders, as well as the Australian Aborigine trade network which brought rare materials and manufactured products from one end of the continent to the other. If objects traversed vast distances, ideas must have traveled also, and much farther and more easily.

Once the first steps to animal keeping and grain cultivation were taken, the complexes of settled living based on the first four—wheat and barley, goats and sheep—spread rapidly in the Near East and around the Mediterranean. On the fringes, however, people kept to earlier ways. Farming brought new material insecurities; animal raising increased psychological ones. Both techniques demanded more labor than the gathering-hunting way of life. One answer was fertility worship to produce more children; another was enslavement by conquest so that subject laborers were acquired. Material insecurities encouraged stockpiling; psychological ones led to hoarding and unequal acquisition, eventually to conspicuous consumption and the establishment of a class system.

20

The Pernicious Analogy: Seed and Semen

The woman is considered in law as the field, and the
man as the grain; now vegetable bodies are formed
by the united operation of the field and the seed.

—*Institutes of Manu*
(Hindu text of 100–300 C.E.)

I have spoken of the need to project purpose outward, the
weakness of humans at the mercy of forces over which they
have no control, and the invention of magic, religion, art, and
science to enable us to cope with the seeming chaos that faces
us. In this disorderly universe, women do have a sense of purpose. Survival and the future of the species depend on them
directly in their capacity as birth-givers.

There are obvious rewards in having children, sensual and
affective ones. Anthropologists report often on the permissiveness and affection bestowed by women and men on their
own and other people's children among nomadic foraging societies. We are a social and friendly species, or at least have the
capacity to be so, and that tolerance for the young observed
among most primate societies seems to obtain in small-scale
human groups.

Children are wanted for different reasons in different societies. Cultures where women are admired for producing many

children and scorned for barrenness appear only after the inception of mixed farming. Many children are a handicap among nomadic foragers; they are even more difficult to carry than material possessions, and birth is self-regulated. In recent times, men may have wanted children as heirs, to bestow on them tangible and intangible possessions, but the idea of children as a hostage for the future, having someone to care for one in old age, when the parent is unable to work, goes back to the earliest of times.

Women had more control over their own bodies in many technologically deprived band societies than in the sophisticated civilizations of patriarchy. Crude methods of birth control have always existed. The most obvious and probably the earliest method is infanticide. Wide-ranging instances have been reported, from the Eskimos to the Kalahari Desert people to tribes of Oceania and Australia. Killing the second twin and presumably two out of three triplets is a widespread custom, extending beyond foraging peoples, as indeed does infanticide, permitted and semilegal. It's an incredibly inefficient method—think of undergoing the discomfort and pain of pregnancy and childbirth, just to dispose of the result!

The demographer Joseph Birdsell cited figures of as low as 15 per cent and as high as 50 per cent for the rate of infanticide among Australian Aborigine tribes at the time they were first contacted by Europeans, and he speculated that Paleolithic humans might also have limited their populations by disposing of newborn children.[1] In most nonliterate groups reported by ethnographers it is women who help women. Birth groups are composed of older women, primarily the mother of the woman giving birth, and men are usually forbidden to appear in the vicinity. Generally the infant is not presented to the group at large until it can be seen whether "the child has come to stay." The Kimberley Aborigines remained apart with their newborn infants for five days, and it was the woman who decided whether or not to keep the child. The same is true of the Kalahari San people and there is no preference for male over female children.[2]

After the birth of the patriarchy, however, evidence for selective female infanticide becomes common, and in many places the decision to keep or kill the infant was made by the father.[3] Though primarily an indication of the devaluing of women, killing females means there are fewer breeders and is effective for long-term population control. Where bride price is required, it raises the price of a scarce commodity, whereas if dowries are customary, poor families may feel they have no other option. Female infanticide existed into the recent past in China, India, and other parts of Asia.

In countries where infanticide is illegal, the overlap between natural mortality and willed destruction is easily blurred. In the baby farms and poorhouses of nineteenth-century England, in foundling homes and orphanages in France, systematic neglect often accomplished the desired aim without openly flouting the law. Even today underfeeding and withholding of medical attention may be responsible for suspicious sexual imbalances—high rates of male infants surviving—in parts of India and Southern Asia.[4]

Abortion also has a long history in human life—acknowledged and sub rosa. Before the discovery of the hormone-containing morning-after pill, most of us were taught that there was no effective chemical method of abortion which did not entail life-threatening dangers for the woman. Civilization has generally underrated and undervalued the intelligence, inventiveness, and ingeniousness of non-Western peoples. Reports on herbs used for abortion and contraception among nonliterate peoples are scanty and usually lack biochemical data. In recent years, however, investigation has shown that folk medicine is often empirically based on sound principles. The Ute Indians of North America were very permissive about sexual liaisons and experimentation among young people. They prevented unwanted pregnancies by using lithospermum, a plant which contained a substance since demonstrated to have a negative effect on fertility.[5]

Many groups in South America, Oceania, and Africa also use local plants to prevent or terminate pregnancy. The Bororo women of Brazil are reported to have a medicine prepared from a local plant which renders them temporarily sterile. In 1974

Marvine Howe wrote that the Christian missionaries had persuaded the women to cease taking the drug and that they were once again reproducing themselves.[6] Thirty years earlier Lévi-Strauss had found the Bororo men to be fine specimens but their women were "small and sickly, with irregular features; it is rare to find among them that bodily harmony which distinguishes their men."[7] If the women really were so inferior in appearance to the men, one wonders whether the drug they took had side effects on their general health, given the fact that men and women share a common heredity and that genetic studies have not so far revealed any sex-linked gene for physical beauty in men and ugliness in women.

Though it was known that abortion was widely practiced, when male anthropologists predominated they were less privy to women's information. In recent years many women anthropologists have brought back reports from the people concerned, the mothers, on the methods used to procure abortions. Jane Goodale tells that among the Australian Tiwi miscarriage-inducing potions are prepared from the bark of a certain tree, women jump from heights, and that they also use pressure and pummeling on the abdomen to bring on abortion. Phyllis Kaberry reports that the tribes of the North Kimberleys use hot stones and beating on the abdomen, while Janet Siskind writes of abortions accomplished by pressure among the South American Sharanahuas.

It is sometimes claimed that childbirth is less painful among "primitive" people than among supposedly tense "civilized" people.[8] In most instances, however, the reason given for inducing abortion was to avoid the pain of childbirth. Sometimes the inconveniences of pregnancy and taking care of a small child were also cited.

Goodale speaks of the Tiwi woman whose marriage has been arranged at birth, who has been living with her elderly husband and gradually introduced to sex, and who now, past puberty, is "of an age to attract the attentions of young men and to arrange meetings with them in the bush at times when she should be hunting for food for her elderly husband. If she is going to accept a lover, this is the age to do so, for as my informants commented, 'Children make such bush meetings difficult.' "[9]

Among foraging peoples living under conditions of minimum material development, the normal birth interval looks like four or five years. Kaberry said that she rarely came across a woman with more than four or five children. Siskind said that the South American women she studied generally have four or five children before they resort to abortion.

Nursing imperfectly controls conception and is much used in cultures which have been affected by the civilizations as well as in those only recently influenced. In many nonliterate societies it is aided by taboos on intercourse during the nursing period.

Given the anticontraceptive slant of most recorded civilizations, only scant evidence remains to show that methods more sophisticated than the Scylla and Charybdis of celibacy and infanticide were in use in the past. Two records from ancient Egypt—the Petri and the Ebers papyri of thirty-eight and thirty-five hundred years ago respectively—tell of contraceptive prescriptions whose operant principles are still in use: sperm-obstructing vaginal plugs or sponges, dipped in honey or olive oil to slow down sperm motility, and a local application of acacia tips, a plant containing lactic acid, the spermicide which is still the prime ingredient of modern contraceptive jelly.[10]

At the time that plant cultivation began, shortly before the keeping of animals, plant and human reproduction would not have been associated. Sophisticated animal breeding came considerably later. The progression of these discoveries was not swift, though in terms of the several million years' duration of the human species it seemed so.

Paleolithic humans did not know that semen played a role in reproduction, as they did not occupy themselves with seeds and planting and agriculture. In the evolution of consciousness, this fact must be considered as an understratum which will shape the future development of human sexual relations and human customs. The discovery of paternity has been likened to the turning on of an electric-light bulb, but it could hardly have happened that suddenly. An understanding of the reproductive process in humans is of very recent date—the mammalian egg was not discovered until 1827—and scientists are still adding to our knowledge. Several writers have detailed the misconceptions which existed in ancient times about the procreation of humans.

The commonest belief was that the child is formed entirely out of menstrual blood retained in the uterus. "Babies need blood when they're inside you, and if you're having a baby, then you don't menstruate. When you're not having a baby then you don't have to save the blood so it comes out."[11] This young girl's explanation from a modern novel by Toni Morrison is echoed on many levels from ancient and ethnographic sources. The Maori of New Zealand say, "The discharge is a kind of human being, because if the discharge ceases, then it grows into a person, that is, the 'paheke' (menstrual blood) ceases to come away, then it assumes human form and grows into a human."[12]

Once it was observed that semen was necessary for conception, the ancients were hard put to explain just how the process worked. Both Aristotle and Pliny the Elder believed the child was formed out of retained menstrual blood. Aristotle said that the male semen supplied some "impulse to movement," and Pliny amplified by comparing semen to rennet, which gathers the uterine blood into a curd so that it grows into a body. An ancient Hebrew midrash states, "The Uterus remains full of blood, which would else flow out as menstrual issue. When it is the will of the Creator, there comes a drop of white seed and falls therein, and the growth of the child at once takes place, exactly as happens when one puts rennet into a bowl of milk."[13]

Aristotle worked out his theory as a philosophical argument for the natural superiority of the male:

> Man is active, full of movement, creative in politics, business, and culture. The male shapes and molds society and the world. Woman, on the other hand, is passive. She stays at home as is her nature. She is matter waiting to be formed and molded by the active

male principle. Of course the active elements are always higher on any scale than the passive forms, and
more divine. Man consequently plays the major role
in reproduction; the woman is merely the passive in-
cubator of his seed . . . the male semen cooks and
shapes the menstrual blood into a new human
being.[14]

This ideology proved useful and was taken on faith for more
than two thousand years, translated into Catholic doctrine by
way of Thomas Aquinas. Only in the seventeenth century C.E.
did scientists begin to use tools to gain an actual understanding
of the process of reproduction. Anton van Leeuwenhoek's use
of the microscope enabled him to observe the spermatazoa in
male semen in 1676. The underlying set made people theorize
that each sperm contained a homunculus, a tiny person capable
of growing into a human once it reached the propitious haven
of the uterus.

It was Lazzaro Spallanzani, in 1775, who demonstrated that
sperm were needed to make frog's eggs develop into tadpoles.
Two thousand years earlier Hippocrates had traced the process
by which eggs develop into chickens and compared their em-
bryos' growth to that of humans. He believed that men and
women have generating seed and that the seed of woman and
man mixed together to form the child. He claimed to have seen
an aborted six-day-old generating seed, though from his description it was a considerably more developed fetus than would result from a six-day pregnancy.[15] However, Hippocrates' theories
did not receive wide acceptance, perhaps because women do
not lay eggs. For centuries the Aristotelian doctrine held sway.

In the early sixteen-hundreds William Harvey's experiments
with dissection did bring him information on embryology, and
he rejected the Aristotelian theory of menstrual blood sparked
by semen with the statement that all animals reproduce by
eggs. Some fifty years later, one Regnier de Graaf operated on
female rabbits and found that, like birds, they had ovaries,
which were covered with tiny pimples, discerned by him as
eggs. Actually they were ovarian follicles. Though the mam-

malian egg—that of a dog—was correctly identified in 1827, the actual fertilization process was not observed until 1875. Knowledge about germ cells and chromosomal union—the equal contribution of male and female—has come only in our own century.

Coincidental with these physiological gropings, however, was and is the belief that while humans may copulate and produce a body it is God who sends the soul needed to vivify an actual human being. As Briffault points out, it is not all that different from the Australian Aborigine conviction that the spirit child climbs into the womb. Some peoples believe in conception without the help of a man; others that the man is an accessory and that divine intervention is needed to assist him.

According to Francoeur, "The Pueblo Indians of New Mexico thought maidens could conceive from a heavy summer shower; the Greeks believed Aphrodite was born of sea foam; the Celtic saint Maedoc was conceived when a star fell into the mouth of his sleeping mother; the founder of the Manchu dynasty was conceived when a maiden ate a red fruit dropped on her lap by a magpie; a pomegranate placed in the bosom of the nymph Nana yielded Attis; and Longfellow records how Winonah was quickened by a western wind and gave birth to Hiawatha."[16] Pliny, Virgil, and St. Augustine believed that mares could be fertilized by the wind, and Plutarch thought the same of birds.[17] Poetry, superstition, ideology, and scientific knowledge mingle in diverse proportions for civilized as well as for nonliterate peoples in their efforts to explain natural phenomena.

Since humans had settled in villages before they began to plant seeds, there was no reason at that time to make any connection between the seed of grain and the sperm of males. The Trobriand Islanders, who planted yams, were ignorant of the function of semen or of any analogy, fancied or real, between plant and human biology. The Australian Aborigines refused to regard seeds as a source of food production even when the whites insisted. Though several of them had been introduced to gardening by white people, they rejected agriculture and the seed-semen metaphor.

All our mighty mythologies are founded on the misunderstanding of the nature of human biology and reproduction, as are the historic interpretations of them. Western religions were frankly reactionary in their effect on women's biology. Judaism vested control over a woman's body in her husband and a rabbinical court, while Christianity flatly forbade any method of birth control but celibacy and preferred the child's life to the mother's in medical emergency. Islam still takes an unequivocal stand against birth control and abortion.

The overt history of women as a force in Western civilization can be counted from the gradual expansion for popular use of birth control, beginning with the vaginal sponge in the eighteen twenties. The vulcanization of rubber in the nineteenth century led to the invention of the Mensinga cap in 1880, the earliest widely used pessary, or rubber diaphragm, as well as to the mass-produced condom. The post-World War II experiments which led to the sequential use of hormone pills have of course revolutionized man-woman relationships. Condoms for men, made originally of linen and later of animal membrane, go back to the sixteenth century—perhaps to the Romans—and they received their original approval as "prophylactics"—still their popular denomination in many languages—protection against venereal disease, to which the man might be exposed by frequenting the equally tolerated, if only semi-approved, prostitute. (The Italian euphemism for brothels, houses of toleration, reveals much about Christendom's illogical attitudes, which label male sexual desire irresistible and designate certain female human beings as necessary sacrifices to its importunacy.)

The situation is reversed in most nonliterate cultures, where it is taken for granted that women will have sex and babies; it is men who must earn these privileges. Reports from Oceania and Australia and Africa stress how this is arranged, after the birth of a girl child, and emphasize that there is no such thing as a woman who has not been married at least once in her life. Women will almost always have sex immediately after puberty; perhaps they will have experimented with it or been gradually introduced to it before their first menstruation.

For boys it is not so simple. There are cultures, like those of Samoa and the Trobriand Islands, where childish sex games turn easily into adolescent freedom before boys and girls settle down into a more stable, possibly arranged relationship. But in many places, the male must go through a complicated initiation ritual, in parts of Australia sometimes of ten or more years' duration, a period when male homosexuality is a not infrequent recourse.

He must also prove himself a hunter before he can arrange a marriage. Among the Mbuti Pygmies he must down an antelope or other large-sized game and present it to his prospective in-laws. Bride payment is common, as are continued obligations to provide the woman's family with meat. A man may have been making gifts to his future wife's mother in the case of the Tiwi, or parents or mother's brother in other cultures, for many years. By this token in most parts of Australia he will be at least fifteen, often twenty or thirty years older than the girl.

Margaret Mead thinks civilization develops out of the need to value male fields and devalue women's. Women achieve naturally and easily through childbirth, while males, seeing no such obvious purpose in the world, have had to invent compensations. Taken to its extreme, and there are some who claim as much, civilization—sometimes all culture—would be a male compensatory device, incited by male envy of the female capacity for generation. This is far from the case, for women have contributed much, though the acknowledgment of their role is scant and hard to document. However, agriculture and animal breeding did bring new anxieties. With the inception of mixed farming, male inferiority and male compensation will be a constant substratum and a constant goad in the shaping of religious and intellectual development. Male resentment at the obvious role women play in nature has led to a host of artificial and inaccurate dichotomies in later history. "Mother earth and father sky" is an early phrasing which has been translated, in more sophisticated times, to the belief that woman is body and man mind: i.e., because women can make babies, intelligence becomes masculine.[18] The one was evident, the other an invention. Man made a virtue of his defects by denying his earthliness beyond that of woman. If women were closer to nature, men must then be more spiritual, eventually closer to God. If women had the babies, it must be men who begot them, created their souls.

Whether paternity is recognized or not, fathering is pretty much a human and a social phenomenon. One of many ways in which men have tried to participate in women's experience is the *couvade*, where a man takes to his bed and simulates the pains of childbirth, for a few hours or days, at the same time his wife is giving birth. For Leacock, the basic principle of humanity is male-female reciprocity, so that men give child care when women are otherwise occupied.[19]

Fathering is extended mothering. For Mead it is a "social invention . . . under which males started nurturing females and their young . . . whether the children are believed to be his, or merely the children of a man of the same clan, or simply the legitimate children of his wife by an earlier marriage."[20] In some cases the children may be those of his sister rather than the woman or women with whom he has sex relations. While it is food sharing which is considered to be the ultimate defining characteristic of human society, there are cultures where the male contribution is slight indeed.

One such are the Malekula, a gardening people who inhabit a small New Hebrides island in Oceania, and who will come up in several contexts. Their food needs are provided by the women, who do the gardening, planting, and harvesting, chiefly of yams. Pigs are raised by the men for their circle tusks and for religious ceremonies in which women do not participate. Women do not eat pork and the men eat it only occasionally.

Sometimes, the extent to which the male participates in familial duties is insignificant: sometimes it is an exchange of services. Fathering has not achieved the importance with which the patriarchy sought to endow it; it is still a pale second to mothering. If necessity is the mother of invention, who is the father?

Another variation on the theme of mothering is the reversal of the mother-child image to apply to the sexual union, with a man in the nurturant role and the female as child. Kaberry cites the protests of an older man who had been making gifts to the parents of a girl-child since birth when the white station manager interfered with his marriage plans: "Me bin grow 'em up." This is also the expression used by the Arapesh; in a society where there is a great shortage of food, it is the husband who "grows his wife" by feeding her with gifts of food.

Since physical fatherhood is such a recent arrival on the human scene, father-daughter incest is not a particularly deep-seated taboo. It occurs far more often than its converse, mother-son incest, and is not always punished or even punishable by law. There are few myths against it; on the contrary, it is a paradigm for desirable man-woman relationships, though the father will be a guardian or father figure rather than a biological father.

When men did not know that they participated in the creative process, they arrogated it to themselves in different ways. Some of this mentality hung over in a culture lag, long after the gap in knowledge had been partially filled. Aristotle's ignorance may be some excuse for his ideology, which by the seventeenth century, about the time Leeuwenhoek discovered the sperm, had been popularized into Samuel Butler's "The souls of women are so small, that some believe they've none at all."

A comparison between the male and female views of spirit children—souls of babies waiting to be born—among the Australian Tiwi is informative here. While most Australian Aborigine tribes are—were—unaware of the connection between sexual intercourse and pregnancy, the Tiwi, who have had contact with Malay pearl fishermen over the past few centuries, have made the connection, but only recently and superimposed on older tradition. The world of the unborn children means very little to the women. If they see them or think about them at all it is as vague little birds. However, it is of vital importance to the imaginative and actual lives of the men. Their art, ritual, and many of their fantasies are bound up with it, and they see the *pitapui* (unborn children) as humans engaging in human occupations.

According to Goodale:

> Although the Tiwi recognize that either a husband
> or a lover can make a baby by having sexual inter-
> course with its mother, they also assert that such ac-
> tivity cannot alone create a *Tiwi* child. A Tiwi must
> be dreamed by its father, the man to whom its mother
> is married, before it can be conceived by its mother.
> To the Tiwi there is no conflict between the two be-
> liefs concerning conception. In fact there is only one
> belief, while there may be two "fathers." . . .
> The *pitapui* take a human form when men see
> them playing on the sandbanks, and when they ap-
> pear to their fathers in dreams. They not only look
> human, they act human, hunting and fighting as well
> as playing. The *pitapui* are symbolically emphasized
> in male ritual roles: the paternal *unandawi's* (fa-
> ther's) kinship dance in the funeral ceremony, the
> spear dance (*tuara*), commemorate the common as-
> pect of a spirit child when seen by its father in dreams
> . . . the sequence of *kakaritjui imunka* songs in the
> kulama ceremony may also be symbolic of the male
> emphasis on this world of the unborn.[21]

The male emphasis on spirit children appears to compensate
for the actual fact of playing such a small, even if recognized,
role in procreation.

Among the major civilizations of the world, this compensation has developed along very different lines. In general, however, since the domestication of grain and of animals began in
the Mideastern heartland, although with variations and possibly in several places, and was then diffused over Europe, Asia,
and Africa, certain broad trends can be traced. I shall concern
myself specifically with the development of Western civilization and the major religions that come from the Near East,
above all Judaism and Christianity, since it is these which have
had the major control over our own world and have, in our
time, influenced the rest of the planet.

Men were the original other; long before philosophers had

begun to speculate on the uselessness of woman save, in Napoleon's words, as a machine to produce babies, it was man who was useless. (Freud lifted from Napoleon the dictum "Biology is destiny.") Now he had discovered that he, too, had a place in the scheme of eternity; it was no longer woman alone who participated in the endless march of generations. Yet, the consciousness was slow in coming and always dragged along with it threads and cords of the past belief.

Feminists often speculate on what miracles might by now have been accomplished if historical energies that went into war and conspicuous consumption, culminating in the massive destructive capacities of nuclear warheads and chemical and biological warfare, had gone into constructive areas of medicine and female biology, birth control, improved techniques of infant nutrition, et al., if they had been exercised initially in these directions, rather than secondarily and often as the by-products of the former aims.

21

Çatal Hüyük and Hacilar:[1] Early Neolithic Towns

When did the Paleolithic respect for women become translated into the Great Mother Goddess of the agricultural civilizations, the fertility figure who inspires the production of children and grain? There is no suggestion that the Paleolithic Venuses and the small early Neolithic female figurines were more than maternal symbols, embodiments of protection, warmth, and sexuality in every sense. Many children are a hindrance to a gathering-hunting people. It is unlikely that the female representations' function was to encourage the conception of children, though by ethnographic analogy they may well have protected mothers in childbirth.

The argument that a matriarchal society preceded patriarchy is often based on a hypothesis of mother-goddess worship in the Neolithic period. Yet in historical times clear reference to fertility goddesses accompanies a progressive decline in the status of women. Emphasis on fertility was an opening wedge in the debasement of the female. The power of generation was removed from the individual woman and credited to a divinity, albeit a female one at first. Fertility worship led to the forced breeding of women; more important, it signified the perversion of sex from pleasure to production.

This transformation of the sexual instinct can be traced through a study of the changes that occurred during the thousand-year occupation of a Neolithic city which came into existence almost nine thousand years ago. James Mellaart's dig at Çatal Hüyük, on the Konya plain of Anatolia in Asia Minor, was one of the most spectacular finds of recent decades.

In 1958 Mellaart spotted a mound comprising 32 acres and began excavating in 1961. As of this writing only preliminary reports have been published, and there have been many contradictions and much changing of minds. The city has been variously described as a trading center, a city of hunting shrines, religious sanctuaries linked with the Paleolithic, and proof of the existence of the matriarchy and the privileged position of women in prehistoric times.

Fourteen layers of occupation have now been uncovered, a fifteenth is visible, and virgin soil has not yet been reached. Only a one-acre portion of the entire mound has been explored, though it is not known whether the city covered the entire 32 acres during any given period of its existence. Still, if it is remembered that some five to six thousand years later historical Jerusalem during the halcyon period of the united kingdom under David and Solomon covered 10.87 acres and that sites more or less contemporary with Çatal range from ten acres (Jericho, in Jordan) to four (Jarmo, in Iraq) to one or two (Ali Kosh, in Iran), the discovery of a 32-acre city that flourished some eight and a half thousand years ago is an astonishing one. Moreover, its location on the western fringes of the Fertile Crescent was formerly considered outside the prime area of the birth of civilization.

The quarter uncovered includes many large, beautifully plastered and decorated rooms which served both ceremonial and living functions and is believed to have been the city's religious center. As yet excavations have revealed no traces of the work rooms needed to produce the intricately crafted ornaments, art, and artifacts so far unearthed.

Careful examination of published reports on Çatal (Hüyük means mound in Turkish, synonymous with Tepe and Tell in other Near Eastern languages) provides evidence for the origins of a strain of sexual repression, leading to the position which women have taken in civilized cultures, most particularly that out of which white Western European and, more recently, American civilization developed.

The earliest levels of Çatal have been scantily excavated—in four rooms the expedition brought their sounding down to Level XII, still about six feet above ground level. Since the thousand-year weight of mud-brick buildings constructed layer by layer on top of each other would press the mound below the ground, it is deduced that there must be still older levels to unearth, probably about twenty feet more of archaeological debris.

Each building level was inhabited for fifty to one hundred years, though the rooms themselves were replastered each year. The people of Çatal were quite tradition-minded, for house design and use were maintained throughout the quarter over the centuries. After one level had been abandoned, swept clean and filled in, another stratum of construction would be built on top of it, the new rooms usually serving the same purpose as the earlier ones and similarly decorated.

In the oldest occupation levels, where fewer and less ornate artifacts were found, carbonized hackberries and acorns told of plant collecting, but no evidence of agriculture remained. Later, carbonized bread wheat and six-row hulled barley demonstrated that the people of Çatal had taken up farming. Both of these plants are cultivars; they cannot reproduce themselves but must be sown by humans. Their presence indicates a long experience with agriculture, either at Çatal or elsewhere.

With the weather conditions then prevailing on the Konya plain, irrigation must have been practiced. From the evidence—remains of marsh plants found mixed in with the grain—it was of the simplest kind. Fields were near a river and the normal spring flooding was encouraged or directed onto the land to be seeded.

Over its one thousand years of existence, Çatal demonstrates the transition from collecting and hunting to planting and animal breeding. Sheep and goats were kept first, some 8,500 years ago at Level X; cattle appear two or three hundred years later at Level VII. Though there were many different animal bones, particularly in the earlier levels, in the aggregate cattle out-number all others.

The kind of cattle domestication practiced at Çatal represents the first phase of animal keeping as opposed to conscious animal breeding. From the evidence, Çatal may have been one of the places where the connection was made between animal and human reproduction, for it contains early representations of the bull as a procreatory symbol. The metaphor of the potent, generative bull persists throughout the Bronze Age and survives in many parts of Africa and India as well as in slang references in our own world.

The people who lived at Çatal had control over their cattle. This has been deduced by analyzing and tabulating the ages at which the animals were slaughtered. A study was made of the bones from Levels VI through II, covering the four hundred years between approximately 8200 and 7800 B.P. The domestication was of an archaic kind, but the fact that the bones were primarily of mature animals cannot be otherwise explained. The young of wild animals are easier to kill than the wily adults; with scientific cattle breeding also there is a selection of young males for slaughter, leaving only a few bulls to service the herd. At Çatal, on the contrary, the cattle were killed only after they were full grown. Presumably they were slaughtered to provide meat after they had been bred or even when they were old. Many cattle-herding tribes in the African Sahel treasure their animals and keep them not for meat but for possession itself, as symbols of one kind or another. The decorations and shrines at Çatal indicate that cattle, in particular bulls, were the focus of a religious cult which may have centered around the mating of a goddess of fertility with the bull of procreation. The females would have been kept for increase; the males may have been sacrificed for their horns; they may also have been used for religio-theatrical games.

The great wild cattle would have been driven into enclosures outside the city itself. Judging by the house plans, all animals, including sheep and goats, were corralled outside the living areas. Here also they were slaughtered for food, but the bulls' skulls and in particular their great curving horns were treasured for ritual and decorative purposes. If the huge aurochs were kept in pens and from them arose both the domestication of cattle and evidence through observation of male participation in the reproductory process, Çatal could be a place where the direct connection between coitus and fatherhood was made.

Judging by the sparsity of cattle bones at most village sites, they were rarely hunted during this period. "The uncomfortably potent aurochs" were difficult to handle—large, frightening, not amenable like the other ruminants—all in all, unlikely candidates for domestication on the face of it. Many archaeologists believe that the cattle were driven into large enclosures, with certain males isolated for sacrifice and the others left free to breed. It is not known whether the taming of cattle arose in Greece or in the Hungarian plains north of the Balkans and then made its way to Asia Minor or vice versa. The only other places where it is certain that cattle were raised at this time were west of Çatal—at Argissa-Maghula in Greek Thessaly (about 8500 B.P.) and perhaps a few hundred years later at Nea Nikomedia in Macedonia.

In historical times goats are associated with less threatening male sexuality—Pan, lust, goatishness—whereas the bull represents the concept of aggressive potency. Divinity is widely associated with both bull and cow in Egypt and Mesopotamia. The cow goddess disappears but the taurine metaphor remains, in Greek mythology, even in the Old Testament.

In the earlier levels of Çatal, the wall decorations showed abstract patterns, believed to be based on the flat-woven Turkish rugs called *kilims*, and various animals, most commonly leopards. In an 8,200-year-old Level VI shrine, two enormous leopards face each other. It is in the conservative tradition of Çatalian architecture, for the room underneath, dated some hundred years earlier, had also been decorated with leopards.

After Level VI leopards no longer appear; now the bull takes over, sharing primacy with a pregnant goddess. A plain undecorated room of the previous century is redecorated with a bull's head made out of plaster; actual horns were inset while the plaster was still damp. Some rooms contain great wall paintings of the bull, but more characteristic shrines are large rooms, sometimes twenty by thirty feet, with plaster bulls' heads sculptured in high relief around actual skulls and massive curving horns, which appear on the north wall. There are about fifty of these shrines and the design is the same. Facing the bull, on the south wall, is a great plaster relief of a female figure with protuberant belly, arms and legs outspread, seemingly in the act of giving birth.

Çatal is often given as an example of the peaceful woman-dominated Neolithic, but the details indicate more complexity. Once the bull and pregnant-woman juxtaposition has been made, other aggressive images also appear. There are rooms decorated by friezes of sculptures representing women's breasts; each breast is molded around the lower jaw of a wild boar. In another room a pair of women's breasts each contained the head of a griffon vulture, whose beak protruded from the open red-painted nipples. Beyond a post was a horn in plaster, evidently a male symbol; and beyond the breasts a huge bull's head crowned a red-painted niche.

Such symbolism is found neither in the Paleolithic nor in contemporary Neolithic sites—small villages and the somewhat larger Jericho. The association of the breast with the hard-pecking beak of the carrion eater contradicts all our benign images of the protective bosom, ever flowing and generous; the boar's jaw, biting not feeding, is another contradictory sadistic image.

Women at Çatal are associated with destructive power; they are also associated with death. Shrines with mural paintings of corpses under gabled shelters and huge winged figures with human feet have been interpreted as depicting religious ceremonies presided over by priestesses of death. Secondary burial has been inferred as part of the religious worship. Dead bodies were first placed outside the city on elevated platforms and left for vultures to pick. The skeletons—in varying states of decomposition—were interred beneath the floors of houses and shrines. Here is woman not only as birth-giver but as destroyer, a common ambivalence of attitudes in farming societies though not among gatherers. The Great Mother of Life and Death, the goddess Kali, Medusa and the Erinyes, Le-hev-hev and her like in Oceania—these are a few of the negative forms into which the Mother Goddess is transformed.

Whatever the role of women at Çatal, and it was an important one, by the time of Level VI, about 8200 B.P., woman is no longer friendly: these are visions of the woman denying and destroying, not in a genital sense, like the biting or toothed vagina, but in a much larger and more primitive sense of the betraying mother.

It was not always so at Çatal, however. The richness of the burials, the objects buried with individuals, and the placing of the bodies are details that can be put together to tell about the social structure of a given site. Originally women were priestesses at Çatal, but after the introduction of cattle worship, though still officiants, they no longer have the authority with which they had previously been endowed. They still have mana, the magic of blood, but now they share it with the bull in its red-painted niche.

During the gathering-hunting period some agriculture would also have been practiced. Çatal was another of those fringe settlements which may have been peopled from the rich mountains. With increasing concentration on farming, more and more labor would be necessitated. Almost nine thousand years ago there may have been a comfortable balance of nutrition. In later centuries, in order to produce the surplus indicated by the remains, trading could have been one source of riches.

At an early level of excavation, Level VIII, a special burial was found, unique for the city and elsewhere. An elaborate shrine with plastered floors painted red had an orange platform at one end. Beneath the platform a mother and a little girl were buried. The woman's body was covered in red ocher, which striped her shoulders and skull also, while the child had been partly stained with red cinnabar. The mother bore extremely elaborate jewelry for the place and period; beside her lay a macehead made of white-veined blue limestone. The little girl's skeleton, partly decayed, rested in a basket about two feet beneath the platform, and she too was richly accoutered. She wore two bead necklaces, one ornamented with mother-of-pearl pendants and deer's teeth. The beads themselves were made from varicolored stones: white, black, and blue limestone, greenstone, as well as dentalium shells. Multicolored bead bracelets encircled her wrists.

Cattle bones were located in Level VII, the stratum above that in which the priestess received her elaborate burial. After the initiation of cattle keeping, the macehead appears beside male skeletons; the priestess of Level VIII was the one female burial accompanied by such a symbol of authority.

Women who are steeped in red color, the symbol of blood and mana, are in later burials also, but they no longer have the ornate jewelry and ritual objects beside them; these now are included in male burials.

What was life like for the people who made these shrines and engaged in the religio-theatrical observances indicated by the sculptures, the wall reliefs, the paintings, and the very special arrangement of architecture? Like certain of the pueblos of Western North American Indians, there were no doors to their homes. They could be entered only through a hole in the roof, which was always on the south side and served both as a smoke hole and a doorway. A fixed ladder led from the roof down into the house; the excavator assumes a canopy or other shelter over the entrance hole and a moveable ladder on the outside leading up to the roof. People lived in the shrines and in residences next door. They cooked at hearths on the same wall as the smoke hole and baked in beehive ovens. The chief furniture seems to have been a large divan-bed, often in the center of the west wall, something like the clay *k'ang*, the couch-bed of a Chinese village home, and not dissimilar to arrangements today in Turkish villages. Underneath this large platform-bed, a woman and several children might be buried. Sometimes there were other platform-beds in the room, but there was always a smaller one in the north corner. Underneath it, a male figure might be buried, described by the excavator as the master of the house, though at this distance there is no way of knowing whether he was master, servant, or neither.

From the burials it is evident that there was a sharp distinction of sex roles in the city. In Australia and Africa men are often more highly decorated and ornamented than women;

they seem like sex objects, while the hardworking, child-raising women spend less time beautifying themselves. At Çatal, it is the women who are accompanied by cosmetic sets and copious jewelry, as well as tools. The latter include awls for sewing, bodkins for basket weaving, knives and hoes.

The men have less jewelry than the women; they have knives but they also have maces with perforated heads of polished stone, daggers and fire-making equipment: flint firestones, sometimes a piece of sulfur.

The women's cosmetics may have been for ceremonial observance: their cosmetic sets contained a palette for mixing, shells filled with powdered red ocher, a bone ointment stick, baskets containing a paste of red ocher mixed with fat, and a small spoon and fork. Obsidian mirrors were found with women's burials exclusively. One man also had a "cosmetic set," but the colors in his were blue and green; life-and-death red was reserved for women.

Many statues have been found, mostly of women, though there are occasional male figures. Several statues show a mother holding a child, and one enigmatic greenstone relief with two scenes may express the new concept penetrating human consciousness. On the left, a couple of equal size are embracing; on the right are a mother and child, possibly the results of the embrace.

There are more women than men buried at Çatal and from this fact as well as the appearance of articles which had to be procured from distant places—copper, carnelian, seashells, and mother-of-pearl are a few—it has been proposed that Çatal was an early trading city. Obsidian was a rare and much desired commodity in Neolithic times, and Çatal had a rich source nearby.

The peculiar burial arrangements at Çatal tell us that families there were not composed of a mother, a father, and their children. There is no evidence for cohabitation in the placement of the bodies under the sleeping platforms. Wives and husbands are frequently buried together, or at least side by side, in many historical excavations and in Western tradition. At Çatal the children are buried with their mothers, not at the feet of the father and mother, as one would find them, for example, in a nineteenth-century cemetery in an agricultural setting or small town in New England or Pennsylvania. Matriliny is indicated by the fact that mother and children were buried together. There are rooms where no adult man was buried. The man frequently placed under the small platform in a far corner could have been a brother, even a grown son, of the woman who lay under the large platform. Still we do not know the nature of the religious observances practiced; possibly the woman and man buried in the same house were both priests of a fertility cult celebrating female and male sex, the smaller proportion of males symbolizing the newly discovered male role in procreation, which is similarly represented in the ratio of statues with its preponderance of females and very few adult male representations.

A medical analysis of skeletons unearthed at Çatal gives much data about life as it was lived some eight thousand years ago in Anatolia. Almost all of the skeletons were from the four-hundred-year period centering about the date 8000 B.P., in particular from Levels VI and VII, the point at which, from other evidence, I have tentatively located the discovery of fatherhood by way of cattle breeding. These were the levels also where those aggressive symbols—plaster breasts incorporating boars' jaws and vultures' beaks—first appeared.

More adult women than men were buried in the only area excavated—the religious quarter. Skeletons of children are difficult, if not impossible, to sex, but the pathologist deduces, within the framework of that statement, that more male children than female children were buried. If more girls than boys survived into adulthood, it may be that boys were more susceptible to *falciparum* malaria in childhood, against which a tell-tale thickening of the skull indicated that the peoples of Çatal Hüyük had developed the protection of Cooley's anemia, as the peoples of Africa were later to develop sickle-cell anemia.

We do not know whether fewer males lived into adulthood, whether the men died and were buried away from home, or whether there were fewer male priests and therefore fewer males buried in the religious quarter.

Çatal may also be one of the earliest societies differentiated by rank, if not class, since people in other quarters—craft, market, etc.—were probably working to provide the priestly quarter with time to engage in religious and artistic activity. However, all or almost all the inhabitants of Çatal will have participated in agricultural pursuits, providing or contributing to the production of a goodly portion of their own food, as was the case in historic Sumer and in Europe down to medieval times.

Life expectancy at Çatal was fairly similar to that found in similar skeletal analyses performed on groups of Paleolithic skeletons—about thirty years. J. Lawrence Angel, the paleopathologist who analyzed the Çatal remains, felt that the women there lived one and a half to two years longer than did the women of Paleolithic enclaves whose skeletal remains he had studied. He used certain pelvic measurements to determine a woman's age at death, as well as marks of wear and scarring on the pelvic girdle to infer the number of children to which she had given birth, figures which supported the thesis of a rapidly growing population in the early Neolithic. These marks and measurements have been tested on skeletons from present-day morgues and hospitals and found to be unreliable. Still, we do know from other evidence—dated village sites in the Near East, not to say the empirical evidence of a cumulative record of geometrical increase into our own time—that village life, agriculture, and the augmentation of what we think of as civilization did result in both steady and spurting population increases, culminating in the twentieth-century explosion of planetary inhabitants.

Angel also finds a chronological trend toward reduction of males buried at home as the levels approach the date of the city's disappearance: "If this trend is valid it suggests stresses of childhood disease, hunting, war, and trading trips as forces to reduce the number of males as possible partial reasons for the end of the Early Neolithic settlement at Çatal."[2]

Not much can be deduced about infant mortality at Çatal, for there is a paucity of newborn skeletons at most of the caches found at Neolithic burial grounds, including Çatal. Ethnographic evidence shows that infants are often not counted as human souls until they have survived a given period of time, varying from five days to several months, and are not given ritual—formal—burial. A sudden drop in burials of children occurred about 8200—from Level VI on—which could indicate a change in religious practices, not inconsistent with my own conclusion that Level VI marks the point at which fatherhood was discovered and male roles in religious observances changed. Angel's conclusion is that infant dead were not given formal burial at Çatal; possibly babies who died at less than a year old were not always buried, a situation he also deduced for a later cemetery excavation at nearby Bronze Age Karatas.

Another site for cattle raising at the time of Çatal, Nea Nikomedia in Greece, had cemeteries in which the number of adult burials equaled those of children and infants, a not uncommon finding. That the ratio of adult skeletons to those of people who died before reproductive age was two to one led Sally Binford to conclude that Neanderthaloids had developed into Cro-Magnon humans while West European Neanderthals, with a one-to-one ratio of immature to mature burials, died out. Ralph Holloway used more heavily weighted statistics to conclude that the species of *Homo habilis* (including *Australopithecus africanus*) survived while *Australopithecus robustus* became extinct. The Çatalians had a lower ratio of immature to mature burials than the people of Nea Nikomedia. Skeletal remains from both towns show signs of endemic malaria, but in other respects the Çatalians seem to have been more healthy than the inhabitants of the European town, who suffered from a higher rate of dental disease and died younger.

Despite the combined evidence for increased population in Neolithic times, the agricultural revolution produced quantitative rather than qualitative advances. The mean life span of thirty years was more or less standard from Paleolithic times well into the nineteenth century.[3] More children lived or were allowed to live into reproductive age, but certain conditions of life were not improved; if anything they probably worsened, with longer working hours, more forced labor, poorer food. According to Angel: "The completely settled and relatively secure life of the trading settlement [of Çatal Hüyük] did not result in any real improvement in quality of diet or in health; in fact, diet and health had deteriorated."[4]

In certain respects this deterioration continued even into our own times. Children may have had a certain stability and protection in life, while childhood diseases had not yet gained a foothold in human existence—as measles and smallpox were unknown to American Indians before they were introduced by European whites. The evidence comes from a comparison of certain striae on the teeth, indications of severe emotional or physical stress caused by, say, sudden weaning or childhood disease. Among modern American whites these marks of childhood trauma are present to a slight degree in 51 per cent of child and adult skeletal remains, to a strong degree in 8 per cent; at Çatal they existed in far smaller percentages—7.5 per cent slight and 5.5 per cent strong.

The people of Çatal were comparatively tall, but slight-boned, except for the pathological thickening of skull and other bones caused by Cooley's anemia. They had more dental and gum disease than occurred in Paleolithic days, no doubt due to the increased starch and lowered protein content of their diets, though less than in modern times. They used their teeth more than we do, both for chewing and, among the women, for what Angel terms "industrial purposes," probably basketry, sewing, weaving, etc. Young children seem to have broken their legs frequently, though the breaks healed well. Despite endemic malaria, the town, estimated at over 5,000 souls, functioned for over 800 years—Mellaart claims more than a thousand. The couches with two to five sets of aurochs' horns plastered along the edges, in five of the shrines of Level VI, as well as undecorated floor benches from other levels, can be seen as healing couches. Angel compares them to the abata of late classical and Hellenistic and Roman times, which were also used during a period of newly increasing malaria. My observation indicates that the horned couches are part of a change in religious observance to worship of the horn as a potency and, possibly, life-giving symbol.

Despite the disease handicap the people of Çatal led an extremely active life. Elbows and arms showed wear and stress, while a certain number of head wounds reflect "social as well as physical wear and tear: warfare and quarrels, hunting and other accidents."[5]

One curious detail explains much and extends the picture of their lives. Almost half the thighbones analyzed show a peculiar formation at the point where the thigh joins the hip: "A special posterior development of the lesser trochanter therefore adds a little leverage in quick turning and poising as in dancing or the animal games shown in the frescoes."[6] In other words, at least half the people found in the priestly quarter of Çatal had highly developed dancer's turnout—suggesting the specific expression of religious ceremonial which was integral to their daily existence. This is not surprising, since dance is the oldest and most universal of the arts, ethnographically synonymous with religious and other festivals. However, it is not often found in the formalized and technically developed art form which must have existed at Çatal. Dancer's turnout is only achieved with much practice and difficult exercises. The tradition of the classical ballet, for example, involved apprenticeship at eight and total dedication throughout the dancer's life. The twentieth-century revolt against the long training necessary for the classical ballet was a revolt also against the discipline and repression of the earlier form, an overturning which produced modern dance and, eventually, revivified the old art. All those injuries, "the wear and tear," the children's broken limbs which Angel ascribed to "falling down the house ladder at night," the knee action and ankle flexion demonstrated by legbones are also evidence for strict athletic training beginning at an early age.

A medical study on present-day ballet dancers showed that they are subject to a wide range of athletic injuries including torn ligaments and fractured and broken bones.[7] It seems likely that the Çatalians in the religious quarter were engaged in similar severe athletic disciplines from a very early age.

On the Anatolian plain some eight thousand years ago extreme rigidity and control must have been necessary to produce a surplus for trading as well as the riches of ornamentation and art evidenced in the city itself, especially with the limited technology then existent. A puzzling feature of the sculptures and reliefs and paintings at Çatal was the absence of sexual representations. No vulvas and no male organs, though the former are prominent in Paleolithic art, and both will turn up in later Neolithic representation. Scholars have frequently interpreted the absence of sexual representation, as in Crete, as an indication of the supremacy of women. At Çatal Hüyük, Mellaart claims the absence of explicit sexual reference as proof that Neolithic woman created Neolithic religion because "emphasis on sex in art is invariably connected with male impulse and desire." The assumption that women have no sexual desire has of course been disproved by copious ethnographic evidence from nonliterate societies where women sing of the clitoris and the penis, the joys of intercourse and of sensuality. The absence of sexual representation does demonstrate the existence of sexual repression, though by whom imposed we cannot tell from this remote distance.

Wall paintings of Levels V and III recently discovered are complicated murals showing tiny figures engaged in athletic feats around and with huge animals, a kind of animal baiting resembling later illustrations of the Cretan bull games, with youths and maidens grappling animal horns, leaping onto their backs, baiting and teasing them. The Çatalian pictures were probably drawn from actual religious festivals, of dance and theater.

One injury from Angel's study indicated a deep bone infection of the left buttock, consistent with the kind of goring that occurs in bullfights—a conclusion substantiated by the animal games illustrated in Levels V and III. These murals have been interpreted as showing reverence for animals. They may tell also of sadomasochistic gamesmanship. In the importance given to animals, the difficulties of taming and killing them, there is a mingling of identification and cruelty which sheds light on the phenomenon of sadomasochism. The bull cult first illustrated at Çatal Hüyük was diffused all across the central areas of Asia, Africa, and Southern Europe. An archaeologist of the future might, indeed, admire the beauty of a bullfight painting in Spain or Mexico—matadors and picadors, brilliant capes and flourishes, the ceremony and athleticism almost a formalized dance—without taking into account the underlying cruelty and horror. Many audiences do so today, enjoying gore and sadism married to panoply and art—one symptom of the particular Spanish cultural history of inhibition, control, and torture that is an outgrowth of the basic contempt for sexuality rooted therein.

Settled life allowed for a development of art, religion, and architecture and crafts which left more complete and visible remains than did the cultures of several thousand years earlier in that area and the contemporaneous culture in other parts of the world.

The material and technological advances at Çatal have been ascribed to freedom from the pursuit of food. Art—beautiful and necessary though it be—is often achieved at the cost of life and lives. Judging by recent ethnographic evidence on the leisure of gathering peoples, there must have been less leisure, more drive and discipline—in sum more sexual sublimation—than in Paleolithic times. I would predicate sexual repression coming from animal breeding, resulting in competitive and sadomasochistic games and pursuits, as well as an early tendency toward material accumulation, read trade, as culture complexes which shaped Çatal's flowering and decline.

Where animals, and particularly the massive cattle, were of less importance, the attitude toward procreation and the position of women was somewhat different. Some 375 miles west of Çatal Hüyük was the village called Hacilar, 3,000 feet up in a well-watered intramontane valley. Very scanty remains of an early Neolithic settlement, predating Çatal, have been found; then a thousand-year gap exists—just the period during which the latter flourished. Hacilar was resettled perhaps about 7,700 years ago, about the time Çatal was abandoned. It was not a large village ever; 7,600 years ago it may have contained about 50 houses, or a minimum of 250 souls.

At Hacilar, both early and late, there is no proof that any domesticated animals except, possibly, dogs, were ever kept. In the remains of the early settlement, where a few bones of fallow deer, hare, wild cattle, and sheep or goats were found, it is felt that hunting must have been practiced. In the late Neolithic settlement, there is abundant documentation of advanced and intensive farming and no evidence of domestic animals. Judging from the sparsity of wild-animal remains unearthed and the lack of weapons, as compared to the richness of the material which told of cultivation, it would seem that the inhabitants of Hacilar were largely vegetarian. They produced a varied farming diet: naked barley and bread wheat, along with earlier forms of wheat, peas, lentils, pistachios, almonds, apples, capers, and an abundance of hackberries, the fruit which *Homo pekinensis* had enjoyed half a million years earlier at Choukoutien. They did little hunting and had to have some method of irrigation to cultivate certain of their vegetables. Religious orientation reflects their cultural and economic life. In extant excavations of prehistoric art from Crete, Greece, Egypt, and the Near East, Hacilar is one of a very few where the male figure is totally absent, while animal references are also scantier here than elsewhere.[8] Surely it is no coincidence that in a village where animals were not kept and hunting was a peripheral activity, all the statues are of women—at every age and stage of maturity: standing with the pointed breasts of youth, reclining with full breasts and distended pregnant bellies, women seated in the birth position, standing women with huge drooping breasts, or, frequently, with hands cupped offering breasts, in a gesture which will turn up again and again, in art and life, in history and ethnography. Among the many statues of baked clay are only two, or possibly three, which show the woman (goddess or talisman) associated with another figure.

One enigmatic fragment is an ample woman with missing arms, a portion of the lower half of a child at her midsection, its leg curled over her thigh. It is described as "Young Woman Playing with Her Son," but the child might just as well be a daughter. Another small unbaked clay figure which shows a woman clasping a fragment of a small animal to her chest and seated on a larger animal is nominated "Mistress of the Animals Holding a Leopard Cub and Seated on a Leopard." And one seated figure with hands cupping breasts who has a portion of what seems to be the long curving tail of an animal across her back is dubiously reconstructed as "Mistress of the Animals Seated on Two Leopards."

This is not to say that no notice is taken of animals alone. A few pottery containers are shaped in the form of animals—theriomorphic vases is the archaeologists' description. The copious finds of richly ornamented pottery are decorated chiefly in geometric patterns, but some of these stylized forms—probably derived from the limitations imposed by earlier ages' basketry patterns—would seem to represent animals and plants. There are even a very few fragments of clay figures and heads of animals. But the "male principle" is conspicuously absent. There are no representations of men or phalli, nor of animal horns or of massive frightening beasts; no association seems to be made between potency and aggression; the concept of potency has yet to appear. Nor is there any emphasis on the Great Mother as a figure of terror and death—surely a projection of male anxiety and hostility.

Hacilar may well exemplify the myth of the peaceful female-dominated early agricultural community. Large rooms in the excavated buildings point to an extended family rather than a nuclear organization. Life was sunnier in this rich. valley between mountains than in the malarial Konya plain where Çatal Hüyük developed. With its small population, every inhabitant at Hacilar would have been able to partake of the fruits of the soil in a basic model of an egalitarian society.

Different strains and different cultural emphases existed at the same time and in nearby locations. Çatalians may have been more quarrelsome and competitive than the peaceful Hacilarians to the west. There is no need to assume matriarchy per se for Çatal or Hacilar even if households centered around the mother. Numerous statues of women have been excavated at Jericho, Beidha, Jarmo, Sawwan, and other sites of the period, both rich and poor. The ambiguous evidence from Çatal is the only positive indication that the male role in generation had been recognized. Judging by the grave goods, it is probable that there was less emphasis on possession, more on sharing, and more sexual freedom in the smaller communities than existed in the larger city of Çatal Hüyük.

Is the myth of the matriarchy a justification for the imposi-tion of the patriarchy? Surely the idea that the patriarchy was preceded by the matriarchy is not only a reverse image of the power wielded by men, but also a metaphor, a childlike phras-ing of the power of the Great Mother. We all desire a great all-giving mother—to suck at the ever-flowing breast—but what poor mortal female can possibly live up to the demands of the infant when closely spaced, forcible breeding has begun to be enforced? Thus we resent weaning, we resent younger siblings, we resent the adult male who sleeps with the mother. Daugh-ters, as well as sons, will harbor all these and more against the also beloved mother. The ambivalence of our feelings, the love that becomes transformed to hate, is more prevalent under the patriarchy and under the heavy socializing of the earlier civili-zations; a substratum capable of development may be hidden in looser and more simply organized societies.

22

Sadism and Masochism: Inherent or Acquired?

Are sadism and masochism inherent in the human animal? Sadism is defined as "a perversion in which gratification is obtained by torturing the loved one" or, in a larger sense, as "a love of cruelty, conceived as a manifestation of sexual desire." Masochism, the obverse of sadism, is the "abnormal sexual passion in which one finds pleasure in abuse or cruelty from his or her associate; hence, any pleasure in being abused or dominated."[1]

The words themselves are of recent origin. *Sadism* derives from the Marquis de Sade, who lived in the second half of the eighteenth century and on into the nineteenth, dying in 1814. *Masochism* comes from the novels written by Leopold von Sacher-Masoch, who died in 1895. Though the human history of torture and cruelty goes back thousands of years, evidently no need was felt to identify the sexual components of these phenomena until the last century or so. Writers on sexuality—Krafft-Ebing and Freud and his followers—brought the words into wide usage, so that in our own time they are familiar if not completely understood concepts.

Freud took it for granted that aggressive impulses were inborn and rooted in sexuality. In his version, the first "crime"

was committed when the son killed the father because he desired the mother. A follower of Freud's, Gregory Zilboorg,
changed the facts but kept the emotional tenor. He said the initial crime was not the murder of the father, it was the rape of
the mother. Both men assumed innate violence and active sadistic sexuality in men and passivity in women, who are being
acted upon rather than acting in both cases. (Until recently,
there was little room for daughters in psychoanalytic formulations of this kind.) Freud's thinking was shaped by Greek
myths, which themselves reflect fairly late stages of political
development. When studies of matrilineal societies were published, like that of the Trobriand Islanders by Malinowski, they
disproved the Freudian thesis. In these societies, it was the
mother's brother who had authority over the son's presumed
object of desire so that Bertrand Russell could imagine the
Oedipal myth reframed with supreme power vested in God the
Maternal Uncle, rather than in God the Father.

Is rape, for example, a sadistic perversion? And if so, does its
seeming ubiquity make a case for the inherently sadistic nature
of men?*

In the same way are woman naturally masochistic? Freud's
initial view of women as incomplete men, feeling themselves
deformed or castrated because they lacked penises, led him to
see them as essentially passive. When they were active, they
were being "masculine"—a view that has been disproved by
ethnographic researches. Masochism as a biological female trait
was only implicit in Freud's earlier writings; he made it explicit
in his later work. It was his followers, among them Sandor
Rado, Geza Roheim, and Helene Deutsch, who further developed the thesis of woman as inherently masochistic.

The wish to inflict suffering develops, I believe, from sexual
energy deprived of outlet. It may also be caused by a need to
control, anxiety projected onto others. But nobody chooses to
suffer unnecessarily. Masochism is an alternative to a worse
suffering, physical or psychic. Sadism can exist in the aggressor

* There are cultures where neither rape nor the concept itself exists—from
the peaceful Arapesh described by Margaret Mead to the Lesu of New
Ireland, to the newly discovered Tasadays of the Philippines.

without masochism in the victim. There is a component of masochism, however, in the sadist's identification (conscious or unconscious) with the object of his or her cruelty.

In his study of Paleolithic art mentioned in Chapter 15, André Leroi-Gourhan divided the representations into male and female. He explicated many mysterious markings in sexual terms, inventing a complicated set of equivalences which made lines, sticks, and plants into weapons, then phalli; rounds, triangles, and other enclosed shapes into wounds, then vulvas. The man-horse-spear image was complemented by that of woman-bison-wound; the male spear and the female wound were seen as symbols of sexual union and death.

Associating the vagina with a wound comes from the Freudian thesis of castration anxiety, in which the small boy takes his and his father's bodies as universal models and assumes that the shape of his mother's and sisters' genitals is the result of castration, that the vagina is a wound, a "gash" in popular terminology, rather than a normal biological manifestation. But this identification is a projection of a violent and terror-filled culture in which the body is hidden so that the first sight of nakedness comes as a shock and everybody's genitals are shameful. It is symptomatic of a recent historic mentality to connect sex with wounds and sadism and to link animals thereto. This comes from the direct linkage between war and sexual oppression in the history of civilization.

In Freud's Vienna, woman's position was manifestly inferior to that of man, so that one might make a case for the penis as a symbol of male power. In the Upper Paleolithic period, however, where there were more representations of females than of males, we cannot prove that a similar situation was already in effect. Morever, as was discussed earlier, Leroi-Gourhan's categorization was based on mistaken identification to begin with, since many of the so-called weapons were probably leaves, branches, and other vegetation. There is no proof that sadomasochistic syndromes were present in the paintings and sculpture or in the people who made them. When war, cruelty, and torture do surface—some millennia after the adoption of agriculture and animal breeding—there is little doubt about their existence. They can be traced in the architecture, the visual decorations, and eventually in the literature, in which last the sexual elements are also revealed.

Many of the factors contributing to sadism and to masochism need not have functioned in the Paleolithic. Psychoanalysts have differed in their views on human sexuality. Freud predicated civilization on its repression. Wilhelm Reich, one of his most gifted students, felt that repressed sexuality was responsible for civilization's deformities rather than civilization itself and broke with the master over this point.

Reich's basic humanity was outraged in particular by the work Geza Roheim had attempted, mixing psychoanalysis with anthropology in a book called *Psychoanalysis of Primitive Cultures*, based on a trip to Australia and New Guinea in the spring of 1929. He quotes Roheim's reactionary outlook on life: "In the purely physical sense their manner of carrying out intercourse seems to be more genital than the Europeans'. They *penetrate more deeply*, work with stronger physical stimuli; with a slight exaggeration, one might even say the woman is only satisfied if after intercourse she feels ill with an inflammation." How can he know?

Reich expostulates, "With a *slight* exaggeration? Has psychoanalysis been founded, the existence of the unconscious discovered, and the morbid sadistic concept of coitus revealed, in order that an official representative of psychoanalysis may summon up the courage and narrowmindedness, to assert such things with authority?"[2]

This was written in 1931. Since then, the expansion of Freudianism, particularly during and after World War II, has given a sanction of seemingly advanced views to what were essentially nineteenth-century ideas on sexuality, and not only in esoteric studies like the work of Leroi-Gourhan. In 1968 Erik Erikson asserted that in every *normal* sexual relationship there was probably some element of sadism, while Irving Singer, writing in 1973, confidently assured us that women need to be banged on the cervix to achieve a preferred kind of orgasm![3]

Reich pointed out "that in the authoritarian patriarchy the genitality of men is considered a proof of potency, while the genitality of women is considered a disgrace." For him, genitality was all, and he saw "a disturbed capacity for gratification" as the pathological basis of sexual aggression.[4] He thought in terms of a primeval age "when love life was free and unrestricted" and traced a line of development which combined Marx-Engels' thinking with the reports of Malinowski on the Trobriand Islanders to project an economic origin for sexual repression:

> With the economic interests of a developing social stratum and the suppression of the sex life of children and adolescents, the sexual experience of the whole community changed. Sexual disturbances and neuroses appeared—sadistic attitudes in the sex life of men and sex negation in the women. . . . Sadism is as prevalent as it is today only when the natural genital functions are hindered or disturbed; in other words, *inhibited genitality changes not only into anxiety but also into sadism and perhaps this is the sole origin of sadism.* . . . Roheim and most analysts view sadism as a natural manifestation in the area of sex, and its origin is therefore biological.

Reich quotes Roheim, declaring that the deepest human sadistic attitudes are linked to the first eruption of teeth and that sadism signifies the desire to devour one's sexual partner. Why, he demands, do not Roheim and the other analysts take account of the differences among peoples in different places since sexual sadism is nonexistent in some cultures and prominent in others.[5]

Reich does not speak of female masochism directly, since he feels that women are the forced victims of male sadism rather than the willing receptors. His theory of forcible inhibition—"sex negation in the women" is his rather judgmental expression—would mean that their masochism is sadistic aggression turned on themselves. Reich clearly acknowledges the sexuality of women: "There is, in this respect, no difference between the healthy man and the healthy woman."[6] Essentially, however, he sees women in relation to or as analogues of men rather than as wholes, with their own specific biology, nature, and history.

Karen Horney and, somewhat later, Clara Thompson also took exception to the view of sadomasochism as inherent in human and animal biology, but from rather different points of view. They focus more on the female, i.e., the masochistic, side of the proposition: male equals aggression equals sadism; female equals passivity equals masochism—and they place more emphasis on cultural conditioning of women under patriarchy.

Horney discusses women's "lowered self-esteem of centuries duration." She points out the factors in Western culture which "predispose to the appearance of masochism in women," including "blocking of outlets for expansiveness and sexuality . . . the estimation of women as beings who are, on the whole, inferior to men (insofar as it leads to a deterioration of female self-confidence.) . . . economic dependence of women on men or on family, inasmuch as it fosters an emotional adaptation in the way of female self-confidence . . . [and] surplus of marriageable women, particularly when marriage offers the principal opportunity for sexual gratification, children, security and social recognition." She concludes "that in our culture it is hard to see how any woman can escape becoming masochistic to some degree, from the effects of the culture alone."[7]

Both Horney and Thompson are cautiously critical of Freud's and his followers' Oedipally based physiological theory of female masochism as the result of penis envy. "Sadism and masochism have fundamentally nothing whatsoever to do with intercourse, but the female role in intercourse (being penetrated) lends itself more readily to a personal misinterpretation (when needed) of masochistic performance; and the male role, to one of sadistic activity."[8]

Writing some years later, in a work not published until after her death, Thompson took an even stronger stand against Freudian "biology":

> Culturally we have been educated to think of women
> as having less sexual drive than men. . . . Observa-
> tion of animals does not seem to confirm this, accord-

ing to Ford and Beach. The sexual drive of the female in heat is *insatiable. . . . One female at that time can exhaust several males . . .* psychoanalysis thus far has secured extensive acquaintance with the psychology of women in only one type of culture. Facts observed by Freud in a particular part of the Western world have been interpreted as an adequate basis for an understanding of female psychology in general and as evidence for a particular theory about specific biological factors in the nature of woman. I have pointed out that characteristics and inferiority feelings which Freud considered to be specifically female and biologically determined can be explained as developments arising in and growing out of Western woman's historic situation of underprivilege, restriction of development, insecure attitude toward the sexual nature, and social and economic dependency. *The basic nature of woman is still unknown.*[9]

Both these women were practicing psychoanalysts, trained by students of Freud, working with male colleagues whose feelings and male bias had to be considered, if not catered to, else they risked total isolation, with a resultant inability to practice their already touch-and-go profession.

It is difficult enough for any artist, thinker, or scientist to be a revolutionary, but a woman is in double jeopardy, assailable because of her sex as well as her ideas. Horney and Thompson pointed out many of the male-oriented ideas in psychoanalytic theory, but they were often forced to adopt a temporizing tone. Like Reich, Horney tended to attack the master's theories by way of his followers' interpretation; it did neither of them any good, for both suffered expulsion from the society of the faithful. Writing after Freud's death, Thompson was able to attack Freud's essay "Economic Theory of Masochism," which was based on studies of male homosexuals: "What a passive male homosexual imagines about the experience of being a woman is not necessarily similar to female sexual experience."[10]

Where in history does the phallus cease to be an organ of enjoyment and become an organ of conquest? How far back can we trace the concept of aggressive sexuality, leading to sadism? One step is the worship of the animal horn as a symbol of male potency. Animal horns are like fingernails, bony growths consisting largely of keratin. Their purpose in animals is largely ornamental, with a secondary function of offense or defense. The phallus is of course made of flesh; blood is responsible for its erection; it is rich in nerve endings and sensation.

Only after humans have begun to control and breed animals, in particular the massive wild cattle, does the horn alone and unmistakably appear in conjunction with fertility worship. The new ideology—envisioning the human penis as a hunk of horn—denies the pleasurable aspects of sexual congress to focus on an ideal of the ever-ready breeder. In a positive view the phallus would be valued in all stages from the excitement of erection to the happy shrinking of realized satisfaction. The whole misplaced construct of the phallus as plow, harrow, sword, or gun begins in sadomasochistic imagery of fertility worship. Women are enslaved by being worshiped as mothers, more specifically as breeders. Men are enslaved to the religion of a massively erect phallus as weapon or producer. Nowhere in these metaphors is it acknowledged that the penis is an organ of exquisite pleasure. Even today, the horn survives as a symbol of luck, or procreation, and of male power. In the Mediterranean countries, one can still buy a good-luck amulet, a twisted horn, usually of red coral—the red, of course, relating to the red ocher used in burials from Paleolithic times on, the red of blood and of life, the whole being an amulet of fortune. On the other hand, when the ascetic antisex Christian religion entered the popular consciousness, the pagan horns of procreation were assigned to the devil, along with the satyrs' goat feet. A man became a cuckold wearing horns when his wife was "unfaithful"; he was reduced to a beast as his wife indulged in sex like the beasts, indiscriminately and without regard to capitalist or Christian possession. The two-finger sign of Mediterranean countries—extended forefinger and little finger signifying the horns which ward off the evil eye and ill luck generally—is another survival of the early religious propitiatory significance of the cattle symbol of male power and potency derived from the great discovery brought about by animal keeping and breeding.

A parallelism between cruelty and animal breeding shows up in many cultures. Pigs were domesticated in Europe and Asia, probably in several places, and are widely used today as food animals. Yet there are islands in Oceania where they figure in special religious worship and their primary importance is hardly for food. The men of Vao, the island off the coast of Malekula referred to earlier, worship an evil female deity, Le-hev-hev, in ceremonies which exclude women. Part of the worship centers around the breeding of boars raised for their circle tusks. Women do not participate in the raising or the eating of pig meat, and the men do not eat the sows—they eat only the male porkers. These animals are, however, reduced to sorry condition by the cruel practices which produce the most highly prized deformations—tusks which may be trained, ideally, to circle twice, even thrice, around, piercing the hapless animal's cheeks and jaws in the process.

The deformation is produced by knocking out the boar's upper canines so that the lower-jaw tusks, which grow in a curve, pierce the cheek flesh and re-enter the jaw. Sometimes they keep growing to form another complete circle, while those which produce a third circle have the highest value. The circle-tuskers are used in religious feasts, the only time they may be eaten. Not surprisingly they produce little meat. Therefore some of the boars are gelded and sacrificed before the tusks re-enter the jaws. According to Cranstone:

> Their value is much less but they provide more meat. For this reason pigs are often killed in pairs, a circle-tusker and a gelding. The circle-tusker is of value only while alive, and only if the tusks are in good condition; if a tusk is broken the pig is worth little. Its physical condition does not affect its value, but after death its tusks are worthless. . . . Tusked boars . . . become almost a form of currency, and a complex network of obligation comes into being. It appears too that the importance of pigs is such that land which

might be used for cultivation is left to provide foraging ground for them.

Sows are not eaten by either sex. Women may not,
because pigs are killed only in the context of ritual in
which women have no part. Men may not, because
sows being female are ritually dangerous to them.
Layard says of the cultivation of tusks: "This practice
lies at the base of the natives' whole overt religious
life, gives rise to the chief form of currency, and so
largely regulates all their economic activities . . . and
permeates every aspect of life."[11]

An effort has been made to link the Megalithic culture of
certain islands in Oceania—including Vao and the larger Malekula, settled from Southern Asia in waves beginning about
two thousand years ago—with the dolmens of Malta, Spain,
and Britain. Direct or indirect though the connections may be,
the parallelism between sadomasochistic practices and selective
animal breeding is found in widely separated areas of human
settlement.

Throughout the Mediterranean the history of sadistic animal
games is an ancient one. From Çatalian rituals to Cretan bull-
vaulting to the Iberian bullfight, there are overlappings of sexual repression, animal-human analogies, and proof of potency.
In Crete women and men participated in the games; in Spain
and Portugal the contest in cruelty is a demonstration of male
courage and ritualized torture.

"Murder is never asexual," said Norman Mailer, and the
butchering of animals we have befriended is also a form of
murder, recognized in the Italian curse, "Go die, slaughtered."†

† "Va a morire, ammazzato."

Part V

———————————

CIVILIZATION AND THE BIRTH OF THE PATRIARCHY

Be fruitful and multiply, and replenish the earth, and subdue it: and have dominion over the fish of the sea, and over the fowl of the air, and over every living thing that moveth upon the earth.

—Genesis 1:28

!Kung San mother and child. (*Photograph Melvin Konner/Anthro-Photo*)

Montagnais-Naskapi woman hunter setting snare. (*Photograph Richard Leacock*)

Venus of Laussel. Paleolithic relief sculpture, circa 24,000 B.P. *(Photograph Jean Vertut)*

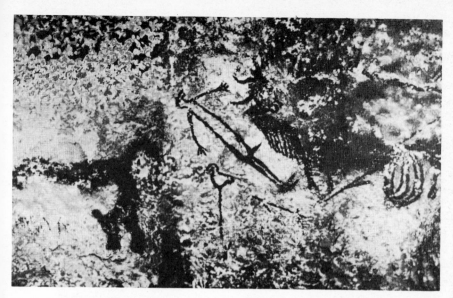

Shaft of the Dead Man at Lascaux. Cave painting, circa 12,000 B.P. *(Photograph Jean Vertut)*

The triune male genital and woman as a potential. Potsherd from Choga Mami, circa 7000 B.P. (uncalibrated radiocarbon date). *(Photograph Joan Oates)*

Uruk vase, circa 3200 B.C.E. Front view showing nude worshipers bringing gifts to the goddess Inanna. *(Courtesy Directorate General of Antiquities, Baghdad, Iraq)*

Bronze Age goddess from the bog at Viksø, Denmark. *(Courtesy P. V. Glob, Arch-eological Society of Jutland)*

The Goddess of War, central European ceremonial sculpture, circa 550 B.C.E
(*Photograph Fürböck, Graz, Austria*)

Defeated Britons—Roman soldier riding down women and children. Stone relief from the Antonine Wall, circa 150 C.E. (*Reproduced by courtesy of the National Museum of Antiquities of Scotland*)

Attis emasculating himself. Bronze statuette, circa 200 C.E. (*Courtesy of the Archaeological Museum of Split, Yugoslavia*)

23

The Power of Procreation:
From Matriliny to Patriliny

Four key factors are pivotal to the development of civilization, cities, and class society. These are plow agriculture, the castration of the bull to produce oxen for drawing the plows, irrigation, and increasing population. To a greater or lesser degree they have been accompanied by the rise of the patriarchy and the economic and sexual subjugation of women. The connections between the four are manifold: the ox is needed for large-scale agriculture made possible by canal irrigation, as well as for moving earth in the construction and control of the canal network, and the encouragement of childbirth results from the need for more labor to work the fields intensively, to watch and feed the animals, and to produce a surplus for the few people at the top of the pyramid which now begins to take shape in organizing human societies. Plow agriculture calls for animal raising and generally results in a switch from female to male cultivators using ox-drawn plows, from matriliny to patriliny, from community ownership to individual ownership of land, which is passed on from father to son.

These four phenomena make their appearance in the three thousand years between the disappearance of Anatolian Çatal Hüyük and the rise of cities in southern Mesopotamia, the home of the first "high civilization" in the history of human-kind. Different observers link the four phenomena in different causal relationships as they attempt to trace their origins. It is not known which appeared first and where, nor which was cause and which was result.

So far, representations of plows and draft animals date back only some 5,200 years ago, though it can be assumed that the animals and tools themselves existed considerably earlier. The earliest known vestiges of canal irrigation have recently been lo-cated in central Mesopotamia at a point more or less midway between pre-existing agricultural settlements to the north and the ancient Sumerian cities where it is believed that written history and the state began. Choga Mami is the name of a dig where archaeologists Joan and David Oates believe they have found traces of artificial water channels. These canals were in use over seven thousand years ago. And at the same time they find that population density was also increasing, as evi-denced by the size and number of settlements in the immedi-ate vicinity of these first earthworks. The presence of wooden plows and dredges and of oxen to draw them cannot be demon-strated at the site, but the existence of canals and of compara-tively large populations supported by a small amount of land is presumptive evidence for their use, as is the fact of a gradual increase in the number of cattle bones—1 per cent at the most ancient layers of occupation, increasing gradually to 9 per cent several hundred years later, at a time when an ambitious canal some fifteen feet wide ran past the largest settlement in the vicinity. Canalization entails digging ditches, moving large masses of dirt, and eventually controlling the flow of water over fields by means of dikes and sluice gates, all calling for an in-creased investment of human and, possibly, animal labor.

A curious fragment of pottery dated to the same period—some seven thousand years ago—was dug up in this settlement of Choga Mami: a potsherd whose design may shed some light on the causes and interrelationship of the above-mentioned piv-otal factors. It shows three geometricalized figures, a woman, a man, and a woman, linked arm in arm, and all display very specific genital areas (see Figure 5). The upper body of the male comprises a large inverted triangle whose point reaches the center of a horizontal bar, and from the bottom of the body triangle append three prongs, the outer ones shorter than the middle one. It looks for all the world like an unbalanced pitchfork and is one of the earliest extant representations of the triune male genital.

In Paleolithic painting and sculpture the emphasis had been on the penis, usually erected, not on the testicles; it was the excitement and activity of the male sex organ which drew attention, not its generative capacity. Clay cylinders from Paleolithic caves, stone cylinders from Siberian mammoth-hunting sites, as well as Neolithic cylinders from Jarmo and Tepe Guran in the Middle East, are often referred to as phalli by the excavators. Any long rolled shape can be seen as a phallus, and, to paraphrase Freud's "Gentlemen, sometimes a cigar is just a cigar," sometimes a cylinder is just a cylinder, a grinder, a spreader, a finger, or an unknown tool or ornament. Cautious investigators refer to these infrequently located artifacts as "possible penis objects."

A nine-thousand-year-old cylinder surfaced at the Deh Luran digs (discussed in Chapter 18) where early transitions between gathering and farming have been traced. A seven-thousand-year-old level produced a small sculpture, a flat-based oval on which a round and a cylinder shape join, looking rather like a clenched fist and upright index finger. A few similar sculptures were excavated at a dig near Choga Mami and contemporaneous with it—Sawwan—where about fifty alabaster sculptures of women were also found. The excavator at Sawwan had no hesitation about terming the six alabaster artifacts penises, though, if they are indeed phalli, it would seem that these early Near Easterners pictured themselves as having one testicle.

At Choga Mami, however, the three-in-one male sexual apparatus is complete and unquestionable. The emphasis on the testicles provides evidence for the new understanding which must have come from animal observation. The connection of the semen producers with reproduction, animal and human, may have been made through experiments in animal castration to produce tractable draft animals.

The two female figures also focus on increase, or at least the capacity for same. The plump little sculpture known as the Venus of Willendorf has a small but distinct mons veneris with the cleft of the vulva clearly incised; in other Paleolithic sculpture the vulva and female sexual triangle might be delineated. But in the clay fragment from Choga Mami, each woman is drawn with a large open diamond-shaped figure between her thighs, seemingly the original portmanteau of womb and vulva, the confusion which causes so many problems in later history.

Throughout the Near East many Neolithic sculptures portray women in every phase of life and maturity. Opulent "mother goddesses" from Çatal Hüyük and nearby Hacilar offer their breasts, embrace children, give birth, and possibly, as in the unique instance of the Çatal plaque, tell a story in two episodes—the embrace of two figures followed by its consequence, a mother and child. On the Choga Mami shard from a shallow bowl, however, where the women are schematically depicted with small upper-body triangles—one of which may have breasts—atop blocky, large-thighed lower halves, woman is seen as a potential, open, empty, waiting to be filled up, not bursting with life and sexuality as earlier and elsewhere. The emphasis in male and female figures is on reproduction rather than fulfillment.

It cannot be a coincidence that this suggestive drawing dates from a time when, according to site surveys, a population explosion was taking place in northern and central Mesopotamia and just before the same thing happens to the south. The emphasis on human increase combines with the results to which this emphasis led. The "penis objects" found at Sawwan and elsewhere may or may not demonstrate a knowledge of the male role in reproduction, but with the potsherd from Choga Mami, the concept of male seed and insemination enters human thought.

Though village life may have lowered the infant mortality rate, population growth was gradual and in certain areas, like Western Europe and much of Africa, barely noticeable for several millennia after the introduction of agriculture. There is a distinction between safe childbirth and survival and the worship of fertility for its own sake. The desirability of the first is unarguable; the second is open to debate. For the woman doing the bearing, many children are a dubious benefit. The more children, the more work; increased fertility of women is not a liberating factor, even if the children themselves are put to work at ever-earlier ages. Archaeological data demonstrate this proposition, showing the unceasing effort entailed by Neolithic peasant life. Where querns or grinding stones and pestles and handstones were found in small quantities during the earliest stage of Ali Kosh—in the Deh Luran excavations discussed previously—they have become omnipresent grave goods at neighboring Tepe Sabz some four thousand years later. Gordon Childe lauded this agricultural revolution, but Bertrand Russell remarked of it, "With the introduction of agriculture *man*kind entered upon a long period of meanness, misery, and madness, from which they are only now being freed by the beneficent operation of the machine."[1]

Here then is an explanation of the demographic fact of geometrically increasing population during the last several thousand years. It has been said that among primates there is an equal division of labor except for childbirth. It is a very unequal division.[2] In most languages, the words we use for reproduction of the species recognize that biology imposes an extra burden of work on women: *labor, carrying, nursing, bearing* . . .

Beginning several thousand years ago in the "fertile crescent," women of the ensuing civilizations and in many parts of the Afro-Eurasian triangle have been selected for fertility. This was not so in Oceania, Australia, and the Americas and may be a partial explanation for the "period of adolescent sterility" which puzzled anthropologists like Margaret Mead and Ashley Montagu. They could not understand why in Australia, the Trobriand Islands, and Samoa, despite seeming sexual freedom, girls did not usually conceive during the first few years after menarche. In Oceania and the Americas the religion of fecundity was not practiced, and women were not pushed into or selected for maximum exploitation of their reproductive talents. They make more ecological sense than we do. Among Australian Aborigines, for example, menarche occurs at about age fifteen, and women do not usually have their first child until age eighteen or nineteen, in contrast to our own society where twelve, eleven, even ten-year-old girls become pregnant and eighteen- and nineteen-year-old women may have already given birth to four, five, or more children.[3]

Animal breeding and its consequences, literal and analogous, were one side of the story; the fertility goddess is the other. Emphasis on fertility and on the mother goddess does not necessarily demonstrate the power of women in Neolithic society. When woman is worshiped for her "natural" powers, woe betide her humanity. Forced breeding and sexual repression go together. Limitations in the area of male-female sexuality led to the overdevelopment of maternal sexuality, and this in turn led to the subjugation of women as it is practiced in the historical Western patriarchy. As Adrienne Rich wrote, "Male domination has been founded on male control of female sexuality and reproduction, on institutionalized male ownership of women and children."[4] From the Near Eastern locus it spread throughout five continents, by a process of diffusion and conquest and in varying forms, superimposed on earlier traditions and with contradictory beliefs surviving or peering through the earlier scheme.

In the past, as in certain existing cultures, it was women who made the decision to prevent or abort pregnancies and to kill newborn children. When did they relinquish the decision-making function? We are taught that people do not willingly give up power. Did women decide to have more children or were they constrained to? How did the sensual and affective pleasure of maternal sexuality become transformed into the brutal institution of forced breeding?

Till recently it had been assumed that geometric population increases were a result of first the invention and then the development of more efficient agricultural methods, technological advances—that, in effect, humans are logical and efficient, and as civilization advances more people are born and survive. This is a hangover from nineteenth-century confidence which saw human evolution as a linear progression of conquest over nature, with industrialized Western white males in the vanguard. Actually, human populations have increased for many reasons: biological, medical, political. They have also been controlled and kept from increasing by women and by women and men in agreement. The demographic problem did not begin in this century, though Malthus' vision of it was a narrow and distorted one, his approach brutal and unnecessarily cruel.

We saw that the adoption of agriculture enabled more people to eat less well, from a small area, if they worked longer hours than the foragers had. Moreover, a gifted United Nations agronomist, Ester Boserup, deduced that, just as foragers spend fewer hours and less labor on feeding themselves than do farmers and modern industrial workers, in the same wise each technological advance in farming has required a higher input of labor per person for the corresponding increase in food production. From long-fallow cultivation using slash-and-burn techniques, through short fallow with hoe culture, plow agriculture using draft animals, and irrigation, under preindustrial conditions each new step necessitates more individual hours per person working and more people working. Only when there are more hands available for a given area of land will people voluntarily adopt the method which requires more labor.

The common impression is that by producing more food farming enabled more people to survive and that the agricultural revolution was the cause of geometrically increasing world populations. New information indicates that it was the increased labor attached to farming that demanded more people. The establishment of fertility worship resulted; it differed from the previous respect for women's generative powers. The breeding of animals suggested the control of women's reproductive capacities. Slaves were also captured to fill the need for more labor.

A steady natural increase of humans occurred during the foraging period of our existence, so small as to be barely perceptible in a ten-thousand-year slice of the whole, but humans did people all six continents before the adoption of farming. Beginning about ten thousand years ago, social factors—religion, politics, and imposition from above by rulers of conquering groups —led to sudden spurts in specific areas, eventually to the perilous condition in which we find ourselves today. The history of women's subjugation is shaped by changing attitudes and knowledge about human procreation. Where fertility is not valued, and birth control is practiced by women, population will not increase substantially. Because of distorting cultural and sexual traits, semistarvation and overpopulation appeared in specific areas thousands of years ago while others were unpopulated or well below their carrying rate, even for foragers, who need access to large areas of land.

Women are more specifically and immediately involved with population increase than are men. Discussants of the demographic problem often overlook this significant fact, given the confusion engendered by the English language's double use of the word *man*, as a generic term and as a specific sexual reference. Birth control and birth attitudes were originally regulated by women. We can trace society's increasing domination over reproduction as social, religious, and political institutions changed.

The linkage of the generative bull and the fecund woman at Çatal Hüyük is an early example of new religious emphasis; the three-pronged male and womb-containing females from Choga Mami are another. From a period several hundred years closer to us (about 4500 B.C.E.) come some provocative finds in cemeteries of two of the most ancient cities in Sumer. In Eridu, traditional home of Enki, the Sumerian god of water and wisdom, a lizard-headed figure with clearly delineated testicles and penis was unearthed in a woman's grave, while in Uruk, later known as the home of the goddess Inanna, several female figures with similar elongated reptilian heads were found.[5]

Peter Ucko, that gadfly of generalizers, has supplied data on the incidence of female and male sculptures found in Mediterranean and Near Eastern excavations during the prehistoric period, including these finds at Eridu and Uruk, sculptures often taken to be indicative of the worship of female or male deities. The great majority of figures are clearly female either with breasts or with "sexual triangle," many are sexless, and a few are male "as indicated by clear secondary sexual characteristics of male beard."[6] Male figures with penises are extremely scarce, while the lizard-headed male with full genital appurtenances from Eridu, like the drawing on clay from Choga Mami, is almost unique. Evidently and in spite of the example of animal breeding, the awareness of male procreatory function, as symbolized by sperm-producers, was indeed slow in arriving. That its arrival coincides with an awareness of property and property rights is not remarkable, since animals were the first self-propelling portable property whereas land stayed in one place and rights to its use would be vested in a communal clan or extended family.

One area where population increased suddenly and irregularly some five to six thousand years ago was ancient Mesopotamia, the land between the rivers. Scholars wonder whether the population increased intentionally so as to have more labor or whether a natural population increase created the new villages which led eventually to the civilization of Sumer. Why do large cities appear first in the unpromising area of southern Mesopotamia rather than in rich wooded areas, mountain valleys with large vegetable resources and much game? Why didn't the upland gatherers with more access to food expand their populations, especially if a few methods of food storage were used? Or, from another aspect, why is it that gatherer-hunters who today regulate their populations did not do so ten thousand or so years ago when the first farming societies began to develop?

The demographic problem goes back to the adoption of agriculture. With the coming of animal breeding and planting came also new concepts. State and religious ideology fosters the worship of possessions and fertility and accumulation. Progeny, both animal and human, are seen as wealth, and the accumulation of wealth becomes desirable only under certain forms of social development. In foraging societies, women controlled their own bodies and there was relatively little emphasis on material accumulation. Nomadic people have to travel light and possessions become a burden. Moreover, foragers know their environment well and have little insecurity about tomorrow's food; they feel no reason to hoard; they may not even have to store.

The insecurities of agriculture produce the emphasis on private possessions, while animal breeding, in telling the human male about his role in procreation, suggests the worship of the male sexual organ. In the domestication of cattle and the discovery of castration lay the roots of a religious development which both solved and caused problems. As I have noted, one bull, many castrates, and many cows set a pattern which influences human psychology for millennia to come. In Sumerian writings of later periods the king is a wild bull who mates with a goddess cow; temple personnel vowed to sexual sacrifice abound, be the sacrifice gelding, chastity, or ritual mating.

The misplaced analogy of seed and semen assigned generation to men. The worship of fertility in animal, plant, and human and the glorification of the phallus as seed producer: these are the religious and utilitarian vectors which influenced the rise of the patriarchy.

The metaphor of mother earth, reducing the female to passivity, was particularly damaging. Earth is soil, a mixture of minerals, air, water, and dead organic matter—hardly the same as the live body of a human woman, with its contribution of 50 per cent of the genes as well as a hospitable active environment which feeds the fetus through a shared circulatory system. In the absence of biological knowledge male semen, actually analogous to pollen, was credited with the power inherent in the fertilized egg; the female became a passive gestator receiving a fertile seed rather than the producer of one of two gametes which must unite, combining reproductive cells in order to produce an embryo, the animal equivalent of the fertilized seed which grows into a plant.

A difficult distinction should be emphasized: that between fertility as generation, the magic of creation, and fertility as production. The one was arbitrarily reassigned to man, the second left to woman in her capacity as childbearer. This was the doctrine used to subjugate the female of the species in most known civilizations. We treated ourselves as breeders treat animals, ignoring psychological, aesthetic, and human and natural principles.

Recent studies claim that a man's sexual capacity is more limited than a woman's, yet civilization has usually assumed the opposite. In absolute terms of physical-aesthetic considerations, the sexes are probably equal in their capacity for sensual enjoyment. Though the ancient Greeks did not think so—Tiresias was blinded by Hera when, having spent time both as a woman and as a man, he testified that women enjoyed the sexual act nine times more than men—I am inclined to agree with Keats: "Who shall say between Man and Woman which is the more delighted." By all accounts, delight is more frequently allowed for in nonliterate, small-scale societies than in our own tradition. Males and females have active physical sexuality, and both can be controlled volitionally. The repressed sexual energy finds outlet either constructively in artistic expression or destructively in sadomasochism. To some extent the sublimation must be voluntary else there is paralysis, numbing, and deadening. Why have women not contributed artistically and creatively in greater measure to historical civilizations? Though some of their contributions are masked behind anonymity or credited to male relations, they have also had their creativity enormously damped by the more rigid restrictions which have been their lot throughout Western, not to say world, history, the written story which begins at the same time as the arrival of severe sexual repression. It is also coeval with the authoritarian state and the patriarchal family, which I see as the state in microcosm rather than as its model.

Early indications of an emphasis on human reproduction are found in the area in which the first historical civilization arose. This is just before major population increases occur in lower Mesopotamia, in Egypt, and in the rest of the nuclear Near East.

Before the domestication of animals sex had been primarily an erotic pastime, though there must always have been some sense of its mystic nature. From the postfestival orgies of the Australian Aborigines to the Dionysian rites of the Greek matrons of classical times, from the sacred prostitution and temple rites of Near Eastern and Oriental religions down to today's gropings in the form of group-sex societies, etc., there has always been some recognition of the potential for transcendence inherent in orgasm. The way in which physical release can take us out of our conscious self and give us an illusion of union with the infinite is related to the human striving of religion, art, theater, ritual experience of various kinds. This is the curious ambivalence which makes sex the highest and the lowest, the most elevated as well as the most profane, of human experiences, the source of life-energy which permeates all nonmaterial and many material creations. It is this that makes orgasm the prototype for all mystic ecstasy (recognized intuitionally perhaps by Wilhelm Reich when he created the artificial construct of the orgone as the mysterious substance, source of healing and creative power for humans). Even when sex is renounced as the direct road, we seek to be transported outside the boundaries of the self, to erase our consciousness in orgies, drunkenness, drugs, religion, art, and varied mystical experiences.

Havelock Ellis recognized this numinous quality, terming it "the miraculous flame of sex." A sacred source of energy, it is connected with religion and art, in festival and in search of the divine. Originally sex was not a means, to be used in fertility rites, but a mystery—one facet of that human striving for transcendence, the which is inherent in orgasm but which is sought and achieved in many other ways, too, that need to escape the conscious self and merge with something larger which characterizes all religious, mystic, and artistic strivings. It is the paradox of humanity that our human, as derived from primate, nature is to be social, but to think is to be alone, and we are always striving to reconcile the conflict.

In the earlier times, as in many non-Western societies today, babies were something a woman produced from time to time, as sex was something a woman engaged in from the earliest age —sometimes even before puberty. In Melville Island and parts of Africa, for example, it is considered that sexual intercourse is necessary for the maturing of the female, to bring on puberty, while the Eskimo children who play at "putting out the lights," the Trobrianders, and the Samoans all engage in sexual play long before they are capable of reproducing themselves. Inhibitions about sex might well be one result of the knowledge that intercourse brings with it babies, so that a woman can choose to be childless by refusing to engage in sex, especially if birth-control methods are suppressed. On the other hand, if a premium is put upon having babies, then a situation may arise where the woman is validated chiefly by her production of children.

When women and men discovered that sex was connected with reproduction, things changed for both of them. Once it became connected with children, it took on a different dimension. Woman became a producer of children, not automatically but through her capacity for intercourse, and children themselves, in a settled agricultural community, became a source of wealth. According to Sandor Bokonyi, "Neolithic *man* recognized quite early that domesticated stock was the basis of 'wealth.'"[7] The analogies between possession of animals and their young and possession of women and children could only come about after the development of farming and animal keeping, and the exploitation of the labor of children as well as the exploitation of women as producers. Hence the beginnings of the materialization of sex and of the objectification of the female.

In a culture where it is taken for granted that all women will bring forth children we can see where women would be more sexually aggressive. Later on, with the results of sexual intercourse being manifest, there is more likelihood of women's being shy—the traditional attitude of civilization with man the aggressor and courter and woman the courted, the hesitant. The enjoyment of sex for the woman is now shadowed by the foreknowledge of its result—feared or desired.

We saw earlier that there is little emphasis on lineage among foragers, though the mother's (the uterine) family has the stronger pull. When people settled down on land, however, there was more reason to be concerned about hereditary rights. It seems likely that the inhabitants of Çatal Hüyük and Hacilar, as well as other villages of the period, traced their lineage from a common feminine ancestor, by way of mothers, the system commonly found among matrilinies in existence in Africa and the Americas.

In the nineteenth century, with the Western white rediscovery of peoples who traced descent through the mother and did not take account of the father's role in procreation, what is today called matriliny was dubbed matriarchy and Bachofen predicated it as a necessary, primitive form of family from which the more advanced and admirable patriarchy had developed. In the more sophisticated twentieth century it was observed that matriliny did not necessarily mean the power of women, and that in cases where descent was traced through the maternal line a woman might often be under the authority of her brother rather than of her husband, but she did not have *political* power herself.

Surviving matrilineal cultures take many forms, and women do not necessarily, nor even often, have what looks like real power in them. In her study *Male Dominance and Female Autonomy*, Alice Schlegel explains that she uses the term *autonomy* rather than *power* because she is not referring to "women's equivalence to men but rather to a woman's control over her person and her activities and her meaningful contribution to society beyond breeding and feeding."[8]

However, the very fact that descent is traced through the female line, rather than the male, gives woman a sense of her own identity in a way that the patriarchal system cannot. The magic of names alone is important. In the Western world a woman gives up her earlier self to shelter behind her husband's for the greater part of her life. In the case of Mrs. Richard Smith, as Dorothy Hage remarked, "it is as if her entire identity is summed up in that 's' tagged onto the man's name."[9] And in the novel *Small Changes*, Marge Piercy describes a woman searching for a woman friend, now married, who must seek her under a new name in the telephone book: "She had to find out that strange name before she could find her. Miriam Berg was no more. Abolished. Women must often lose a friend that way and never be able to find each other again."[10]

Contrast the advanced West with the Australian Tiwi culture, wherein each human being has her or his own name—a name carefully chosen which belongs only to that person, has never before pertained and never will pertain to any other Tiwi. Name magic exists everywhere—from the San to the Iroquois—though with us it would seem to be an evil magic which serves to erase the female. Only under special aristocratic circumstances is the name of the female line preserved. Spanish and Italian systems may include the names of both parents in the surname, postponing the erasure for one generation. Afterward, the mother's name is dropped, the father's perpetuated. (In Italy, it is customary to merge a woman's name into that of her husband when she marries: Maria Barone in Gambino.)

Under matriliny, however, the woman has both concrete and abstract perpetuation of the species vested in her and in the fruits of her belly. Even in male-dominant societies where, by Schlegel's criteria, female autonomy is low, it would still be higher in a matrilineal culture than in a patrilineal one. Comparing the better position of Ambo women with the generally low status of women among the patrilineal Herero, neighboring peoples in Southwest Africa, Schlegel reasons that when women are the link between the past and the future they have a dignity which is otherwise lacking and that both men and women must think differently about the status and importance of women in such cases. Descent systems thus are influential in setting up the image of oneself as a woman or as a man and determining how one behaves to one's fellows, of whichever sex.

From the long millennia of Neolithic agriculture, we have only tantalizing archaeological hints—the burial arrangements at Çatal Hüyük, the size of the houses at Neolithic Jericho, the finding of so many female figurines, the composition of the grave goods—on which to base speculations about Neolithic households. Imperfect as they may be, analogies are often made with recently existing matrilineal groups. One of the most thoroughly studied matrilinies was the group of American Indians banded together as the Iroquois League. They provided evidence for the nineteenth-century anthropologist Lewis Morgan, and the book he wrote in turn influenced Engels and in consequence the way in which Marxists today think about early groupings. Certainly women among the Iroquois did, at the time of the first contact with whites, have enormous power and prestige. Even after their economy had been influenced by the introduction of alien elements like the gun and fur trapping—both of which strengthened the male role at woman's expense—these women continued to retain their influence.

In questions of economy and inheritance Iroquois women were more important than men, in religion their equals. Skilled agriculturalists in a fertile region with ample land to draw on, although men helped in the forest-clearing of the fields, it was the women who did the planting, cultivating, and harvesting of crops. This was accomplished by means of "mutual aid societies" consisting of all of the women of the village. The women managed the households, and were in charge of the succession of family titles. They were matweavers, carvers of bark utensils, and makers of clothing. Men had different specialties—they made weapons and were warriors (although war seems to have arrived chiefly with white conquest), and they carved wooden ornaments. In religion and ceremony, offices were divided equally between the sexes. Some of the medicine societies were composed exclusively of men, some of women, while in others equal numbers of women and men participated.

The matrilineal Iroquois family consisted of a head woman (the matron) and her daughters and sons, the daughters and sons of her daughters, and so on. There were matrilineal families consisting of three or four living generations which numbered fifty or less, while others were composed of one hundred and fifty or more members.

With women taking care of the economic responsibilities, it is believed that the men were free to engage in political organization, which may have led to the founding of the Iroquois League of the Six Nations. As for hunting, a Jesuit observer wrote in 1653, "The Hurons and other peoples distant from the sea, who are sedentary, hunt only for pleasure, or on extraordinary occasions."[11]

As with so many other American Indian peoples, our view of the Iroquois has been colored by the Western white conquest mentality as well as by changes wrought in their culture and the impetus to war introduced by the European conquerors. The Neuters, a tribe of Indians bordering the League's western territories, state that Iroquois women "held political offices alternately with men." It seems more probable that it was the women, the elder matrons, who appointed the sachems—the peace chiefs—who were the prime political powers before the expansion of the warrior complex that occurred during the hundred years between 1650 and 1750. Buell Quain wrote:

> Coming to a unanimous agreement the women of the maternal line chose the child successors to a series of names which might culminate in high administrative titles of community or nation . . . in former times women carefully watched and censured the behavior of their titled men. If a sachem expressed opinions contrary to what they considered the general welfare, and persisted in his misbehavior, they removed him from office. . . . At marriage it was the principle matrons of each participating family who arranged and decided the matches.[12]

It is the contention of the same author that, as with so many other nonliterate peoples, it was white contact which destroyed the Iroquois, not only by direct conquest but also by corruption of their earlier pattern of existence. By the time of the Revolutionary War the importance of the class of warrior chieftains had so increased that sachems, or civil chiefs, were little more than honorary titles. The rise of militarism, if not completely dependent on European contact, did receive a powerful stimulus from it. The two sets of ideals—peaceful co-operation toward national ends and competition for individual war glory—oppose each other. The growth of the latter was a symptom of the former's decay. Military emphasis was a mutation which grew in inverse proportion to the decline of the old order.

Only at the end of the nineteenth century did the United States Government succeed in breaking the men's resistance to agriculture. Before that, the Iroquois women, with their mutual aid societies, enjoying the pleasure of group work, their co-operative living, and group councils, would seem to have been a

prime example of women's talent for leadership and co-operation, the nonexistence of which was claimed in a book that had
a certain popular success some years ago.[13]

The Iroquois women were not the only Indian women to
own property and houses and to delegate power. This is true of
the Hopi women to this day, and was true of Eastern woodland
Cherokees and of the Mandans, who were farmers and bison
hunters on the Missouri before the introduction of the horse
on the North American continent completely changed the
economy and psychology of many Amerindian groups. Though
anthropologists who studied North American Indians during
the nineteenth and twentieth centuries found both matrilineal
and patrilineal groups, there is evidence that bands which had
been matrilineal often changed to patriliny under white
influence and as a result of changes created by the European
market for furs.[14]

Despite the flourishing economies created by Amerindian
groups like the Iroquois and the Cherokee, there is a widely
prevalent view today that matriliny exists only in stagnant agricultural backwaters similar to the earliest periods of Neolithic
agriculture, while patriliny is a necessity for growth and
efficient use of resources. Mary Douglas questions this assumption in an essay examining matriliny and patriliny in recent
ethnographic contexts. Equating growth with increase of
wealth, differentiation, and inequality, she notes that anthropologists believe descent is traced through the mother only in
poor, egalitarian economies. Matrilineal groups are organized to
recruit members by means other than direct inheritance. The
Ashanti have ranking systems and hierarchies, but they emphasize descent from a common womb rather than close lineal connections. Douglas finds that in matrilineal systems the emphasis is on alliances between groups rather than on exclusiveness
of individual groups. Matriliny does not, of itself, provide a
strong authority system. Leadership by achievement is encouraged. An open authority system is not necessarily disad-
vantageous. If it encourages achievement in some circumstances, it can have great adaptive value.[15]

One would think that the qualities inherent in matrilineal groups, "open recruitment of talent and *man*power, strong intergroup alliance, scope for achievement," would indeed be of great adaptive value, and yet a majority of groupings in the last five thousand years of the planet's history have been in the opposite direction. How did this happen? Patriliny, we note, is commonly found with the plow, with the raising of animals, with the herding of animals. Animal breeding set off a chain of events, an unhappy and augmenting combination of psychological and economic elements, with the result that civilization was based on an economy of scarcity in the same wise that the Pyramids were built on the backs of slaves, of laborers forced or convinced to donate their time.

Patriliny is more effective for growth only where things are more important than people and where people are produced as things, tools to be used for the aggrandizement of others, be they priests, warrior kings, or fathers. This is the etiology of patriarchy, and of all known civilizations, using *civilization* in the narrow technical sense of societies embodying cities and technology and writing, not in the broad idealistic sense with which the upper-class beneficiaries of these factors have often endowed the word.

Patriliny maximizes possession; matriliny maximizes group co-operation and recruitment of hands. Patriliny is effective for growth where there is a shortage of food and other resources. Combined with polygyny it produces maximum increase of population, who are then available to hierarchical powerholders for increased production of goods inequitably divided. Matriliny opens up the authority system and makes more effective use of human initiative and ingenuity. It would probably have been more flexible than patriliny, but once males discovered their role in fathering children, an overcompensation developed. In a mistaken notion of biology, seed and semen were equated. Male seed then came to be worshiped as a source of prosperity, of grain, animals, and above all children. Patriliny and its concomitant, patriarchy, are more efficient for producing a large number of children than either matriliny, even with men wielding power, or matriarchy, if such ever existed. The system in use today in our own society, bilateral inheritance, is weighted in favor of patriliny through names, preferential inheritance, and other prerogatives, but it incorporates some advantages of the earlier system.

24

Women in Sumer

Sumerology, a study that began only in the last fifty years, has shown that the Sumerian network of city-states—Uruk, Nippur, Lagash, Ur, Eridu, Umma, and Kish are a few of them—was the first truly urban civilization, as opposed to the castle ruling over the countryside of ancient Egypt or Crete. Many of our laws and customs are incipient in the Sumero-Akkadian state, and a direct line can be traced by way of the Old Testament, which reflects and borrows from Sumero-Akkadian writings— laws and business transactions and literary works—as well as from subsequent records in other areas of the ancient Near East.[1] Sumer in the south was the earliest urban center; Akkad in the north developed subsequently and merged with the older civilization.

Sumer is axiomatic, not because it necessarily represents the first civilization—we do not know what was going on elsewhere at the same time—but because a clear line can be traced through Sumer and Babylon to the Hebrews and certain neighbors of the Sumerians, the Hittites, the Greeks, and other Indo-European nomad tribes, leading to our own civilization and customs. Hence my focus on extant details of Sumerian writings, mythology, and archaeological finds. Most of history is known through the viewpoint of those in power, and Sumer is no exception. The story of the decline of women and of the underclasses is written between the lines; often it must be deciphered in reverse, like mirror writing.

The role of women in early Sumer compared favorably with that of women in later history: Hebrew, Greek, even Victorian women could not avail themselves of many of the rights of the Sumerian woman. She could be a religious officiant, own property, sign contracts, engage in business, be a witness. Compare this with Jewish law, where one hundred women do not equal one male witness, or the English common-law concept of *feme covert*, which made married women nonexistent, their legal status encompassed by the phrase "married women, infants, and lunatics." Her position was strongest in the earliest period and progressively deteriorated.[2]

On the face of it, Mesopotamia was an unpropitious land for the developments which there occurred, lacking in raw materials like lumber and metal, subject to sudden severe storms, extremes of heat and cold, swirling dust clouds and drought, and generally unpredictable weather. Complex irrigation systems, the use of ox-drawn plows and dredges, and a large supply of labor were needed to produce the twice-yearly returns of barley which formed the basis of its economy. It rose to preeminence through a combination of trade, conquest, and sheer organization.

Essential to this development was an expanding population, today seen as a prerequisite for rather than the result of Sumerian technological advances.

By the middle of the fourth millennium, about 3500 B.C.E., the southernmost part of Mesopotamia, the land of Sumer, was a network of small fishing, herding, and agricultural villages, of modest material development, governed by an assembly of elders, women and men, with a leader, elected or volunteer, who had to be careful in asserting authority not only to shape but also to reflect the will of the assembled townspeople.[3] This is "primitive democracy," the system used by many small-scale gathering and horticultural societies, and it is believed that the earliest governing bodies in the southern cities grew out of these first councils.[4]

Within the next two or three centuries a sudden change took

place. Throughout the Near East population had been gradually increasing over the thousands of years—sixteenfold in 4,000 years in the area of the early Deh Luran villages. In Sumer, however, site surveys show that about 3300 B.C.E. the number of inhabitants doubled within a very brief period—say, a hundred years. The reasons for this sudden spurt are not known. People from agricultural villages like Choga Mami and Sawwan may have emigrated south, bringing with them their knowledge of irrigation and cattle raising, mixing with or swamping the local inhabitants. Gathering nomads may have taken up farming and animal keeping. Herdspeople may have settled down in the area in some symbiotic relationship with existing villages or combined the herding way of life with complementary means of subsistence such as fishing.[5] Or a combination of two or more of the above factors may have led to economic, political, and ideological change.

Shortly after this change, another shift in population density took place, possibly as the result of the first increase. This was the growth of cities, unrelated to increasing population.

Uruk is characteristic. Around 3500 B.C.E. it was a ceremonial center with two temples, the Eanna (house of the goddess Inanna) and the White Temple, surrounded by many small towns and villages of equal importance. Within the next few hundred years Uruk's population grew from 10,000 to 40,000. This did not represent a regional increase; it resulted from the abandonment of outlying settlements during these centuries. A defensive wall requiring "prodigious labor" was built at the turn of the millennium, and villages were either "compelled or persuaded" to move within its precincts.

Elsewhere in Sumer similar events were taking place. Whole districts outside the city centers were seemingly abandoned: in Nippur, several hundred miles to the north, perhaps even earlier; in Larsa, in Ur, in Umma and Lagash, several hundred years later and by slightly different processes. After 3000 B.C.E. intercity warfare, kingship, and class differentiation can be traced—for the first time.

The earliest form of government for the cities of Sumer was theocratic; the city was organized around a temple, for it was the gods who brought protection and ensured fertility. Reflecting the common tendency toward teleological reasoning, most historians say that the theocracy in Mesopotamia, the rule of priests and a temple, arose in part from physical hardship since the temple was a storehouse of food, given the chancy nature of farming in the southern Mesopotamian flood plain. However, Sumerian religion early focused on reproductive plenty—of harvest, of animals, of humans. With the increase of anxiety after agriculture, it seems to me that once the hoarding mentality occurred, the development of fertility worship was a response, a syndrome which led to expanding power.

Fertility worship set the stage for the temple as an institution—and the Sumerian cult of fertility worship goes back into the fourth millennium. The Uruk vase pictured in Figure 7, dates from that era and is a three-foot-high alabaster vessel. It shows the city goddess Inanna, or a priestess representing her. Clothed and crowned, she welcomes a procession of naked men bearing gifts to the village storehouse. Behind her is the temple, signified by the reed gateposts, the altar with its vases, animals, and fruits, and, on lower registers, the cattle, sheep, and grain that represent material plenty.

Two essays of Thorkild Jacobsen set forth the evidence enabling us to project "primitive democracy" as the governing system of the southern cities. Jacobsen looks to the myths written down more than a thousand years later in his explanation, but he supports his assumption with archaeological findings from the end of the fourth and the beginning of the third millennia. In the myths the gods and goddesses are organized into a bicameral assembly: sometimes it is the fifty senior deities and seven lawmaking gods and goddesses who meet; at other times the fifty elders constitute an upper house and the rest of the gods and goddesses the lower house. In any case, it is an assembly in which "goddesses as well as gods played an active part."[6]

In researching the archaeological evidence, Jacobsen points out that the Sumerian word *unkin*, meaning a general assembly of all the citizens, occurs in the earliest documents, the Uruk tablets from protoliterate times (before 3000 B.C.E.). An-

other word appearing in these earliest texts, in which only individual words, not records or sentences, can be distinguished, is
en, which in later days means priest or priestess, sometimes lord
or delegate. The word for the autocratic military leader, which
came to denominate the hereditary office of king, is *lugal*, and
this word does not appear until several hundred years later, in
the Early Dynastic I tablets found at Ur. The words for the
king's palace and for the earliest forms of military organization
—soldiers, sergeants, company, and colonels—also appear for
the first time on these Ur tablets, whereas the cuneiform symbol for a temple has been a constant since the very first appearance of written words.

The first control was that of elders over youngers, which
could and can verge on tyranny. While decisions over general
welfare were probably made by a council of elders (note, however, that among the Iroquois it was a council of women), it is
likely, both from literary mythic references and from ethnographic analogy, that marriages and sexual unions had been arranged by mothers, who could be expected to have some degree
of understanding for their children, and that fair amounts of
choice and experimentation were allowed for. As the landhold-
ing and property-accumulating system developed, control became fiercer, especially when centered in an autocratic head
rather than in a council of wise elders. These latter would have
some understanding of the foibles and desires of youth, even if
they insisted on respect for their own privileges. They might
also exercise tolerance, since their own positions were not
achieved by force but derived from mutual respect and were
subject to the will of the group. A regime dependent on the
pleasure of the ruled—one in which the leaders follow the
wishes of the group almost as often as they impose their own—
differs in essence and application from one supported by armed
force, and the latter appears only after about 3000 B.C.E.

In the south records attest to clan ownership of land. Farming was made possible only by large-scale reclamation, diking,
and clearing of land, necessitating community co-operation.
Marsh dwellers in reed huts and island settlements lived largely

on fishing, with hunting and gathering as supplements, though cattle herding came to be practiced later.

According to Sumerian tradition, their oldest city was Eridu, located on a fresh-water lagoon in the southernmost part of Mesopotamia, a tradition supported by archaeological findings which have traced Eridu's temple building to before 4000 B.C.E. Eridu's population and importance had already begun to decline by the time Nippur and Uruk had achieved temporal status, but it kept its prestige as the home of Enki, the god of water and wisdom, and of his mother, Nammu, the goddess of pools and of the deep, the fresh water beneath the land. In third-millennium cylinder seals, Enki is depicted with streams of fish cascading from his shoulders, and a layer of fishbones on an early temple altar substantiates the hypothesis that Eridu was originally a fishing village. Nammu figures in myths which were written down only after 2000 B.C.E., and there is good reason to believe that she originally played a much more important role than those ascribed to her in the myths.

The earliest indications of private property, in the form of individual seals dated to circa 4500 B.C.E., came from northern Mesopotamia. This was the land which had had the earlier development of mixed farming—animal keeping and grain cultivation. On the fringes of the settlements, sheep and cattle herders, recently converted from foraging, may have had symbiotic relationships with the farmers. Patriliny is the likely form of social organization in either case.

In the south, communal ownership of land, later attested by contracts and inheritance records, hung on long into the third millennium. The earliest development of cities in south Mesopotamia may have come out of group co-operation and out of group ownership of resources centering on matrilineal clans with the temple as organizer.

By historical times northern private ownership had combined with southern organization to produce the league of city-states known from tradition and record. Initially it was a league of states centered around the city of Nippur, whose god Enlil became important in the Sumerian pantheon. This league broke up into competing warring states. Eventually, temporary rulers appointed by the council seized power and achieved domination over other city-states.

Mesopotamian history used to be given as a record of conflict between Sumerians in the south and Semites, peoples of the northern agricultural and mountainous part of Mesopotamia as well as of the western deserts of Syria and Canaan, who spoke languages belonging to a common family—Akkadian, Assyrian, Babylonian, and the later Aramaic and Hebrew. Some scholars felt that the Sumerians were more democratic and more pro-woman than the Semitic peoples. Thorkild Jacobsen has demonstrated, however, that Sumerians and Semites had lived peacefully together from the earliest times, with conflict breaking out only as the city-state develops. The north is earlier associated with animal keeping and private property, the south with group ownership.

The causes of the shift were probably economic rather than racial. The imposition of a superstructure, first theocratic, then military and monarchical, led to demands for the expansion of tribute. The surplus for this tribute was not inevitable; it was an artificial exaction, requiring either force or ideological imposition by the state, which demanded labor and goods. Hence the change from matriliny, which utilizes talent, to patriliny, which maximizes possession and production and control.

This change in the status of women in Sumer is taking place during the third millennium, the time when the first kingdoms arose.

In the words of *1066 and All That*, was civilization "a Good Thing"? Until recently, with a few exceptions, the answer was always positive.* Even now we hear of the great inventions of

---

* Tacitus saw clearly how civilization functioned for the conquerors: "To induce a people, hitherto scattered, uncivilized, and therefore prone to fight, to grow pleasurably inured to peace and ease, Agricola gave private encouragement and official assistance to the building of temples, public squares and private mansions. . . . He trained the sons of chiefs in the liberal arts. . . . The result was that in place of distaste for the Latin language came a passion to command it. In the same way our National dress came into favor. . . . And so the Britons were gradually led on to the amenities that make vice agreeable—arcades, baths, sumptuous banquets. *They spoke of such novelties as 'civilization,' when really they were only a feature of enslavement.*" Or, in Engels' words: "From its first day

writing, metallurgy, urban configurations, trade, etc. But, looking at the record, it would seem that it was a good thing for a
relative few. Robert M. Adams remarks on the increasing emphasis on militarism, as reflected in the construction of fortifications, in the mustering and equipping of large bodies of soldiers, in the emphasis on martial equipment in the "Royal
Tombs of Ur," and in the many myths, epics, and historical
inscriptions which tell of fighting and battle among the city-
states themselves. He concludes that the early Mesopotamian
cities were "amalgams brought together to increase the economic well-being and offensive and defensive strength of a very
small, politically conscious superstratum." For the vast majority, he adds, the advantages of the city—protection for one's
personal and household goods within the walls, as well as access
to the temple stores of food in case of enemy siege or natural
disaster—had to be balanced against heavy demands on the individual for taxes and military and work (corvée) service. Most
of the population was tied to the city only under varying degrees of duress and was only marginally affected by the most
characteristically urban institutions.[8]

The war leader appointed by the council of the earliest times
—perhaps about 3000 B.C.E.—was transformed into a king some
hundred or two hundred years later. One of the early kings,
Gilgamesh, entered literature as the hero of a group of tales
describing his adventures. He is credited with having built the
huge walls encircling Uruk, Inanna's city, and in the epic
that bears his name the warfare between Inanna and Gilgamesh—the female deity and the semi-divine or later deified
male—reflects the decline in status of the female, both goddess
and mortal.

The institution of kingship took shape over the next few
hundred years. Our information comes from the Sumerian
King List, which often attributed reigns of obviously mythical

---

to this, sheer greed was the driving spirit of civilisation; wealth and again
wealth and once more wealth, wealth, not of society but of the single
scurvy individual—here was its one and final aim. If at the same time
the progressive development of science and a repeated flowering of supreme
art dropped into its lap, it was only because without them modern wealth
could not have completely realized its achievements."[7]

length—36,000 years to one of Gilgamesh's forerunners, Dumuzi, who turns up in mythology as the husband of the
goddess Inanna and is subsequently worshiped as a dying fertility god. Though the data in the King List are fictionalized,
building inscriptions demonstrate that most, if not all, of the
people named were based on historical personages. There was
one queen on this list—Ku-Baba, who reigned for a hundred
years and founded the dynasty of Kish, in the north. As "a
woman of wine"—a tavern keeper and wine seller—who became
queen, she was the legendary patroness of the alehouse, the
wineshop, and of alcoholic beverages. Though Ku-Baba may
have been a real queen, she is sometimes identified with the
later Anatolian goddess Cybele, worshiped with wine and rev-
elry, as well as with the fertility goddess of Çatal Hüyük.

Sometimes, leaders or would-be kings would seize power by
claiming to restore justice to the people. One such was Urukagina of Lagash, whose *apologia pro vita sua* has been preserved
and translated. It provides further evidence to suggest that matrilineal egalitarianism preceded patriarchal hierarchy. Claiming inspiration from Nanshe, the goddess of justice and mercy,
the king boasts of restoring freedom—*amargi*—in relieving the
people from encroachments and impositions which had developed in recent times.[9] As pointed out by Adam Falkenstein
and reiterated by Samuel Kramer in accepting his translation,
the word *amargi* means literally "return to the mother." But,
says Kramer, "we do not know why it came to signify freedom." Feminists have no problem with this concept. The return to the mother is a return to the mother-centered family of
matriliny.[10] I would theorize that it refers to a folk memory of
a time when there was a preclass, prepatriarchal society—a
golden age with no slavery, no kings, no employer in the form
of temple or private landowner, no forced labor or forced military service, no heavy produce appropriations (taxes) by temple
or king.

It has been pointed out that there is a certain amount of distribution even in egalitarian economies, when the food gathered, hunted, or grown by one or several individuals is shared
out around the hearth or among close relatives. It does not,

however, grow more complex than the pooling and reallotment of stored food for an extended family—the presumed matrilineal clan of Neolithic days. The key role in the initial form of redistribution is often played by the oldest woman in the active generation, since she usually administers the household and runs the kitchen.[11] On the Uruk vase of the fourth millennium the woman who stands at the temple gate welcoming the procession which bears grain and fruit and animals to the storehouse is a personification of the guardian of the stores, though seen as a young divinity, the goddess Inanna.

Thus freedom would have been associated with the weak and open authority system that, as Mary Douglas pointed out, is a characteristic of matrilineal society, rather than with the tight restriction of the first hierarchies, which produced the early forms of civilization in Mesopotamia. Return to the mother did not mean freedom in any absolute or modern sense. *Amargi* referred to the relative freedom that had existed under the theocracy and under the extended-clan family system that preceded it, as both preceded the war-leader-turned-king of the dynastic stage. This evolution—from village, to temple state, to monarchy—began in the middle of the fourth millennium, a thousand years before Urukagina's edict, and was substantially completed some five hundred years later at the time of the building of the Uruk city wall during the legendary reigns of the first kings.

Sumero-Akkadian royal edicts and law collections tell about their mores and the changes which took place over the millennia. Urukagina's Reform is the earliest extant record, currently dated to about 2450 B.C.E. One is reminded that when Hitler took power his initial speech proclaimed, "We must have law and order!" In the same way, Urukagina claims to have triumphed over the power of the priests. He tells of lands unfairly appropriated, of high taxes, and of other abuses, from all of which he has relieved the people. One provision makes it seem likely that selective monogamy, bearing more heavily on the woman than on the man, was a fairly recent development in third-millennium Sumer. It would seem that in the fourth millennium both serial monogamy and polyandry existed, as well as polygyny, as they often do in non-Western small-scale societies. Urukagina forbids women to take two husbands, as they had been wont to do in previous times, on pain of being stoned to death.

After Urukagina, a progressive deterioration occurs in the rights and role of women. Sumerian myth usually has the goddess refer to her mother's house or ask her mother's permission in marriage; the later Akkadian myths refer to a father's permission, though the house may still be the mother's. In third-millennium writings, too, one reads of fathers and mothers arranging marriages, while later law collections refer only to fathers.

Divorces were obtainable in Urukagina's time; his edict eliminates the fee demanded by the chief priest in granting them, without specifying other conditions. Four hundred years later, a collection of laws testifies to the value placed on women: men pay for the privilege of marriage with bride price, and a man who divorces his wife must also give her alimony—"a mina of silver."[12] Two hundred years later, in another set of laws both bride price and dowry exist and a man who leaves his wife for another woman must continue to support the wife.[13]

By the time of Hammurabi, the Babylonian king who reigned from 1785 through 1759 B.C.E. (circa), a husband could divorce his wife at will, though he had to return her dowry.[14] (Five hundred years later, under the Middle Assyrian laws—applying to the northern Mesopotamian kingdom of Assyria—he could divorce his wife at will, and "if he wants, he may give her something."[15])

There are instances in Sumer of women acting as regents for their sons or ruling by themselves for brief periods, but nowhere near as many as in ancient Egypt, where, for example, Queen Hatshepsut ruled for some forty years. Her rule was an exception even in Egypt, however, as shown by sculptures where Hatshepsut is depicted with a long, curled beard, the symbol of male authority. Though female autocracy is not necessarily better than male autocracy, for ordinary women the rule of queens and the worship of goddesses allows for a stronger self-identity.

In the earliest times women and men were high priests, with political and religious power. Sometimes a man would be priest for the goddess, a woman for the god. By historical times, in the period when the kingship had evolved, the office of high priestess was an honor reserved for the daughter or wife of a king. Her duties would be chiefly ceremonial, though there were exceptions. Sargon of Agade, the first Akkadian ruler, unified north and south Mesopotamia about 2400 B.C.E. and built the capital city of Agade, from which came the name Akkadian. His daughter Enheduanna was a poet whose work was copied down and transmitted through the centuries. As high priestess, she may have played a political role in her lifetime. In general, however, it was the priests who wielded temporal and administrative authority in the goddess' service, or the king might hold the offices of king and priest together. About 2000 B.C.E., under a later king, Shulgi, there were many women appointed to administrative duties in the collection of animals for the temple, a form of taxation. A few hundred years later, by the middle of the second millennium, however, the custom of appointing priestesses as high officiants seems to have disappeared; only high priests figure in the service of goddesses and gods.

The participation of women in work is not to be taken as an index of equality. In Sumer and Akkad as elsewhere women worked hard and along with men, in the fields and in manufacturing. By the middle of the third millennium certain humble occupations had a predominance of women workers. Women invented and specialized in producing barley beer and later wine, made in southern Mesopotamia from dates, and are cited as keeping wineshops and taverns.[16] In palace and temple there were probably always more women in service than men. Many women were employed in the temple industries connected with the main needs of food and clothing, in the stores and kitchens, in the flour mills and as spinners and weavers in the cloth factories, most of whom appear to have been slaves. If they had children, they received a small allowance for these helpers or dependents. A superior order of attendants—personal maids, hairdressers, nurses, and cooks—waited on the chief priest's wife and children.[17]

A provocative article by Assyriologist I. J. Gelb[18] gives some indication of the minimal existence of these workers, slave and semislave, from about 2500 to 2000 B.C.E. on, and what it meant to be a woman captive, slave or "semi-free." During that epoch, women received half as much food as men; both were paid in monthly rations of barley, yearly ones of wool, and regular—perhaps four times a year—distributions of oil, and occasionally paid also in peas, dates, and fish. During the period before Sargon's conquest of Sumer, during his reign, and later, in the Sumerian revival known as the Third Dynasty of Ur, the systematization of rations applied in widespread areas of Mesopotamia and neighboring Elam. Forewomen received more than did ordinary slaves and "semi-free" workers.† The former received forty "quarts" of barley per month as opposed to thirty for ordinary workwomen, though less than the sixty commonly allotted to men, both ordinary workers and foremen. Peasant farmers—free men—received 125 quarts of barley a month as pay, in addition to the normal food allotment. Old men received less than other adult men but more than ordinary women, who in turn received more than old women. Sometimes male children were allotted more food than female ones, but not always.

In the dispute over which came first between the sexes, larger size and strength for males or differential feeding, Gelb, like most male historians, opts for the former by stating that those who did harder physical work received more food. However, the Mesopotamian ration system would certainly result in selection of females for smallness. In this scheme, which is followed, if less rigidly and systematically, in many parts of the world today, genetically tall women would be less likely to survive to reproductive age on minimal rations than those whose inheritance demanded less protein and caloric intake for full

† The phrase is Gelb's and the distinction is not clear, for the same word, *geme*, literally "mountain woman," is variously translated "captive," "slave," and "worker" attached to a household, temple, workshop, or palace.

growth. All women would have been stunted in comparison to men, since the difference in size between male and female humans is not 50 per cent, but more like 10 or 11, similar to that between female and male chimpanzees but unlike, say, the hamadryas baboons.[19] Small wonder that femininity and femaleness became synonymous with weakness, softness, tenderness, while the dictionary defines male as "robust, strong."

The first authoritarian and controlling governing bodies, centered on matrilineal clans, with marriages arranged first by mothers and later by mothers and fathers, were, then, over a period of centuries perverted to the service of individual strong leaders. As class stratification set in, women could, in the beginning, keep up with their males and achieve positions on their own, though usually on a somewhat lower or more insecure footing. The categories of class and caste with regard to women —you're always in the caste of women no matter how high you rise on the ladder of class—are taking shape in this period.

25

The Decline of the Mother Goddesses

Life-giving semen, life-giving seed,
King whose name was pronounced by Enlil,
Life-giving semen, life-giving seed,
Ninurta whose name was pronounced by Enlil.
—Sumerian hymn (circa 2000 B.C.E.)[1]

Most of us were brought up to believe that monotheism was a great advance over polytheism, while for some of us atheism was the next step forward. Leaving aside the question of theology and comparative religion, it strikes me that as there is no progress in art so there is no progress in religion (matters of the spirit), which can be seen as an intensely serious aspect of art if not its original expression.

Before it could be said that God created *man*, humans had to conceive of God. We invented divinity, not vice versa. The mother goddess was imagined not by one or the other of the sexes but by women and men locating the power of creation outside the material body of the human being on earth who was born, fucked, gave birth, and died.* That the deity was

---

* It is a measure of our English language and attitudes that there is no simple matter-of-fact verb like the Australian Aborigine *muna-muna*—apart from the biological "copulate"—only awkward circumlocutions like "have sexual intercourse" or harsh and male aggrandizing vulgarisms. (In Partridge's Dictionary of Slang, we are told that a woman can be fucked, she

female meant that woman herself partook of some divinity as childbearer identified with a female creator, though it was a divinity that hedged and circumscribed her activities. Whether the worship of the supreme mother goddess everywhere preceded the worship of the father god is impossible to determine at the moment. It is certain that there was a mother goddess, that she was worshiped, and that her worship declined, not to say disappeared, with the rise of patriarchal religion, though it was never possible to stamp it out completely.

It seems likely that before the concept of a queen or king of heaven appeared, some few thousand years ago, the universe was viewed as a pantheistic collection of forces inherent in nature, forces that were female and male, animal and human, and combinations of both. The Mesopotamian pantheon of the fourth millennium showed the gods as immanent in nature, not rulers but expressions. There were the mountain range, Hursag; the sky, An (sometimes female, sometimes male) with its flowing breasts, the clouds; the plenty within the storehouse of dates, Inanna, later the storehouse itself; the divine cow, Ninsun or Nintur; Nammu, the goddess of the deep; and a host of other goddesses—nourishing, fostering, birth-giving, human- and animal-creating.

In the later ordering of the pantheon the goddesses and gods were paired; still later most of the goddesses fade or disappear, leaving only the questionable Inanna, of whom more later. In protohistorical and into historical times, each village or town had its own goddess or god or a pair of tutelary deities.

Changes in Sumerian religion reflect changes in Sumerian politics. Following, paralleling, perhaps symbolizing the shrinking status of the earthly woman in Sumer and Akkad is the gradual disappearance of the mother goddesses and the elevation of the gods in hierarchical order, culminating in the victory of Marduk over Tiamat, a version of Nammu, in what was essentially a state political instrument, the late Akkadian creation myth *Enuma elish*.

Mesopotamian religion can be schematized in outline over

can fuck, but she cannot fuck a man, though he can fuck her: "fuck" is defined as "verb, intransitive, transitive only with a male subject.")

the millennia. In the earliest time—the fourth millennium—it was a celebration of fertility and production, enduring aspects that were to be incorporated into later religious development. In the third millennium there was a struggle between the diffuse mother goddess image and the ruler god, between loose authority, self-achieved or assumed, seconded by the unanimous endorsement of the village council, and pyramidal hierarchy. At the beginning of this millennium or the end of the previous one, women may have been eliminated from earthly decision-making groups, though goddesses still participate in the divine assembly.[2]

In early times the creation of life was separate from the sexual meeting. During the third millennium the gods were paired in marriage, and male imagery and male metaphors of vitalizing powers and generation became common though the birth-giving and nourishing female deities struggled for expression. By the second millennium the male god had prevailed over the female. The mother goddesses were reduced in role, supplanted by a daughter god, who owed her existence to a father. Her image was contradictory: sometimes she embodied the loving and life-giving qualities of the earlier goddesses; more often she was wilful sexuality seen as betrayal, cruelty, destruction. She represented procreation through intercourse.

The early polity disappeared; one god became prominent. The first images of the male god were as ruler of the state, receiving his authority from the divine assembly of gods, in particular from An, the sky, and Enlil, Lord Wind, though Enki, Lord Earth, was also prominent. Not fatherhood was emphasized as much as lord, master, ruler, and the heavens were administered like a feudal estate, with various gods and goddesses assigned their tasks by the rulers, just as the worldly administration of the temple estates was arranged.

During the second millennium the autocratic ruler god was translated into the powerful but caring father. The God we know from Hebrew and Christian sources was taking form, though as yet he merely ruled, he did not create. To this millennium also can be traced the constitution of the extended family wherein the father derived his authority from the model of the

king, the family is the state in miniature. We who have been
brought up on the tradition of the ruler at the top of the pyramid of authority see monotheism as an advance over other
religions, for it reflects historical forms of government centering
on the rule of one male.[3]

Monotheism is authoritarianism. The worship of a single
male ruler is a cultural projection of specific historical events.
This does not constitute progress over the earlier beliefs in immanent and transcendent natural forces. Even if the Old Testament God of Wrath can sometimes be seen as the God of Love,
he is still paternalistic and we are dependent on his character
and whim.

Returning to the fourth millennium, we can trace the evolution of the fertility theme in the festivals and traditions centering around Inanna.

Originally Inanna was the goddess of the date palm, which
grew well in the brackish soil of southern Mesopotamia,
wherein her city Uruk was located. An early representation of
Inanna appears on the Uruk vase described in Chapter 24 and
illustrated in Figure 7.

The worship of Inanna ensured both vegetable and animal
procreation, and the sacred marriage rite—ceremonial intercourse enacted by the king as Dumuzi and a priestess who
represented the goddess—was to ensure plenty for the coming
year. Plants, animals, produce spring from it, and the people's
rejoicing in the gifts of the land is a much repeated theme.
When Inanna is angry all mating ceases, the ewe does not
bring forth lambs, the cow does not calve, the land is bare of
vegetation. The sacred marriage rite was practiced in other
cities, and with other goddesses and gods, but in its development the relationship between female and male is gradually reversed. Eventually generation is credited exclusively to
the male, whether he is envisioned as the heart of the date
palm or date cabbage, the bull of heaven or earth, or the human
himself.

The female then becomes a passive instrument of production
fecundated by the male, and Inanna is often referred to in the
literature as a storehouse heaped up with fruits and grain. After

the act of coitus, a banquet would be offered to the city's citizens; slaves would have extra rations—fish, oil, fruit—distributed to them. It is during this period that the distinction between fertility as generation-creation and fertility as fecundity-production is becoming confused in human thought.

Inanna was wedded to Amaushumgallanna, the big central bud in the palm (the date cabbage), whose pollen must be dusted on the flowers to make them fruitful. It was during the third millennium that heavy irrigation and intensive cultivation made it impossible to grow wheat in the southern part of Mesopotamia. Eridu may have been the first city to become deserted as a result of the exhaustion of the soil. From about 2700 B.C.E. on, barley, which is more tolerant of increasing salt levels, had become the principal crop in the south. After it was no longer possible to raise barley, date palms were still practicable. A wine was made from the fruit, and dates in their natural state provided a concentrated supply of sugar and calories. To cultivate dates it is necessary to understand and practice the principles of plant cultivation. The union of the goddess with the god in the sacred marriage rite symbolized the process of plant reproduction.

Eventually Amash was seen as the shepherd-god of sheep, Dumuzi, as Damu, the power of growth in trees and vegetation. He was also identified with the historical king, Dumuzi, mentioned in the King List as having reigned some time before the legendary Gilgamesh, i.e., shortly after 3000 B.C.E. These male gods, Dumuzi, Damu, Amaushumgallanna, have in common that they are always referred to in song and myth as husband, son, or brother; the male parent is unnamed and unheeded. In true matrilineal tradition there is no concern over a father. This is the original view of the male role, and it is perpetuated in popular religion. The cult of Damu or Dumuzi is a curious blend. There is the official fertility rite, the sacred marriage; there is also a masochistic cult wherein the remaining goddesses—mother, sister, wife—mourn a dead god.

This element appears again and again in transmuted form in future history. The mourning for the dead King Dumuzi, who later becomes Tammuz, is related to the worship of Orpheus,

Osiris, Dionysus, and Christ—sacrificial male figures originally worshiped above all by women.

The best-known sacred marriage rite was that between the goddess Inanna, played by a human woman as priestess, and the king, Dumuzi (probable date, circa 2800 B.C.E.), who had married Inanna in legend, and whose role was enacted by later kings as his earthly incarnation. Other parties might also be the principals. After the Akkadians became prominent, Inanna and Dumuzi were translated into Ishtar and Tammuz, Akkadian counterparts, as the protagonists of the yearly drama in which the king took on the god's identity, a priestess that of the goddess.[4]

One early text describes Inanna, the bride, decorated for her wedding with freshly harvested date clusters—her jewelry and personal adornments—standing at the lapis lazuli door of the *giparu* (the storehouse within the temple which, in later centuries, becomes the sacred cult chamber). She goes to receive her bridegroom Dumuzi at the door of the *giparu*—the opening of the door for the bridegroom was the main symbolic act of the Sumerian wedding—and he is led into the *giparu*, where the bed for the sacred marriage has been set up.[5]

From the earliest records—in cylinder seals dating to the middle of the fourth millennium—celebrating the participation of the male in nature's round to the sacred marriage rite of Neo-Babylonian days, about 700 B.C.E., is a jump of some three thousand years, longer than the total duration of Christianity. Not surprisingly the transformation is enormous. Just as the Roman Catholic mass changed over two millennia and varied in different places where it was celebrated, so the *hieros gamos* (the sacred wedding) must also have evolved and changed in the two or three, perhaps even five, thousand years in which it existed. (A present-day report by Elizabeth Colson on the Plateau Tongas, a matrilineal group from Southeast Africa, tells of the ritual coitus performed once yearly by the headman and his wife, which ensures fertility for the coming spring.[6])

In a poem known as the "Herder Wedding Text," of about 2000 B.C.E., the role of the woman—maid, goddess, queen, priestess—is clearly delineated; she is a seducer in a drama which admits of no self, for she exists only to rouse the male and effect the act which will bring plenty to the land. The literal translation by Samuel Noah Kramer contrasts with the more chaste version by Thorkild Jacobsen. In the former, Inanna baldly describes her vulva, "the piled-high hillock," and asks who will plow it for her, the maid? Her vulva is well-watered ground for men, she says, who will station his ox there? The chorus replies that the king, Dumuzi, will plow it for her and, seemingly content, she asks the man of her heart to plow her vulva, not a happy thought, certainly, in contemporary terms.[7]

Jacobsen has Inanna praising "her parts," the entire pubic area. She describes her sexual triangle as a ceremonial barge, and as the cosmic barge of heaven that is the new crescent moon. She then uses a series of landscape metaphors that culminate in fields, hillock land bordered by levees and moist lowland, both ready for plowing. Here the agricultural imagery is more specific and more convincing. Inanna's body is land waiting to be cultivated, and, the translator explains in a note, since a woman can own land but does not operate the plow, she needs the king to be the plowman and to bring his oxen to the fields.

Apart from the varying interpretations, it must be remembered that the English language has a built-in prejudice which tends to make male sex active and female passive. There is no way of knowing how far back these attitudes go. The songs of Australian Aborigine women, which hymn the clitoris, as well as African and American Indian ethnographic material, provide a manifest contrast. That the eminent organ of female pleasure should be ignored in a hymn to sexual joy would be indeed strange, but these are not odes to pleasure, they are official politics, in male versions, exhortations to male potency and the material produce it is deemed to symbolize. The "Herder Wedding Text" ends on the same note as earlier agricultural texts. Inanna rejoices in the great abundance that Dumuzi brings; she has asked Dumuzi the Wild Bull to bring her rich yellow milk, and so he does. Before that, however, Dumuzi's response to Inanna's love-making produced a monster erection, according to Jacobsen, with salutary effects on nature: "With the exalted rising of the king's loins rose at the same time the flax, rose at the same time the barley, did the desert fill as with delicious gardens."[8]

We stand witness at the birth of the phallarchy, the origins of phallus worship, the pernicious effects of which are still with us, operating to the detriment of women and men. Though "plow my vulva" may be the imagination of the twentieth-century translator, the image of utilitarian sex and women's passive role is implicit in both versions.

Shulgi, the Sumerian ruler mentioned earlier in connection with the employment of women tax collectors, has left many hymns which describe the sacred marriage rite specifically in its state form. Presumably written by males attached to the court, several are in the king's own voice, as though he himself had composed them. Shulgi was the son of Ur-Nammu, the first king of the newly reconstituted line of Sumerian rulers (the Third Dynasty of Ur), who had recaptured control of Sumer and Akkad about 2100. Described by historians as a fulsome braggart, Shulgi left many self-glorifying hymns—about thirty are extant in whole or in part—and some of their extravagant praises may have been written by the king himself.[9] In these texts, and in several from succeeding Sumerian reigns, the goddess still has powers to bestow, a contradictory hangover from the past. Her gifts reveal the values of the period, however, in their mingling of the sexual act with the warlike leadership powers that now result from the consummation of the sacred mating between the priestess-goddess and mortal king.

In one sequence, Shulgi has gone by boat from his city of Ur to Inanna's shrine at Uruk. Inanna describes how Shulgi will caress her, bringing life to her with his hands, taking her on the bed. In return, she says she will embrace him and decree his fate—he will be the faithful shepherd, a figurative title for the kings of Sumer, and receive the shepherdship of all the lands. In battle she will be his leader, in combat always present. She pronounces him fit to hold his head high on the dais and to sit on the lapis lazuli throne, validating his realm through their act of coitus. Hence he bears the crown on his head, carries the mace and the weapon, guides straight the long bow and the arrow, fastens the throwstick and the sling at his side. These and many other powers are his because Inanna holds him dear. The hymn ends with a ritual exordium, stating that he is the beloved also of the moon goddess, Ningal.[10]

In later epochs, Hebrews, Christians, and Moslems also invoke their deity, Jehovah or Allah, to sanctify bloody deeds and repression. The situation is more ambiguous in Sumer and early Mid Eastern theology. The goddess is both over and in the service of the king, to whom she is object and for whom she does all: "When for the wild bull, for the lord, I shall have bathed/ . . . When in his fair hands my loins shall have been shaped . . ."[11] The poet put the all-powerful Inanna into the service of the mortal king, who receives his office and temporary godship through being her spouse. By 2000 B.C.E. Sumerian religion was entwined with politics and, like Sumerian society itself, vertically organized.

Though the king received his power from the goddess, she was a woman and therefore ambivalently viewed. Several other compositions, from this period and shortly afterward, reflect this fact: "Inanna, most deceitful of women," runs a line from a song to Inanna in which Dumuzi, the "wild bull," is himself counseling Inanna to deceive her mother.[12] And in one of the several versions of the epic of Gilgamesh, this one written in Akkadian, Inanna, here Ishtar, is taunted by the hero-king, Gilgamesh: "What lover did you ever love constantly?"[13]

The subjugation of female sexuality was in process of accomplishment during the thousand years before these texts were written down, and it is delineated in the myths.

The Sumerian tale of Inanna's descent into hell reflects the ambivalence of attitudes toward her. Inanna's sister Ereshkigal ruled in the nether land, the home of the dead. When Inanna ventured into her sister's domain, Ereshkigal had her seized, stripped naked, and hung from a stake like a side of rotting meat, there to stay. Inanna was finally released through the agency of wily Enki, her grandfather, but she had to provide a substitute. This substitute turned out to be Dumuzi, her husband. Till fairly recently it was thought that Inanna had gone

down to the land of the dead to bring Dumuzi back to life, but
newly translated tablets have proved differently. She had not
gone down to rescue Dumuzi; rather she had had him captured
and brought to hell as her replacement when she discovered
that he was not mourning her death but seated high on a
throne celebrating. This rivalry between divine female and
semidivine or deified male will culminate over the millennia
with the (seeming) disappearance of the female and the reign
of male divinity. But more than a thousand years before monotheism has emerged, the battle between male and female elements in the divine pantheon is still being played out.

Women have a worse time of it in Akkadian mythology,
which stems from a later period. A late Akkadian tale tells how
the Queen of the Underworld was brought to bed and dominated by a man, who then came to rule as Nergal, the King of
the Underworld. Originally autonomous and independent,
Ereshkigal was undone by sex, dragged from the throne and
forced into coitus. It is the beginning of a long literary tradition describing the humbling of female pride and self-expression, best exemplified perhaps by *The Taming of the Shrew*.

In the exordium to the sacred marriage text quoted earlier,
Inanna's invitation to Dumuzi was variously interpreted by
different translators. A chaste metaphor drawn from the
farmer's experience in one version became an encouragement to
sexual athletics in another. The myth called "The Marriage of
Enlil and Ninlil" has been presented as a case of rape.[14] Careful examination of the various translations raises doubts about
the episode and larger questions about translators' ability to
penetrate the Sumerian material. I have mentioned that Sumerology dates back only half a century. The study of one dead
language, accessible only through faint wedge marks left on ancient clay, and reached through three other dead languages—
Akkadian, Elamite, and Old Persian—poses enormous difficulties. *Traduttore-traditore*—"translator-traitor"—is an Italian saying about live languages; how much the more so in this instance where so little is known about the peoples whose work
and lives we presume to interpret.

Two versions of the myth have been published. In Jacobsen's, a maiden goddess, Ninlil, is warned by her mother *not* to walk by the stream, for she might be seen by the god Enlil, and "forthwith, he will embrace thee, he will kiss thee!" In the better-known version by Samuel Noah Kramer, whose popularizing books on Sumerian culture and mythology have received wide circulation since *From the Tablets of Sumer* was first issued in 1956, Ninlil's mother expressly sends her to walk by the stream (or canal), a more unlikely occurrence. In any event Ninlil is approached by Enlil as her mother, Ninshebargenu, has predicted. She protests her inexperience: "My vagina is too little, it knows not how to copulate; my lips are too small, they know not how to kiss."[15]

Whether he persuades her or rapes her, she is impregnated by him. This is deduced from a passage also under debate, in which Enlil strolls through the Kiur, the assembly in which the fifty great gods and the seven lawmaking gods meet. These cause Enlil to be arrested and sentence him to banishment, terming him *uzug*, and it is on the strength of this word that both scholars deduce the rape of Ninlil. *Uzug* appears in different contexts and is translated variously as ravisher, rapist, immoral one, sex criminal, and menstruating woman. Jacobsen tells us that *uzug* means "one who is under a sexual taboo, who is sexually unclean . . . dangerous to the community. This term may be used of a menstruating woman or—as here—of a person who has committed a sex crime, rape."[16] Since Ninlil follows Enlil after his banishment and since only the word *uzug* (menstruating woman, sex criminal, rapist!) and Enlil's banishment testify to the act, the rape is not proven. My interpretation is that the taboo Enlil broke was that of having intercourse with, and marrying, Ninlil against her mother's wishes— that the word *uzug* refers to the fact that marriages were to be arranged by the mother, as was customary among matrilineal peoples like the Australian Tiwi and the American Iroquois.

Most translators assume that the taboo of menstrual uncleanliness, so strongly regulated by Hebrew, Moslem, and Hindu law, goes back to Sumerian days. From the temple archives at Ur, about 2500 B.C.E., tablets referring to the employment of women as weavers are translated: "Payments for the sick, for the days of absence (when unclean [*uzug?*]) and sundry expenditures of female workers for one month."[17] That women did not work while menstruating is likely, but to call the menstrual period unclean is probably a projection from later days. In similar wise, Egyptologists influenced by Judeo-Christian prudery write that the god Atum created the world through *self-pollution*, though the actual text of the fairly late myth reads, "I copulated with my fist; I masturbated with my hand."[18]

Though neither scholar boggles at the thought, I find it difficult to believe that the same word would be used for a rapist and a menstruating woman. Even the phobic Hebrews, who equated menstruation with disease—it was "an issue," as were pus from leprosy, running sores, and other signs of infections— and who ordained similar ritual cleansing after "pollution" by childbirth, did not go that far. (Sexual fluids were also considered "polluting," but the measures of purification were less stringent and of shorter duration.) Jacobsen does question Kramer's characterizing as a "delightful myth" a story which "tells how Ninlil's mother deliberately makes her daughter expose herself so that she may be raped by Enlil, how Enlil abandons her as soon as he has raped her, how she follows him and is seduced three times in succession by men whom she meets on the road—all of them, as it turns out, Enlil in disguise."[19] Evidently the myth of Enlil and Ninlil still escapes our Western understanding.

Much about Sumer must, of necessity, escape our Western understanding, especially since the culture continuum summed up under the rubric Sumero-Akkadian, Assyrian, and Babylonian was constantly changing during its three-thousand-year existence. In an early Sumerian tradition the sky is female and male. An the sky god is married to An the sky goddess. In the earliest times the sky may have been female alone or female and male combined; in Akkadian translations, however, Anu the sky god is married to the goddess Antum. This can be compared to the conflicting and coexisting Egyptian traditions where, in the one, the sky goddess Nut overarches the earth and, in the other, the sky goddess named Hathor is the divine cow, whose teats send down the milk of heaven. In Sumer An is often referred to as the bull of heaven or the fecund breed bull, with his wife An as the divine cow. A later tradition reflecting the agricultural image has An the sky god married to Ki the earth. On the other hand, Enki, the god of wisdom and water, is also seen as Lord Earth, produced by An's marriage to his mother Nammu. In other Sumerian traditions An married Ninhursag, the goddess of birth, and eventually he is named as the husband of Inanna (the only goddess permitted to survive into the late historical period), although, following earlier genealogy, she would have been An's great-granddaughter.

The persistent tradition of a female sky identifies Inanna as the rain goddess—her breasts are the clouds pouring out the beneficent rain—overlapping with visions of her as the thunder goddess and her later evolution into the patron of war. "I step onto the heavens and the rain rains down/I step onto the earth and grass and herbs sprout up," says one hymn.[20] She is shown riding a lion or in a chariot drawn by seven lions; sometimes she is herself the lion. Enheduanna, the poet daughter of Sargon the Great, writing circa 2350 B.C.E., invokes her as the destroyer of mountains: "O my lady, at your roar you made the countries bow low. . . . With the charging storm you charge,/with the howling storm you howl."[21]

A series of myths found on many different tablets reflects the competition between gods and goddesses for the creation of humanity, a competition that ended with the decline of the mother goddesses and the assignment to the males of the major role in both power and creativity. The myths have been arranged by Jacobsen to present a sequential origin story, giving both a chronological and etiological picture of the Sumerian world view.

The initial myth tells of the gods' reluctance to labor. Tired of working so hard, they appeal to Enki's mother Nammu for relief. Nammu instructs Enki on what to do, and working in combination with Ninmah, the goddess of birth, they create humans to do the gods' work. People are made from the clay of the deep—Apsu—the source from which Enki himself had issued, engendered on it by Nammu. In one version Ninmah, lit-

erally August Lady, a variant of Ninhursag—Lady Mountain—
or Ki, the earth goddess, stands over Nammu to receive the
child, made of silt, when Nammu gives birth, while Enki is a
helper, representing the sweet water that moistens the clay.[22]

In a more complex tablet of later date, Enki instructed his
mother to have two womb goddesses pinch off pieces of the
clay for her. She then put limbs on each lump and thus gave
birth to human beings, assisted by Ninmah and eight other
goddesses.

Afterward there was a feast to celebrate the delivery. The
Sumerian gods and goddesses were an uproarious lot, given to
celebrations and to drinking, sometimes too much. At this banquet, Ninmah and Enki both drank heavily, and they began to
exchange boasts. Ninmah said she could change humanity's
form at will from good to bad. Enki dared her to do her worst;
he would find a role for whatever warp of nature she could
create. Ninmah began to make all kinds of strange and defective creatures—a blind man, an incontinent person, a barren
woman, a human with neither male nor female genitalia, and
so on, six in toto. Enki found a place and a livelihood for all.
The creature who had no genitals became the eunuch he set to
wait upon the king; the barren woman a lady-in-waiting to the
queen, and each freak Ninmah had created he inserted into the
Sumerian social order.

Then Enki proposed that they change places. He would
create the imperfect beings; let Ninmah fit them into society.
He proceeded to make a creature so warped and distorted that
life was barely present: his eyes were diseased, his liver and
heart hurt, his hands trembled, he was too feeble to take nourishment. His creation was so ailing—prematurely senile, unable
to eat and to move—that Ninmah was unable to do anything
for it. Helpless to alleviate this epitome of human misery, she
was horror-struck. She shrieked with rage and despair. So it
turned out that Enki was more efficient at evil than Ninmah.
As Jacobsen puts it, when the goddess decides to create imper-
fection, something can still be made of the warped humans she
molds, but when clever Enki decides to be malign, he wins the

contest. Thus the goddess makes life but the god excels at misery and death.[23]

The male takes center stage, and male imagery predominates, in the writings that date from 2000 B.C.E. on. The same word, E, served the Sumerians for water and semen, as in the "life-giving semen, life-giving seed" referred to in the epigraph to this chapter. Enki lifts his penis and ejaculates, and the Tigris River is filled with sparkling waters. The verse from the sacred marriage hymn in which Dumuzi's mighty erection produced the harvest was cited earlier. Elsewhere, rain from the mountains is seen as seminal water, bloodied in a deflowering, according to Jacobsen.

The evolution of Sumerian customs is reflected also in the description of the king's antecedents which prefaced royal edicts and announcements. In the third millennium kings might not name a father, they boasted of their descent from a goddess; but they named their gods as patrons, proclaiming themselves servant of a god. Ur-Nanshe was the son of Ninsun, the goddess of justice; Gudea was also the son of Ninsun; and Ur-Nammu was the son of Nanshe, goddess of mercy. Eventually this ritual exordium would tell of a king whose mother was the goddess of justice or of mercy, who was nursed at the breasts of Ninhursag, the dairy goddess, beloved of Inanna, and was sustained by An and Enlil of Nippur, with other gods who were patrons of individual cities. The goddesses represented the king's moral and fecundating qualities, the gods the worldly authority conveyed on him by the rule of the different cities necessary to validate his reign over the kingdom.

Further evidence of the decline of the mother goddesses comes from the change in personal names over the millennia. Matrilineal references were frequent in the third when goddess names were incorporated into the kingly appellation. Ur-Nanshe was an early ruler of Ur named after a goddess of mercy and justice; Ur-Nammu was the first of the newly reconstituted dynasty of Ur, which sought to return to earlier tradition.

The last king to use a goddess name was Lipit-Ishtar, shortly after 2000 B.C.E. In the second and first millennia, both kings and male commoners use god names only. Ninurta of the plow, Suen or Sin the moon god, Dagan and Adad the Assyrian weather gods, Asshur and Nabu—these were some of the royal favorites.

In the third millennium Nammu and other mother goddesses were giving place to Inanna, the goddess of fertility through sexual intercourse. In cylinder seals of the period the fertility goddess is on top in depictions of ritual mating.[24] Later representations show her facing her consort; finally she is dominated by him. Thus Inanna's uneasy union with Dumuzi.

Where early kings had boasted of their goddess mothers, in the millennia to come the creating goddess is reduced; Nammu —"she who gave birth to heaven and earth"—becomes the housekeeper of Enlil, Ninhursag a mere wet nurse. Inanna-Ishtar remains, but the ambivalence of need-resentment is always present and ever stronger; eventually the whore overpowered the virgin-madonna aspects.

From the time of the first unification of Mesopotamia in mid third millennium, Inanna is associated with Ishtar, the Akkadian goddess of war and harlotry and sexuality, and by the first millennium the warrior-conqueror god Marduk has achieved primacy.

For the Sumero-Akkadians, the Babylonians, the Assyrians, and other associated Near Eastern religiocultural groups, there was no need to dichotomize woman into madonna and whore. Inanna-Ishtar combined the two in one envelope, though she was conceived more as virgin whore than as madonna mother. She is the type of daughter goddess who remains a virgin because she never gives birth. Initially the term *virgin* can be seen as a synonym for *maid* or *young girl*. It refers to the original sexual freedom—the permissive customs that preceded the patriarchal period and were characteristic of so many of the small-scale cultures to which I have earlier referred. *Milady* persists as a form of address in Sumero-Akkadian and Babylonian prayers and invocations, but to read into it the significance and associations of the Catholic Madonna (*ma donna*—my lady) is a projection of a later cultural ethos.

Inanna is not an all-giving mother, she is a questionable and irritating necessity to *man* in the peopling of the world and the consequent acquisition of material goods through production or conquest. Later on, Hebrew and Moslem religion will attempt to do without her; they do not succeed, for she sneaks into the folk religion in several guises, as the Shekhina, as the Matronit, and, in her most negative aspects, as Lilith. In Christian mythology Mary was made a mere vessel, a passive recipient for the son of God, but future generations idolized her anew in the cult of Mariolatry, while a whole pantheon of gods and goddesses crept back into worship in the form of saints. Then Protestantism came along and firmly cleaned house, expelling saints, sometimes the Virgin herself.

26

The Authoritarian State and the Family

I will create man. Let him be burdened with the toil
of the gods that they may freely breathe.
            —Akkadian myth (circa 1500 B.C.E.)[1]

The father-headed family was a relatively late development in
Sumer, preceded and suggested by the authoritarian state. Selective monogamy, permitting concubines and second wives to
men while demanding chastity for women, arose during the
third millennium, the period when the authoritarian state was
taking shape. The battle for male supremacy was symbolized by
myths showing an uneasy battle between the goddesses and the
gods, in which the gods established precedence and a pyramidal
organization centering on An, the sky god. Matrilineal egalitarianism disappeared, but, judging from the subtext of historical inscriptions and myth, matrilineal descent with males holding power probably hung on well into the millennium. The
authoritarian state was the model from which individual fathers derived power. Present-day observations of surviving
foraging peoples and simple groupings support this hypothesis,
based on analysis of Sumerian religion and writings.

Nineteenth- and early-twentieth-century thinkers assumed
that the authoritarian family preceded and set the pattern for
the stratified state. Historically, they come on the scene to-

gether; but there is today more evidence for the authoritarian state preceding the power of fathers—patriarchy—than vice versa. We are more aware of just how much anthropological evidence of the nineteenth and twentieth centuries was skewed by Western observer bias, preconception, and misconception. In the early nineteenth century, theorists were still conditioned to think of the Old Testament as describing ancient history, with some leavening from Greece and Rome. Later nineteenth-century political philosophers based their theories on the historical civilizations of Greece and Rome. Only recently has information on the earliest states become available.

Just as the Sumerian king lists began in the dim past with mythology and then recorded actual reigns as the chroniclers came closer to their own times, as Herodotus and Tacitus preface their histories with mythical geneses, so Old Testament beginnings in the mists of myth, proceeding through historically recognizable events, were generally accepted as the preface to our own past. Hence our acceptance of the wandering-shepherd patriarch as prelude to the state ruled by a father-king, the world ruled by a father-god. Most of nineteenth-century and much of twentieth-century thinking is still underlain and influenced by these assumptions of history and prehistory, despite the facts and principles made available by the natural sciences—physics, biology, astronomy, archaeology, et al.—during the past few centuries.

One Sumerian myth in which the gods grew tired of labor and created humans as slaves to do their work was cited in Chapter 25. Several other Sumerian and Akkadian myths iterate the motif of people made to serve the weary gods.[2] This was a convenient explanation, an ideology which justified the power of priests, who were the earthly representatives of individual divinities. Originally kingship had been a temporary office, received as an appointment from the council. The soldier king who represented himself as the chief priest of the city god either created or adapted this world view and built a bureaucracy around it. Whether it justified the theocratic rule, the power of priests, and was perverted to the king's use or was the creation of the war leader himself cannot be stated with

the information on hand. Since written material is late, after
the process itself had begun to take form, we can only speculate on just how it happened. However, the way in which Sumerian and, later, Akkadian mythology was ordered, along with
its transformation over the centuries, does demonstrate the
three-thousand-year shaping of power in Mesopotamia.

The ruler metaphor—humans created to serve the gods—appears later than the fertility motif and is related to social and
political forms which develop only after 3000 B.C.E. If one believes that form follows function, the progressive changes of
religion in Sumer and then in Akkadia, Babylonia, and Assyria
tell something about their social structure and the directions in
which they evolved.

The process began in the third millennium. By the beginning
of the first millennium, religion was constructed as a militarist
state, and it was indeed inextricably mingled with the worldly
state, metaphor, model, and justification for its form and functioning.

We saw how the sacred marriage rite came into the monarchy's service by the time of the Third Dynasty of Ur, about
2100 B.C.E. The mother goddess disappeared or became a
nurse, and the battle was joined between Inanna-Ishtar—
goddess of sexuality—and the male gods. These last changed as
the kings of different cities achieved power over the country.
Since state ideology is supported by religious observance, the
king was the temporal embodiment of the chief god, just as in
later epochs emperors and kings often wore the mantle of divinity, claiming election by God through his worldly representative, the pope, partaking of the aura, sometimes the actuality, of godship. The king was his city god's earthly
representative, taking his place in festivals, and while some
kings validated themselves with official religion, later ones
brought their own city gods into prominence, finally changing
the order of the pantheon as the power center shifted.

Initially, the religious festival of which the Akkadian creation
myth became an integral part was probably a simple harvest
festival. A version in which the king participated has been
traced back to the middle of the third millennium. It centered

around the city god's visit to a temple in the open country outside the walls and his return home to the city temple.[3]

Near Eastern culture was being shaped in increasingly warlike, materialist, and inequitable directions: the religious ceremonies reflect what was happening in the state. By 700 B.C.E. the sacred marriage rite of the New Year had been combined with the harvest festival, but the festival had become a complex ritual celebrating the victory in battle of one warrior god over the whole pantheon, but above all over the mother of all living things—Tiamat, an Akkadian name for our old friend Nammu, she of the primeval waters, the watery deep, who was originally a leading element in the fertility cult, now enslaved and put to use. "Don't kill our mother," said the Australian myth, and yet in genesis after genesis, tale after tale, from every quarter of the world, the mother is slain, reduced, consumed, yet never dies.

The creation battle and the sacred marriage rite were one long ten-day festival which culminated in the union of Marduk, conqueror of the great mother Tiamat, with a goddess who had added the patronage of war and of harlotry to her original fertility powers. The focus of the festival was the recitation and re-enactment of the Akkadian creation myth, sometimes cited as a decisive station on the road to patriarchal religion.[4] Actually the steps had been charted in the previous millennia, beginning in the third, when the female deities were espoused and reduced. The tale is usually referred to as *Enuma elish* from its opening words: "When above." It continues, "the heavens had not been named/below the earth had not been called by name" and recounts the victory of Marduk, the young warrior god, over the old order, led by Tiamat, the mother of all the gods and goddesses. Tiamat is a transmuted version of Nammu, the goddess who begot Enki, wisdom god of Eridu, that early city of Sumer long since disappeared.

During the early third millennium An was the most important god in the Sumerian pantheon. Though he always retained the shadowy aura of authority he was gradually supplanted in decision-making by his son Enlil of Nippur, probably at the time Nippur became the leading city and meeting place of the Early Dynastic (2800 to 2400 B.C.E.) league of Sumerian cities.

Nippur remained the ceremonial center of Sumero-Akkadia long after the dwindling of its temporal importance.

The version of the Akkadian creation myth which has come down to us is a late one, found in the library of Assurbanipal of Nineveh (660–638 B.C.E.), and the tone and content are far removed from Sumerian genesis myths. Fragments of copies of the myth have been found in other cities, including Assur in Assyria, where the Assyrian storm god is substituted for Marduk, but none of them predates the first millennium. When the festival began, probably about the middle of the third millennium, it may have been Enlil, the Sumerian air god of Nippur, who was represented by the king.

Scholars feel that though it may have been Sargon the Great —the first Sargon—who began the transformation of the harvest festival into a battle celebration, it is more likely to have been Hammurabi, a Semite king descended from Amorites (West Syrians), who re-united North and South Mesopotamia about 1850 B.C.E. and who made his capital at Babylon, where Marduk was city god. In the surviving account, dating about a thousand years later, "the king in symbolic action fought and won as the embodiment of Marduk the battle against chaos which established the ordered cosmos for the new year as it had done primevally."[5]

The symbolic battle justifies the warlike rule of a single leader, unifying the disparate parts of the land under a strict bureaucracy. It is a tale of bloody combat resulting in established order. *Enuma elish* probably dates from the second half of the second millennium; it is a cautionary tale glorifying the rule of Babylon in the south, Assyria in the north, or whatever regime chose to adapt it for its own uses. Two descriptions give details of the ritual, the sacrifice of first a sheep and on another day a bull (white in Babylon and black in Assur, where Assur, the storm god, was the male protagonist), the recitation and acting out of the myths, culminating in the creation of humans, no longer from clay vitalized by water nor from sexual intercourse, but from the blood of Tiamat's consort Kingu.

Marduk's decisive victory over Tiamat is told in all its gory detail:

Tiamat became as one possessed. She lost her reason; uttered wild piercing screams; trembled; shook to the roots of her limbs; pronounced an incantation; and all the gods of the battle cried out. Then Tiamat advanced; Marduk, as well: they approached each other for the battle. The Lord spread his net to enmesh her, and when she opened her mouth to its full, let fly into it an evil wind that poured into her belly, so that her courage was taken from her and her jaws remained opened wide. He shot an arrow that tore into her, cut through her inward parts, and pierced her heart. She was undone. He stood upon her carcass and those gods who had marched by her side turned for their lives. He encircled them with his net, destroyed their weapons, made them captive, and they wept.

The poisonous monsters to which Tiamat had given birth and assigned splendor, Marduk flung into fetters, arms bound behind, and trampled underfoot . . . returning to the carcass of Tiamat, mounting upon her hinder quarters, with his merciless mace [he] smashed her skull. He cut the arteries of her blood and caused the north wind to bear it off to parts unknown . . . Marduk now paused, gazing upon the dead body, considering the foul thing, to devise an ingenious plan. Whereafter he split her like a shellfish, in two halves; set one above, as a heavenly roof, fixed with a crossbar; and assigned guards to watch that her waters above should not escape.[6]

Marduk takes the lower half of Tiamat's body for the earth, establishing the zenith in her belly. The warrior-god has created the universe from the body of the conquered goddess.

Enuma elish is a decisive recounting of the victory of the male world of battle over the female world of creation, with Marduk treating Tiamat as raw material, making humans himself, not by generation but by killing, out of the blood of a slain enemy. The form in which it endures was written down long after the appearance of another Sumero-Akkadian phenomenon, the ambivalent and peculiar institution whereby woman's sexuality is a sacrifice, a prize which she no longer enjoys for its own sake. Along with its other inventions, Sumero-Akkadian civilization may have invented the phenomena of sex for money, sex for sacrifice, and the sacrifice of sexuality by men as eunuchs and by women vowed to chastity as high priestesses.

The origins of prostitution lie in the destruction of woman as an active entity. She is neuter, existing for the enjoyment of men. "The attitude of a society toward prostitution," says Eleanor C. M. Laughlin, "can be seen as a barometer of the degree to which woman is reduced to mere instrumentality."[7] At this stage and place in history most people are being reduced to instrumentality, women as breeders, men as soldiers, both as workers, witness the myth in which human beings are created by the gods as their slaves, which enables kings to treat their subjects as the gods treat kings. There are degrees, however, and as the priestess is to the king, the wife to the husband, the slave girl to her mistress, the "harlot of the square" is the instrument of lowest grade, the bottom rung in a series into which each human is now slotted.

Popular tradition of prostitution has it that it is the oldest profession and pimping the second oldest. Marx, Engels, G. B. Shaw all took prostitution as a paradigm of modern capitalism, on the basis that if you could sell sex for money, you could reduce anything to material terms. How indeed did it come about that the man was the buyer, the woman the seller? In sacred prostitution, sex is a symbolic act; each time the man has intercourse, he is planting his seed, ensuring a material return. The prostitute takes the risk: she may become pregnant, whether the children are wanted or not. Children are a commodity, and sex itself has become a symbol of production, with the woman's sexuality promising a delivery, never mind that it is not necessarily or perhaps not at all desired in a specific instance. The seeds of Western materialism are sown in Sumer, which is why we study their culture for causes and explanations of present-day sexual, familial, and economic phenomena. The sale of one's sexual charms and attractions, in various guises, still influences all of female life in Western culture. Prostitution was used as a metaphor for the situation of women, who had the choice of selling their sexual services in the respectability of marriage or on the open market in prostitution, with many intermediate degrees of life and half-life interposed, both hidden and recognized.

In literature about the origins of prostitution, tracing a religious etiology to the sacred marriage rite in honor of Inanna or some other goddess of sexual love, procreation, and harlotry, male writers tend to express a prurient joy or a puritanical horror at the supposed sexual freedom—what has been called the school of history as pornography. Actually, it should be seen as the invention of woman as object, a literal sacrifice on the altar of male desire, rather than any kind of equal meeting of desires. In the chicken-egg controversy of which came first, monogamy or prostitution, the prevailing male viewpoint has always called prostitution a necessary sop to male desire, given the tradition that male sexuality is irresistible and uncontrollable, whereas females either have none or are essentially passive respondents to male importunacy. In fact, it is women not men who have the greater physiological capacity for active sex. But if sex is practiced as a symbol for reproduction, not for pleasure, even in prostitution, then the woman becomes an instrument. And with the help of oil, saliva, or other lubricant, time is the only limitation on the number of tricks she can accommodate, and instances are told of soldiers lining up, being allowed a few minutes apiece for what has to be the merest shade of expression on the male side as well. By Goodall's account chimpanzees manage better, while Kate Millett's sculpture "The Brothel," with its pairs of female legs extending from a row of urinals, makes a metaphoric point about human sexual debasement.

In the class society which evolved in Sumer and Akkad, the temple had been organized to serve the gods, the people served the temple and the king. I spoke of the validating myths which had it that humans were created as slaves to the gods, so that the gods could enjoy themselves while people labored, a metaphor which was applied all the way down the hierarchy. In exchange for labor the gods—and their worldly surrogates, priests,

kings, and designated representatives—offered fertility and protection in the form of food, clothing, and other material appurtenances, in severely regulated amounts. In the temple there
were many grades of priests and priestesses, several of which involved sexual functions. Eunuchs and priestesses were employed in large numbers, though it is not known exactly what
their duties were.

The sacred marriage rite, with its emphasis on female fertility
and male generation, was quite different from the earlier participatory sexual celebrations, which may well have continued in
rural areas. The orgiastic festivals described for Grecian women
may not differ all that much from periodic group sexual experiences which are written about by Malinowski (the *katayausa*),
Phyllis Kaberry, and others cited in earlier chapters. The ritualized coitus of king and goddess before a passive audience is
an early spectator sport, while phallus worship and glorification
of male seed become more and more insistent with ensuing
millennia. Even profane acts of male coitus become symbols
for the fructifying religious one.

Thus male sex is deemed necessary and good while female
sex is evil, inasmuch as it threatens inheritance, male dominance, and other characteristics of the patriarchy. Moreover, if
a woman experiences many men, she has a standard of comparison and can criticize the sexual adequacy of the one to whom
she is chained in a marriage based on materialist-accumulative
considerations.

Did the people feel that they participated vicariously in the
sacred marriage rite, so that each man who went to a prostitute
was enacting the rite with each act of coitus and each woman
seduced the man with conscious arousal as the prostitute-
harlot-courtesan's role developed over the ages? It is as if the
male must be courted to produce the people, the animals, the
grain so desperately needed for an accumulative society whose
surplus—often exacted and more artificial than actual—paid for
conquest and for the conspicuous consumption of a ruling elite.
It was an ideology in which it was the product that counted,
not as formerly the enjoyment, and it was reinforced by the distribution of luxury items—fish, dates, extra oil rations—to

slaves, semislave workers, and peasants that was a feature of the annual or semi-annual holiday.

In the second and third millennia before Christianity the class of sacred prostitutes may have lived in a brothel on the temple precincts. In Neo-Babylonian times, during the first millennium, prostitutes were permitted to live near the temples of Ishtar in Uruk, according to Leo Oppenheim, who describes the streets of the cities of Babylon as "teeming with domestic animals, cripples and prostitutes."[8]

Temple prostitution had begun as sex servicing the religion of procreation. In a materialist religion, the next step put copulation into the service of the material. Thus temple prostitution and common prostitution evolved out of a similar etiology: sex put to service—of the gods and of the religion of procreation. The fertility of land and animals and people depended on the religious rite.

The highest priestess, who played the role of Inanna or, earlier, the local city goddess, was often the daughter—sometimes the wife—of a king. Her role was highly circumscribed. She was vowed to chastity except for the one yearly ceremony, which at some periods may have been unconsummated. There were other, lesser priestesses who were also enjoined to chastity; they came from the upper classes and might be married but evidently did not have children, for their marriage contracts mention both their inheritance and other rights and that they might supply concubines to their husbands in order to produce children. At the lower levels were prostitutes available in brothels or in their own premises to anyone who paid—the poor man's concubine, according to H. W. F. Saggs.

The earliest known reference to prostitutes is in the Laws of Lipit-Ishtar (circa 1934–1924 B.C.E.): "If a man's wife has borne him no children but a prostitute from the street has borne him children, he shall provide for that prostitute her corn, oil, and clothing, and the children which the prostitute has borne him shall be his heirs; but as long as his wife lives the prostitute shall not reside in the house with the wife."[9] In the same code, reference is made to the marriage of prostitutes —"If a man marry a harlot . . ."; but the conclusion is indecipherable. While historians state that no stigma attached to the resort to temple prostitutes or to the keeping of concubines, both occupations certainly meant low status for the women themselves. In advice to a son, a father says: "Do not marry a temple prostitute or make a slave-girl mistress of your house, for besides being accustomed to accepting other men she would make an unsympathetic and intractable wife." Elsewhere a father advises his son not to go with "a harlot of the square."[10]

In other texts, the classes of temple prostitute—literally, hierodule or sacred slave—vary from the hierodule of heaven, Inanna herself, through several gradations of priestesses vowed to chastity and priestesses of the lower class, vowed to the service of male sexuality. What all these provocative references have in common is that chastity and sex on demand are linked, which is not as strange as may first appear, since both preclude any spontaneous sexual activity of the woman's own choice and for her own pleasure. One might add eunuchs as a depressed group, since they would seem to have taken part as actors, possibly in female dress, in cult performances and were equally deprived of sexuality, exemplified by a text referring to "the Kurgarru and Issinu whose virility Ishtar has changed into femininity to wear the mask before the people."[11]

Much has been made of the libidinous activity permitted women in Sumero-Akkadian life.[12] This is a misinterpretation of the formal chains put on them by the time of written history, about 2000 B.C.E., which probably developed during the preceding thousand years. The symbolic union of king and priestess did not result in children, as far as we know. In certain surviving contracts, provision is made for the children of priestesses. Again, we do not know what were the rules governing their sexual relations. In later centuries it was assumed by Roman and Hebrew literature and tradition that prostitutes practiced birth control, sometimes equated with movements in intercourse. Documents like one from first-millennium Babylon providing for the adoption of a prostitute's child, not to mention the afore-cited law of Lipit-Ishtar, demonstrate that whatever methods were in use, they were far from foolproof.[13] Despite the law, infanticide, abortion—self-induced or midwife-administered—and folk remedies of more or less efficacy and threat to life have been and still are widely used, be it in present-day Italy and Morocco, Ancient Greece and Rome, or medieval Denmark. No doubt they were employed in Sumer and Akkad also.*

By 2000 B.C.E. Sumero-Akkadian civilization registers its fear of free sexuality in strict rules controlling the priestess and in contempt for the prostitute.

This is the nub of the ambivalent attitudes—alternating reproaches and supplications—toward Inanna-Ishtar which characterize the mythic and epic texts from 2000 B.C.E. on. Originally Inanna was a free maid. Inanna chose and Inanna enjoyed, an intolerable situation in the development of a hierarchy characterized by a male warrior class directing a primarily male bureaucracy.

The temples themselves began as economic institutions. Over the millennia they developed into huge bureaucratic and parasitic organizations which engaged in symbolic theater—rituals of conspicuous consumption—as a means of uniting and controlling the cities' inhabitants, of assisting the military in enforcing inequity.

Several writers have commented on the materialist, joyless ethos of Mesopotamia and the ambivalence of the temple as holy and practical. Certainly it gave an organized shape to life, as slavery is organized. Why was this ethos accepted, to the extent to which it was? Freud predicated the existence of civilization on sexual repression and sublimation. Succeeding theorists amplified or modified his original dicta. It was pointed out that the relationship is not a direct one; i.e., you don't produce more civilization or more art in direct proportion to the amount of sublimation. I have noted that the sublimation must be volitional to some extent. Psychoanalytic scholars as diverse as Reich and Marcuse and Fromm all observed that authoritarian and militaristic regimes always base themselves on severe sexual repression. The repressive nature of civilization

* Abortion became legal in Italy in 1978.

produces alternate responses of numbing paralysis and a chain of self-perpetuating tyranny, whereby each level of the ranking pyramid passes on to a lower level the cruelty and domination received from the one above. The thousands of years of Mesopotamian history are a clear example of the linkage between militarism and war and the division of people into classes of more and less privilege, more and less prosperity, more and less sexual expression. Sexual deprivation of women is combined with the invention of a class of women who exist only to serve male sexual desire, to provide sex on demand or as propitiation, regardless of their own wishes. The mass of men are also controlled by difficulty of access to women or by the price which is put on them, in marriage or in fleeting encounters.

27

—··—··—··—··—··—··—··—

War and Sex and Animals

For a nation to be civilized, it has to abolish its standing army.

—Immanuel Kant

Inanna—better known under her Akkadian name Ishtar—is the Sumerian goddess who has most penetrated Western consciousness, the only one to survive into later times and the commonest in writing. The character and functions of earlier female deities were assimilated to her Akkadian name so that the word *ishtar* became a synonym for *goddess*. Essentially, however, she was "the goddess of war and whore," her chief concerns being battle, also known as the dance of Inanna, sexual love, and procreation.

Inanna is often confused with the prototype mother goddess. Actually she is quite different from Nammu, Ninhursag, Nintu, Nanshe, and a host of other mother figures who originally gave birth on their own, unaided by male impregnation, who suckled gods and kings, and were powerful as mothers without heterosexual undertones. Though Inanna, too, was probably a mother goddess in earlier times, when we encounter her in myth and poetry from 2000 B.C.E. and later she is a daughter not a mother, born of the union of male and female, and is characterized by her relationship to male gods—her grandfathers Enki and Enlil, her husband Dumuzi—while her mother is present but peripheral. She represents the fertile impulse involving a male and is regarded with mixed feelings. Other daughter goddesses from neighboring countries relate to her: Anat, Antit, Anath, Astarte, Ashtoreth, and Isis overlap many of her functions. Her Akkadian version brought in the battle aspects; indirectly Ishtar may come from the Hittite Arinna, Lady and Queen of Heaven and Earth. It was Ishtar who marched before the Assyrian armies in battle; on one occasion she is said to have manifested herself bodily to the whole army. Anath, known as the "Violent Goddess"—the Hebrew Ashtoreth—was regarded with awe and fear and distaste, in contrast to her mother.

These daughter goddesses descend from the supreme god, but they still have a mother, Asherah in the case of the Canaanite goddess of harlotry and war combined. Later Greek goddesses will be born asexually from the father alone, Athena springing from the brow of Zeus while Aphrodite was born of the water out of Uranus' sperm awash in the billowing wave— the old sea metaphor which appears in dreams and poetry as a symbol of sexual intercourse. For the Greeks war was perhaps too important to be entrusted to the goddess of profane love; it became the department of Aphrodite's brother Ares. Our own nonrationalist Western ethos, however, has comfortably assimilated the juxtaposition of war and love under one heading; we have a romantic tradition which equates love, sex, pain, suffering, and death, as in the line by Ronsard, *"Car l'amour et la mort n'est qu'une même chose* (for love and death are the same thing), or the description of orgasm as *la petite mort*.

We saw in Chapter 25 that by about 2000 B.C.E. Inanna had conferred the prerogatives of kingship on Shulgi including the appurtenances of office and the weapons of war, and that she was his leader in battle. She had become the patron of war only after she was synthesized with Ishtar a few centuries earlier, when Sargon I unified northern and southern Mesopotamia as the kingdom of Agade—Akkad—and greatly extended its hegemony.

I mentioned that the concept of the peaceful Sumerians conquered by warlike Semites was disproven by the researches of Thorkild Jacobsen. He demonstrated that Sumerian and Semitic names were mingled in the historic inscriptions of the Sumerian city-states long before the first recorded conquests by Semitic rulers—Sargon I in the third millennium and Hammurabi of Babylon in the second. There is still a tendency, however, to think of the advanced culture of Sumer invaded by warlike pastoralists of a lower material level of culture, the "haves" conquered by the "have-nots."

It is a part of Western tradition to give high marks to any culture which produces bigness and material objects—be it the Moguls, the Incas, the Chinese, the Babylonians, the Assyrians, or the Egyptians—and to dismiss as primitive those cultures whose legacy is measurable only in abstract terms of imagination. The ancient Hebrews are a curious exception: their history has been much distorted, the ambivalent relationship with the dominant cultures which owed existence to their gift—the Book or what is usually termed the Judeo-Christian heritage—alternating between persecution and uneasy tolerance or appreciation.

In the twenty-five hundred years before Babylon fell to the Persians, waves of conquest back and forth between north and south Mesopotamia and neighboring countries brought the northern Assyrians, the northeastern Kassites, the western Syrians, as well as descendants of the Akkadians into prominence in Mesopotamia, with interim periods of anarchy, fighting, or alliances (including, by 1000 B.C.E., with the Hebrews), in which vassal kings pledged themselves with tribute to one ruler or another. There were attacks not only by the Semitic Akkadians and Amorites and Assyrians, but by the Lullubi and the Gutians, the Indo-European Kassites, Hurrians, and Hittites, the Mitanni and the Urartu. The chronicles of Sumer and Akkadia, and later Babylonia and Assyria, speak about the lawless invaders; the Gutians, for example, are characterized as stinging serpents of the north.

But history is written from the point of view of those writing it. It may well be that the invasions were provoked by predations and demands made for tribute in the form of goods and labor, as well as conflict over immigration and boundaries. Translators point out that the Sumerian word for slave, *geme*, meant, literally, mountain woman, meaning that women were taken from the mountains to serve in temple workshops, in king's palaces, and eventually on private estates.[1] A temple record from Lagash during the third millennium shows that women and children were brought back from war expeditions.[2] Male war prisoners may have been killed or women, particularly young women, and children may have been more vulnerable to capture, and could always be put to use—sexual or otherwise.[3] In any event, the incursions were not a one-way street.

In some instances the conflicting interests of herdspeople and farmers may have been involved. Foraging peoples may be converted to animal raising by choice, merely by contact with the farmers and exposure to their knowledge, but frequently necessity enters. It was shown earlier that as people of mixed practices—farming and animal keeping—settle on the land, they change the ecology, so that it is no longer possible to live by foraging—gathering and hunting. Different plants grow, game is killed or unable to graze; the wide range of land necessary for the foragers' subsistence is occupied and enclosed so that the previous round of wandering is no longer possible. Herdspeople are more dependent, however, than either foragers or mixed farmers. Like the former, they need a wide area of land, but they are also constricted by the demands of their animals. They must travel where the grazing is good. Moreover, theirs is a specialized way of life; they cannot exist autonomously. They obtain some of their own food, raw materials, and manufactured goods from the settled peoples.[4]

Whether the pastoralists were already herders or were forced to turn to animal keeping during the late Neolithic and Bronze Age, the herding way of life demanded access to pasture lands. The basically agricultural organization, with clan or temple or private ownership of land, in Sumer, Akkad, and the northern part of greater Mesopotamia later known as Assyria impinged on this access. The herdspeople were forced to change their ways. They either had to settle down on land of their own or develop symbiotic relationships with the farmers, as happens much of the time. On the other hand they might take to raiding, given the development of different psychological values engendered by animal breeding. The stress of conquest and insecurity fostered by the new relationships between animals and humans gave rise to accumulative values that encouraged raiding and warlike traits. This turn was further encouraged when central governments appropriated tribute and labor.[5]

Myths about the competition of the shepherd and the farmer for Inanna's favors show that the Sumero-Akkadian story is not a history of settled farmfolk against warlike herders. The final outcome makes it clear that there are no hard feelings: Inanna chooses the farmer, but she needs the shepherd too. In good times, agricultural and herding peoples combined in symbiosis, until the balance was disturbed by aggression-predation on one side or the other.

The history of the back-and-forth movement of nomadic herdspeople, whose waves of invasion press on the "peaceful advanced civilizations," is a stereotype commonly presented by historians influenced by conventional Western thinking, as in the recounting of the Mesopotamian story. In truth, incursions were made by kings and city-states for produce, for military service, for labor; wanderers and immigrants were captured and enslaved, women carried off as booty. Long before we hear about their successful conquests, historical references are made to Amorites and Gutians in lowly occupations, employed in the temples as fishermen and weavers, and to the other "semi-free" persons whose rations were so parsimoniously doled out.

Recent history has left detailed accounts of the chain of events set off when a culture with advanced technology swamps people who live by simpler means.

It was, for example, the invasion of whites and the pressure of land expropriations which transformed the American plains into a welter of warring tribes in the nineteenth century. The initial step had occurred several hundred years earlier when horses and guns were introduced into North America by the Spaniards, elements which set off a new pattern of bison hunting on the Great Plains. As noted earlier, the introduction of simple animal keeping introduces sadistic patterns into human lives. In this case, a lethal weapon and the animal most closely associated with the waging of war were introduced by mounted conquistadors. Not surprisingly, new warlike traits, raiding, sadistic cruelties, and changes in sexual relationships also developed among the Amerindians.[6] Changes not completely dissimilar can be found in ancient history also.

On the North American continent, gathering tribes like the Navajos and the Comanches were transformed into raiders and warriors in less than one generation. The Comanches had lived for unknown centuries on the northern plains, subsisting on wild vegetables and small game. They were famous for their cowardliness; their response to threatening strangers was to run away with all possible speed. After they obtained guns and horses from the Europeans who entered the plains, they moved southward and changed tactics. They became a scourge, harassing other Indian populations and Europeans, inflicting terror from the Mexican frontier to Louisiana.[7]

Agricultural or semi-agricultural Indians were driven out of forest lands by white invaders, pressing on the gatherer-hunters who had inhabited the Great Plains. Formerly these tribes trapped buffalo in periodic group hunts, in which women, children, and men participated. When men were mounted and equipped with guns, in imitation of the whites, hunting methods changed and new patterns of sexual relations emerged.

Under the new brutalizing pressures, religious cult centered around cruelty, sacrifice, self-mutilation, and deeds of vengeance. Sexual restrictions and emphasis on chastity were also part of the complex which followed on the adoption of the horse, animal castration, the lasso, the saddle, and the stirrup.[8] Scalp-taking had been a restricted practice existing chiefly in eastern North America. This barbarous custom—used here in the literal Greek sense, since the first known scalp takers were the Scythians of the Eurasian plains, barbarians because they spoke a language which sounded to the ignorant Greeks like bar-bar or the barking of dogs—was encouraged and spread by the whites, who paid a bounty for each Indian (or enemy white) scalp taken. Scalping was incorporated into the new masculine mystique taking shape in the period after white penetration of North America. We are more aware today that the white stereotype of cruel and bloodthirsty Indians developed in a time when they were fighting a desperate and losing battle in defense of their homelands.

Though we have sparse evidence of the events taking place several thousand years earlier when Mesopotamian culture began to radiate out and interact with peoples to the north and west and east in Europe and Asia, similar processes may have been set in motion. Male bureaucracy was established during the third millennium in Sumer and Akkad. To what extent neighboring egalitarian foragers were influenced cannot be determined, but another recent example from the North American continent indicates what could happen. In recent years anthropologists have studied American Indian groups and documented the change-over from loose authority systems to stricter male-headed ones imposed by male-dominant conquerors. The gathering Navajos had retained their tradition of loosely ascribed authority, egalitarian female roles, and sexual permissiveness among young people even under the influence of the Spaniards and the Catholic Church and after the adoption of sheepherding. There was even more pressure on them to take up Western ways in the second half of the nineteenth century when they came under the aegis of American governmental authorities, who preferred to deal with one male leader and lamented "anarchic" Navajo customs.

Sumerian influence reached out without gunpower and the other post-Renaissance developments brought into the Americas by Western white conquerors. It did radiate in all directions, though ideas flowed in as well as out. Sumerian cylinder seals have been discovered in ancient Egypt, and the Egyptian system of hieroglyphs, formerly thought to be the oldest method of writing, is now believed to have been suggested by cuneiform, which predates it by a few centuries. Contacts between the two cultures became increasingly frequent during the pre-Christian millennia, though they were basically different in aspect and outlook. In both cultures writing was a tool of the elite. In Sumer it was initially and primarily an instrument of economic order, not to say enslavement, used by the bureaucracy, whereas in Egypt originally it served a formal and ritual religious function in tomb inscriptions and on palace walls.

Materials were exchanged between Mesopotamia, Arabia, and the Indus Valley during the third millennium. Fourth-millennium stones with sign writing that looks like cuneiform have been unearthed in Romania. Discoveries in Turkmenia of third-millennium buildings resembling the Mesopotamian temple (the ziggurat), of bronze implements, and of four-wheel carts, as well as of traces of writing, were recently announced by Soviet archaeologists.[9]

As in the earlier case of cattle domestication it is not always known which of the areas originated a given culture trait. The fifth-century historian Herodotus pointed out that the Eurasian-African land mass is, in effect, one continent, and, as I noted in earlier chapters, contact and exchange have been maintained within it from the earliest beginnings of the human story. Some discoveries began in nonliterate areas and were adopted and expanded by literate ones, the lands we call civilized, then re-exported into the nonliterate areas of their first utilization. Thus ironworking and horse breeding, which began to the north of the first states, were integrated into the repressive order of civilization and influenced the conduct of war.

In the history of civilization animals and war became increasingly entwined in a causal crescendo of power and domination, act and symbol. The first use of oxen was for plows, but close on the heels of the plow was the ox-drawn cart, to be followed by the war chariot—described by militarist historians as the first tank. The wheel may have been invented in northern Mesopotamia, where private property seals first surfaced—the area later known as Assyria—on the presumptive evidence of clay disks from Tepe Gawra (circa 4000 B.C.E.); clay models of wagons and chariots appear in Tepe Gawra levels of about 3000 B.C.E. The first clear evidence of the use of carts in Sumer is in pictograms from Uruk of about 3100 B.C.E. From about 2900 on vehicles appear frequently, as models, in paintings on pottery, and in chariot burials at Ur, Kish, and Susa. These carts were drawn both by oxen and by onagers, an almost extinct wild ass which was domesticated at some period in the fourth millennium and used as a draft animal until the introduction of the horse some thousand years later. The onager was a difficult animal to use, not well adapted for draft purposes. Those in use must have been either castrated males, or females, judging by the history of the more tractable horse.[10]

Horses were domesticated on the Eurasian steppes, as draft animals initially. Introduced into Mesopotamian patterns of war by the Hittites, they were substituted for the onagers and oxen that draw the battle carts of third-millennium sculptures.

Tribes who combined a nomadic pastoral way of life with horseback riding emerged on the central Eurasian steppes almost a thousand years after the first records of large-scale warfare in Sumer. The Scythians are the first people known to have ridden horses; they were mistaken for man-horses by Mesopotamians, probably laying the basis for the fabled centaur of Greek mythology. With the spread of warlike traits, the riding horse was integrated into the new patterns of life. In the developed states of the Mid East, it was, at first, a treasured show animal, traded and bred for kings, but not ridden by them. Only stableboys and trainers are shown mounted on horseback in, for example, second-millennium Egyptian art.

Mounted horsemen played an important role in the Kassite conquest of Old Babylonia in the late second millennium. The Assyrians picked up the use of the animal from the Kassites, and swift war carts and mounted cavalry subsequently enabled them to expand their conquests and impose power over large domains.

Proudhon's proposition "Property is theft" has been amended by latter-day anarchists to "Property is murder." The connection works two ways. Trade, the nineteenth-century dictum had it, follows the flag; four thousand years ago, as today, all too often it was the flag and murder which followed trade. Long lines of caravans were characteristic of the earlier period, and trade networks linked much of Europe and Asia, even Africa, to the Near Eastern heartland. Individual settlements of traders in Kanesh, in Bogazhkoy, and in other far-flung outposts of Mesopotamian culture preceded conquest. Exchange of mores, demands for tribute, and murder in the form of warfare and captured slaves followed. References have shown that the custom of capturing and selling human beings goes back at least five thousand years. Historians write that slavery was minimal, with the slaves limited chiefly to women and children, whether describing Sumer or Amerindians of the Pacific Northwest, but it is hard to see what was minimal about it for the human beings involved.

As mentioned earlier, historians concluded that male war prisoners in Sumer five thousand years ago must have been killed, judging by Old Testament and Greek references to similar customs. In later days, Sumerians seem to have blinded male war prisoners, to discourage running away, another practice followed also by the Greeks. While slavery was different in these ancient times from the eighteenth- and nineteenth-century European and American enslavement of blacks, as well as from, say, the widespread Roman use of slave labor, it cannot ever have been a good life. One difference is that in ancient times many people seem to have sold themselves into slavery, permanent or for a term of years; the custom of parents' selling their children because they couldn't feed them was also widespread, testimony to the increased hardship brought about by the spread of agriculture. Judging from art and literature, Bronze Age life expectancy would seem to have been considerably shorter than it was during both the Paleolithic and the early Neolithic.[11] It has been speculated that seventeen years was the average life span. I noted that analyses of skeletons at Çatal Hüyük and of various Paleolithic group burials gave roughly thirty years as the average life expectancy for those periods. If these figures are indicative, they are a remarkable verification of the effective substitution of quantity for quality engendered by civilization and its concomitant, forced breeding.

Organized warfare and the cruelty it brings in its wake began some five thousand years ago in Mesopotamia, as documented by the presumptive evidence of city fortifications, like the walls of Uruk and Nippur. More exact testimony comes from the Vulture Stele of Eannatum of Lagash (circa 2500 B.C.E.), a large limestone marker which describes and illustrates Eanna-tum's victory over the neighboring state of Umma. Sculptural reliefs show him leading his soldiers over the enemy dead and riding in his chariot, with dead bodies caught in a net and armed soldiers in phalanx. An inscription of his nephew En-temena tells of the slaughter of 3,600 Ummaites.

Scenes of warfare were pictured perhaps a century earlier on the Standard of Ur. This ivory panel inlaid with shells and lapis lazuli consists of several registers, telling the story of a suc-cessful battle charge. The king rides in an onager-drawn cart; he is followed by carts bearing armed soldiers; after the victory, armed foot soldiers drive the defeated—soldiers and captives, bound, wounded, and in disarray—before them.

Literary works from the following millennium fill out the bare historical evidence of earlier times. Epics and laments de-scribe the war campaigns and the hostilities, the famine and suffering inflicted on the people: dead bodies melting in the sun, people not brought to burial, those who died on the roof, and those who died inside the house, the blood which flowed, of the brave and the fearful, of the loyal and the treacherous, the people who starved and those who resorted to eating their children. War and siege know little discrimination.

One commentator has compared the Sumerians in their ma-terialism with present-day Americans, noting that they valued "rich harvests, well-stocked granaries, folds and stalls filled with cattle large and small, successful hunting on the plain and good fishing in the sea."[12] Sumerian materialism spreads in exagger-ated form all over the Near East and thence westward, east-ward, southward. Shylock's "My daughter! O my ducats! O my daughter!" is foreshadowed in the second millennium by many of the Sumerian lamentations. A passage from "The Destruc-tion of Ur" wails, "My possessions like heavy locusts on the move have been carried off, O my possessions I will say/ My possessions, who comes from the lands below, to the lands below has carried off . . . O my possessions, I will say,/ My precious metal, stone and lapis lazuli have been scattered about,/ O my possessions I will say."[13]

The Babylonian creation story discussed in Chapter 26 recorded the final hardening of the state, as exemplified by the victory of one permanent leader, the young battle god Marduk. *Enuma elish* was a martial tale ending in mass slaughter; it reflected a battle mentality. The Gilgamesh epic may have earlier roots than Marduk's victory over Tiamat; fragments of this string of tales go back to Sumerian days, and the Sumerian version differs from the later Akkadian recensions. One substory, "The Taming of Enkidu the Martu"—the Sumerian word for Amorite—tells about the conflict between the gatherer-hunters and the grain producers and reveals how so-called civilized countries' attitudes toward women were involved in this clash of cultures. Schematized, it may be a prototypal unfolding of how foraging people changed their ways after contact with the Sumero-Akkadians.

Both Akkadian and Sumerian versions are told from the very male viewpoint of the second millennium B.C.E., but within their contradictions are echoes of earlier popular tales. The Akkadian epic is confused and contradictory, with much switching of viewpoints. Male friendship—that of Enkidu and Gilgamesh—is glorified, and women are ambiguously viewed. Undoubtedly, many separate folk tales and myths are here combined; archetypal explanations hint at earlier themes and ethical problems, and substories interject. In the prior, Sumerian recension, Enkidu was not the friend but the loyal servant of Gilgamesh, his leader.

Enkidu is an early characterization of the "noble savage," who gives up the freedom of the primal way of life for the attractions as well as the corruptions of civilization; he pays with his life. He lives in harmony with nature, an *enfant sauvage* who lies down with the beasts and sucks of their milk, who knows not bread or alcohol. Initially, the city folk send out a harlot to entrap him; she wraps her legs around him and they bed down for several days, after which the beasts will no longer tolerate him, for he is ruined by his contact with a woman. She is a softening civilizing influence. He goes back to Uruk with her and there makes friends with Gilgamesh, the legendary builder of the Uruk city wall. They go off on a series of adventures, as a result of which he is killed in punishment for his part in a fight with the Bull of Heaven. The archetypal story has been repeated ever since: the effete joys of civilization soften and destroy; but the myth has it that the delights of culture are worth the price, which is to die for one's conquerors.

Mortal women are instruments or are absent from this fable. Only the goddess Inanna-Ishtar appears, and she is powerful, independent, and treacherous. Gilgamesh turns her down because of her sexual freedom, because she has been to bed with so many others, all of whom he says have come to a bad end. However, while he resents a powerful and independent woman, as will all men in subsequent history, it is still dangerous to flout her. Because he has refused her, Inanna asks her father Enlil to send out the Bull of Heaven to do battle against him. Gilgamesh and Enkidu kill the bull. In consequence sterility falls on the land, the trees do not fruit, animals stop bearing, and the people are punished for Gilgamesh's sin. Inanna-Ishtar is allowed to retain traces of her earlier compassion. She weeps for her children, shrieking like a woman in childbirth, though it was through her intervention that this early bullfight took place and she had participated in the divine decree that resulted from the animal's death.

Though mortal women are subservient, weakening, or instruments of corruption, they are necessary. Gilgamesh's faithful and loving mother appears in one of the final episodes; and toward the end the temple harlot reconciles Enkidu to his approaching death.

Buried within the many themes and incidents of the Gilgamesh epic is an adolescent-male myth of the wonderful world without women which still surfaces in male writings. It is the earliest extant tale of male bonding and the diabolic influence of women, describing a string of individual feats of heroism and posing moral questions about the inevitability of death, not only for the human Enkidu but for the hero-king himself.

Enuma elish was ancient agitprop in support of a martial king. The Gilgamesh epic has mingled elements of folklore and philosophy; it is a comment on nature and civilization and mortality, the unconquerable powers of the ancient gods. In the battle of Enkidu and Gilgamesh against the Bull of Heaven we get a foretaste of the Greek hubris, and of brutal animal games which carry over into the sadistic competitive pursuits to which males are still encouraged. The references are to actual events, the change of Enkidu from forager to shepherd, and the development of *friendship* as a form of pledging and subservience, perhaps even vassalage, since by Akkadian times Enkidu had been transformed from a servant to a friend.

By the next millennium, with the destruction of Tiamat, all traces of woman as the supreme creator disappear from official state religion. Never again in the civilized world will woman have the primary importance even of an Inanna, though she may sneak in as a kindly suffering mother in the stories of Isis and Osiris, Mary and Jesus, and as a beneficent spirit in the medieval Shekhina.

The changing stories show the threat posed by woman's sexuality and how she was tamed. Enkidu feared the harlot and cursed his original entrapment by her, though at another point she was admiringly compared to the wife. There was fear of Inanna-Ishtar, and the way in which that fear was handled demonstrates what has happened to sexuality. From a peaceful and joyous encounter it was translated into a symbol of warfare. This curious mixture of attitudes toward women is a constant in Western culture, and its roots can be found in the perversion of sex into war and killing and sadism for man, while the basic stratum of masochism is set for woman.

The average man was forced as well as encouraged to participate in actual warfare; the violence of outlet there provided was a perverse compensation for the restrictions on activity, long labors which took away leisure and spontaneous sexuality. In military service, men were deprived of women for long periods of time, with the promise of booty in compensation—concubines and possessions, or simply rape and rapine. Sex becomes one of a series of material rewards. Prostitution increases at this period, for life is reduced to labor, possession, reward, rather than participation. Necessity and psychological impetus combined in a particular way to suggest the exercise of sadistic power to some and to facilitate its imposition on and acceptance by masses of others, both male and female. No wonder freedom meant return to the mother!

The kind of sexual repression which was demanded of great numbers of humans at this time and which was to become the rule throughout the course of "civilization" (*pace* Freud and his followers) has no counterpart in ethnographic data from foraging peoples, or even great numbers of simple small-scale societies. In the degree to which it was accomplished (always imperfectly), it could never have been enforced on or accepted by women, had it not been for the existence of maternal sexuality. For most women, that aspect was strengthened at the expense of adult sexual expression. This shifting of focus was originally imposed from outside and always with a most uneasy balance. As for men, their acceptance of severely repressive structures was based on a transference of sexual energies directly into the perverse expression of violence and cruelty which is necessary to wage war and to establish dominion over others. A chain of suffering is created: pass it on, pass it on. This deflection of sexual energies is not basic to humanity: it grew out of a given cause-and-effect which, once established, tends to be self-perpetuating.

At this time in history, possession has entered the arena as a substitute for feeling. Despite ambivalent historicoreligious efforts to establish spiritual and affective dimensions in life, it remains a constant throughout five thousand years of Western history.

The confusion between sexuality and war and the introduction of daily violence into relations between men and women are everywhere demonstrated—in large scale by the goddess; in small by beatings, tearing off of ears, and other brutalities specifically referred to in the kingly edicts which have been preserved. The Middle Assyrian Laws of about 1300 B.C.E. are particularly harsh. Mention was made earlier of self-abortion; the punishment decreed for the woman who has taken the liberty of regarding her body as her own possession is to be impaled on a stake and left unburied. In marriage, apart from punishments prescribed for adultery, when wives go out with their heads uncovered the husband is given carte blanche to flog his wife, pull out her hair, split and injure her ears. "There is no legal guilt in it." Commentators point out that these laws are crueler than those promulgated by Hammurabi four hundred years earlier, with many of the penalties involving mutilation: a slave girl who presumes to wear a veil shall have her ears cut off; if a husband does not choose to kill his adulterous wife and her lover, he may cut off her nose and should then castrate her lover and slash his face. If a man's daughter was raped, the father might then violate the despoiler's wife; if the rapist was unmarried, he might merely force him to marry the daughter; small comfort to either of the women involved.

A few hundred years earlier, the laws of Hammurabi had also provided for death and mutilation in several of the punishments. In line with earlier statements about uterine relations and paternal ones, we note that mother-son incest is punished by a fiery death at the stake for both, whereas for father-daughter incest the penalty is comparatively mild—exile for the man. Can this be put down to patriarchy, the power of fathers, with daughters considered as only one more possession to dispose of? I think not. Despite the overcompensating importance being given the male at this period, the visible facts of biology still have greater influence. (On the contrary, among the Hittites, the Indo-European people who introduced not only draft horses and horse chariots but also iron technology and the spoked wheel into the Near East, the punishment for incest with mother, daughter, or son was death to the man; sodomy with sheep, pigs, or dogs was also accounted a capital crime, though permissible with horses and mules.)

All the law collections had class distinctions—lighter penalties for offenses against common men and women than for those against gentlemen and gentlewomen, and still lighter ones where slaves were concerned. The sins of the father are visited on the daughter—"if a gentleman strike a pregnant gentlewoman, causing her to miscarry, and she dies as the result, his daughter shall be killed"—and on the son: "if a builder's work is defective, with the result that the house collapses and the houseowner's son is killed, the builder's son shall be put to death."[14]

The usual explanation for the increasing severity of laws from Urukagina's reforms through Ur-Nammu and Lipit-Ishtar of Sumer and Akkad to Hammurabi of Babylon and, lastly, to the Middle Assyrian Laws is that each nomadic herdspeople introduced their barbarian cruelties to the civilized Sumerians; but the actualities are more complex. The salient point may not be whether Sumer or Akkad or Assyria is responsible for the progressive drop in the status of women. Examination should be made, rather, of the way in which forcibly colonizing states developed, for warfare is dependent on the perversion of sexuality into sadism and violence, a linkage that is made increasingly evident as we look at the spoils of war—booty and rape and concubinage.

Part VI

THE FATHERLAND

The common want of logic . . . this merciful provision of nature, this buffer against collisions, this
friction which upsets our calculations but without
which existence would be intolerable, this crowning
glory of human invention whereby we can be blind
and see at one and the same moment, this blessed
inconsistency, exists here as elsewhere.

—Samuel Butler, *Erewhon*

28

Gifts from the Greeks

About five thousand years ago the first hierarchical, exploitative societies arose in Mesopotamia. They spread out over the next few thousand years and made their influence felt in much of the Afro-Eurasian land mass. Integral to the success of the first organized bureaucracies was the distortion of human sexuality into actual and symbolic production, the repression of· female sexuality, and the linkage of war and sex for men. With the worship of material accumulation, people were reified to be used as tools and frequently were treated as possessions themselves. In autocratic societies children were the possessions of their parents; women were first valued as producers of children, later transformed into property. The sexual nexus became an expression of the dominance hierarchy, perhaps the most widespread, the most pervasive, and the most difficult to root out.

Before the middle of the second millennium, the Near East was parceled off into spheres of influence, owing tribute to warring central powers, which built cities and temples and administered a heavy bureaucratic and military superstructure based on the surplus production engendered by that mixture of technology and organization which we call civilization. Agriculture and animal breeding, bronze and copper casting, writing, the ability to construct huge buildings, and above all the imagination and means to utilize human and animal labor—for the benefit of a very few—were among the techniques invented or adopted. All this was accomplished—and we, the products of a materialist society, have been brought up to admire it—on the sweat, the blood, the deprivation of a great many people, who lived fewer years, labored longer, and ate less well than the smaller number of people who occupied the area before these developments.

By 1000 B.C.E. ancient societies incorporating diverse elements from these earliest stratified societies are located around the Mediterranean and feed into what eventually becomes our own tradition, the Western world. Christian antecedents are found in ancient Israel—the land of the Old Testament—and in the Greco-Roman area; what we call the Judeo-Christian tradition can be seen as an amalgam of ethical Hebrew monotheism, late Greek and Egyptian mystery religion, Greek philosophy, and Roman law.

In a world where acquisition was a supreme value, war was viewed as a legitimate means toward this end. Odysseus' description of his raid on Ismarus—"I sacked the city and killed the men; taking the women and many goods, we divided them"[1]—is echoed by many passages in the early books of the Old Testament, which view the land of Canaan as a place to be exploited, where slaves, polygyny, and the accumulation of goods were taken for granted as the divinely ordained organization of the world. If a city does not surrender the Israelites are to besiege it, "smite every male thereof with the edge of the sword: But the women, and the little ones, and the cattle, and all that is in the city, even all the spoil thereof, shalt thou take unto thyself . . ."[2]

Attitudes toward women were well established by the time the Greeks came on the historical scene, shortly after 1000 B.C.E. A collection of city-states often at war with one another, though capable also of alliance to fight foreign invaders, they resemble the much earlier Sumerians in that they think of themselves as one people, the Hellenes (the Sumerians had called themselves the Blackheads). Basically the Greeks are in the mainstream of the development we have so far been tracing: warlike, slave-based, male-dominant, with an increasing strain of misogyny. The good life is outlined for a male upper class; it includes slaves and cattle as basic necessities. Women are objects, whether for the production of children or for sexual diversion. Speakers of an Indo-European language related to that of the Hittites before them, in some cases they may have merged with the earlier inhabitants of the peninsula; in others, as in Sparta, they would seem to have made the indigenes a subject class, the helots, who worked the land while Spartan overlords occupied themselves with war.

The position of women varied from state to state; the harshest laws may have been in Athens, associated for us with the early development of philosophy, science, and history. Paradoxically, Spartan laws, which served as the model for Plato's *Republic*, were kinder to women, allowing them education, athletics, and an equal start in life, and as much food for female as for male children. (In Athens, boy babies were nursed twice as long as girls, and there were differentials in feeding throughout childhood.) This anomaly, whereby a constant state of war, efficiently waged, may result in more strength, more self-expression, and more autonomy for women, will be examined again when we look at the peoples of northern Europe and the Eurasian steppes.

Athenian women were kept sequestered; they were not educated and were under the complete control of fathers, brothers, and eventually husbands. They were not allowed to own or inherit land, to sign contracts, or to engage in business. Married, ideally, at about fourteen to men of about thirty, their role was to produce a male heir. Athenian attitudes toward women produced two cultural phenomena which later gave the Greeks a reputation for liberal sexuality: male-male relations and a complex system of institutionalized, state-licensed prostitution.

State and private prostitution flourished in many Greek states. In classical Athens, the polis maintained brothels staffed with slave women, both in the city itself and in the nearby port of Piraeus; they were a tourist attraction and a high-yield source of government income. Individual harlots were registered and subject to a special tax; these might be non-Athenian citizens born in another Greek state or in a foreign state or former slaves who had been manumitted or had accumulated enough money, sometimes with the help of former clients, to buy their freedom. There were severe fines for inducing Athenian citizen women to become prostitutes, indication that it did happen. Some of the poorest Athenian women whose families had been unable to arrange dowry marriages for them might well prefer the more lucrative trade of prostitution to the occupations otherwise open to them: spinning and weaving wool, washing clothes, selling food or articles of clothing or ornamentation produced in the home, nursing, and midwifery.

In an early instance of the victim being punished for the crime, a married Athenian woman who had been raped or seduced was equally disgraced; her husband had to divorce her and she was returned to her family to live in seclusion, though surely some women must have escaped to the underworld. The rapist was less severely punished than the seducer, who had breached the family's confidence. In classical Athens, the rapist merely paid a fine while the seducer's life was at the disposition of the offended husband.

Custom and law were less severe in two other parts of Greece, particularly in earlier times. In Sparta adultery seems to have been regarded with a tolerant eye. Male citizens were often away at war, and a chief concern may have been increasing the supply of soldiers. Spartan women were much derogated by later Athenian writers for their licentious ways and promiscuity. Spartan husbands were also accused of lending their wives to friends, in order to produce heirs for them. Analogizing with modern Western white views of relaxed Eskimo and Indian sexual customs, it is quite possible that many of the women's escapades may have been undertaken on their own initiative. In one instance, during the eighth century, they undoubtedly took advantage of their husbands' absence on campaign to have relations with their helot laborers, an episode which produced numerous offspring euphemistically recorded as "children of unwed mothers." These were not, however, admitted to full Spartan citizenship; they were sent off to southern Italy, where they founded the colony of Tarentum, today's Taranto.

The law code of Gortyn, on Crete, dated to the sixth or seventh century B.C.E., treated women in some respects with a liberality equal to or exceeding that of Sparta. In Gortyn adulterers were fined, as were rapists of men or women, though if the adultery had been committed in the home of the woman's husband, father, or brother, the fine was doubled.

As a means of free enterprise, one of the few open to women in ancient Greece, the sale of one's person was then, as later, an avenue of social mobility. From a common prostitute, a woman of intelligence and talent might become a hetaira, companion to men, the equivalent of *les grandes horizontales* of the late nineteenth century. But though the hetairai emerged in public and become known through the important men they influenced, as respectable Greek wives did not, their position was a risky one, subject to restraints different from those on the sequestered wife and not unfamiliar to women of later periods. Lose your protector or your looks, tread on officialdom, and all is lost. No wonder they had a reputation for being grasping and mercenary, since money was the sole protection that endured.

Infanticide was common practice in Greece, as later in Rome. In Sparta the object was eugenic; boy babies were examined for physical defects and unfit infants disposed of. All girl children seem to have been kept, however, for Plutarch merely reports that newborn females were consigned to the women's care. In Cretan Gortyn, the child was presented to the mother's husband and the decision as to whether it should be kept or exposed was his. In Athens the purpose may have been birth control. On the basis of demographic statistics, scholars believe that selective female infanticide was practiced from very early times; studies show a preponderance of male children in classical Athens. In one instance the ratio is five males to every female, though the lesser importance given to women probably led to their being underreported as well.[3]

Exposed girl children had a special economic value. Young girls could be bought or abandoned children adopted to be reared as hostages for the future, prostitutes whose earnings would support the superannuated whore or the independent merchant willing to make a long-term investment. Aspasia was a foreign-born hetaira who lived for some years with Pericles, orator and political leader of fifth-century Athens, then with an Athenian citizen named Lysicles, and ended her days as a brothel keeper.

Rare prostitutes who achieved favor as hetairai have been recorded by history; the great majority must have lived bleak and unrewarding lives. Feminists note that there are no records of citizen wives desiring to become hetairai, but there were women of the latter class who attempted to live as respectable wives, confining though that status was.

Historians have often romanticized Greek attitudes toward sexuality. Erotic paintings on wine cups date from the sixth century B.C.E. on. Frequently they show scenes of group sex, either the satyrs and maenads who formed the wine-god Dionysus' entourage or depictions of the men and women who attended the parties at which the wine cups were used. These would have been upper-class men and prostitutes; the wives, daughters, and sisters of privileged men were never invited to these *symposia*. A wide range of male sexual activity is portrayed on these cups, some homosexual, but more heterosexual. Intercourse in many positions is illustrated. Numerous scenes show women giving pleasure to men in fellatio, very few show its analogue, cunnilingus, while there are no extant portrayals of the two acts performed together, in the position popularly called "sixty-nine."[4] Anal sex occurs frequently with women and men as object. There is little reason to believe that Greek sexual freedom was concerned with women's satisfaction. According to Plutarch, the lawgiver Solon, himself a homosexual, advised the husbands of heiresses to have marital relations with their wives three times monthly. Plutarch endorses this recommendation, extending it to marriage in general, on the ground that it takes off petty differences and keeps small quarrels from growing into large breaches.

Greek misogyny is well documented, beginning with Hesiod in the eighth century B.C.E.: "Do not let a flaunting woman coax and cozen and deceive you; she is after your barn. The man who trusts womankind trusts deceivers."[5] The seventh-century poet Semonides of Amorgos was perhaps the coarsest of woman's vilifiers. In *On Women*, he catalogues their vices, describing the characteristics of the different kinds of women Zeus created from divers animals, including the sow, the donkey, the weasel, and the fox, from soil and from the shifty sea. The one made from the sow wallows in the mud, rolls on the ground, and keeps her house like a pigsty; the weasel woman is insatiable in her sexual demands—"she is wild to make love, but her husband wants to vomit when he comes near her." The one from the monkey "has the ugliest face imaginable, hardly any ass, and skinny legs. She knows every kind of monkey trick and routine and doesn't mind being laughed at." He concludes that, despite rare exceptions, Zeus designed women as the greatest of all evils, especially to their husbands, even if they seem to be useful in some way.[6]

In the fifth century B.C.E. Aristotle considered the female state as being, as it were, a deformity, though one which occurs in the ordinary course of nature. Prefiguring Freud, he pronounced the female a mutilated male and declared it inappropriate in a female character to be manly or clever.

Plato is often considered to be more friendly to women, but on closer examination he turns out merely to be less hostile than his compatriots. As Sarah Pomeroy puts it:

> A chasm gapes between the beastlike women in the verses of Semonides and the female watchdogs of Plato's Republic; yet, upon closer analysis, the attitudes of one of the most celebrated misogynists and one of the greatest philogynists of antiquity show more similarities than differences. Even Plato—of ancient authors the most sympathetic to women—found that one sex was in general inferior to the other, although he allowed for exceptions. . . . the views of Aristotle were more representative; he elucidated in detail the range of woman's inferiority, from her passive role in procreation to her limited capacity for mental activity.[7]

It was from the Greeks rather than the Hebrews that Christianity received its strongest antiwoman impetus, while Greek misogyny also influenced the Romans. The patriarch honors women in their place, while the misogynist dislikes and fears them whatever they do. The worst fault a woman can have is to have none at all. Thus, Juvenal, writing shortly after the beginning of the Christian era, asks, "Who could endure a wife that possessed all perfection?"[8]

As elsewhere, we know more about what well-to-do Greek men did and thought than about the practices of the uneducated, which includes women of all classes in Athens, if not in Lesbos or Sparta. What little we know of Greek popular religion has come to us filtered through literature, as in the *Bacchae* of Euripides, in which Pentheus, King of Thebes, disguises himself to spy on the women in their annual expedition to the country to celebrate the feast of Dionysus.

Jane Ellen Harrison, the famous classical scholar at Cambridge University, wrote about Greek popular rites by carefully picking her way through allusive references in Greek drama and prose, supplemented by her interpretation of vase paintings. Her *Prolegomena to the Study of Greek Religion* was first published in 1903; in the three quarters of a century since then, new information enables us to see links between Greek and Hittite mythology, as well as adjacent Near Eastern religions. Harrison examines ancient harvest festivals allowing for sexual license and traces the development of several cults over the centuries, culminating in the eventual asceticism of the late Orphic rites, just prior to and contemporaneous with early Christianity. In a world of increasing differentiation between classes, with the enormous mushrooming of slavery under the Roman Empire, with little free outlet for women of any class and men of the lower classes, the appeal of puritanism and of a belief in a future world where the unhappiness of the present will be redeemed was manifest and widespread. Orphism was only one of several mystery religions which arise at almost the same period, the prelude to our own epoch. These religions emphasizing ecstatic rites appeal to women of all classes and to men of, above all, the underclasses.

Many of the cults centered around fertility worship, death, and resurrection. Interpreters usually claim that they recapitulate the round of nature in agricultural society. However, the

particular form of worship for a dead god-child-man—Attis-
Adonis, Tammuz-Dumuzi, Orpheus, Osiris, Dionysus-Bacchus,
Christ, as the case might be—frequently showed strong elements of masochism and of sadism. The ecstasies of sorrow and
of joy provided much needed outlet in a severely repressive society. In the beginning, the cults of Dumuzi-Tammuz, of the related Attis-Adonis, of Dionysus, and of Osiris were especially
popular with women. Adonis was the beloved of Aphrodite, as
Attis was loved by Cybele, and Tammuz by Ishtar; the
goddesses are usually linked as goddesses of fertility. While
Cybele and Inanna-Ishtar were directly invoked as war deities, I
noted in Chapter 27 that Aphrodite occupied herself with love
and beauty, leaving bellicose activities to Ares, her sometime
brother and sometime husband.

Characteristic of the festivals is the celebration of a sacred
marriage rite, whether of actual sexual union or of symbolic
merging in mystic oneness, and a period of great weeping and
mourning for the death of the god. Relationships are confused;
though the god is beloved, he is frequently seen as a child, and
he may be invoked as brother-son-husband. It is hardly surprising that with such strong restrictions on man-woman relationships women's affective energies are expressed in terms of
mother-son love. Thus in Christianity we hear of the beloved
Christ child, or Baby Jesus, who is worshiped like Tammuz, the
darling of his mother, yet at the same time the ideal of mystic
union is celebrated when a nun becomes the "bride of Christ."

The Dionysian cult is one of the earliest popular religions.
An ecstasy cult practiced chiefly by women, it spread from
northern Thrace over all of Greece. The women left their
houses and work and roamed about in the mountains, whirling
in the dance, swinging thyrsi and torches. At the height of the
ecstasy they seized upon an animal or, according to the myths,
even a child, and tore it into pieces, which they devoured raw
and bleeding. This is the so-called omophagy—a sacramental
meal. The maenads incorporate the god and his power within
themselves by devouring the animal's parts.[9]

In a world of exceeding cruelty, religion was equally extreme. There were cults of weeping, mourning celebrations of

death, pain, and deprivation. Other masochistic cults, for men, involved sacrifice and self-mutilation, as in the castration practiced by the priests of Attis.

From the period around the turn of the Christian epoch, descriptions of the Hellenist cult of Isis have come down to us with more concrete information. The mingling of asceticism and eroticism documented for the cult of Isis was probably characteristic of many of the mystery religions. Isis herself was supposed to have been a prostitute in Tyre for ten years. When her brother-husband Osiris was killed and dismembered by Set, Isis searched for the various parts of his body and found everything except his penis. Osiris was often represented by his missing part—as a phallus. The temples of Isis were located in the popular neighborhoods, near brothels and marketplaces, and were reputed to be meeting places for prostitutes. Vows of abstinence, from given foods and from sexual intercourse, were a feature of the worship. These vows were made for brief periods or for life; women might dedicate themselves to perpetual virginity in the service of Isis. Her cult was an egalitarian religion open to all. There were slaves who converted their owners, but though it spread to the upper classes the Isis cult always retained its associations with lower classes. At the time of the Mysteries of Isis, the celebrants enacted first the lamentations of Isis and then her joy when she found Osiris' body, exchanging embraces, dancing in the streets, and inviting strangers to dinner parties.[10]

At the beginning of the first millennium before our epoch the Greek world was confined to a small corner of the Balkans and a few toeholds on the Anatolian coast of the Aegean Sea. Greek colonies spread out, but they were always centered around the Mediterranean—"Our Sea," the Romans called it. "We inhabit a small portion of the earth, from Phasis [on the east coast of the Black Sea] to the Pillars of Heracles [Strait of Gibraltar], living around the sea like ants and frogs around a pond."[11] When Greek culture merged with and was incorporated into Roman civilization, the degree of domination and the extent of hegemony spread widely. By the time of Trajan's death, in 117 C.E., the Roman Empire stretched from the Atlantic Ocean to the edge of the Caucasus, nearly 3,000 miles; from Britain and the Rhine in the north it extended south to a line running more or less along the border of the Sahara Desert and thence to the Persian Gulf.[12]

One part of this world was the small area at the time known as Judea, the Roman colony which had previously owed allegiance to Assyria, Babylonia, Egypt, and Persia and which for a very brief time, perhaps a little over a century, had its own hegemony and empire.

29

The Puritan Strain

The Hebrews' written literature is an exception to that of the Near East and the Mediterranean. For the first time we are permitted to catch glimpses of the other side of civilization, the underclass who are the people encroached upon. The Greeks, like the Sumerians before them, lauded agriculture and had only contempt for those people in their eyes too incompetent or too ignorant to practice it. Not so the Hebrews; they remembered their own past too vividly. The picture of the Garden of Eden, where food is gained without toil, is like a folk memory of a foraging people. Not long before they turned to the wandering shepherds' way of life described in the middle chapters of Genesis, they may have been nomadic foragers, dispossessed from a part of their range or otherwise forced to abandon their earlier way of life. Abraham's father, Terah, was an idol maker, who came originally from Ur of the Chaldees—that is, southern Mesopotamia. Abraham sojourned for a long time in Haran, a caravan station on the route between Syria and Babylon.

It took three thousand years before science corroborated the biblical tale—a metaphor for the preagricultural human adaptation—by studying the leisure and pleasures of recently existing gatherer-hunters, with the results described in earlier chapters.

After the expulsion from Eden, and the compressed history of human origins, Genesis depicts the early Hebrews as an underclass of nomads, living on sufferance among the Canaanites,

sometimes permitted to camp and draw water, at others forced
to move on. When Abraham left Haran for Canaan he took
his wife "and all the substance he had gathered"—slaves, cows,
tents. The descriptions of the Hebrew way of life in the early
books, in which kine and women and children are valued as
wealth, is reminiscent of many African cultures in the Sahel—
the Masai, the Watusi, the Fula or Fulani. As was pointed out
earlier, it is almost impossible for nomadic pastoralists to be autonomous; they must have symbiotic relations with settled
neighbors from whom they obtain commodities not supplied
by their own way of life. Sometimes it is peaceful coexistence
on more or less the same level; more often the relations are vertical. In the biblical description of the Israelites' conquest of
Canaan, with the Israelite tribes wandering, living in tents, allowing some of their neighbors to live as bondspeople, servants,
and concubines, but killing many, one is reminded of the class
structure which recently fell apart in Zambia. The Watusi, now
called the Tutsi, were invaders who had conquered the Hutu,
while the Twa were at the very bottom. These last were evidently the indigenous occupants of the area into which first the
Hutu and later the Tutsi had penetrated. It is a pattern which
emerges in many other places. In Britain the Saxons, themselves conquerors of the native Celts, become the lower classes
to the Norman invaders. Earlier the Royal Scyths and the Cim-
merians in their migrations probably established similar relations with the indigenes they encountered in their wanderings
on horse and in wagons.

The Israelites conquer the land of Canaan, shortly before
1000 B.C.E., and are briefly an overclass, still living among local
indigenes but with the power relationship reversed, now landowners and agriculturalists as well as herdspeople. Five hundred years later they are subjects again, the ruling oligarchy ex-
iles in Babylon, many others in flight to Egypt, and the
remnant still on the land paying taxes to the Babylonian Empire instead of to their own monarchy. And their great contribution, the Old Testament, was written down and edited after
the Babylonian exile (586–538 B.C.E.) when they are once more
an underclass, though it included earlier writings and reflects

events from the previous millennium until about three hundred
years before the birth of Christ.

Scholars date the composition of the diverse material—tales,
rules, preachments, proverbs, and poems—to a period between
1200 and 300 B.C.E. The actual writing down probably occurred
between 900 and 300 B.C.E., with the earliest surviving text, one
of the first five books only, dated to a fifth-century Samaritan
version. Other early versions are the Greek Septuagint of the
third and second centuries B.C.E., fragments of the Qumran
texts (the Dead Sea scrolls), and the Masoretic Hebrew texts of
many centuries later.

This sequence of powerlessness and power and again powerlessness influences the special contribution of first the Hebrew and then its much more powerful offshoot the Christian
religion. Concepts like "Blessed are the poor" were alien to
Greco-Roman thinking. The preachings of the reforming Jewish rabbi were an outgrowth of the Hebrew concern for fair
dealing and charity, initially among themselves, but also in
their relations with the outer world. The ethical approach of
Judaism was expanded in Christianity, in principle, if not in
practice. Paradoxical strains were set up: fierce acquisition was
countered by asceticism and holy poverty, and conquest had to
be justified by conversion.[1]

Like the Greeks the Hebrews shared in the common values
of the Near East. Recent scholarship has traced how many of
the law codes and customs and myths of earlier Near Eastern
societies were incorporated into the Bible.[2] The Song of Songs
is probably a version of a Canaanite sacred marriage hymn
which slipped through almost in toto—and in contradiction to
most of their writings on marriage and sexual relations. What
the Jews added to the existent Near Eastern and Mediterranean ethos was an emphatic rejection of sex as a numinous
activity and a certain distaste for it even in its profane aspects.
They also introduced a revolutionary concern for ethics. "An
eye for an eye" reflects Near Eastern laws of long standing, but
"Thou shalt not kill" was new.

In a world where sexuality was already being defined from
the male viewpoint so that women were, at best, highly suspect

and, at worst, completely ignored, a world where women had been reduced to instrumentality, the puritanism of the Hebrew religion, combined with the Hebrews' concern for fairness, was not completely nocuous. Within the framework of a male-oriented society, paternalistic kindnesses toward women were invoked.

On the other hand, sex is profane and polluting in the two books of ritual law, Leviticus and Deuteronomy, both of which were recorded when the Hebrew religion was shaping as an expression of identity against oppression, notwithstanding its own inegalitarian attitudes. Barbarous punishments are decreed along with milder restrictions. Women are defined as unclean in their biology; in fact, the word "unclean" tolls out repeatedly in an almost orgiastic rejection of all the creeping and crawling things that are abominations, in the complex prohibitions on what can be eaten and what can be used, and with regard to the pollutions which deny one access to the community.

The Old Testament is a man's book: a compendium of writings from a male-dominated society. It portrays a man's world and describes activities and events conducted primarily or exclusively by males—war, cult, and government. It tells of a jealously singular God, who is described and addressed in terms normally used for males.[3] Its injunctions are to men, and when it speaks of the people, it uses the Hebrew term Am, meaning men, not men and women.

Ethical rules—"Thou shalt neither vex a stranger nor oppress him for ye were strangers in Egypt"—are intermixed with sexual and health regulations.

Leviticus, the first book of the law, dated somewhere between the eighth and fifth centuries before Christianity, but written down after the return from Babylon, expresses the priests' distaste for the female, as well as for biology itself. With Chapter 11, we begin to get the particular insistence on clean and unclean, pure and impure, the search after holiness which will set aside the humiliated people, make them superior inside to those who oppress them outside. And part of this self-depriving search is the antibody part. We are often told that

the Christians introduced the ascetic element into the Judeo-
Christian tradition, but scripture does not entirely support
this thesis. From the first word "unclean," to be cried after
lepers, there is a paranoid intensity: "Every swarming thing
. . . is an abomination; it shall not be eaten . . . I am the
Lord your God; consecrate yourselves therefore and be holy, for
I am holy. You shall not defile yourselves . . ."[4]

Natural body processes are lumped indiscriminately with
sickness, menstruation with illness: "This is the law for him
who has a discharge and for him who has an emission of
semen, becoming unclean thereby; also for her who is sick with
her impurity; that is, for any one, male or female, who has a
discharge, and for the man who lies with a woman who is
unclean."[5]

The strictures on sexual intercourse and menstruation follow
directly on the prohibitions on lepers and the definition of a
running issue: "Whether his flesh run or his flesh be stopped
from his issue it is his uncleanness."[6] Sexual intercourse is also
polluting: "If any man's seed of copulation go out from him
then he shall wash his flesh and every garment and be unclean
until the even."[7] Menstruation makes a woman unclean during,
and for seven days after, her monthly period—i.e., twelve days
out of each twenty-eight-day cycle. Combined with the longer
period of uncleanness enjoined after childbirth, this meant that
for much of her adult life a woman was not allowed to participate in religious ceremonies or enter the temple. Small wonder
that Ezekiel found women weeping for Tammuz at the entrance to the holy place. With such restrictions they may well
have been attracted to more welcoming local cults.

A man who lay in the same bed with his wife during her
menstrual period was unclean for seven days, and intercourse
"with a woman having her sickness" was punishable by exile;
"if she has uncovered the fountain of her blood; both of
them shall be cut off from among their people."[8]

Women are not addressed directly but through fathers and
husbands. "*You* shall not lie carnally with *your* neighbor's wife
. . . *You* shall not lie with any beast and defile *yourself* with it,

neither shall any woman give herself to a beast to lie with it, it is perversion."[9]

It is made clear, through the differential rules for purification after childbirth, that girls are more defiling than boys. A mother is unclean for seven days after the birth of a male child, but for fourteen days after that of a female. Moreover, to the initial uncleanness in the case of a male child's birth, another thirty-three days are added for further purifying before a woman is allowed to "touch any hallowed thing, or come into the sanctuary."[10] For a female child, the additional purification rites take twice as long, sixty-six days after the earlier fourteen. (This regulation has been compared to Aristotle's pronunciamento that it took forty days for a male fetus to develop a soul, but ninety days for a female "ensoulment," since both demonstrate a belief in female inferiority.)

While there are precedents from nonliterate societies for isolation during natural processes, for the dangerous power of menstrual blood, the particular emphasis on disgust, uncleanness, impurity belongs to civilization, be it Hebrew, Moslem, Christian, or Hindu.[11]

Many of the laws of earlier times are repeated—some, like the regulation about the ox that gores, almost verbatim from Hammurabi's Code. The Hittite law on rape is also that of the Hebrews: when a woman is raped in the city, she is adjudged guilty of co-operating with the attacker, for she could have cried out and gotten help, and both are to be stoned to death. If the rape, however, occurs in the country, "then the man only that lay with her shall die: But unto the damsel thou shalt do nothing . . . For he found her in the field, and the betrothed damsel cried, and there was none to save her."[12]

In premonarchic days, virginity may not have been valued as highly as in later times. In Exodus, "If a man entice a maid that is not betrothed and lie with her, he shall surely endow her to be his wife. If her father utterly refuses to give her unto him, he shall pay money according to the dowry of virgins."[13]

By the time Deuteronomy, the second book of laws, was recorded, several centuries later, there is no longer a question of enticement. A man may demand proof of his bride's virginity,

and if she is not a virgin, she is to be stoned to death. Therefore, all unmarried women are by definition virgins and it is
only rape which is legislated. "If a man find a damsel that is a
virgin and is not betrothed and lay hold on her and lie with
her, and they be found; Then the man that lay with her shall
give unto the damsel's father fifty shekels of silver, and she
shall be his wife, because he hath humbled her, he may not put
her away all his days."[14] The law reflects earlier law codes,
Hammurabic and Assyrian, with the slightly more kindly addition of an injunction against divorce.

In all cases, however, the woman is not consulted; it is the father who decides how to dispose of his daughter. Life does not
always follow the law; one instance in the Bible where a daughter contrived to marry at her own desire occurs in the first book
of Samuel: ". . . Michal loved David: and they told Saul, and
the thing pleased him."[15]

The injunctions against prostitution—"Thou shalt not sell
thy daughter to be a whore"—were later extended into analogy
with Israel abandoning the true Jehovah and playing the whore
with strange gods. The Hebrew condemnation of intercourse
outside marriage, for men as well as for women, was in contrast
to most of the cults surrounding Israel.

I have pointed out that prostitution, sacred or profane, is to
not be equated with women's self-expression. We saw how the
introduction of the sacred marriage rite as a symbol of production led to the worship of male sexuality and the instrumentality of the female. Temple prostitution was practiced in
many cities of the Near East and the Mediterranean. In Israel,
particularly in the later writings, whores and whoring are constantly being held up as an abomination. But it is clear from
many biblical references that the prostitute existed on the margins of society, tolerated if not encouraged. It was sin for a
daughter of Israel to be a whore (as Athenian citizen-women
were not to be sold into prostitution) but the hero Jephthah,
"a mighty man of valor," was the son of a harlot. Rahab, the
whore who hid the Hebrew spies from Jericho's king, played a
helpful role in Israel's destiny. In gratitude, when the city was
taken, she and her family alone, of all the inhabitants of Jeri-

cho, were spared, "and," in the chronicle's words, "she dwelleth in Israel unto this day." Samson visited a whore before being undone when he fell in love with the foreign harlot Delilah. The prophet Hosea was married to Gomer, a prostitute, though he was abasing himself as an example to Israel: "The Lord said to Hosea, Go take unto thee a wife of whoredoms and children of whoredoms; for the land hath committed great whoredoms departing from the Lord."[16] Still, on the face of it, the only opportunity a woman had for sexual initiative was to play the part of a whore; Tamar, in the Book of Genesis, had no choice but to pose as a sacred prostitute in order to entice her father-in-law into making her pregnant.

Though Tamar was a foreign woman, sacred prostitution was practiced in the Temple of Solomon at various times, probably by Hebrew and foreign women. The Hebrews had adopted many of their neighbors' customs—they worshiped idols, practiced Baal worship, and prostrated themselves to both Asherah and Ashtoreth. What we know as Jewish religion emerged only after the return from the Babylonian exile, under the aegis of a fierce male priesthood. The Old Testament's frequent injunctions against idol worship are *ex post facto* explanations for Israel's misfortunes; the priests reproved the people and pointed to their sins in the attempt to enforce their harshly exclusive monotheism.[17]

30

Shall He Treat Our Sister as a Harlot

In a patriarchal society, rape and prostitution can be seen as two sides of a coin, conjoined through the glorification of virginity and chastity. The Old Testament and Greek literature tell of many rapes, though the act of violence itself is usually inferred. Only the brutal gang-rape by the Benjamites, which resulted in a concubine's death, has realistic details. Even here, it is like a war report: she is abused all night and in the morning has the strength left only to stagger to the doorstep and die. As a concubine "who had played the whore" she was sacrificed when the rowdy Benjamites threatened homosexual rape of her master, the Levite. The old man who was his host, mindful of the duties of hospitality, enjoined them not to do "so vile a thing." In place of the Levite, a member of the priestly clan, he offered the rioters his own virgin daughter, along with his guest's concubine, but they satisfied themselves with the woman who was the lowest of all three on the social scale. A whore—loosely, any woman who has been accused of sexual misconduct—is always fair game.

Rape is so institutionalized in Western tradition that women's responses are not recorded.[1] It is a crime against the man who has authority over her, not against the woman.

When Zeus wanted a woman, he took her; the myths do not distinguish as to whether a mortal woman is raped or accepting of divine love; we are more likely to hear about her husband's displeasure, as Amphitryon resented Alcmene's visits from Zeus. Yet, in the Sumerian tale "Shukalletuda and the Shade Garden," when the goddess Inanna lies down to rest and wakes to find that the gardener has "taken advantage of her in her sleep," she is furious and punishes humans in consequence.[2]

In Genesis 34:31 the answer of Jacob's sons, "Shall he treat our sister as a harlot?" when Jacob remonstrates with them after their treacherous attack on the Shechemites points up the intimate association of rape and prostitution. If a whore may be raped, since there is no man to protect her, a woman who has been raped automatically becomes a whore. Once her virginity has been breached she loses value on the marriage market. Women, being passive and possessions, are déclassé if they have relations with a man other than the one who has been given authority over their sexuality, never mind whether with or without their consent. In Hebrew law, as in most other Near Eastern law codes and in Mediterranean custom until very recently, the only remedy open to an unmarried woman after rape was to marry the criminal. If a woman refused to obey her family, she had few options; often prostitution was her only recourse. In the mass rapes of Bangladesh a few years ago, many women were disowned by their families; this is prefigured by the European servant girls of the nineteenth century who were first abused by the son or father of the family, then dismissed without references for profligacy. In Sicily until the early nineteen seventies it was common to kidnap and rape a young woman, who then had no choice but to marry the perpetrator of her dishonor.

In another sense, also, rape and prostitution become allied once a market value has been placed on sex. A woman may sell her sexual services in prostitution; a man may steal them in rape. In the world of the early civilizations theft was recognized and honored in war, as long as one stole not from one's fellow nationals but from another group, the speakers most likely of another language—in Deuteronomy described as "all the cities which are very far off from thee." Rape is also socially approved; it is getting something for nothing. When the men of the cities conquered by the Greeks or the Hebrews are put to the sword, the women are taken as concubines or bondswomen; probably the difference is that upper-class women like Cassandra are concubines, the servants are subject to the will of the men though not dignified by concubine status. By extension therefore rape is a sign of manliness; to the victor belong the spoils, to the conqueror the women, and to take a woman by force means being a conqueror.[3]

Deuteronomy does, however, have kindly instructions about how the captive is to be treated. She is to be given a month to mourn her parents before she is forced into sexual relations. If she does not please her master, she is to be allowed her freedom. "Thou shalt not sell her for money, thou shalt not make merchandise of her because thou hast humbled her."[4] What other recourse she would have besides prostitution is difficult to imagine. Women in this cruel and authoritarian society are given Hobson's choices: give in to rape or be dishonored in prostitution. No doubt some chose the latter, with its illusion of freedom, while others would have settled for the protection of the former if the master were at all tolerable.

With woman as instrument, we saw how the physical gratification in prostitution is reduced to a minimum. The woman is performing a service, not expressing her needs and feelings, and the man is deprived of a truly reciprocal and therefore participatory experience. What then is the gratification in rape? It is perversion in the most literal sense; instead of pleasure, the gratification is in the conquest. Like the imprisoned animal who diverts his or her sexual energy into attack, so does the human, only in this case civilization has made the outrage a convention. Many a nineteenth-century Western white thought that rape was the savage way of making love. This is not true. Recent studies have shown that rapists are often sexually impaired; they suffer from disfunctions, such as impotence and delayed ejaculation. The realization that rape is a crime of violence and has little to do with sexual gratification is just beginning to penetrate the popular consciousness.[5] Though the male organ is envisioned in macho fantasies as an extension of man's other weapons—sword, gun, or club—the living penis is quite inadequate to such a purpose. In individual rape, the injuries to the woman are usually wrought by the arms—literal or otherwise—not by the precious male triune. The Deuteronomic law which forbids "taking a man by the secrets"—a woman who does so in order to help her husband in a fight is to have her hand cut off—must have had an inhibiting effect in other cases, too, an effective injunction against the most potent self-defense a woman has, as cinematographer Nelly Kaplan demonstrated when she had her heroine kick an assailant in the genitals to fend off attempted rape.[6]

A common way to force a woman into prostitution, past and present, was to kidnap and rape her, once or repeatedly, to break her will and deprive her of her sense of self, as well as to impress on her that her sexuality is not hers but at the disposition of others. If it's going to be taken by force, it might just as well be sold at a profit, though, as we noted in Greece, the profit might not accrue to the woman herself.

It is not clear whether Dinah, the sister to whom Jacob's sons referred, was raped or seduced by Prince Shechem. It is an index to these warrior societies' indifference to women as human beings that we know so little about the woman's feelings. As with Ninlil, who became Enlil's loyal wife, so with Dinah and the many mortal women taken captive and carried home in the victors' train: not only is woman a passive field to be plowed, she is also portable. As the tale tells it, while Jacob and his family were camped outside Shechem, Dinah went out to visit with the daughters of the land and "Shechem the son of Hamor the Hivite saw her, he took and lay with her and defiled her." According to the Hebrews' own laws, Shechem did what was legal after the rape or seduction of a virgin: he sent his father with a marriage proposal and generous bride gifts. Moreover, Hamor proposed that Hebrews and Hivites exchange wives, that the Hivites marry the daughters of the Hebrews—unspecified sisters and nieces of Dinah—and the Hebrews the daughters of the Hivites. When the Jews insist that their kin must be circumcised, the Hivites undergo the painful operation, and "on the third day, when they were sore," Dinah's brothers "came upon the city boldly, and slew all the males." Not only do they repossess themselves of their sister, now living with Shechem, but they "spoiled the city . . . took their sheep, and their oxen and their asses . . . all their wealth, and all their little ones, and their wives took they captive," subjecting the Hivite women to worse treatment than Dinah's.[7] Their response to Jacob points up the lack of distinction which prevails when women's active sexuality is forbidden.

And yet there were strong women in the Old Testament. Jael was one, the wife of a Kenite not a Hebrew, who offered Sisera a sup of milk after the battle and then took a nail and hammered it into his head. This was before the monarchy, when Israel was ruled by judges, and "Deborah a prophetess judged Israel at that time." Deborah's stirring song of victory, believed to date from the eleventh century, is one of the earliest extant poems in the Bible.[8] And Jael's action was cited only recently as the inspiration for a black woman prisoner who killed the prison guard attempting sexual liberties with her.[9]

Judith's assassination of Holophernes, when she entered his tent in the guise of a seductress and then proceeded to behead him, is, however, relegated to the Apocrypha, while Esther, the dutiful daughter of Israel who won Ahasuerus' love on her uncle's instructions and then saved her people from destruction, is in the canon itself, a less fiery example. In either case, they are acting as sex objects, using their sexuality as a prostitute does, though the end was to the Hebrews' advantage. From a woman's point of view, the real heroine in the Book of Esther is Ahasuerus' first wife, Vashti, who refused to come at the King's command. The women who served the chroniclers' purposes were written about. Other women must have resisted patriarchal imposition, as Chinese women were wont to commit suicide in the bridal chair rather than be married against their wishes, but we hear nothing of them.

Once a woman's "virtue" has been lost, whether involuntarily or by her own actions, she is damaged goods. No more is said about Dinah after the episode with Prince Shechem. Presumably she was kept in isolation, like a Greek wife who had been divorced by her husband. If she did escape, there were few occupations open to an unprotected woman; her choice might have been to become one man's servant or a harlot. And the latter path must have been taken by many, for there was no dearth of prostitutes.

Ancient society was based on war, on exploitation, on greed. According to Aristotle one of the reasons why statesmen should know the art of warfare was "in order to become masters of those who deserve to be enslaved."[10] These attitudes were as true of the earliest Hebrews as of the Greeks and the Romans. They were, however, less successful empire builders than either of the latter. In consequence, it was only after the return from Babylon that they formulated an ethic which went beyond the materialism of the ancients, that showed a concern not only for their fellow Hebrews, but even for non-Hebrews.

By the time the laws were written down, Jewish society had long passed its material apex. The United Monarchy of David first and then Solomon (circa 1000–930 B.C.E.) had broken into northern and southern kingdoms after Solomon's death. The Assyrian conquest in 721 permanently dispersed the larger fragment, and Nebuchadnezzar's infestation of Jerusalem destroyed the southern portion—all that was left of Solomon's empire—in 586 B.C.E.

Thus on the basis of a tribal ethos which served to unify a small kingdom that broke down within a century is constructed a book which has lasted for two thousand years, a book created out of defeat and dispersal and conquest. Somewhere within this book a new synthesis was created, which took the concepts of the power kingdoms—conquest, bureaucracy, and naked force—and added another more viable dimension. One aspect was sexual puritanism, superimposed on the sadomasochistic underpinning of the previous two or three thousand years. While rape and booty were taken for granted in the versions whose composition was earliest in time, in later editings rules were formulated, not only for the treatment of captives, as we saw, but for that of bondservants, Hebrew and stranger, for fairness in business dealings, and for charity. In contrast to earlier Near Eastern law codes, class distinctions were elimi-

nated in the Bible, except for the blanket one between Hebrews and foreigners. Frequent is the reminder "because ye
were slaves in Egypt" or "because ye were strangers in a strange
land." It is this feeling for the underclass, initiated in the Old
Testament and developed further in the New Testament, the
book created by a reforming sect of Jews, which has made
Christianity effective in its broad appeal to subject peoples
over the past two millennia.

Where women are concerned, the Hebrew record is mixed.
Their laws and attitudes were kinder to women than those of
the Assyrians if harsher than those of the Sumerians. Some
commentators make a case for women being stronger and more
active in the earliest period, before the monarchy and the establishment of a bureaucratic government, which would be consistent with observations made elsewhere in the Near East and
the Mediterranean.[11] The Greeks and the Romans recognized
prostitution and slave concubinage as legitimate for men. They
licensed the former and made money for the state from it. The
Old Testament appears to disapprove of sex outside marriage,
but it accepts polygyny, concubinage, and, in the sending in of
Rachel's and Leah's maids to Jacob, the master's sexual rights
over all the female servants, common practice throughout the
Near East. It does not explicitly forbid prostitution—only the
selling of one's own daughter as a whore, and the practice of
prostitution on temple precincts.

The transported Africans in nineteenth-century America
adopted Old Testament tales for their own self-esteem. If
looked at in the light of compensatory literature, when the
"chosen people" were powerless slaves, tolerated and allowed to
exist but no more, at the impressive court of Nebuchadnezzar,
the boastful and self-righteous tone of the historical books becomes less offensive. The insistence on seed and multiplicity
and on their apartness and identity was shaped to fit the needs
of an oft-conquered people. The sources for "Let My People
Go" and "Joshua Fit the Battle of Jericho" were wishful para-
bles to the Jews long before they spoke to enslaved blacks.
Their actual history in relation to the powers around them is
somewhat different from the dramatic tales of the book. They

built no huge cities like Babylon and Uruk and Assur, left few splendiferous ruins. Babylon's two thousand five hundred acres under Nebuchadnezzar are in sharp contrast with the ten acres compassed by the Jerusalem city walls under Solomon (circa 970–930 B.C.E.).[12]

During the diaspora, attitudes changed and influences were now received from Hellenist and Roman Christian sources, as earlier they had come from Near Eastern neighbors. Concubinage disappeared, though polygyny was practiced well into the Christian era in the West, even into the nineteenth century in Moslem countries. Adultery was forbidden with the punishment of death for man and woman, but the judgment was based on the violation of property rights, not sexual equality.

Men were literally valued more than women. One example is that the payment to release a male from religious vows is almost twice that for a woman. The general distaste for the body cited earlier, the almost phobic attitudes about life processes, comes down much more heavily on the childbearers, the producers of life. The exclusion of any female reference in religious imagery—where formerly it was Inanna who had prevented all bearing and fertility in the land, now it is the Lord who has "fast closed up all the wombs of the House of Abimelech" at the time the latter took Sarah into his harem—had to have an effect on the way men and women thought about themselves.

On the other hand three references to earlier matrilineal tradition remain in Genesis, the first book of the Old Testament, and one hung on into the recent past, in the rabbinical definition of a Jew as the child of a Jewish mother. On the face of it, this judgment seems to show the rabbis' mistrust of women, since only the woman knows for sure who is her child's father. I believe it reflects the heritage of foraging times, possibly retained on a pragmatic basis, since Old Testament Hebrew men had a tendency to marry out. Though the practice was frowned upon initially, they were always bringing in the daughters of neighboring groups. Tamar is only one of several examples. Sarah and Abraham sent back to Haran for a cousin to marry their son Isaac, but Esau displeased his parents by marrying an Edomite. Jacob went back to Haran and there fell in love with his cousin Rachel, though Laban trapped him into marrying both sisters. Moses, it will be remembered, married the daughter of a Midianite priest, and there was conflict back and forth about the problem, since the Jews' exclusiveness was at odds with the emphasis on increasing their numbers—especially in latter days.[13]

The customs accepted by their Near Eastern and Mediterranean neighbors were anathema to the Hebrews. Homosexuality, typified by anal sex, was an abomination punishable by death and, as we saw in the story of the Levite's concubine, in practice considered a worse sin than the rape of a virgin. Moreover, the injunctions against "unnatural ways" and the sin of Onan—masturbation or coitus interruptus—became a rigorously restrictive, not to say anti-sexual, code, which was further developed in Talmudic times, the centuries just before and for several hundred years after the birth of Christ, when the interpretation of religion was hardening into dogma. The strict rules were a prohibition on experimentation and elaboration in heterosexual practice also. Women were not to approach their husbands to initiate sex, because of their modesty and Eve's sin: "Thy desire shall be to thy husband and he shall rule over thee."

Positions in marital intercourse were legislated by the Talmudic rabbis. In one part of the Talmud, "A man may do all that he will with his wife," but most other sources condemn "intercourse not in the usual way." One second-century rabbi issued a fiat against intercourse where the woman is above the man.[14] In line with Jewish emphasis on multiplying the people, however, marital relations were approved—in fact, the number of times per week, as well as the length of time a husband could stay away from his wife, was legislated according to the husband's profession. Only Talmudic study excused the man from *onah*, the wife's right to sexual intercourse. On the other hand, the woman was to satisfy her husband's sexual needs.

The Talmud assumed that an unmarried man would be unable to resist sexual temptation. The wife's function was to give him pleasure, thus helping him to resist his natural tendency to commit immoral acts. Even after marriage, however, he is thought of as waging a continuous battle against his sinful desire for extramarital sex.[15]

The precious male seed was believed to be equivalent to humans, and the Babylonian Talmud (500 C.E.) has a strong condemnation against masturbation. One third-century rabbi felt that "whoever emits semen in vain deserves death."

Though Christianity would carry the sexual bind much further, the ascetic strain was prefigured by the dissident Hebrew sect known as the Essenes. (Recent archaeological discoveries indicate that this group may have been the actual as well as the spiritual source of the new synthesis that, in later centuries, would become the Christian religion.) Writing about 100 C.E. the Jewish historian Josephus describes two orders of Essenes, the one practicing celibacy, the other marital restraint, which included avoiding intercourse when wives were pregnant since, according to Josephus, their purpose in marriage was reproduction and not "self-indulgence."

The first-century Jewish philosopher Philo also believed that intercourse should be only for procreation, explicating thus the biblical condemnation of homosexuality and of intercourse during menstruation, when, he thought, conception would produce deformed infants. Philo criticized immoderate and insatiable desire, deeming unchaste "the rage for sexual intercourse," even with one's own wife, and condemned the "passion of love."[16] As with most other patriarchal pronouncements on sexual impulses, he writes from the male viewpoint, ignoring any feelings or desire a woman might have. Her contribution was to receive the male seed and to give it shelter and sustenance.

Because of these attitudes Jewish men were not allowed to practice birth control, but women, by their very inferiority, were spared certain prohibitions. Moreover, as the emphasis on survival under outside domination increased, there was a tendency to encourage all practices that would increase the people. This meant that the woman's life was preferred over that of the fetus—you don't kill the cow to save the calf. On occasion, the rabbis permitted sterilization or the use of a *mokh*—a sponge or wool tampon inserted into the vagina to occlude the opening of the uterus—for married women: when the woman's life would be endangered by pregnancy or when she suffered excruciating pain in delivery. It is assumed that there are certain other conditions under which a woman will use a *mokh*. The slave, the convert, and the captive, who do not know what fate is in store for them, are described in the Talmud as having recourse to contraception. And Rabbi Naman, a teacher in Babylon at about 330 C.E., quotes another rabbi who permitted the use of a *mokh* in three cases: for minors—that is, girls under twelve—nursing mothers, and pregnant women.[17]

The Gemara, a part of the Babylonian Talmud, which probably dates back to the first or second century C.E., makes an oblique reference to coitus interruptus during a mother's two-year nursing period, taking it for granted that the man "will thresh inside and winnow outside." The severe and literal emphasis against the spilling of male seed, inferred from the story of Er and Onan, the brothers who practiced coitus interruptus with Tamar and died shortly thereafter, may postdate this particular passage. In medieval days the demon Lilith was blamed for even such unconscious sins as nocturnal emission, a possible reflection of the more intensely antibody, antifemale, and antisexual attitudes of the dominant Christians, who surrounded the small sect of Jews, now struggling to survive the persecutions of their more powerful offspring.

It was assumed that harlots practiced birth control, either with a *mokh* or by moving during and after the act of coitus, which is interpreted as serving to expel the seed.[18] In effect, this may have meant that a married woman was expected to lie still, just as the Latin writer Lucretius averred that the customs of prostitutes were not fitting for Roman wives. According to him movements in intercourse made it difficult to conceive; surely, he counseled, our wives have no need of such effeminate movements.* The equation of female sexual pas-

* Lucretius advises that the proper position for conception is *a tergo*, from the rear, "after the manner of wild beasts and quadrupeds because the seeds in this way can find the proper spots in consequence of the position of the body. Nor have wives the least use for effeminate motions; a woman hinders and stands in the way of her own conceiving when thus she acts; for she drives the furrow out of the direct course and path of the share, and turns away from the proper spots the stroke of the seed. And thus

sivity with respectability seems to predate the Victorian era by at least two thousand years. The entire male domination of sexual acts must have had severely inhibiting effects on spontaneous expression for woman, a heritage that is still with us.[19] Love was directed toward children; woman's functions in marriage were "to grind corn, suckle children, be a beautiful wife, and bear children."[20]

Even more than in the Old Testament, Talmudic quotations can be found to justify diverse conclusions about the position of women. The patriarchal tradition in Jewish heritage needs no exegesis—women's inferiority is a given within and without the Hebrew world. What is specific to Hebrew theology is the bind in which the Jews found themselves once they rejected female imagery in creation, despised the body and its functions, and at the same time emphasized the value of fair treatment, charity, and kindness. They were caught in ambivalences which in Christianity turned into almost pathological double binds. Talmudic Judaism developed rabbinical courts which decided on all questions of life, from the most intimate to the most formal. The heritage of puritanism is passed on to the Christians and there combined with asceticism to produce an even more body-hating schema. The Jewish tradition decrees marriage for all; only a rare prophet or rabbinical scholar was excused from this obligation. In practice, the usage was to arrange early marriages for men and women.

If the Greeks hated women, the Hebrews had contempt for them. But the patriarchal problem is that no one has yet figured out a way to eliminate women from actual life, despite the theoretical ascription of holiness and spirituality to men, the innumerable inventions of myth which ascribed creation to men, seduction and sin and evil to women.

In the Old Testament we see an early dichotomization, which underlies two thousand years of patriarchy and which is still operant in our cultural tradition—the profane and the holy. The spirit is considered superior to and separate from the body. Women, however, are more nakedly connected with the

---

for their own ends harlots are wont to move, in order not to conceive and lie in child-bed frequently, and at the same time to render Venus more attractive to men. This our wives have surely no need of."

body's role in maintaining life—and the process of patriarchal inversion is spelled out in a series of prohibitions and punishments, rules and taboos. It is only one of a series of dichotomies which have formed the bases for much of Western thinking and are accepted by women as well as men. With the Jews, nature is profane, worship holy. This dichotomy of spirit and body is peculiarly unworkable in the case of women, who are necessary and yet inferior and suspect. The Talmud expresses it thus: "With the Jews one great consideration of life is to have children and more especially male children; because when a boy is born all rejoice over him, but over a girl they all mourn. When a boy comes into the world he brings peace with him, and a loaf of bread in his hand, but a girl brings nothing." The tractate *Niddah* (The Menstruous Woman), says: "It is impossible for the world to be without males and females, but blessed is he whose children are boys, and hapless is he whose children are girls."[21]

The attitudes of the Talmudic writers were passed on to the early Christians. The Jews were harshly patriarchal, but they valued women too highly as wives, producers of children, preferably sons, to permit themselves the total misogyny in which several Greek writers indulged. Katherine Rogers points out that the Bible itself is most misogynistic where it has been influenced by Greek thinking in the apocryphal books of Ecclesiasticus and Esdras and in the writings of Paul. Later Christian commentators distorted the Old Testament to make it more misogynous than it was. St. Paul harped on the Adam and Eve story as the basis for women's inferiority. In the original Old Testament tale of David and Bathsheba, the emphasis was on King David's adulterous desire when he accidentally saw Bathsheba naked as she was bathing and on his murder of her husband. The Christians shifted the blame onto Bathsheba, so that she has come down to us as a seductress.[22]

Moreover, where the Jews were concerned with numerical survival, the new religion no longer felt it necessary to increase by sexual means. In the first place, the end of the world was imminent; the coming of the Kingdom of God was expected at any time. Christianity increased by conversion; it reached out rather than forward. So the new emphasis was on chastity for both women and men; marriage was good, but virginity was better. Celibacy as a choice for women was one road away from the impasse which has been made of the male-female meeting, a rather drastic one.

The new religion was never revolutionary. From "Render unto Caesar the things that are Caesar's" to "Servants, obey in all things your masters," it preached accommodation to the external powers. But within itself the initial impetus was toward egalitarianism.

The early organization was informal and there were many women among the first converts. Women, in the beginning, enjoyed positions of leadership, as prophets, deacons, and patrons who provided shelter and a meeting place. Acts, particularly, has many references to single women and wife-husband teams who worked for the new religion.[23]

By the end of the first century c.e. it was clear that the Parousia—the end-time or the second coming of Christ—was not imminent. The Church reverted to some of the Jewish and Greek feelings about women. The pseudo-Pauline letter to Timothy, with its clear definitions of men's authority over women, is generally dated to the early part of the second century.† In Paul's letter to the Colossians, husbands were to love their wives, but wives were to submit to their husbands. It was not that the first Church planned to revolutionize men-women relations—it was just that relative status on earth would be of no importance in Paradise, so that Paul could say, "There is neither Jew nor Greek, there is neither slave nor free, there is neither male nor female, for you are all one in Christ Jesus."[24] But Jesus Christ had not returned, and the microcosm which was the persecuted Church, home of slaves and women, began to imitate the macrocosm around it. More and more, the early egalitarianism gave way to an accommodation with the forces around it. The process was, of course, enormously facilitated when Constantine converted to Christianity in the early fourth century.

† Paul's first letter to Timothy is believed by modern scholars to have been written after Paul's death.

31

The European Connection

To the north of the "civilized world" of the ancients, in
Europe and Asia, lived the people lumped together by the
Greeks and Romans under the name "barbarians." Their forebears had indeed given rise to the classical states of Greece and
Rome, in the various waves of post-Minoan invaders, as well as
to the Aryan invasion of India and to the languages, if not the
peoples, of most of Europe and eventually the Western white
world. By the middle of the first millennium B.C.E. a complex
society had taken shape, influenced by earlier developments in
the area as well as by the technologies of the ancient civilizations.

At this point the distinction between nomadic foragers of
the earlier periods of human existence and herdspeople—pastoral nomads—should be restressed. Foraging peoples still
existed in Eurasia as recently as one thousand years ago—a very
few exist even today in remote parts of India and Southeast
Asia.[1] By three thousand years ago, however, the majority had
been converted to agriculture and/or animal keeping. I explained earlier that animal breeding did not precede agriculture
and that pastoral herding was not a primitive state of development, a bridge between food collecting and farming. On the
contrary, nomadic herdspeople utilize complex systems, choosing a mixture of animals matched to the different kinds of

grasslands they encounter: cattle, horses, and camels need long grass, while sheep and goats crop close.

As agriculture and animal breeding spread through much of Europe and Asia different combinations developed, to take advantage of the different ecologies found there. The horse was domesticated during the third millennium, somewhere in the region of the Hungarian plains, the south Russian steppes, and the Caucasus. As noted in Chapter 27, it had been introduced into the civilized Near East from the north by about 2000 B.C.E. In the meantime, a complex system of pastoralists who knew agriculture but lived mainly on animals was taking shape across the steppes of inner Asia and Central Europe. In the development of the specialized mode of existence which characterized the Indo-European herdspeople, the use of horses was a necessity. They developed the technology for full utilization: harnesses, bits, even carts, and finally iron stirrups. Their subsistence, largely based on pastoral nomadism, stemmed from the invention of horseback riding.[2]

True nomadic pastoralists are limited in their material equipment. Like foragers, they must travel light. They rarely use pottery, have very few metal containers, and possess only the simplest of household goods. Their homes are portable, and they are unlikely to have ritual or decorative art objects. Clothing and artifacts are often made from animal products of horn, bone, wool, and skin. On the open plains which provide grazing land for their animals, wood is scarce. Many of their tools are of perishable materials. For these reasons, it is difficult to trace their history by archaeological methods. They do not own land and they cannot afford concubines, servants, and the conspicuous consumption which characterized the established bureaucracies in the Near Eastern kingdoms. In the beginning at least, the nomad tribes of the Eurasian steppes could not bring to bear the efficiency of domination exercised by their civilized neighbors.[3]

I spoke earlier of how the horse was integrated into the practice of war and of how horse breeding facilitated the expansion and the efficiency of warfare, while, at the same time, it strengthened the underlying psychological motivation. In the case of Greater Mesopotamia and Syria, Palestine, even Egypt, what had happened was that already settled warlike, materialist, accumulative peoples adapted to their own uses the techniques introduced by the nomadic herdspeople. The Hittites, who lived in Anatolia during the third millennium, used horses for draft purposes and knew iron technology. The first people to use the riding horse as a war machine may have been the Kassites, who lived in the mountains to the northeast of Greater Mesopotamia and conquered the Old Babylonian kingdom founded by Hammurabi shortly after the middle of the second millennium (1500 B.C.E.).

Modern scholars have shown how the aggressive way of life fostered by horse riding spread throughout Europe and Central Asia. Horsemen went south, conquering the Near East; the Kassite wave was the first; the Persians were later Indo-European invaders. Other mounted warriors went north, plundering the pastoralists of the steppes, who did not usually ride. Helpless against cavalry attacks, the latter either gave up their flocks and herds to the invaders or paid tribute. The only way to resist was to adopt the enemy's methods and to take to the horse themselves.

Thus raiding complexes were transmitted to the steppes, wherein arose communities of mounted warriors who controlled subject tribes and huge flocks and herds. The more people took to the steppes, the more nomadic they became. Horses needed extensive pasture, so there was more reason to conquer more areas. The herdspeople spread in all directions. Where the steppe would not support agriculture, they adapted to life on the open land; elsewhere, as in South Russia, they exacted tribute from the settled agriculturalists. Forest people who lived by gathering and hunting were recruited or converted to a different way of life—by example or necessity—when the pastoralists encroached upon areas from which the foragers had previously drawn sustenance at certain times of the year; mass migrations occurred only when folk were driven from their lands by invading groups.[4]

Within this complex mixture of interrelationships are comprised the peoples variously described under the names Scyths and Teutons, and eventually the Celts, all of whom spoke Indo-European languages. They are not usually considered civilized, for although they had complex technologies, they did not use writing and they had no centralized dominating bureaucracies; their settlements never become cities on the scale of Babylon, Assur, Athens and Rome.

It is difficult to trace their movements over the millennia before they enter written history, during the conflicts with the Greeks and the Romans and the later conversion to Christianity.

First source of information is Herodotus, writing in the fifth century before our epoch. Variously termed the "father of history" and the "father of lies," he is today recognized as the world's first anthropologist, a rousing tale-teller whose work still provides confirmatory material for archaeologists, anthropologists, and historians. He jumbles many tribes together under the general name Scyths, though he also gives specific tribal identities and explains that there were Scyths who were settled agriculturalists and others who were horse-riding pastoralists living in the special way of life described above. In one place he describes them as "a people without fortified towns, living in wagons which they take with them wherever they go, accustomed one and all, to fight on horseback with bows and arrows, and dependent for their food not upon agriculture but upon their cattle."[5] Elsewhere, however, he mentions the agricultural Scyths, the nomadic Scyths, and the Royal Scyths. These last had picked up conspicuous-consumption customs from the Middle Eastern and Mediterranean civilizations: they practiced a form of suttee, with sumptuous royal burials in which wives, horses, and chariots were interred with the dead king; they were also the dominators of subject agricultural tribes, occupying the extreme high side of the vertical interrelationship that usually existed between the settled agriculturalists and the horse-and-cattle raisers.

At the extremes of the Scythian territory were peoples Herodotus called hunters, the Thyssagetae and the Iyrcae, though we imagine that in today's terminology foragers or gatherer-hunters would be a more accurate description. Beyond them, to

the north and east, was another Scythian tribe, the Argippaei,
described by the historian as living on fruit from a tree he calls
ponticum—a kind of cherry. They strained the ripe fruit
through cloths and got from it a thick dark-colored juice, which
they lapped up with their tongues or mixed with milk for a
drink, making cakes from the remaining sediment. He writes
further:

> They have but few sheep, as the grazing is poor. Ev-
> ery *man* lives under *his* ponticum-tree, which *he* pro-
> tects in winter with bands of thick white felt, taking
> them off in the summer. These people are supposed to
> be protected by a mysterious sort of sanctity; they
> carry no arms and nobody offers them violence; they
> settle disputes amongst their neighbors, and anybody
> who seeks asylum amongst them is left in peace.[6]

The different peoples varied in organization as in subsistence techniques. A careful reading of Herodotus on Asian peoples, and of Tacitus, writing about the Germans some six hundred years later, brings evidence of peaceable egalitarian band
societies—with the equality going across sex lines—existing in
northern reaches of the Europe and Asia of their times.

The Fenni described by Tacitus are clearly egalitarian gatherers and hunters. They have "neither arms nor homes; their
food is herbs, their clothing skins, their bed the earth . . . the
men and women are alike supplied by the chase; for the latter
are always present and demand a share of the prey."[7]

In some places the social organization was what we would
call "rank society," with some people owning more than others,
but no real stratification.[8] Tacitus describes the German moots,
which are typical of this form of government, one of the bits of
evidence which gave rise to the theory of primitive democracy
deduced by Jacobsen for early Sumer: they are a sort of town
meeting where "the final decision rests with the people . . . the
chief is heard more because he has influence to persuade than
the power to command."[9]

In other places class societies like that of the Royal Scyths
took shape. Graves with treasure hoards of gold ornaments and

weapons and rich tumulus burials appear throughout Eurasia, from England to the steppes, by the middle of the second millennium before our epoch. In some areas, as under the Scyths of Central Eurasia, agricultural tribes were kept in subjection by mounted peoples; in others, groups lived by fishing (Northwest Europe, particularly Scandinavia), by gathering and hunting (parts of the forest lands of Germany and Poland), or by mixed practices of farming and animal raising (the Swiss lake dwellers).

Trade connections were, however, maintained from the extremes of Europe into Asia, not only within the "barbarian" area but between the barbarians and the civilized peoples. The Scyths had Greek craftsmen working for them, and Greek, and later Roman, objects are found as far away as Germany and Scandinavia, just as amber found its way south to the Mediterranean. Technologies were also passed in both directions; it took almost a thousand years for the wagon to travel from Mesopotamia to England and Holland, while I have noted that the use of the horse and of iron was transmitted in the opposite direction.

In all these societies, ancient writers were surprised to find woman's position was rather different from the repressive situation typical of their own worlds. Herodotus tells of the Sauromatae, eastern neighbors of the Scyths, who were descended from the union of a group of Amazons with some of the free Scyths. The women had been shipwrecked within Scythian territory, at Cremni on the shores of the Sea of Azov (Lake Maeotis). When the Scyths discovered, after a battle, that their opponents were women, they sent out an equal number of their youngest men to make acquaintance with the Amazons. "Neither party had anything but their weapons and both lived the same sort of life, hunting and plundering." They struck up friendships, using sign language, and the young men and women paired off. The Scyths never managed to learn the language of the Amazons, but the women learned to speak that of their husbands. "Ever since then the women of the Sauromatae have kept to their old ways, riding to the hunt on horseback, sometimes with, sometimes without their menfolk, taking part in war and wearing the same sort of clothes as their men."[10]

The Sauromatae are believed to be the same people mentioned centuries later by Tacitus as the Sarmatians. By the time he wrote, they had migrated westward from the shores of the Sea of Azov in Asia to what is now Bulgaria, on the eastern fringes of the lands of the Germani, but they still lived in wagons and on horseback. (A modern writer believes the customs of the Sarmatians are—or were until recently—still extant in the lives of the Gypsies or Romany.[11]) Tacitus also reports on the Veneti, who, though they have fixed habitations, "have borrowed largely from the Sarmatian character; in their plundering expeditions they roam over the whole extent of forest and mountain."[12]

Also like the Sauromatae are the Issedones, who allowed equal authority to women and men. Herodotus mentions the peculiar sexual customs of the Massagetae, whose queen, Tomyris, led them to a victory over Cyrus the Persian: "Though each person has a wife, all the wives are used promiscuously . . . if a man wants a woman, all he does is hang up his quiver in front of her wagon and then enjoy her without misgiving." Greek fashion, Herodotus makes the sexual choice at male initiative; with our newfound awareness of how much ethno- and androcentric views have colored nineteenth- and twentieth-century writings about foreign cultures, we can safely conclude that Massagetae women enjoyed more sexual freedom than was allowed to the women of the Greeks. Similarly, he speaks of the Agathyrsi who "live in luxury and wear gold on their persons. They have their women in common so that they may all be brothers and, as members of a single family, be able to live together without jealousy or hatred."[13] The Agathyrsi remind us of the Nayars of India, discussed earlier as a warrior caste who practice a form of polyandry in which a woman is, in effect, married to a group of brothers, any of whom may cohabit with her.

According to Herodotus, the Scyths' chief deity was the goddess of fire and the hearth—the Greek Hestia—whom they called Tabiti. They also worshiped Zeus, under the name Pa-

paeus, and the earth—Papi—believed by them to be the wife of Zeus.

The German tribes had been under Roman attack for more than two hundred years at the time Tacitus wrote about them. Since he was writing a moral tract for the benefit of Roman readers, some of his strictures on German chastity are today viewed with distrust. However, his statement, "They even believe that the sex has a certain sanctity and prescience, and they do not despise their counsels, or make light of their answers," is supported by other sources, ancient and modern.[14]

In recent years archaeologists have turned up increasing confirmation for these and other ancient writers' observations on the relative freedom enjoyed by women among the barbarians. Silver cups and fragments of pottery depicting women on horseback have been found at several places in Central Europe. Male and female burials at a site in Saarbrücken, dated to 450 B.C.E., were accompanied by grave goods of equal richness. Several cemeteries in Czechoslovakia, the earliest dated to 700 B.C.E., yielded wagon burials in which women and men were found inside or on top of four-wheeled vehicles.[15]

More recently several burials have confirmed the ancients' reports that women of the Germans were trained and fought as soldiers along with their men. A grave dated to 350 B.C.E. containing the bodies of three women and eight men was excavated in Tecklenburgh, Westphalia. All the bodies were buried with shields, swords, and spears. The women had died of wounds; they also had bows beside them. Other graves with women warriors dressed in trousers and bearing arms, who were killed by sword strokes, have been found in various places in West and East Germany and Czechoslovakia.[16]

Tacitus, when telling of Queen Boadicea's revolt against the Romans in Britain, explains that the royal line admits of no distinction of sex. Celtic warrior tales tell of queens who participate in war and decide whom they will bed, who are in every sense mistress of their own persons. Queen Maeve boasts to her husband of her position before she married him: she was mistress of one of the provinces of Ireland, had her own castle and her own, exaggeratedly large army at her disposal. She married him only on condition that she retain her sexual freedom, and she makes use of this freedom when it serves her purpose, as in the tale about the Brown Bull of Cooley, to whose owner she offers "the freedom of her own upper thighs" in exchange for the use of the bull for one year.[17]

Keeping women in inferior positions has always been inefficient. Thus in Sparta, the women managed the estates while their husbands were away at war. Tacitus reports that the management of the household, the home, and the land was left to the German women even when the men were not fighting: "They [the men] pass much of their time in the chase and still more in idleness, giving themselves up to sleep and to feasting, the bravest and most warlike doing nothing."[18]

In our own country, in World Wars I and II, mobilizing the country's full resources enabled women to enter occupations previously reserved for men. Sometimes, after the war, women were forced back into their previous isolation in the home; in other instances they retained newly acquired participatory social roles.

In the loose societies of Europe before Christianity, class differentials seem to have been more strongly enforced than sex restrictions. Increasingly, theories which see the subjection of women as the basic one from which other class stratifications arose are being called into question.[19] New tools of science and scholarship have produced imaginative researches into previously masked areas of our nonliterate past. A picture of increasingly complex caste-class relationships emerges from them, substantiating the strength and breadth of roles exercised by women in barbarian Europe. Ruby Rohrlich-Leavitt deduces a class society in Minoan Crete, with women playing leading roles.[20] Evidently class identification transcends sex loyalty. Women also enjoyed stronger and more autonomous positions in the "uncivilized" pre-Christian parts of Europe than were permitted them after the benefits of Roman Christianity had been extended to the whole of Europe.

32

The Christian Contradiction

It was the first time I could do something I could respect myself for. Until that time I was nobody. If
God had wanted me to die because I saved Jews, I
was ready to go on the cross, like Jesus.
—Katarzyna Kalwinska, explaining why she had
sheltered Jewish fugitives from Nazi death
camps at the risk of her own life. *New York
Times*, April 20, 1978.

The period of ferment during which Christianity began to
spread throughout the area of Roman domination, comprising
what had previously been Hellenistic civilization in Asia
Minor, Egypt, and Greece, was, as I have said, characterized by
many other-worldly cults. Women were prominent in many of
these as worshiper and worshiped, from the religion of Isis, who
was mother and wife and who had been a whore, to a wide variety of syncretistic Gnostic sects.

In *The Golden Ass* of Apuleius, Isis introduces herself: "The
Phrygians, first born of men, call me Mother of the Gods, goddess of Pessinus; the inhabitants of Attica, Minerva of Cecrops'
city [Athens]; the Cypriots living amid the sea, Venus of
Paphos; the arrow-bearing Cretans, Diana of Dictynna; the tri-
ple-tongued Sicilians, Proserpina of the Styx; the original Eleu-
sinians, Ceres of Attica, some call me Juno, others Bellona,
some Hecate, others the One from Rhamnus."[1]

Isis here has assimilated many of the great mother goddesses, though they also retain their own special qualities. She was named first the Mother of the Gods, otherwise known as Cybele, who has been identified with the first goddess of birth represented on the walls of Çatal Hüyük. In the form known in Classical times she was worshiped as Cybele, the great goddess of nature, mother of all living—plants, animals, gods, and humans. She did not rule but she created new beings.

By the second century C.E. she is described as a daughter goddess, child of Uranus and wife of Cronus. Originally, in Asia Minor she had been wild and savage, like Dionysus himself, and her cult was celebrated with dance and tambourine. Two hundred years before the beginning of the Christian era, during the Hannibalic Wars, her image and her cult were brought from Pergamum in Asia Minor to Rome, and she became a national Roman goddess, who granted victory and protected the state. Over the centuries image and rites changed. She became associated in myth with Attis, a young shepherd, who castrated himself for love of her. In consequence Cybele's priests performed the same operation on themselves, becoming eunuchs in her service. Statues of Attis performing the sacrificial act, with his belly exposed and a flint or knife held high in his right hand, are found all the way from Asia Minor to as far west as England. It was under the Roman rule that cults of this sort, focusing on pain and deprivation, spread throughout their provinces.

I have pointed out that Christianity can be seen as a combination of Hebrew and late Greek and Roman mystery religions. Jane Ellen Harrison showed how much Christianity owed to the Greek mystical cults—Dionysian rites and the later development of Orphism. We saw that the tradition of masochistic women's cults went back to Sumer, at least, and was perhaps intensified under the Akkadian impact with the increasing severity of male dominance and class and sex oppression. These cults provided outlet and ecstasy. They stem from the first harvest festivals, which in turn relate to the still earlier and universal traditions, documented from ethnographic records, of celebrations allowing for ritualized sexual promiscuity. After agriculture and animal breeding had fostered anxieties and, with the first civilizations, created property and class differentials, these orgiastic celebrations were often translated into the masochistic cults referred to earlier—Inanna-Dumuzi, Ishtar-Tammuz, Cybele-Attis, Isis-Osiris, et al. The cultic rituals, which usually involved the weeping of the mother for the lost child who is also husband-son-brother, took different forms in different countries, allowing for more or less self-expression and more or less aggression or weeping and self-laceration.

Dionysus of Thrace and the Bacchanales came from a central European tradition and seemed to permit more expression and a fiercer outlet, whereas in the heavily socialized civilizations the cults were "gentler," focusing on sacrifice and self-reproaches and suffering.

As the worship of Attis developed over the centuries, taking away from Cybele's influence, a blend of both traditions evolved. In Rome the rites of Attis were celebrated in March, over a period of weeks. Nine days of fasting and sexual abstinence preceded the enactment of Attis' fatal deed. The pine tree under which Attis collapsed and died after he had emasculated himself was brought into the city. Then came a Day of Blood during which the priests ran through the streets flagellating themselves till they drew blood and the celebrants wept and tore their clothes. The tradition of self-attack and mourning exists in other sects, and the medieval *penitentes* need not be in a direct line of descent from Attis worship; they were, however, an expression of similar psychological needs.

In some sects women were the chief participants—in the Greek and Roman traditions the only ones permitted to join in certain celebrations. However, during the first centuries of the Roman Empire the masochistic strain intensifies. Civilizations extend their bureaucratic and hierarchical organization, and sexual deprivation as well as class and caste domination increase. More democratic cults arose, which allowed slaves and lower-class men to participate along with women of every social stratum. Upper-class men also were attracted to them. Eventually the Orphic and Isis streams merged with Gnosticism and flowed into early Christian tradition. The Attis custom of self-emasculation was emulated by the early Christian monks who also castrated themselves in the ultimate act of sexual renunciation.

How Christianity prevailed eventually, to be adopted as the official religion of the Roman Empire in 320 c.e., is outside the scope of this book. Some say that Constantine made it the state religion in response to the conversion of many of his troops, conquered barbarians impressed into the Roman army of domination, though it is his mother, Empress Helena, who is officially credited as the instrument of his conversion.

The counterrevolution by which the initial impetus toward class and sex equality was subverted had occurred almost two hundred years earlier. During the second century after Christ a male bureaucracy had already emerged. The first- and second-century orthodox tradition produced the pseudo-Pauline letter to Timothy: "Let a woman learn in silence with full submissiveness. I do not allow any woman to teach or to exercise authority over a man; she is to remain silent."[2] It also produced a political structure which claimed to have the authority of God —the familiar figure of the Lord, King, Ruler, Master, Judge, and Father.

As Elaine Pagels points out, it was no coincidence that the orthodox insisted that this father-god figure could be represented only by men. Furthermore this devolution occurs just at the time—about 140–200 c.e.—when some churches were developing a hierarchical structure of organization. At the head of this orthodoxy stood the bishop, described in orthodox sources as God's representative. Below him were the priests—all men— and beneath them the third order in the hierarchy, the deacons, who by this time were exclusively male. A striking correlation now exists between the exclusively masculine image of God, the social structure of domination, and the political structure of the community.[3]

The fatherland is well-trodden ground for mainstream historians, and feminists, too, have usually begun their explorations of the hidden story with the period on which there is the largest body of accessible record. I have chosen to highlight specifics

I felt were specially relevant to the points I have been discussing.

Almost a thousand years ensued before Christianity penetrated the whole of barbarian Europe. Scanty reports on the position of women during the Dark Ages—the early medieval period—tend to confirm the observations of Herodotus and Tacitus from earlier times.

Women appear frequently in the record in a wide variety of occupations. Their position seems to have been strongest in the period between 700 and 1200. Although it is a sparsely documented era, several scholars make a case for the significant role they exercised in the economy. In southern France and Spain Burgundian and Visigothic laws allowed women to administer their own property, to participate in the administration of family property, and, when widowed, to act for their families. Women were landowners and managers elsewhere in Europe; they were also heads of families. The wives of warriors and of priests were prominent in the records; they acted in their own names, managed estates and businesses, and their children were often known by their mothers' names rather than their fathers'. Since early medieval laws gave even married women personal title to property, they figure frequently in the documents. Many of the surviving sources refer to women's public acts. They do not seem to have been relegated to domesticity, nor were their activities determined by or subordinated to their sexual functions, and this holds true well into the medieval period.[4] In France women kept relatively equal status with men until the entry of Christianity. In England women of the feudal classes functioned in a considerable number of public capacities almost to the end of the Middle Ages. They appear in manorial registers as property owners, brewers, bakers, cultivators, weavers, and as plaintiffs or defendants in business matters.[5]

During the Middle Ages, moreover, both before and after the conversion to Christianity, a war society existed within Europe, and the wars continued for centuries, with brief periods of truce or relative peace. There were wars between nations; there

were wars against "infidel" invaders and rebellions after conquest. The eighth century saw the Arab conquest of Spain. The
Moslem—Saracen—penetration of France provided a rallying
point; Charlemagne united his country in the battles which
stopped the Moorish penetration into Europe, after which the
Crusades were organized. Expeditions in the opposite direction
took men away from their homes in Christian holy wars, by
which kings and popes attempted to expand their domains
under the emblem of the "true faith."

I spoke earlier of the anomaly by which a state of war can
lead to a strong position for women, as in Sparta, and of the
relative autonomy enjoyed by women in the Scythian lands and
under the Germani at the time of the Roman invasions. As a
consequence of the endemic conditions of war which prevailed
during the Middle Ages, women also had to perform a variety
of functions on the home front, especially in view of the limited energy sources available in a preindustrial society.

Partly as a result of the spread of Christianity, Roman law,
and with it Greek philosophy, came to influence the barbarian
kingdoms of Europe. The Roman concept of the family
strengthened male power and the paterfamilias governed the
position of women in Christian Europe. The tradition known
as the "Perpetual Tutelage of Women" comes from early
Roman law. The concept that women are perpetual children
and only men are adults has had its ups and downs and has
been more or less enforced. In essence, however, the definition
of women as minors who never grow up has been perpetuated,
in modified form, to this day; vestiges of it can still be seen in
our legal system. Perpetual tutelage means that woman's relation to man is designated by the concept of *manus* (hand),
under which the woman stands (*feme covert*). Women do not
exist under the law—they can only go from under one hand to
another—hence the still extant practice of "asking for a
woman's hand in marriage." Technically it is the father who is
being asked. Some of the most restricting aspects of Roman
law were incorporated into canon law—the rules of the Church
—whence they passed into English common law.[6]

The contrast then was of a class society where women enjoyed economic participation and varying degrees of social autonomy with the more strictly enforced Mediterranean attitude inherited from Greeks, Romans, and Jews. Christianity took the Jewish mistrust for women and added its own repressions, in a much stricter interpretation of Hebrew mores. Significant was the fact that the idealization of chastity was transformed into a loathing for the body and a severe condemnation of sexual acts.

The Christian distaste for the female and her physical functions went far beyond the already phobic attitudes of the Hebrews. Sex was rarely accepted even as a profane activity. The establishment of a celibate male hierarchy gave an added prurience to the authority the Church assumed over people's private acts.

The history of the early Church Fathers' *pronunciamenti* against masturbation, against coitus "not within the fit vessel," turns up extremes which make the Talmudic judgments mild indeed. Comparisons of penances for sexual and criminal offenses inflicted from the sixth to the eleventh century show some extraordinary equivalences. Some bishops ordered equal penalties for intentional homicide, for abortion, and for oral intercourse; seven years of fasting on bread and water, along with renunciation of marital relations, was typical. One ecclesiastic, in office from 690 to 710 C.E., decreed penances of seven years, fifteen years, even life for such sins as oral and anal intercourse, but only seven years for intentional homicide. Even if the punishment's duration was reduced through prayers, the value scheme is manifest.[7]

The principle which sacrificed the mother's life to that of the fetus is early set forth and long maintained. In twelfth-century Paris a theologian named Peter Cantor is asked about a woman who has suffered "a rupture of the navel (umbilicus) in a previous childbirth. The doctors say that if she bears another child she will die. May she 'procure sterility' for herself?" Peter gives a brusque negative. "This last thing is not at all lawful, because this would be to procure poisons of sterility; that is prohibited in every case."[8]

In the twelfth century the Augustinian doctrine of original sin based on the line in Psalm 51, "In iniquity my mother conceived me, in sin was I born," was carried even further. Ecclesiastics like St. Albert decreed that a husband who was too ardent a lover of his wife treated her as a harlot.[9] Intercourse should be only for procreation; to delight in the sexual act was a mortal sin.[10]

The doctrine of the Church changed over the centuries, but not for the better till much, much later. It was sin "when a woman is known in a different way from what nature requires." In the thirteenth century Thomas Aquinas condemned any semination "outside the vessel," any departure from the normal mode (the missionary position), and equated coitus interruptus, the most accessible method of birth control, with sodomy. The fit way according to Thomas was with woman beneath the man, because of man's natural superiority to woman. Moreover, it was believed that this position facilitated conception. If the woman was above the man, the seed "would pour out of the matrix."[11] After Thomas, any other position was condemned as unnatural and adjudged mortal sin. Authority was found in the Old Testament, the New Testament, and Aristotelian theories of women's inferiority, which Thomas Aquinas adapted to Christianity.

The Talmudic writers had been troubled by sexual desire, the distinction to be made between lust and procreation. Christianity carried the sexual bind much further. With many Christian theoreticians sexuality was lust; all intercourse carried some degree of sin.

The twelfth-century bishop Huguccio said that coitus "can never be without sin, for it always occurs and is exercised with a certain itching and a certain pleasure; for, in the emission of the seed, there is always a certain excitement, a certain itching, a certain pleasure." His pupil Innocent III amplified: "Who does not know that conjugal intercourse is never committed without itching of the flesh, and heat and foul concupiscence, whence the conceived seeds are befouled and corrupted."[12] Husbands, love your wives was translated as pure spirit; sex was best avoided. A small undercurrent admitted the possibility of husband-wife love expressed also in sexual relations.

Christianity attempted to apply a single sexual standard to men and women, which can be summed up in the word *no*. Husbands were told what to do; wives were addressed chiefly by being asked to report any "unnatural practices"—usually assumed to be anal intercourse—to their confessors.

In later centuries priests were instructed to question their parishioners as to whether they used forbidden means of intercourse, but they were cautioned to couch their questions in a form that would not suggest to the confessant methods effective for birth control (or pleasure) of which she or he was unaware. They were to avoid "imprudently questioning the young of either sex, or others, about matters of which they were ignorant, lest they be scandalized and learn thereby to sin."[13]

When Christianity adapted Greek philosophy and tied it to Jewish theology, the dichotomization of mind and body was enormously strengthened; it was the culmination of a process that had begun several thousands of years earlier. In the philosophical system based on dualities, mind, spirit, objectivity were usually assigned to men; body, emotion, and subjectivity to women. If woman is all body she is of course incapable of resisting her body's impulses. As the weaker vessel she cannot bring to bear the strength of her missing intellectual and spiritual qualities and therefore easily succumbs to lust, being at the mercy of her passions, her desires, above all her bodily functions. In this respect, the derogation of sex involved also an enormous increase in the derogation of women.

Goddesses were now represented by the mother of Christ, who was not God the Mother but a mere vessel for the gestation of the divine child, in accordance with already well-established belief about women's role in reproduction. In Catholic theology, Mary had never known sex. Her impregnation by God's Holy Spirit was an ethereal process with no bodily—that is, sexual—connotations. Even the suggestion that she had subsequently had sexual relations with Joseph in order to produce the siblings referred to in the early Gospels aroused great rage among the Church Fathers.[14] Medieval Christian dogma insisted that Mary was *virgo intacta*. "Clean maiden that she is/And with man never did amiss," runs a couplet in a mystery play of the period.

This is the official side, recorded in religious writings, in church documents. We saw earlier that the Old Testament spoke, above all, to a propertied class, to the masters, men who had bondservants and possessions. And yet, it was noted in Chapter 29, scholars believe that until the Babylonian exile the Jews engaged in local cults, worshiped the fertility gods of their neighbors, and practiced sacred prostitution, as evidenced by archaeological discoveries and by the constant condemnations in the Bible. In the same way, the fact that priests are condemning the poisons of sterility, unnatural practices and positions, harlotry and fornication throughout the Church's history indicates that they never succeeded in stamping out these practices. Fornication was considered less sinful than practicing unnatural methods of coitus in marriage: in principle contraception equaled murder so that in the sixteenth century Pope Sixtus V decreed the same penalties for both acts.[15] The realities, however, differed from the written ideal, the practices from the *pronunciamenti*.

In similar wise, a constant duality existed between the antimaterialism of Christian philosophy and the materialist power of worldly authority, papacy and monarchies. Like most successful religions the new faith was elastic enough to permit of varying interpretations and to be adapted by many power structures for their own uses. What was constant was the sexually repressive, sadomasochistic underpinning, with religious devotion offered as an outlet. The identification with Christ's suffering on the cross and with Mary's loss of her beloved son, the otherworldly rewards in the New Testament, promised in exchange for the pains of this one, had—have—a universal appeal, given the oppressive syndromes that characterize the war civilizations.

The people themselves never really accepted official doctrine. Though the Church—official Catholicism—was male-run and misogynous at its center, the clerics could not stamp out certain pro-woman tendencies in popular worship. Women, in particular, identified with the Virgin as a suffering mother and addressed special prayers to her. Moreover, one of the strengths of Catholicism—like Roman religion before it—has been its ability to accommodate to diverse tendencies among the various peoples it proselytizes and to follow as well as to lead, enabling it to merge with or absorb local religions like those of Bahia in Brazil and various African meldings. In southern Europe, particularly in Italy, paganism was integrated into the Church by way of the institution of sainthood. On a regional level, local miracles and saints could be comfortably assimilated. Temples to the Great Mother, as at Paestum, could incorporate churches for Our Lady, and towns and shrines dedicated to Venus were renamed in honor of "St. Venus." The Feast of the Assumption, a special day to celebrate the taking up of the Virgin Mary into heaven, originated in the East and came to Rome through Byzantine influence. It was universally celebrated by the end of the Middle Ages, though only in 1950 did Pius XII declare that the doctrine was "revealed."

To those who had no privilege over their own bodies, women who must obey fathers and husbands, slaves who must obey masters, Christianity did offer the dual ideal of celibacy and chastity.

For women, celibacy was a fairly new concept. Under the Hebrews women and men could vow themselves to God for brief periods of time. In Sumerian religion a few upper-class women were priestesses and hierodules dedicated to chastity during their reproductive years only, or to the once yearly intercourse of the sacred marriage rite. The vestal virgins of Rome were twelve women from noble families who tended a sacred flame and on whose abstention from sex Roman honor and prosperity depended. In both Rome and Sumer these were positions open only to a few women from aristocratic strata, and the obligation ended at menopause. In the cult of Isis and in other mystery religions of the period just before and after Christ's birth women—and men—of all classes might vow celibacy for shorter or longer periods, occasionally even for life.

Christianity, however, recognized and encouraged lifelong celibacy—for men and for women—although the latter were always subject to the former.

In actual practice, however, celibacy, as well as voluntary chastity, even monogamy, tended to be luxuries available above all to the propertied classes, and within them to men more than to women. Daughters were subject to fathers and often could not enter convents without dowry payments. In slave society also control over one's own body had been reserved for middle- and upper-class males. The great underclasses of the past are little recorded, be they slaves or bondspeople, serfs or peasants.

The woman slave was at the disposition of her master, and the man slave had to satisfy himself with the leavings. When Odysseus returned to Ithaca, he was more concerned with the damage Penelope's suitors had wrought on his house than he was with the rape of the maids. Where property considerations were not involved, provisions for marriage were often sketchy; the records of marriage contracts tell about the customs of the upper classes, those who were disposing of property along with women. Imaginative Greek and Roman studies today can sometimes infer, from lists and dates and gravestones, bare statistics of birth, death, occupation, and number of children of slaves, even their marriages. Of their feelings we know less. Similarly, in the sparsely documented medieval era, scholars today examine church records, notarial archives when they first appear, available tax rolls, and estate censuses.

Like the slave, the serf was lucky to be able to have a wife. In feudal times it was unlikely that he could worry about whether his wife was virgin or not, especially since the *droit du seigneur* gave the lord of the estate sexual privileges over the women serfs as previously the Hebrew, Greek, or Roman slaveowner had enjoyed sexual rights over his or, among the Romans and then rarely, her human possessions.

Sexual deprivation was the rule, not the exception, for many members of the war society that characterized Christian Europe. Serfs were disposed of by their lords; soldiers might be away from home for months or years. The feminist scholar

Heath Dillard has deduced that in one area of Europe, northern Christian Spain, throughout the Middle Ages marriages lasted on the average ten years, and that half the combined population and over 60 per cent of the men never married.[16] Men died in war, women in childbirth, made much less safe by enforced breeding; both died of disease and malnutrition.

In two Spanish towns studied by Dillard, rape and adultery were the subject of severe and complex legislation. Of all the crimes a woman could commit, interracial—that is, interfaith—sexual intercourse was the most harshly punished. It was not an offense for a Christian man to sleep with a Moslem or a Jewish woman, but Christian women who slept with Moslems or Jews were sullied by the contact and the whole Christian community was disgraced thereby. In line with my earlier comment about male sex as conquest, intercourse between Christian men and Jewish and Moslem women was justified as an insult to inferiors and a demonstration of Christian prowess. Sexual conquest of Jewish and Moslem women was thus a legitimate form of aggression, an expression of Christian superiority. It was legal to strike the shameless woman (*muger male*) who insulted or verbally dishonored a reputable person, and if it was discovered that she had slept with two or three men she might be killed without penalty. Public prostitutes were totally without honor and could be defamed or raped with impunity.[17]

These were harsh times for Spain, but the legacy of sadism in the interconnection of war and sex, rape and prostitution reached out to affect all of European, not to say Western, mores.

At the lower levels of society, however, people could sometimes come together out of mutual need, even affection. The ideal of chastity and arranged marriages applied chiefly to the propertied classes, perhaps the upper two thirds of the population.

Comparing the family lives of rich and poor, historian Diane Hughes studied the copious notarial archives of Genoa. She examined records of notarial acts such as marriage contracts, dowry pledges, divorce proceedings and legitimizations, wills, estate inventories, and apprenticeships and guardianships, beginning in 1156 and continuing through 1400, in order to extrapolate information about the life styles of artisans and aristocrats. At this time in Genoa, particularly in the earlier period covered by her study, the artisans were chiefly humble folk, with modest holdings and little property. Artisan women's lives were often based on a working partnership with their husbands; wills show that the business was not infrequently left to the widow rather than to the male offspring. Such was not the case with aristocratic women. Property considerations were primary in their marriage arrangements, and when husbands died, the property would be left to sons or peripheral male relatives, and widows often returned to their natal families.[18]

Affection was also more likely to develop between children and mothers in poorer families, where children were nursed by their mothers, often for several years, and infancy was spent in the home. The aristocratic custom of sending children away to nurse at the breast of a countrywoman seems to have been common not only in upper-class Florence and Genoa but in several other parts of Europe.[19]

Among the lower classes the actuality of life asserted its own pressures. Society sets up a theoretical norm, but the practice is influenced both by the exigencies of everyday life and by the refusal of humans to fit themselves into the abstractions society tries to impose. Similarly we saw in Chapter 1 that the complexities of the Australian horde system of marriage, which so intrigued anthropologists Radcliffe-Brown and Lévi-Strauss, were found by later field anthropologists to be observed largely in the breach. When they did a statistical rundown of actual marriage arrangements there was very little correspondence with the postulated rules, just as few Western people observe the Ten Commandments religiously in their daily living. In the same way, human beings contrived to evade the excessive rigidities of Christian morality erected on the basis of Roman law. In Genoese documents, the mamma, the affection name for the woman with whom a small child might spend anywhere from one to four years, was often mentioned in a will; bequests of money, property, or a treasured article were made to their wetnurses by both women and men.

Prolonged nursing—up to four years—continued into the early twentieth century among peasant and lower-middle-class households of Europe. Since ovulation does not usually occur while a woman is producing milk, breast-feeding served as a partial birth-control measure, enabling these women to space births almost as far apart as non-Western foragers do.

When the custom of putting aristocratic children out to nurse was discarded and poor women were brought into the home to breastfeed the offspring of the well-to-do is not clear from the records. Whether children were sent away or wet-nurses brought into the home, the fact that wealthy women did not nurse their own children meant that they often became pregnant again almost immediately after giving birth. Forced breeding resulted from the combining of Christian morality and normal human sexual desire.

In fourteenth-century England a confessor writing to his bishop explained that among his flock the men fornicated because they could not afford to set up homes and to have children.[20] It is probable that some form of birth control was practiced by these couples; coitus interruptus or abortion, self- or midwife-administered, would have been the most effective and accessible means.

Poor women could—and often did—take the fullest advantage of the partial protection offered by lactation; well-to-do women were deprived not only of this safeguard, available to the poor, but also of the sensual pleasures involved in breast stimulation and mother-child contact. These gratifications were all the more important in women's sensual and affective lives, given the shambles the Church had made of sexuality between adults.

The idealization of the seemingly innocent joys of nursing—of mother love—in the Madonna image and in the worship of Mary offered women a guilt-free outlet, though their pent-up passion might well prove suffocating to the children. The boy, in particular, was likely to be laden with all his mother's starved sexuality since society valued males more than females, and the projection of the woman's feelings about herself might well work to the detriment of the mother-daughter relationship. In addition, a mother's biological pull toward the opposite sex may have been more easily transferred to the infant male. The idealization of the Madonna and the infant Jesus incorporates characteristics from many of the pagan mother-son cults referred to in earlier chapters.

The religious life did offer some refuge from a martyrdom of incessant pregnancies, to the more prosperous classes particularly. It was one way to avoid being literally bred to death. The grandmother of the famous French letter writer Madame de Sévigné had entered a convent after her husband's death, abandoning her four young children to the care of others. Sévigné herself, widowed at twenty-six, with two children, prudently refused to remarry. She lived her full complement of threescore and ten years—hale and hearty and productive—dying at seventy and then as a result of a fever caught nursing her daughter through one of her innumerable illnesses. Françoise-Marguerite, the beloved child to whom most of the letters were addressed, survived her mother by only seven years, her health ruined, her beauty destroyed by numerous pregnancies, many of which miscarried. She had been a great beauty, but when she died, she must have been much reduced. The letters frequently refer to her lamentable situation. Sévigné was criticized for her coldness, but, once safely widowed, she seems rather to have decided to spare herself the kind of martyrdom that was to be inflicted on her daughter.

The Comte de Grignan married Françoise-Marguerite de Sévigné in 1669; she was twenty-two and he was forty-one. By 1670 she had already had one miscarriage, and a daughter, Marie-Blanche, was born in November of that year. (Marie-Blanche entered a convent young and survived until 1745—the longest lived of the Sévigné-Grignan progeny.) A son was born in 1671, and another daughter, Pauline, adored by her grandmother, in 1674. Between and after the successful pregnancies there were many miscarriages, as well as poor wizened infants who did not survive their first year. Throughout this period Madame de Sévigné frequently refers to Françoise-Marguerite's ill health and to the disfigurements suffered by her beauty. Her letter of March 4, 1676, is written a week after she has congratulated the countess on being safely over her lying-in:

I am addressing myself to you, dear Count, for you are reported to have said that my daughter's confinements were the models of what confinements should be, and the oftener she does it the better. Dear God! She never does anything else. I must, however, warn you that unless you call a halt to this business out of common humanity, and if this poor machine is never allowed a pause, you will destroy it utterly, which would be regrettable. I am putting this to you for your serious consideration—the subject can scarcely be called hilarious.[21]

In 1678 she refers to "my daughter's weakness and emaciation . . . the loss of weight is due to the condition of her lungs . . . if this should continue she is not long for this life . . ."[22]

The Comte de Grignan had already killed off two wives before he inflicted those incessant pregnancies on Françoise-Marguerite. Later centuries deduced that the cause of this havoc was syphilis. The count is believed to have infected Françoise-Marguerite and the children, which accounts for the many illnesses and frailty of the son, who survived only into his twenties, for the beloved Pauline's "blemishes," which so greatly troubled her grandmother, and for all those miscarriages and infant deaths.

In England, Ann Fanshawe bore twenty-one children in the twenty-three years and twenty-nine days during which her marriage lasted. Her childbearing career was brought to a close only by the death of her husband in 1666, and she survived to write an autobiography that describes her many activities as well as the births, deaths, and burial places of her children, only five of whom outlived their mother.[23]

The custom of forced breeding was continued, not to say exaggerated, by later centuries. The composer Pleyel, founder of the still existent French piano-manufacturing establishment, was one of forty-some children of his father, though history does not tell us on how many wives these infants were wrought. Enrico Caruso was the eighteenth child of his mother, the first to survive past infancy.

33

Women Have Always Worked

The arrival of Protestantism, with the Reformation, did little to ameliorate the situation of women and the expression of sexuality between adults. The single authority of God was stressed, replacing the papal hierarchy. There was a renewed focus on the Old Testament, strengthening the master-ruler father-god image. As the ruler was God's earthly representative on earth, so the father of the family represented supreme authority in the home. Individual autocracy was strengthened. The king ruled his country in the name of God; the father repeated the pattern in a smaller scale. In Wilhelm Reich's words, "The authoritarian state had its representative in every family, in the figure of the father, and the family became the most important instrument of power."[1]

Like the Hebrews before them, Protestants dispensed with the female image in religion, minimizing the importance of Mary and, in most cases, eliminating the saints. Obedience to males was further stressed. Moreover, many Protestant sects rebelled against the ritual and aesthetic splendor of Catholicism, leaving their practicants free to focus on materialist aims —the business of making money in the world. Protestants often rejected the golden visions of a future life implicit in

Catholic mythology, as well as the theatrical, artistic element in Catholicism which, even if translated into material terms, did allow for a certain expression of sublimated sexuality.

In England, for example, pagan festivals had slipped into the official Church, with church-ales, periodic drinking fests and gatherings held in connection with church festivities—"when the sweet bagpipe doth draw forth the damsels to frisque about the maypoles." Even before Puritan times, English Protestantism legislated against this kind of spontaneous expression: in 1572 the Elizabethan canons ordered that "the church wardens shall suffer no plays, feasts, banquets, suppers, church-ales, drinkings to be kept in the church."[2]

The celebration of the First of May with the dance around the Maypole is, of course, a relic of pagan fertility rites. The orgiastic rollick around the phallic pole is an agricultural society's adaptation of the more universal periods of promiscuity characteristic of human beings both before and after the adoption of agriculture and animal breeding.

Despite the seventeenth century's prohibitions against church-ales, in 1743 they still exist, but are described as occasions "when people go from afternoon prayers on Sundays to . . . some publick house where they drink and be merry."[3] One wonders whether, at this time, the people include the "damsels" of earlier centuries.

Beginning about 1500, the father's authority was strengthened, and his power over both wife and children increased. Lawrence Stone has found overwhelming evidence of the change in parent-child relationships and of attitudes whereby children were seen as little animals whose will must be broken and who must be kept in total subjection to the authority of elders and superiors—primarily the parents, father first, then mother. More interest was taken in the rearing and education of children, but the process was considered similar to that of breaking in a horse or training a hunting dog.

Even in the Middle Ages, education—consisting chiefly of the learning of Latin—had been a forced process. The schoolmaster's equipment was a rod or a bundle of birch twigs rather than a book. However, very few children received these benefits, whereas, by the late fifteenth century, more children of all classes were being taught to read and write. In the beginning of the sixteenth century, flogging became routine punishment for schoolchildren regardless of rank or age. Severe physical punishment was used in the home, the school, and the university. Whipping was so common that when, in 1671, a didactic clergyman wished to characterize hell to young people, he described it as "a terrible place, that is worse a thousand times than whipping. God's anger is worse than your father's anger."[4]

This institutionalization of sadism and cruelty and violence meant that the children who had been maltreated themselves internalized the maltreatment and later passed it on to those over whom they had power, creating that chain of oppression earlier referred to, in which the wife and the children of the brutalized male become the victims of the victim, the phenomenon which we today call battered wives and children. In the sixteenth century both wife-beating and child-beating seem to have been accepted practices.[5]

To these trends in family relationship should be added the weight of guilt felt by children whose mothers bore child after child at the cost of health and life. Sévigné describes the death of the Dauphine after childbirth: "She blessed her little ones, adding, 'I bless you as well, my little Berry, although you are the cause of my death.'"[6] Similarly, an orphan of my acquaintance who was asked when his mother died answered, "I killed her. I mean she died borning me." In adulthood, this guilt and its consequent shame are often transformed into brutality and incorporated into the sick, sadomasochistic heritage of civilized heterosexual relationship.

We saw earlier that the dictum, "No lady moves," was prefigured in Talmudic and Roman sources. An aspect of civilized Europe's attempts to deny women's active sexuality is the belief that movement or enjoyment by women in sex will always have a negative effect, whatever the desired end. If she wants to conceive, Musitanius, writing on the diseases of women in 1709, advises:

Passionate coitus is to be avoided, for it is unfruitful. Sometimes the woman does not draw back her buttocks, and conquers, as is the custom of Spanish women, who move their whole body while they have intercourse, from an excess of voluptuousness (they are extraordinarily passionate), and perform the Phrygian dance, and some of them passionately sing a song, which in Spanish is called Chaccara, and on account of this Spanish women are sterile.[7]

On the other hand several folk traditions decree that if a woman wishes to avoid pregnancy, lying still and holding the breath during intercourse will prevent conception.[8]

The full weight of Christian sexual repression and European materialism was probably felt less in the lower levels of society, though the prohibitions filtered down in somewhat attenuated form.

The custom of living together without benefit of marriage was common among the very poor—perhaps the lower third of society—from the time of the Middle Ages and the introduction of Christianity. It continued in many parts of Europe, enduring at the bottom of the social scale into the comparative present.* Just as the exigencies of life did not always permit of the legitimization of marriage, so the ideal of parental power and premarital chastity was not always enforceable under the disorganized conditions of poverty. When there was no money or land to leave, no professional preferment to use as a club, it was more difficult to exercise authority over children. "We poor men must marry where we love," Mozart wrote to his father in the eighteenth century, explaining his marriage to the penniless Constanze Weber.

These same poor men brought—bring—their damaged psyches and the internalization of society's double standard

---

* In Partinico, Sicily, in the early nineteen sixties, young couples who could not afford the *corredo*—trousseau and housekeeping equipment—that local mores required as a prerequisite to marriage would elope, run away, and then return and live together unmarried for years, producing children and raising a family, always planning to be married in church when circumstances permitted.

into their relations with the opposite sex. It is more difficult to trace the harm done to women, since their responses and reactions are for the most part reported by male sources, strained through male eyes, and Church and state assume they are passive in love, the respondents to importunate male needs, despite or perhaps because of the Christian contradiction which makes them all body and no body.

Before industrialization, on the lower levels of society—among the peasants and laborers—all members of the family contributed work to eke out their meager subsistence. New opportunities arose with the spread of technology, but women often continued their traditional pursuits under different circumstances. The occupations named in Chapter 28 as open to women in classical Greece—the manufacture of textiles and clothing, the service trades of laundry and food preparation, the fabrication and sale of items of ornament—were still filled largely by women, sometimes translated into factory labor or piecework done at home. They were always ill paid, and if the woman lived at home or kept contact with her natal family, she was expected to contribute the major portion of her earnings to the common funds to help support the household.

By the eighteenth and nineteenth centuries, poor families were in movement, and there was less stability and less control of young people. The old tradition of living together before marriage was brought with them by young girls who went to cities to work—in service or in the new factories.[9]

When women left their families to earn money, emigrating from country protection to city anonymity, opportunities and pressure to engage in "illicit" sex increased, but there was no family or community support to assist the young woman in gaining the protection of the legal ceremony. Servants were victimized as they had been throughout history, but by the nineteenth century, with the growing middle class, there were more of them, and they were more likely to be cast adrift, seduced and impregnated by the sons of the house, fired for immorality by the elders. Working-class women who took up with men of their own class, thinking that the liaison would, as in earlier times, be a stable one, with or without marriage, often found themselves abandoned by their lovers, unable or unwilling to maintain their promises.[10]

The contradiction between Judeo-Christian moral attitudes and Western materialist ones carried less weight among the very poor. The only commodity the poor man had to sell was his labor, while the poor woman had two, her labor and her sexual services. Prostitution was always an alternative, a corollary of women's inferior economic opportunity. Female sexuality had more market value than other skills or labor. Women prostituted themselves to feed their families and to feed themselves. Asked if she let men fuck her for sausage rolls, one young girl replied, "Yes, meat pies and pastry, too."[11]

One way or another sexuality was sold or bartered for property, in arranged marriages and on the open market.

In nineteenth-century England it was felt that women's employment in the new industrial system, as instanced by fourteen-hour days in cotton mills and dragging coal cars underground in mines, disturbed the order of nature, and reform commissions took up their cause, with the idea of keeping women in the home. But the majority of women had always worked alongside men. That they were so ill paid made prostitution attractive, for as long as their physical attributes endured. Among the poorest classes chastity hardly existed after the age of fourteen. Social attitudes deprived women of their own physical expression, whether among the respectable middle- and upper-class women who were, by Victorian days, considered to be without sexual feelings or among the lower-class women who were believed to be all body and made contemptible thereby. In the eyes of the women who practiced it, prostitution was a legitimate road away from poverty and exploitation.[12]

In the nineteenth century lower-class women crossed over the line from respectability and back again fairly easily, particularly in the anonymity of cities. The popular idea that "the harlot's progress is short and rapid, and that there is no possible advance moral and physical and once abandoned she must always be profligate" was contradicted by the researches of Henry Mayhew and William Acton.[13] Women grew old in prostitution and, according to Acton, himself a practicing physician, they were rather more healthy than their socially approved sisters, who slaved fourteen hours a day in the factory and bore endless children. Mayhew's and Acton's writings show that for the poor there was no sharp distinction between respectable society and the "depraved underground." There were women who prostituted themselves on occasion or in addition to other work, merging inconspicuously with the respectable poor. Prostitution was often a stage in a woman's life or a part-time profession with which she added to her bare earnings as a shopgirl, a factory worker, a housemaid, or a needlewoman. In Acton's words, "poverty, evil training, and seduction" drove women into prostitution; its consequences forced them to resort to infanticide, baby-farming, and abortion.

The ambivalence of attitudes about women's sexual expression and the peculiar contradictions which have made the most transcendent physical act into a commodity continue into the present. Prostitution of women and young men is presumably based on the principle that women do not need sex enough to pay for it on the market and that men need it so much they are willing to buy it. It is also premised on the idea that sex is a service unilaterally offered by the female or by males playing a female role and bought by the male rather than a participatory process involving two human beings. On the one hand prostitutes are despised as the lowest rung on the social ladder, as they were back in Sumerian days. On the other, hustling has become the master metaphor of our materialist society where we are all measured for sale in business, profession, even marriage, and tempted to treat ourselves as commodities in a vertical climb for advancement. Hustle is used variously to mean straight prostitution, pimping, hurrying, selling oneself, pulling off a confidence trick, or using devious methods and charm to gain one's end.

Only in our own century have we finally begun to shape new concepts about women's and men's sexual rights. The result is the ferment and confusion in which we now find ourselves, with five thousand years of the materialization of sex hanging over us. We may doubt whether civilization has entailed progress over the so-called savage state in several abstract senses. But any woman who looks back to her grandmother and great-grandmother cannot doubt that within Western society some advances have been made, imperfect as they may seem. The more we penetrate the past roots of oppression, and its resultant superstructure, the more we shall be able to build toward a future of true human intercourse.

Epilogue and Prologue:

The Machine Stops

. . . I accept the Universe.
  —Margaret Fuller

. . . she'd better.
  —Thomas Carlyle

In the course of writing this book, I suddenly understood the meaning of the myth of Medusa. To look into her face was to be turned to stone. When Perseus cut off the gorgon's head, Pegasus, the winged horse of poetry, leaped upward out of the blood spurting from her neck. And as a particularly exciting thought hit me, I realized that Medusa was reality, and I felt the terror of single awareness. Similarly, to face the position of women over the last several thousand years can be paralyzing. Only in art, and then infrequently, have poets been able to approach its awesome injustice.

Even though she gave in eventually, Margaret Fuller was right to question the universe. Almost a century later Ellen Glasgow wrote that she had never been able to accept the universe. Her novels were her answer to the givens with which she was confronted.

In the late nineteen sixties and early nineteen seventies women came together in the new feminist movement. We shared our insights and realized that we are right not to accept the universe, at least as it has been presented to us by male authority, in terms corrupted by a greed-based civilization. Shored up by our sisters, we were able to face the extent of our disadvantaging, to see the metaphors based on mistaken biology, to strain out some of the assumptions that masquerade as science. Our intellectual world was full of misnomers and mis-analogies which have shaped poetry, philosophy, thought itself. The tool of thought, language, was suspect, based on premises of aggression and false dichotomies, so that a serious and useful agricultural scientist could say that scientists seek power over nature as politicians seek power over men when in truth science must seek penetration and understanding of, collaboration with the forces of the natural world to which we humans belong, rather than domination over them.[1] The great dichotomizing tradition of Western civilization begins with the supposed passivity of the female, with woman as earth and man as vitalizer. From thence come the others: dominance-submission, body-spirit, mind-body, etc.

History and writing emerge with the reification of people and of sex, with vertical relations. In the state it was the king who ruled subjects, the subjects who ruled slaves; in the family, the father who ruled wives and children. Five thousand years of the substitution of acquisition for feeling and of the glorification of aggression have entered our very marrow. The most beautiful form of communion is described in smirched and derogatory terms and used as an execration: so-and-so is a slimy fuck, a cunt; he screwed me; she sucks.

That initial impetus fell apart. We've gone off, some into oblivion or survival enclaves, others into well-paid niches, which may make their explorations less compelling. Many just got tired. For one thing, the times did not immediately improve. The parousia has not arrived; on the contrary.

Feminism has survived and entered the mainstream of American culture, but no longer is there any implication of sweeping political or societal changes; reformism is the order of the day. There were always many strains in the movement, and in a competitive, materialist world it is not surprising that more and more women are attracted to the idea of grabbing power for themselves. If the choice is between being pushed around and pushing other people around, one would prefer to be the pusher not the pushee. During the nineteen seventies, as political change became ever more illusory, more and more women settled for the individual line of self-advancement.

Statistically, the new feminism of the late sixties and early seventies did not change the economic situation of women. There are a few more women in high places. Some professional barriers have been breached. The distribution of money has become even more unequal and more concentrated in the hand of an elite than it was some thirty years ago. Income figures still reflect lowest incomes for black women, then white women, and then black men, and the proportions have improved only slightly in the last decade.[2] Many women have entered the labor force but primarily in the lower-paying jobs. They form a pool of low-paid workers, those with the least skills, and they serve rather to shore up the inequities of the system. The gap between the earnings of women and men has also increased. A report of the Labor Department published toward the end of 1976 showed that men earned 75 per cent more than women today, whereas twenty years ago the difference was 50 per cent.[3]

"Are you a feminist?" I asked a woman of my acquaintance recently.

"Who has time to be a feminist! With my job, three children, and all I have to do in the house. When I retire, I'll be a feminist." This particular woman lives in Pennsylvania and has a full-time job, her pay raised, in 1978, from $3.50 to $4.00 an hour. She has three children ranging from eleven to eighteen years in age. I have seen various estimates of the American woman's work week—those employed outside the home and those whose work entailed *only* housework, cooking, and child-raising—placing their work load as high as seventy but never less than forty-five hours a week. Compare these with the life of the Australian Aborigine woman of the Pitjandjara, described in 1933 as arduous drudgery sometimes consisting of as much as four to six hours a day—a work week of twenty-eight to forty-two hours.[4] Which, if either, is the liberated woman I leave to the reader to decide.

The most hopeful thing to come out of the women's movement has been the larger percentage of women in graduate schools, in medicine, in law, in disciplines of the humanities and science. The insights that were so blinding to us have been taken up by women in academia. At many levels they are turning the magnifying glass on the human story as it used to be taught, removing the male prism. On the other hand, once graduated, they are still subject to a discriminatory system. Despite the showy individuals, the new Ph.D.s and M.D.s earn less and advance more slowly than their male counterparts. And five years after the Federal government issued an order against discrimination in educational institutions, the percentages of women faculty members remain dismally low.[5]

Meanwhile the world outside has moved farther away from idealism. The uneasy balance of material acquisitiveness and aspiration toward ethical behavior has tipped decisively toward the materialist side. "If I can't take it with me, I ain't going," said a bumper sticker I saw the other day. In an exploitative society people are advised to get ahead by beating on someone else. Interpersonal relations have broken down. Everything is for sale: warmth, support, and understanding from therapists or self-help books; instant riches from state lotteries; anodynes in the form of alcohol, marijuana, tranquilizers; individual salvation in a wide range of new and old religions. The media package and sell politicians and ideas; abstract concerns are translated into purchases, as in the *Whole Earth Catalogue,* the *Jewish Catalogue,* and the Buycentennial of 1976. Feminism is no exception. Solutions are individual—up the organization (the corporate woman), self-assertion, freedom through underwear, devices for masturbation, the joys of gay sex—everything is marketable. Salesmanship is the means, power-through-possession the end by which feeling and caring are subverted. The pathology of loneliness increases. Business and personal relations are like a constant state of war.

An early slogan of the movement was, "None of us are liberated until all of us are liberated." Magazines and newspapers may talk about the new sexual freedom, describe individual women as liberated, but there are only varying degrees of personal accommodation and personal expression. Given the heritage of five thousand years of treating sex as a power relationship, with male sex as aggression and female as submission, it is not surprising that the new relaxation of attitudes brought with it more libertinism than liberation. Ever increasing numbness is countered by sensation and violence in the popular arts. The sexual revolution has meant money in the pocket for entrepreneurs.

The whore issue is still very much with us. That prostitution exists, despite the relaxation of attitudes, shows that it is still a power symbol. "The enslavement of women lies simply in the fact that people desire, and think it good to avail themselves of her as a tool of enjoyment." Thus Tolstoy in the eighteen-sixties.[6] Where men used to take women, now women are being instructed to do the same with men. Fortunately not many of them can. Most of the women who answered *The Hite Report* questionnaire felt that the sexual revolution is a myth.[7] It has left them free to say yes but not to say no. The double standard is still with us. The quantity of sex has gone up; the quality has not. We are encouraged to use each other as masturbatory devices; the new emphasis on sexual prowess further dehumanizes physical intimacies.

It was Reich who introduced the revolutionary yet obvious concept that not all orgasms are alike, that some sex is better than others. Today, when orgasm for women is recognized as a desirable end, few of us acknowledge that orgasm has a wide variation, for women and for men. (Ejaculation is not synonymous with orgasm.) In line with our other materialist attitudes, we go by the numbers instead of by the depth of the experience. In the past and for much of Western history, it would seem that deep and gratifying sex was not of common occurrence.

In a period where women are granted more expression, sexual acts still retain the aura of conquest and violence; rape increases; hustling is omnipresent as image and reality.

On a very different scale the social breakdown can be translated into economic dilemma. At the very moment we reach an apogee of materialism, the profit motive is becoming untenable. It was like a vast chain letter, promising things that were taken from other people; it cannot be indefinitely extended. Space may be infinite—there are questions about this—but our planet is finite. The profit motive could function on conquest and expansion till we reached the limits of earth and of material resources. We are close to these limits now. The debate about whether human ingenuity and imagination in the form of technology will be outrun by human greed will be resolved by the events of the next thirty or forty years.

The principles of sharing and caring are our only hope, in the large sense as well as in the small, in the relations between individuals, as in the relations between nations. Autocratic control increases internationally, and live or die becomes a world alternative. Reports from Chile, from Argentina, from Iran, to mention only a few, show how sadistic tactics are used to control people against their will.

Socialist claims that woman's subjection to man is a function of capitalism and that destruction of the class system under socialism would solve problems of male-female inequality have not been validated by existing socialist states. In the two largest, the Soviet Union has a class system based on a bureaucratic elite, and as of 1978 China was moving in that direction. In both states, women have come nowhere near achieving parity in political and economic institutions and still do double work, in the home and outside. There are no indications that they have gained sexual equality, nor signs pointing toward positive change in the near future.

In 1964 Mao Tse-tung told André Malraux that the Chinese Communists were the first group in China to address themselves to women, to the young, and to the peasants and that in consequence every one of them felt involved. Since his death Maoism has been largely abandoned; a return to earlier Chinese hierarchical attitudes is reported. In the country, arranged marriages and wife selling still exist.[8] In the cities, late marriage, sexual abstinence, and hard work had been the Maoist solution to the ages-old degradation of women in

China. Even if temporarily effective, no permanent restructuring of society can be achieved by this kind of imposition from above. As with early Christian ideals, new forms of repressive sadism will emerge. Puritanism and asceticism inevitably lead back to dominance and control and materialism again. Sex cannot be repressed and eliminated; it finds outlets, usually destructive. It must be incorporated. The answer is to integrate. Only when the power nexus is removed, when the whore issue disappears from attitudes and language, can we hope for an approximation of equality between the sexes. An approach must be made toward seeing sexual meetings as equally body and mind-spirit, toward valuing active female and male sexuality, toward achieving a holistic philosophy.

I have tried to shed some light on the sexual roots of sadism and the desire for dominance which spread throughout the world beginning at a given moment not too long ago in human existence. Solutions must be multilevel, but there will be no solutions, only increasing hierarchy and lack of freedom if we do not get at the causes, the oppressive principle growing out of the relation between man and woman which has mushroomed to be the greatest danger to the world's survival. As I see it, the dominance hierarchy is the underlying problem.

We cannot go backward; we must start from where we are. And where we are could be the beginning; we may be in the infancy of civilization. There is, for example, uncultivated land which can be developed to feed the hungry people in Asia, Africa, and Latin America. On the bases of wasteful aims, we have created complex technologies. How much further we could go if instead of power domination, with its pump-priming of war and armaments, we could achieve co-operative forms of social encounter! If even a portion of the almost 300 billion dollars the world spends annually on armaments were diverted into agricultural and educational improvements for the earth's four billion inhabitants, food could be produced, suffering relieved, relations between people and nations transformed.

It may take a quantum leap. What we are working for is the time when out of a sufficiency of material things—as once out of a minimal amount—sharing and living, doing rather than accumulating, will once again become modes of behavior. Then the process, not the end; the journey, not the arrival; the experience, not the possessing will be paramount.

If we consider that our species existed for some two hundred thousand years without imposing burdens on a subject class, and that the phenomena discussed in these pages have existed only for a little over five thousand years, during which survival has been rocky and imperfect, it is clear that the stages traced in Parts IV, V, and VI were not inevitable in form. At the moment, it looks as if even the liberality of the evolutionary process has been stretched. Not only were the divisions into caste and class, by sex and occupation, respectively, unnecessary ones —they were antiproductive and the catastrophic results are upon us. Imminent destruction threatens from several sides— nuclear explosion, pollution, expanding population, et al. Patriarchy had a long run for its money. Human ingenuity devised all kinds of compensations for its seemingly intolerable customs, but the point of no return is close. Apocalypse or change are our only alternatives. Given the long prehistory of our species, I imagine the second will prevail.

In the nineteenth and early twentieth centuries, most writers assumed that the stages of human social development— whether the horde of Darwin, Spencer, and Freud or forms of matriarchy postulated by Bachofen, Engels, Briffault, Neumann, etc.—were predetermined and a progression from a lower to a higher state. In our twentieth-century sophistication, and with the help of comparative ethnography, we know these were not inevitable stages. Social developments were a combination of happenstance, and of vectors of environment and psychology. They were unnecessarily cruel. If our sexual and social evolution had happened along other lines—and limited cases exist, refuge areas in the face of hostile odds, where some material advance and, above all, survival were accomplished in opposition to the prevailing trend toward hierarchy—it would have been quicker, easier, more productive. One problem, however, is the self-perpetuating nature of aggression and conquest, the killing off, subjection, or conversion to dominance-submission ideology of the gentler peoples when they are exposed to the hierarchically organized dominators. There is hope for humanity, however, if we acknowledge that patriarchy, sadism, and fighting are not inherent in the nature of either civilization or the species.

We have had five thousand years of war and hierarchy; ten thousand years of anxiety leading to sadomasochism, dominance-submission, and power through possession; and, on a conservative estimate, two hundred thousand years of being a sharing and friendly species. The prognosis is not an easy one. We must change characters and change society. Multilevel goals—inner and outer, objective and subjective—are involved. But the possibilities exist, within ourselves in our brains, our nervous systems, and our genes, and outside, in the planet's resources. I have hope of human survival and amelioration given our spread under such inimical circumstances as were created by the first civilizations. Both direct voice and social pathology indicate increasing awareness of the dead ends that face us if we continue on our doomsday path. The incentive for change is there, and adaptation has been the hallmark of the human genus throughout its several-million-year existence.

Nothing ever ends: the end is the beginning.

Source Notes

CHAPTER 1 SCIENCE IMITATES SOCIETY

1. Schlegel, *Male Dominance and Female Autonomy*, p. 21.
2. See Briffault, *The Mothers*; Campbell, *The Masks of God*; Graves, *The White Goddess*; Neumann, *The Great Mother* and *The Origins and History of Consciousness*; others influenced by Jungian concepts.
3. See Davis, *The First Sex*; Diner, *Mothers and Amazons*; et al.
4. Wickler, "Socio-sexual Signals and Their Intra-Specific Imitation among Primates," in Morris (ed.), *Primate Ethology*, p. 109.
5. Goodall, "A Preliminary Report on Expressive Movements," in Jay (ed.), *Primates*, pp. 351–52; Jay, "The Common Langur of North India," in DeVore (ed.), *Primate Behavior*, p. 226.
6. Lévi-Strauss, *The Elementary Structures of Kinship*.
7. Cf. L. R. Hiatt, "Gidjingali Marriage Arrangements," M. J. Meggitt, "Marriage Classes," A. Yengoyan, "Demographic and Ecological Influences," F. Rose, "Australian Marriage," in Lee and DeVore (eds.), *Man the Hunter*, pp. 165–208.
8. Rose, op. cit., p. 205.
9. Meggitt and Yengoyan, op. cit., pp. 171, 187–88; see also Goodale, *Tiwi Wives*; Kaberry, *Aboriginal Woman*.

CHAPTER 2 THE IDEA OF DOMINANCE

1. Jay, "The Common Langur of North India," in DeVore (ed.), *Primate Behavior*, p. 221.
2. K. Yoshiba, "Local and Intertroop Variability," in Jay (ed.), *Primates*, p. 228.
3. Imanishi, "Social Behavior in Japanese Monkeys," in Southwick (ed.), *Primate Social Behavior*, p. 77.
4. Cited in Kolata, "Primate Behavior," p. 55.
5. Darwin, *The Descent of Man*, p. 225.

6. Lorenz, *On Aggression*, p. 271.
7. J. P. Scott, "Agonistic Behavior of Mice and Rats," in Southwick (ed.), *Animal Aggression*, p. 110.
8. Kolata, op. cit., p. 55.
9. Carpenter, "The Howler Monkeys of Barro Colorado," in DeVore, op. cit.
10. S. Eisele, quoted in Hahn, *On the Side of the Apes*, p. 82.
11. Tiger and Fox, *The Imperial Animal*, p. 31; Hall, "Behavior and Ecology," in Jay (ed.), op. cit., p. 83.
12. Goodall, *My Friends the Wild Chimpanzees*, p. 21; Goodall, "Chimpanzees of the Gombe Stream Reserve," in DeVore (ed.), op. cit., pp. 425–73; Goodall, "A Preliminary Report on Expressive Movements," in Jay, op. cit., pp. 313–14; Goodall, "Mother-Offspring Relationships," in Morris, op. cit., p. 325.
13. William Greulich's experiment has been reported widely: see Judy Fireman (ed.), *Cat Catalog* (New York: Workman Publishing Co., 1976), p. 173, for a recent account.
14. Morris, *The Naked Ape*, pp. 78–79.
15. See Chevalier-Skolnikoff, "Male-Female, Female-Female, and Male-Male Sexual Behavior," for comprehensive data on laboratory observations of orgasms in female monkeys.
16. Herschberger, *Adam's Rib*, pp. 11, 201.
17. Weisstein, "Psychology Constructs the Female," in Gornick and Moran (eds.), *Woman in Sexist Society*, pp. 138–39.

CHAPTER 3 OUR PRIMATE RELATIVES

1. The Gombe Stream Research Center in the Gombe Stream Reserve, Tanzania, was closed in 1975 because of local terrorist action and reopened in 1977 (see *New York Times*, May 22, 1975, and Oct. 15, 1977).
2. Goodall, *My Friends the Wild Chimpanzees*; Goodall, "Chimpanzees of the Gombe Stream Reserve," in DeVore (ed.), *Primate Behavior*, p. 429.
3. V. and F. Reynolds, "Chimpanzees of the Budongo Forest," in DeVore, op. cit., pp. 415–16.
4. Pilbeam, "An Idea We Could Live Without," p. 68.
5. *New York Times*, May 7, 1975.
6. Goodall, *My Friends the Wild Chimpanzees*.
7. Goodall, "Mother-Offspring Relationship," in Morris (ed.), *Primate Ethology*, pp. 287–337.
8. V. Reynolds, *The Apes*, pp. 270–74.

9. Engels, *The Origin of the Family, Private Property and the State*, p. 44.

10. Briffault, *The Mothers*, Vol. 1, pp. 119–20.

11. Schaller, *The Mountain Gorilla*, pp. 283–84.

12. Tanner and Zihlman, "Women in Evolution," p. 594.

13. Fossey, "More Years with Mountain Gorillas," p. 580.

14. Zuckerman, *The Social Life of Monkeys and Apes*, (London: K. Paul, Trench, Trubner, 1932), pp. 233–34.

15. Hall and DeVore, "Baboon Social Behavior," in DeVore, op. cit., pp. 71–72.

16. DeVore and Washburn, "The Study of Primate Behavior," in DeVore, op. cit., pp. 1–13.

17. Eaton, "The Social Order of Japanese Macaques," pp. 97–106.

18. Goodall, *In the Shadow of Man*, pp. 112–15. See *New York Times*, Apr. 20, 1978, for Goodall on chimpanzee war, and *New York Times*, May 2, 1978, for Montagu's response.

19. Kropotkin, *Mutual Aid*, p. 3.

20. "Monkeys, Apes, and Man," CBS Television Network, Oct. 12, 1975.

21. Pilbeam, op. cit., pp. 66–67.

22. Hall, "Behavior and Ecology of the Wild Patas Monkey," in Jay (ed.), *Primates*, pp. 32–119.

23. J. S. Gartlan and C. K. Brain, "Ecology and Social Variability in Ceropithecus aethiops and C. mitis," in Jay, op. cit., pp. 253–92.

CHAPTER 4   AGGRESSION AND MALENESS

1. Lore and Flannelly, "Rat Societies," p. 113.

2. Moss, "A New Image for Hyenas," p. 38–45.

3. D. E. Davis, "Physiologic Factors in Aggressive Behavior," in Southwick (ed.), *Animal Aggression*, p. 148; R. Blier, "Bias in Biological and Human Sciences: Some Comments," *Signs*, Vol. 4, no. 1 (Autumn 1978), p. 160.

4. Ibid., p. 150.

5. Kolata, "Primate Behavior," p. 55.

6. Eaton, "The Social Order of Japanese Macaques"; see also Lore and Flannelly, "Rat Societies," p. 115.

7. Blier, op. cit., pp. 160–61; see also H. H. Lambert, "Biology and Equality: A Perspective on Sex Differences," *Signs*, Vol. 4, no. 1 (Autumn 1978), pp. 99–102.

CHAPTER 5   MATERNAL SEXUALITY

1. N. Newton and M. Newton, "Psychological Aspects of Lactation," p. 1180.
2. Rossi, "Maternalism, Sexuality and the New Feminism," p. 25.
3. See Imogen Howe, letter to the *New York Times Magazine*, Apr. 1, 1973, p. 69.
4. Rossi, op. cit., p. 26.
5. Ibid., p. 27.
6. Goodall, "Mother-Offspring Relationships in Free-ranging Chimpanzees," in Morris (ed.), *Primate Ethology*, p. 302.
7. Briffault, *The Mothers*, Vol. 1, p. 133.
8. Jay, "Primate Field Studies and Human Evolution," in Jay (ed.), *Primates*, p. 495.
9. Eaton, "The Social Order of Japanese Macaques"; Kolata, "Primate Behavior."
10. Pilbeam, "An Idea We Could Live Without," p. 66.
11. Horney, *Feminine Psychology*, pp. 60ff.
12. J. B. Miller, *Psychoanalysis and Women*, p. 10.

CHAPTER 6   FROM MAN THE HUNTER TO WOMAN THE GATHERER

1. W. S. Laughlin, "Hunting: An Integrating Biobehavior System and Its Evolutionary Importance," in Lee and DeVore (eds.), *Man the Hunter*, p. 304.
2. Lee, "What Hunters Do for a Living," in Lee and DeVore, op. cit., pp. 40–48.
3. Holloway, "Australopithecine Endocasts," pp. 195–200; Holloway, quoted in the *New York Times*, Sept. 26, 1975.
4. Quoted in Montagu, *Man and Aggression*, p. 5.
5. E.g., the illustration of a small male monkey evolving into a taller ape man carrying a stone dagger and then into a tall bearded muscular male with a spear that was featured in the brochure for a 1976 course on evolution at the American Museum of Natural History in New York City.
6. Cited in Balikci, "The Netsilik Eskimos: Adaptive Processes," in Lee and DeVore (eds.), op. cit., p. 81.
7. Buettner-Janusch, *Origins of Man*, pp. 359–60.
8. Pilbeam, *The Evolution of Man*, p. 33.
9. Leakey and Ardrey, "Man the Killer, a Dialogue," pp. 73–85.
10. Jolly, "The Seed-Eaters," pp. 4–24.
11. Turnbull, discussions, in Lee and DeVore, op. cit., p. 341.
12. J. D. Clark, *The Prehistory of Africa*, pp. 66–67.

13. Montagu, op. cit., pp. 9–10.
14. Chomsky, *Language and Mind*, p. 82.

CHAPTER 7   THE CARRIER BAG THEORY OF EVOLUTION

1. Laughlin, "Hunting: An Integrating Biobehavior System," in Lee and DeVore (eds.), *Man the Hunter*, pp. 304–20.
2. Lee, "What Hunters Do for a Living," in Lee and DeVore, op. cit., pp. 41–43.
3. J. D. Clark, *The Prehistory of Africa*, pp. 76–79.
4. Tanner and Zihlman, "Women in Evolution," p. 597.
5. Bryant and Williams-Dean, "The Coprolites of Man," pp. 100–10.
6. Tanner and Zihlman, op. cit., p. 600; Lancaster, "Carrying and Sharing in Human Evolution," pp. 85–87.
7. Cf. J. D. Clark, op. cit.; Lancaster, *Primate Behavior and the Emergence of Human Culture*; Slocum, "Woman the Gatherer: The Male Bias in Anthropology," in Reiter (ed.), *Toward an Anthropology of Women*; Tanner and Zihlman, op. cit.
8. Simons, "Ramapithecus," pp. 31–32.

CHAPTER 8   WOMAN THE POTTER

1. *New York Times*, Dec. 12, 1975.
2. Laughlin, "Hunting: An Integrating Biobehavior System," in Lee and DeVore (eds.), *Man the Hunter*, p. 318.
3. J. D. Clark, *The Prehistory of Africa*, pp. 69–70.
4. Tanner and Zihlman, "Women in Evolution," p. 590.
5. J. D. Clark, op. cit., p. 91.
6. Ibid., p. 99.
7. Harlan, *Crops and Man*, p. 29.
8. Boserup, *The Conditions of Agricultural Growth*, p. 12.
9. Abramova, "Paleolithic Art in the U.S.S.R.," p. 170.
10. Leacock, introduction, in Engels, *The Origin of the Family, Private Property and the State*, p. 39.

CHAPTER 9   WOMAN THE HUNTER

1. J. D. Clark, *The Prehistory of Africa*, p. 72.
2. Yellen and Lee, "The Dobe-/Du/da Environment: Background to a Hunting and Gathering Way of Life," in Lee and DeVore (eds.), *Kalahari Hunter-Gatherers*, pp. 32–46; L. Mar-

shall, "The !Kung Bushmen of the Kalahari Desert," in Gibbs, *Peoples of Africa*, pp. 249–50.

3. Pilbeam, "An Idea We Could Live Without," p. 69.
4. Goodale, *Tiwi Wives*, pp. 151–82.
5. Landes, *The Ojibwa Woman*, pp. 135–43; J. Mirsky, "The Eskimo of Greenland," in Mead (ed.), *Cooperation and Competition Among Primitive Peoples*, pp. 54, 83–84.
6. J. D. Clark, op. cit., p. 73.
7. Teleki, "The Omnivorous Chimpanzee," p. 36.
8. Tanner and Zihlman, "Women in Evolution," p. 600.
9. Reid, *A Law of Blood*, p. 68; B. Quain, "The Iroquois," in Mead, op. cit., p. 269.
10. Herbert Basedow, quoted by Meggitt, " 'Marriage Classes' and Demography in Central Australia," in Lee and DeVore (eds.), *Man the Hunter*, p. 176.
11. Silberbauer, "The G'wi Bushman," and Watanabe, "The Ainu," in Bicchieri (ed.), *Hunters and Gatherers Today*, pp. 305, 469–71; Woodburn, "An Introduction to Hadza Ecology," in Lee and DeVore, op. cit., p. 54.
12. E. F. Gombrich, "Zebra Crossings," *The New York Review of Books*, Vol. XVIII, No. 8 (May 4, 1972), p. 35.
13. Jobson and Moore as quoted in Grant, *The Fortunate Slave*, pp. 13, 22.

CHAPTER 10   THE FIRST TEACHERS

1. A. Jolly, *The Evolution of Primate Behavior*, p. 212.
2. Tanner and Zihlman, "Women in Evolution," p. 597.
3. J. D. Clark, *The Prehistory of Africa*, p. 72.
4. Lancaster, *Primate Behavior and the Emergence of Human Culture*, p. 80; Tanner and Zihlman, "Women in Evolution," pp. 585–608.
5. J. D. Clark, op. cit., p. 71.

CHAPTER 11   EARLY STAGES OF EVOLUTION

1. *New York Times*, Nov. 10, 1972.
2. Bordes, *The Old Stone Age*, p. 47.
3. *New York Times*, Dec. 5, 1975.
4. *New York Times*, Oct. 31, 1975.
5. *New York Times*, Apr. 12, 1975.
6. Reported in "Science and the Citizen," *Scientific American*, Vol. 234, No. 2 (Feb. 1976), p. 54.

7. Holloway, "Australopithecine Endocasts"; Holloway, quoted in *New York Times*, Sept. 26, 1975.
8. Leacock, personal communication; see *New York Times*, Sept. 12, 1976, for report on Fore.

CHAPTER 12 SEX AND CONSCIOUSNESS

1. Tiger and Fox, *The Imperial Animal*, p. 76; Sherfey, *The Nature and Evolution of Female Sexuality*, pp. 96–100.
2. Singer, *The Goals of Human Sexuality*, pp. 159–94.
3. Freud, *The Basic Writings of Sigmund Freud*, pp. 612–13.
4. Money and Ehrhardt, "Gender Dimorphic Behavior and Female Sex Hormones," p. 736.
5. Sherfey, op. cit., pp. 141–42.
6. Salzman, "Psychology of the Female: A New Look," in J. B. Miller (ed.), *Psychoanalysis and Women*, pp. 204–6.
7. A. Jolly, *The Evolution of Primate Behavior*, p. 200.
8. Jay, "Primate Field Studies and Human Evolution," in Jay (ed.), *Primates*, pp. 487–503.
9. A. Jolly, op. cit., p. 186.
10. Kolata, "Primate Behavior," pp. 55–58; Pilbeam, "An Idea We Could Live Without," pp. 63–70; Rohrlich-Leavitt, *Peaceable Primates and Gentle People*, pp. 3–4.
11. Eaton, "The Social Order of Japanese Macaques," pp. 97–107; Goodall, *In the Shadow of Man*, pp. 82–88, 182.
12. Tanner and Zihlman, "Women in Evolution," pp. 606–7.
13. Wickler, "Socio-sexual Signals," in Morris (ed.), *Primate Ethology*, pp. 77–78.
14. Jay, "Primate Field Studies and Human Evolution," in Jay, op. cit., p. 492.
15. Pfeiffer, *The Emergence of Man*, p. 160.
16. Goodall, *In the Shadow of Man*, p. 191.
17. Sherfey, op. cit., p. 138.
18. Smith, *The Brain*, p. 320.
19. Ibid., p. 260.
20. Ibid., p. 30.
21. P. Breggin, "The Return of Lobotomy and Psychosurgery," *New York Times*, Feb. 24, 1972; B. Roberts, "Psychosurgery: The 'Final Solution' to the 'Woman Problem'," *The Second Wave*, Vol. 2, no. 1 (1972), pp. 13–15, 43.
22. *New York Times*, Nov. 1, 1975.
23. Morris, *The Naked Ape*, p. 63.

24. C. R. Carpenter, *Naturalistic Behavior of Nonhuman Primates* (University Park: Pennsylvania State University Press, 1964); Wickler, op. cit., pp. 69–147.
25. Goodall, "A Preliminary Report on Expressive Movements," in Jay, op. cit., pp. 313–74.
26. Slocum, "Woman the Gatherer: The Male Bias in Anthropology," in Reiter (ed.), *Toward an Anthropology of Women,* p. 44.
27. Marshall, "Sexual Behavior on Mangaia," in Marshall and Suggs (eds.), *Human Sexual Behavior,* p. 110.
28. Holloway, "Australopithecine Endocasts," p. 194.

CHAPTER 13   THE BRAIN IS THE HUMAN ADAPTATION

1. Chomsky, *Language and Mind,* p. 83.
2. *New York Times,* Sept. 26, 1975.
3. Holloway, "Culture: A Human Domain," p. 404.
4. Holloway, "Australopithecine Endocasts," pp. 196–200, 201–2.
5. E.g., Ralph Solecki, "Neanderthal—Worthy Ancestor," in Fried (ed.), *Explorations in Anthropology,* pp. 182–88.
6. Cf. Ardrey, *The Hunting Hypothesis.*
7. Pfeiffer, *The Emergence of Man,* p. 221.
8. Washburn, foreword, in Lee and DeVore (eds.), *Kalahari Hunter-Gatherers,* p. 4.
9. Holloway, "Australopithecine Endocasts," p. 187.

CHAPTER 14   HUMAN LIKE US

1. Kraus, *The Basis of Human Evolution,* pp. 243–44.
2. Kurtén, *Not from the Apes,* p. 115.
3. W. Straus and A. Cave, "Pathology and Posture of Neanderthal Man," *Quarterly Review of Biology,* Vol. 32 (1957), pp. 348–63.
4. G. Clark and Piggott, *Prehistoric Societies,* p. 50.
5. G. Clark, *The Stone Age Hunters,* p. 42.
6. Goodale, *Tiwi Wives,* pp. 3–4.
7. Dr. E. S. Crelin, cited in Hahn, *On the Side of the Apes,* p. 217; Ralph Solecki, "Neanderthal—Worthy Ancestor," in Fried (ed.), *Explorations in Anthropology,* p. 187.
8. Kahn, personal communication.
9. Goodall, *In the Shadow of Man,* pp. 226–31.
10. Firestone, *The Dialectic of Sex,* pp. 53ff.; G. Rubin, "The

Traffic in Women: Notes on the 'Political Economy' of Sex,"
in Reiter, *Toward an Anthropology of Women*, pp. 185ff.

11. E.g., G. Zilboorg, "Masculine and Feminine: Some Biological
and Cultural Aspects," in J. B. Miller (ed.), *Psychoanalysis
and Women*, pp. 96–131.

12. Campbell, *Primitive Mythology*, p. 315.

13. Pilbeam, *The Ascent of Man*, pp. 74ff.

14. S. R. Binford, "A Structural Comparison of Disposal of the
Dead in the Mousterian and the Upper Paleolithic," pp.
139–48; also personal communication.

15. Brace, *The Stages of Human Evolution*, pp. 90–92.

16. Kurtén, *Not from the Apes*, p. 129; Brace, op. cit., pp. 63–64,
66–67, 89–90; etc.

17. J. Helm, "The Nature of Dogrib Socioterritorial Groups," and
J. Woodburn, "The Stability and Flexibility in Hadza Resi-
dential Groupings," in Lee and DeVore (eds.), *Man the
Hunter*, pp. 118–31, 99–102; Lee, "Male-Female Residence
Arrangements and Political Power in Human Hunter-
Gatherers," pp. 167–74.

18. M. Shostak, "A !Kung Woman's Memories of Childhood," in
Lee and DeVore (eds.), *Kalahari Hunter-Gatherers*, pp.
275–77; Leacock and Lurie (eds.), *North American Indians in
Historical Perspective*.

19. Malinowski, *The Sexual Life of Savages*, pp. 56–57.

20. R. Berndt, "The Walmadjeri and Gugadja," in Bicchieri (ed.),
Hunters and Gatherers Today, pp. 182–88.

21. Campbell, *Primitive Mythology*, pp. 339–41.

22. S. R. Binford and L. R. Binford, "Stone Tools and Human
Behavior," p. 78.

23. Discussion based on S. R. Binford, "A Structural Comparison
of the Disposal of the Dead," "Late Middle Paleolithic Adaptations," and personal conversations.

24. Suggested to me by Ellen Harold in 1972; see also Birdsell,
Human Evolution, pp. 523–25.

25. Brace, *The Stages of Human Evolution*, pp. 3–6.

26. G. Clark and Piggott, *Prehistoric Societies*, pp. 89–104.

CHAPTER 15 PALEOLITHIC ART

1. E.g., G. Clark, *The Stone Age Hunters*; G. Clark and Piggott,
Prehistoric Societies; Pfeiffer, *The Emergence of Man*.

2. J. Hawkes in Hawkes and Woolley, *Prehistory and the Begin-*

nings of Civilization, pp. 283–86; Levy, *Religious Conceptions of the Stone Age*, pp. 3–28; Campbell, *Primitive Mythology*, pp. 286–89, 299–312, 374–83.

3. G. Clark in G. Clark and Piggott, op. cit., pp. 70, 78–79, 84.
4. Pfeiffer, op. cit., pp. 251, 265.
5. Ucko and Rosenfeld, *Paleolithic Cave Art*, p. 135.
6. Kaberry, *Aboriginal Woman*, p. 206.
7. Ucko and Rosenfeld, op. cit., p. 52.
8. G. Clark in Clark and Piggott, op. cit., p. 84.
9. Cited by Ucko and Rosenfeld, op. cit., p. 43.
10. Campbell, op. cit., pp. 303–4.
11. Levy, op. cit., p. 21n.
12. Hawkes in Hawkes and Woolley, op. cit., pp. 276–77.
13. Hays, *The Dangerous Sex*, p. 30; Y. Véquaud, *The Women Painters of Mithila* (London: Thames and Hudson, 1977); Lévi-Strauss, *A World on the Wane*, pp. 155ff., 161ff., 173ff.
14. Ucko and Rosenfeld, op. cit., p. 42.
15. Ibid., p. 52.
16. Marshall, "The !Kung Bushmen of the Kalahari Desert," in Gibbs (ed.), *Peoples of Africa*, p. 275.
17. S. R. Binford, personal communication.
18. Ucko and Rosenfeld, op. cit., p. 39.
19. A. Savelli, personal communication.
20. *New York Times*, Mar. 3, 1977.
21. Ucko and Rosenfeld, op. cit., p. 100.
22. Ibid., pp. 174–95, 229.
23. Marshack, *The Roots of Civilization*, p. 173.
24. Ibid., p. 219.
25. Abramova, "Paleolithic Art in the U.S.S.R."
26. Campbell, op. cit., pp. 327–28.

CHAPTER 16 THE MANA OF BLOOD

1. Levy, *Religious Conceptions of the Stone Age*, p. 68.
2. Kaberry, *Aboriginal Woman*, p. 94.
3. Birket-Smith, *Primitive Man and His Ways*, p. 59.
4. Ibid., p. 51.
5. Hays, *The Dangerous Sex*, p. 13; Weideger, *Menstruation and Menopause*, pp. 105–7; see also B. Bettelheim, *Symbolic Wounds* (New York: Collier Books, 1962).
6. Birket-Smith, op. cit., pp. 16–17.
7. Ibid., p. 48.

8. Hogbin, *The Island of Menstruating Men*, pp. 88ff.

9. Mead, *Male and Female*, pp. 103–4.

10. Schlegel, *Male Dominance and Female Autonomy*, p. 25.

11. Kaberry, op. cit., p. 238–39.

12. Schlegel, op. cit., p. 90.

13. Schlegel, op. cit., p. 93n2.

14. Ibid., p. 93.

15. Kaberry, op. cit., pp. 204, 206, 207.

16. Goodale, *Tiwi Wives*, p. 226.

17. Goodall, *In the Shadow of Man*, p. 237.

18. Kaberry, op. cit., pp. 54–60.

19. Ibid., p. 122.

20. Goodale, op. cit., pp. 228–29.

CHAPTER 17   EARLY HOUSEHOLDS

1. Pfeiffer, *The Emergence of Man*, p. 141.

2. Turnbull, "The Importance of Flux in Two Hunting Societies," in Lee and DeVore (eds.), *Man the Hunter*, p. 135.

3. Lee, "Work Effort, Group Structure and Land-Use in Contemporary Hunter-Gatherers," in Ucko, Tringham, and Dimbleby (eds.), *Man, Settlement, and Urbanism*, pp. 182–83.

4. Ibid., p. 182.

5. Turnbull, discussions in Lee and DeVore, op. cit., p. 156.

6. Lee, "Male-Female Residence Arrangements and Political Power," p. 173; Leacock, "The Changing Family and Lévi-Strauss."

7. Leacock, introduction, in Engels, *Origin of the Family, Private Property and the State*, pp. 36, 38.

8. Ibid., p. 31; see also Leacock, "The Changing Family and Lévi-Strauss," in Leacock and Lurie (eds.), *North American Indians in Historical Perspective*.

9. Kaberry, *Aboriginal Woman*, pp. xi, 277.

10. Ibid., p. xxx.

11. Ibid., p. 144.

12. Ibid., p. 103.

13. Ibid., pp. 152–53.

14. Powdermaker, *Life in Lesu*, pp. 244–45.

15. Ibid., p. 144.

16. Ibid., p. 227.

17. Woodburn, "Ecology, Nomadic Movement and the Composi-

tion of the Local Group Among Hunters and Gatherers," in Ucko, Tringham, and Dimbleby, op. cit., pp. 196–97, 203.

18. Landes, *The Ojibwa Woman*, pp. 91–94.
19. Goodale, *Tiwi Wives*, pp. 335–36.
20. M. Fortes, cited in Bohannon and Middleton (eds.), *Family and Residence*, p. 322.
21. Reported in *Off Our Backs*, June 1973.
22. Leacock, introduction, in Engels, *Origin of the Family, Private Property and the State*, p. 38.
23. Cf. Boserup, *Women's Role in Economic Development*.
24. Fried, *The Evolution of Political Society*, pp. 86–87. Goodale compares her findings in *Tiwi Wives* with those in earlier studies and discusses discrepancies.
25. Schlegel, *Male Dominance and Female Autonomy*, pp. 143–44.
26. Rohrlich-Leavitt, B. Sykes, and E. Weatherford, "Aboriginal Woman: Male and Female Anthropological Perspectives," in Reiter (ed.), *Toward an Anthropology of Women*, pp. 123–24.
27. Anthropologists who write of the freedom with which foragers and some horticulturalists change partners in their early adulthood also note the existence of long-term sharing relationships among older couples.

PART IV

1. Translated by J. A. Wilson, in Pritchard (ed.), *Ancient Near Eastern Texts Relating to the Old Testament*, p. 4.

CHAPTER 18   GATHERING TO FARMING

1. See Harlan, *Crops and Man*; Isaac, *Geography of Domestication*.
2. Mellaart, *Earliest Civilizations of the Near East*, p. 22.
3. Harlan, op. cit., p. 23.
4. Cited in K. Flannery, "Origins and Ecological Effects of Early Domestication in Iran and the Near East," in Ucko and Dimbleby (eds.), *The Domestication and Exploitation of Plants and Animals*, pp. 80–81.
5. Childe, *Progress and Archaeology* (London: Watts and Co./Thinkers Library, 1944), p. 12.
6. Childe, *Man Makes Himself* (New York: New American Library/Mentor Books, 1951), p. 61.
7. Campbell, *Primitive Mythology*, p. 139.

8. Lee, "What Hunters Do for a Living," in Lee and DeVore (eds.), *Man the Hunter*, pp. 30ff. (One of the earlier statements of a situation since extensively discussed; cf. Flannery, op. cit., p. 75.)

9. L. R. Binford, "Post-Pleistocene Adaptations," in S. R. and L. R. Binford (eds.), *New Perspectives in Archeology*, p. 328.

10. Lee, op. cit., p. 33; F. Eggan, discussions in Lee and DeVore, op. cit., p. 95; quoted in Harlan, op. cit., p. 49.

11. Flannery, op. cit., p. 98, n. 71.

12. Site surveys are cited by Hole, "Social Organization in Western Iran 8000–4000 B.C.," in S. R. and L. R. Binford, op. cit., pp. 253–56. See also Adams, *Land Behind Baghdad*; Adams and Nissen, *The Uruk Countryside*; Hole, Flannery, and Neely, *Prehistory and Human Ecology of the Deh Luran Plain*.

CHAPTER 19   THE DISCOVERY OF FATHERHOOD

1. Lévi-Strauss, *The Elementary Structures of Kinship*, p. 14.

2. Though the timetable is reversed, this Marx-Engels thesis still holds up. Cf. Harlan, *Crops and Man*; Isaac, *Geography of Domestication*; Joan Oates, "Prehistoric Settlement Patterns in Mesopotamia," in Ucko, Tringham, and Dimbleby (eds.), *Man, Settlement, and Urbanism*, pp. 299–310; Sacks, "Engels Revisited," in Reiter (ed.), *Toward an Anthropology of Women*, pp. 215–17.

3. Harlan, "The Plants and Animals that Nourish Man"; D. Perkins, "Prehistoric Fauna from Shanidar, Iraq" (*Science*, Vol. 142, pp. 1565–66), the one report with early evidence of domesticated sheep.

4. Flannery, "Origins and Ecological Effects of Early Near Eastern Domestication," in Ucko and Dimbleby (eds.), *The Domestication and Exploitation of Plants and Animals*, p. 87.

5. See note 12, Chapter 18, above.

6. Cf. Kaberry, *Aboriginal Woman*, pp. 42ff.

7. Malinowski, *The Sexual Life of Savages*, pp. 190–91.

8. Tom Buckley, "When Secretariat Stands at Stud," *New York Times Magazine*, Sept. 23, 1975, p. 94.

9. S. R. Binford, personal communication. See also Piggott, *Ancient Europe*, p. 36.

10. E. Isaac, "On the Domestication of Cattle," pp. 195–204; Isaac, *Geography of Domestication*, passim.

11. Lorenz reported rape among enclosed greylag geese. More recently it has been claimed for mallard ducks at the University
of Washington Arboretum, "a seminatural suburban environment." Barash, "Sociobiology of Rape in Mallards," p. 738.

12. Cf. Sacks, "Engels Revisited," in Reiter, op. cit., pp. 211–34.

13. E. Wilson, *To the Finland Station*, p. 223.

14. R. E. Chaplin, "The Use of Non-morphological Criteria," in
Ucko and Dimbleby, op. cit., pp. 240–41.

15. P. Ducos, "Methodology and Results of the Study of the
Earliest Domesticated Animals," in Ucko and Dimbleby, op.
cit., p. 272.

16. M. Eliade, "The Yearning for Paradise in Primitive Tradition," in H. A. Murray (ed.), *Myth and Mythmaking*, p. 65.

17. S. Bokonyi, "Archaeological Problems and Methods of Recog-
nizing Animal Domestication," in Ucko and Dimbleby, op.
cit., pp. 219–27.

18. B. A. L. Cranstone, "Animal Husbandry: The Evidence from
Ethnography," in Ucko and Dimbleby, op. cit., pp. 255, 256,
257, 258.

CHAPTER 20   THE PERNICIOUS ANALOGY

1. Birdsell, "Predictions for the Pleistocene Based on Equilibrium
Systems Among Hunter-Gatherers," in Lee and DeVore
(eds.), *Man the Hunter*, pp. 236–40.

2. Kaberry, *Aboriginal Woman*, p. 242; Marshall, "The !Kung
Bushmen of the Kalahari Desert," in Gibbs (ed.), *Peoples of
Africa*, p. 263.

3. Rich, *Of Woman Born*, pp. 119–20; Mead, *Sex and Temperament*, p. 49; Firth, *We, the Tikopia*, p. 374; Pomeroy,
Goddesses, Whores, Wives, and Slaves, pp. 164–65.

4. Boserup, *Woman's Role in Economic Development*, p. 49.

5. Noonan, *Contraception*, p. 12.

6. *New York Times*, Aug. 2, 1974.

7. Lévi-Strauss, *A World on the Wane*, p. 200.

8. N. Newton, quoted in Rossi, "Maternalism, Sexuality, and the
New Feminism," p. 28.

9. Goodale, *Tiwi Wives*, p. 130.

10. Himes, *Medical History of Contraception*, p. 64.

11. Toni Morrison, *The Bluest Eye* (New York: Holt, Rinehart
and Winston, 1970), p. 31.

12. Quoted in Briffault, *The Mothers*, Vol. 2, pp. 413ff.

13. Ibid., p. 417.
14. Translated in Francoeur, *Utopian Motherhood*, p. 9.
15. Hippocrates, *Diseases of Women* 1, translated by A. E. Hanson in *Signs*, Vol. 1, no. 2 (Winter 1975), p. 582.
16. Francoeur, op. cit., p. 7.
17. Briffault, op. cit., p. 418.
18. Cf. Briffault, op. cit.; Neumann, *The Origins and History of Consciousness*.
19. Leacock, introduction, in Engels, *The Origin of the Family, Private Property, and the State,* pp. 33, 39.
20. Mead, *Male and Female*, p. 189.
21. Goodale, *Tiwi Wives*, pp. 138ff.

CHAPTER 21 ÇATAL HÜYÜK AND HAÇILAR

1. This chapter is based on Angel, "Early Neolithic Skeletons from Çatal Hüyük"; Helbaek, "First Impressions of the Çatal Hüyük Plant Husbandry"; Mellaart, *Çatal Hüyük, Excavations at Hacilar*, "A Neolithic City in Turkey," "Excavations at Çatal Hüyük, 1962," "Excavations at Çatal Hüyük, 1963," "Excavations at Çatal Hüyük, 1965."
2. Angel, op. cit., p. 90.
3. Brothwell, "Human Nutrition," in Ucko and Dimbleby (eds.), *The Domestication and Exploitation of Plants and Animals*, p. 540.
4. Angel, op. cit., p. 94.
5. Ibid., p. 92.
6. Ibid., p. 93.
7. Reported in *New York Times*, December 4, 1975.
8. See Ucko, *Anthropomorphic Figurines*.

CHAPTER 22 SADISM AND MASOCHISM

1. Definitions from Webster's New International Dictionary of the English Language, 2d Ed., unabridged (Springfield, Mass.: G. & C. Merriam, 1959).
2. Reich, *The Invasion of Compulsory Sex-Morality*, pp. 192–93.
3. Erikson, *Gandhi's Truth*, p. 236; Singer, *The Goals of Human Sexuality*, p. 94.
4. Reich, op. cit., p. 36.
5. Ibid., pp. 193–94.
6. Reich, *The Sexual Revolution*, p. 7.
7. Horney, *Feminine Psychology*, pp. 229–31.

8. Ibid., p. 232.

9. Thompson, *On Women*, pp. 22, 141.

10. Ibid., p. 144.

11. Cranstone, "Animal Husbandry: The Evidence from Ethnography," in Ucko and Dimbleby (eds.), *The Domestication and Exploitation of Plants and Animals*, pp. 248–49.

CHAPTER 23   THE POWER OF PROCREATION

1. Russell, *The Conquest of Happiness* (New York: Horace Liveright, 1930), p. 152.

2. Engels, *The Origin of the Family, Private Property, and the State*, p. 58n.

3. Reports in the *New York Times*, Jan. 12, 1976.

4. Rich, *New York Times*, Nov. 20, 1976, Op Ed page.

5. M. A. Mallowan, "The Development of Cities from Al 'Ubaid to the End of Uruk 5," in *Cambridge Ancient History*, Vol. I, Part 1, Ch. VIII, pp. 348ff.

6. Ucko, *Anthropomorphic Figurines*, p. 174.

7. Bokonyi, "Domestication and Exploitation of Animals," in Ucko and Dimbleby (eds.), *The Domestication and Exploitation of Plants and Animals*, p. 222.

8. Schlegel, *Male Dominance and Female Autonomy*, p. 23.

9. Hage, "There's Glory for You," p. 7.

10. Piercy, *Small Changes* (Garden City, N.Y.: Doubleday, 1973), p. 344.

11. Quoted by Quain, "The Iroquois," in Mead (ed.), *Cooperation and Competition Among Primitive Peoples*, p. 241n2.

12. Ibid., pp. 243, 258, 259.

13. Cf. Lionel Tiger, *Men in Groups* (New York: Random House, 1969).

14. Leacock, introduction, in Engels, *The Origin of the Family, Private Property, and the State*, p. 36.

15. Douglas, "Is Matriliny Doomed in Africa?" in Douglas and Kaberry (eds.), *Man in Africa*, pp. 123–37.

CHAPTER 24   WOMEN IN SUMER

1. Extensively documented in Pritchard (ed.), *Ancient Near Eastern Texts Relating to the Old Testament*. Cf. Kramer, *The Sumerians*, and Jacobsen, *The Treasures of Darkness*.

2. Saggs, *The Greatness That Was Babylon*; M. A. Mallowan, "The Development of Cities," in *Cambridge Ancient History*,

Vol. I, Part 1, Ch. VIII, and C. J. Gadd, "The Cities of Babylonia," ibid., Part 2, Ch. XIII.

3. Saggs, *The Greatness That Was Babylon*, p. 37; Fried, *The Evolution of Political Society*, p. 161; Tacitus, *The Agricola and the Germania*, p. 47.

4. Jacobsen, *Toward the Image of Tammuz*, pp. 139ff.

5. Adams, "Patterns of Urbanization in Early Southern Mesopotamia," in Ucko, Tringham, and Dimbleby (eds.), *Man, Settlement and Urbanism*, pp. 735–50; Adams and Nissen, *The Uruk Countryside*.

6. Jacobsen, *Toward the Image of Tammuz*, p. 164.

7. Tacitus, *The Agricola and the Germania*, pp. 72–73; Engels, *The Origin of the Family, Private Property, and the State*, pp. 235–36.

8. Adams, op. cit., p. 743.

9. Gadd, op. cit., pp. 141–42.

10. Kramer, *The Sumerians*, p. 79; Rohrlich-Leavitt, "Women in Transition," p. 40.

11. Fried, "On the Evolution of Social Stratification and the State," p. 716.

12. *Laws of Ur-Nammu*, in Pritchard, op. cit., p. 524.

13. *Laws of Lipit-Ishtar*, in Pritchard, op. cit., p. 160.

14. *Laws of Hammurabi*, in Pritchard, op. cit., p. 172.

15. *Middle Assyrian Laws*, in Pritchard, op. cit., p. 183.

16. Hawkes, *The First Great Civilizations*, pp. 104–7.

17. Gadd, op. cit., p. 129.

18. Gelb, "The Ancient Mesopotamian Ration System."

19. Lancaster, *Primate Behavior and the Emergence of Human Culture*, p. 82.

CHAPTER 25 DECLINE OF THE MOTHER GODDESSES

1. Translated by Kramer, in Pritchard (ed.), *Ancient Near Eastern Texts Relating to the Old Testament*, p. 576.

2. Saggs, *The Greatness That Was Babylon*, pp. 37–39.

3. This development is traced in Jacobsen, *The Treasures of Darkness*, though his interpretation differs from mine.

4. Jacobsen, *Toward the Image of Tammuz*, p. 94.

5. Ibid., pp. 375–76.

6. Colson, "Plateau Tonga," in Schneider and Gough (eds.), *Matrilineal Kinship*, p. 50.

7. Kramer, *The Sacred Marriage Rite*, p. 59.

8. Jacobsen, *Toward the Image of Tammuz*, p. 95.

9. Gadd, "Babylonia c. 2120–1800 B.C.," in *Cambridge Ancient History*, Vol. I, Part 2, Ch. XXII, pp. 605ff.

10. Kramer, op. cit., pp. 64–65.

11. Ibid., p. 63.

12. Kramer, *The Sumerians*, p. 251.

13. Jacobsen, *The Treasures of Darkness*, p. 143.

14. Kramer, *History Begins at Sumer*, pp. 84–88.

15. Kramer, *The Sumerians*, p. 146.

16. Jacobsen, *Toward the Image of Tammuz*, pp. 207, 356.

17. J. Hawkes, *The First Great Civilizations*, p. 115.

18. J. A. Wilson, in Pritchard, op. cit., p. 6.

19. Jacobsen, *Toward the Image of Tammuz*, p. 153.

20. Jacobsen, *The Treasures of Darkness*, p. 136.

21. Loc. cit.

22. Jacobsen, *Toward the Image of Tammuz*, p. 117; *The Treasures of Darkness*, pp. 80, 131–32.

23. Jacobsen, *The Treasures of Darkness*, pp. 113–14.

24. Cf. Frankfort, *Cylinder Seals* (London: Macmillan, 1939); Campbell, *Oriental Mythology*, pp. 41–44.

CHAPTER 26   THE AUTHORITARIAN STATE AND THE FAMILY

1. Jacobsen, *The Treasures of Darkness*, p. 181.

2. Ibid., pp. 116–18, ccp. 180–82.

3. Saggs, *The Greatness That Was Babylon*, pp. 383–84.

4. Campbell, *Occidental Mythology*, pp. 75ff.

5. Jacobsen, *Toward the Image of Tammuz*, p. 9.

6. Campbell, *Occidental Mythology*, pp. 82–83.

7. E. Laughlin, "Equality of Souls, Inequality of Sexes," in Ruether (ed.), *Religion and Sexism*, p. 226.

8. Oppenheim, *Ancient Mesopotamia*, p. 141.

9. Translated by Kramer, in Pritchard (ed.), *Ancient Near Eastern Texts Relating to the Old Testament*, p. 160.

10. Quoted in Saggs, op. cit., p. 442.

11. Quoted in Saggs, op. cit., p. 348.

12. Kramer, *The Sumerians*; Hawkes, *The First Great Civilizations*.

13. Translated by Kramer, in Pritchard, op. cit., p. 547.

CHAPTER 27   WAR AND SEX AND ANIMALS

1. Gadd, "The Cities of Babylonia," in *Cambridge Ancient His-*

tory, Vol. I, Part 2, Ch. XIII, pp. 127, 129ff.; Saggs, *The Greatness That Was Babylon*, pp. 169ff.

2. Gadd, op. cit., pp. 129–30.
3. Ibid., p. 152.
4. Cranstone, "Animal Husbandry: The Evidence from Ethnography," in Ucko and Dimbleby (eds.), *Domestication and Exploitation of Plants and Animals*, pp. 248–62.
5. Oppenheim, *Ancient Mesopotamia*, pp. 82–83.
6. Birket-Smith, *Primitive Man and His Ways*, pp. 66ff.
7. Fried, "On Human Aggression," in C. M. Otten (comp.), *Aggression and Evolution* (Ann Arbor, Mich.: Xerox College Publishing, 1973), p. 360.
8. Birket-Smith, op. cit., p. 68.
9. *New York Times*, Dec. 7, 1974.
10. Nobel, "The Mesopotamian Onager as a Draft Animal," in Ucko and Dimbleby, op. cit., p. 483.
11. Cf. Brothwell, "Dietary Variation and the Biology of Earlier Human Populations," in Ucko and Dimbleby, op. cit., p. 534.
12. Kramer, *The Sumerians*, p. 263.
13. Ibid., p. 263.
14. Pritchard (ed.), *Ancient Near Eastern Texts Relating to the Old Testament*, pp. 164ff.

CHAPTER 28   GIFTS FROM THE GREEKS

1. Quoted in Finley, *The Ancient Economy*, p. 126.
2. Deut. 20:13, 14 (King James).
3. Pomeroy, *Goddesses, Whores, Wives, and Slaves*, pp. 40, 46, 69–70.
4. Ibid., pp. 142–43.
5. Quoted in Rogers, *The Troublesome Helpmate*, p. 24.
6. Pomeroy, op. cit., pp. 49–52.
7. Ibid., p. 230.
8. Quoted in Harold, "More Thinking About Feminism," p. 57.
9. As described in The Oxford Classical Dictionary, 2d ed. (Oxford: Clarendon Press, 1970), p. 352.
10. Pomeroy, op. cit., pp. 222–23.
11. Plato's *Phaedo*, quoted in Finley, op. cit., p. 30.
12. Ibid., p. 29.

CHAPTER 29   THE PURITAN STRAIN

1. Cf. Finley, *The Ancient Economy*, p. 29.

2. E.g., Pritchard (ed.), *Ancient Near Eastern Texts Relating to the Old Testament.*

3. Bird, "Images of Women in the Old Testament," in Ruether (ed.), *Religion and Sexism,* pp. 41ff.

4. Bible quotations in this chapter were originally taken from an old family Bible, the American Standard Version of 1901, based on the 1881–85 revision of the 1611 King James Version. I have retained certain of these quotations, either for euphony or as having influenced our view of sexuality and the female; others I have conformed with the 1952 Revised Standard Version of the Old Testament, indicating in the note which source I am using. Lev. 11:41–44 (RSV).

5. Lev. 15:32–33 (RSV).

6. Lev. 15:3 (ASV).

7. Lev. 15:16 (ASV).

8. Lev. 20:18 (RSV); cf. ASV's "with a woman while she is in her menstrual uncleanness."

9. Lev. 18:20, 23 (RSV).

10. Lev. 12:4 (ASV).

11. Cf. Hogbin, *The Island of Menstruating Men,* wherein menstruation is considered a necessary cleansing, despite the pollution it brings, and where its analogue is artificially induced by men.

12. Deut. 22:25–27 (ASV).

13. Ex. 22:16–17 (ASV).

14. Deut. 22:28–29 (ASV).

15. I Sam. 18:20 (RSV).

16. Hos. 1:2 (ASV).

17. Cf. Patai, *The Hebrew Goddess;* Russell, *A History of Western Philosophy;* et al.

CHAPTER 30   SHALL HE TREAT OUR SISTER AS A HARLOT?

1. See Brownmiller, *Against Our Will,* and Griffin, "Rape," for complete exegeses of this institutionalization.

2. Kramer, *The Sumerians,* pp. 162–63.

3. Brownmiller, op. cit., and Griffin, op. cit., both stress the ways in which historical society encouraged rape.

4. Deut. 21:10ff. (King James).

5. Rougemont, *Love in the Western World,* p. 298; *New York Times,* Oct. 6, 1977.

6. *A Very Curious Girl,* a film written and directed by Nelly

Kaplan. The passage in Deuteronomy reflects earlier Assyrian and Hittite laws.

7. Gen. 34:13–29 (King James).
8. Patai, *The Hebrew Goddess.*
9. Joan Little, reported in the *New York Times,* Jan. 7, 1975.
10. Quoted in Finley, *The Ancient Economy,* p. 136.
11. Bird, "Images of Women in the Old Testament," in Ruether, *Religion and Sexism,* pp. 61, 68; Patai, op. cit., *passim.*
12. Oppenheim, *Ancient Mesopotamia,* p. 140; Kenyon, *Archaeology in the Holy Land,* p. 121.
13. In Books of Ezra and Nehemiah the taking of strange wives is anathematized; on the other hand, the convert Ruth is praised, in the book named for her.
14. Cited in Noonan, *Contraception,* pp. 50ff.
15. Hauptman, "Images of Women in the Talmud," in Ruether, op. cit., p. 198.
16. Noonan, op. cit., pp. 50–55.
17. Noonan, op. cit., pp. 10–11, 50–55; Himes, *Medical History of Contraception,* pp. 72–78; see also Feldman, *Birth Control in Jewish Law.*
18. Himes, op. cit., p. 75.
19. Cf. testimony cited in Hite, *The Hite Report.*
20. Quoted by Parvey, "The Theology and Leadership of Women in the New Testament," in Ruether, op. cit., p. 120.
21. Cited in *Hebraic Literature,* p. 14.
22. Rogers, *The Troublesome Helpmate.*
23. Parvey, "The Theology and Leadership of Women in the New Testament," in Ruether, op. cit., pp. 137, 142–46.
24. Gal. 3:28 (RSV); cf. Pagels, "What Became of God the Mother?"

CHAPTER 31   THE EUROPEAN CONNECTION

1. The Birhors and the Paliyans of India are described in Bicchieri, *Hunters and Gatherers Today,* pp. 371–447, with passing reference to other foragers of Southeast Asia.
2. Piggott, *Ancient Europe,* p. 182.
3. Bridget Allchin, "Hunters or Pastoral Nomads" in Ucko, Tringham, and Dimbleby (eds.), *Man, Settlement and Urbanism,* p. 115–19; Cranstone, "Animal Husbandry: The Evidence from Ethnography," in Ucko and Dimbleby (eds.), *The*

Domestication and Exploitation of Plants and Animals, pp. 260–62.

4. E. D. Phillips, "The Royal Hordes: The Nomad Peoples of the Steppes," in Stuart Piggott (ed.), *The Dawn of Civilization* (New York: Holt, Rinehart and Winston, 1961), pp. 303–28.

5. Herodotus, *The Histories,* p. 286.

6. Ibid., p. 278.

7. Tacitus, *The Agricola and the Germania,* p. 46.

8. Fried has developed this concept in his paper "On the Evolution of Social Stratification and the State," and the subsequent book *The Evolution of Political Society.*

9. Tacitus, op. cit., p. 111; cf. Reid, *A Law of Blood,* for a description of Cherokee society, in which women and men participate in the governing body.

10. Herodotus, op. cit., pp. 306–8.

11. Piggott, *Ancient Europe,* p. 196.

12. Tacitus, op. cit., pp. 140–41.

13. Herodotus, op. cit., pp. 128, 305.

14. Tacitus, op. cit., p. 108; cf. Julius Caesar, Suetonius, and other Roman historical commentaries, as well as modern archaeological findings.

15. Piggott, *Ancient Europe,* pp. 179, 181, 196–99.

16. *New York Times,* July 26, 1976.

17. Campbell, *Occidental Mythology,* pp. 36–40, 303.

18. Tacitus, op. cit., p. 114.

19. E.g., Stewart and Winter, "The Nature and Causes of Female Suppression"; Lewis, *Psychic War in Men and Women,* Ch. 8, 10; Sacks, "Engels Revisited," in Reiter (ed.), *Toward an Anthropology of Women,* pp. 211–34.

20. Rohrlich-Leavitt, "Women in Transition," pp. 10–29.

CHAPTER 32   THE CHRISTIAN CONTRADICTION

1. Apuleius, *The Golden Ass,* p. 264; quoted in Vermaseren, *Cybele and Attis,* p. 10.

2. 1 Tim. 2:11–12 (ASV).

3. Pagels, "When Did God Make Man in His Image?", p. 38.

4. David Herlihy, "Land, Family, and Women in Continental Europe, 701–1200," in Stuard (ed.), *Women in Medieval Society,* pp. 13–42.

5. Catherine Silver, personal communication; Barbara Hanawalt,

"The Female Felon in Fourteenth Century England," in Stuard, op. cit., p. 127.

6. Jo Freeman, quoted in Harold, "More Thinking About Feminism," p. 61.
7. Noonan, *Contraception*, pp. 143–70.
8. Ibid., p. 177.
9. Ibid., pp. 287–88.
10. Ibid., pp. 240ff.
11. Ibid., pp. 76–77.
12. Ibid., p. 194.
13. Ibid., p. 375.
14. Rogers, *The Troublesome Helpmate*, p. 18.
15. Noonan, op. cit., p. 362–63.
16. H. Dillard, "Women in Reconquest Castile," in Stuard, op. cit., p. 73.
17. Ibid., pp. 80–89.
18. Hughes, "Domestic Ideals and Social Behavior," pp. 115–43.
19. Ibid., p. 131; see also Piers, *Infanticide*.
20. Noonan, op. cit., pp. 229–30.
21. Sévigné, *Letters*, p. 150.
22. Ibid., p. 205.
23. D. M. Stenton, *The English Woman in History* (New York: Schocken, 1977), pp. 153–55.

CHAPTER 33   WOMEN HAVE ALWAYS WORKED

1. Quoted by Stone, "The Rise of the Nuclear Family," p. 25.
2. Ibid., p. 29.
3. Quotations in this and an earlier paragraph from Oxford English Dictionary description of church-ales.
4. J. Janeway, quoted in Stone, op. cit., p. 37.
5. Stone, op. cit., pp. 34–57.
6. Sévigné, *Letters*, p. 364.
7. Quoted in Himes, *Medical History of Contraception*, p. 172.
8. Ibid., pp. 21, 22, 118n, 121, 161.
9. Scott and Tilly, "Woman's Work and the Family in Nineteenth Century Europe," pp. 152ff., 161–65.
10. Basch, *Relative Creatures*, pp. 103–40, 195–209; Scott and Tilly, op. cit., pp. 166ff.
11. Quoted in Scott and Tilly, op. cit., p. 170.
12. Basch, op. cit., pp. 198–206.
13. Cf. Walkowitz, "Notes on the History of Victorian Prosti-

tution," pp. 107ff.; Marcus, *The Other Victorians*, pp. 137–38, 141ff.; Scott and Tilly, op. cit., p. 170; Basch, op. cit., pp. 123–40, 195–209.

EPILOGUE AND PROLOGUE

1. R. Revelle, quoted in *New York Times*, Oct. 26, 1975.
2. *New York Times*, May 31, 1976; Mar. 6, July 24, 1977.
3. Ibid., Nov. 29, Dec. 5, 1976; Apr. 3, 1977.
4. Tindale, "The Pitjandjara," in Bicchieri (ed.), *Hunters and Gatherers Today*, p. 261.
5. *New York Times*, Jan. 26, Dec. 6, 1977.
6. L. Tolstoy, "The Kreutzer Sonata," in E. J. Simmons (ed.), *Short Novels* (New York: Modern Library, 1966), p. 147.
7. Hite, *The Hite Report*; see also review of *The Hite Report* by E. Jong, *New York Times Book Review*, Oct. 3, 1976.
8. *New York Times*, Sept. 12, 1977.

Bibliography

Bibliographies can serve two purposes. They buttress the writer's findings, documenting research and telling scholars and professionals what one's sources were and how much study went into the book. The other purpose is to point the way for interested readers so they can find out more about specific areas which have stimulated their curiosity. I have settled for a selected bibliography showing some of my sources and pointing also to books and papers where readers may find more information on material I have been unable to treat in as much detail as I would have liked. Books, articles, and papers I found particularly exciting in the shaping of my theories are starred: sources where the reader will find useful detail and amplification I was unable to include are double-starred. Some sources referred to in the notes are also in the Bibliography, not necessarily because they are good, or even useful, but for the record.

BOOKS AND PAMPHLETS

Adams, R. M., *Land Behind Baghdad*. Chicago: University of Chicago Press, 1965.

——, and H. J. Nissen, *The Uruk Countryside*. Chicago: University of Chicago Press, 1972.

Ardrey, Robert, *The Territorial Imperative*. New York: Atheneum, 1966.

——, *The Hunting Hypothesis*. New York: Atheneum, 1976.

Bachofen, J. J., *Myth, Religion and Mother Right* (1861), trans. Ralph Manheim. Princeton, N.J.: Princeton University Press/ Bollingen Series, 1967.

**Basch, Françoise, *Relative Creatures: Victorian Women in Society and the Novel*. New York: Schocken, 1974.

Beard, Mary R., *Woman as Force in History: A Study in Traditions and Realities*. New York: Collier, 1971.

Beauvoir, Simone de, *The Second Sex*. New York: Bantam, 1961.

Benedict, Ruth, *Patterns of Culture*. Boston: Houghton Mifflin/ Sentry, 1959.

*Bicchieri, M. G. (ed.), *Hunters and Gatherers Today*. New York: Holt, Rinehart and Winston, 1972.

Binford, S. R. and L. R., *New Perspectives in Archeology*. Chicago: Aldine, 1968.

Birdsell, J. B., *Human Evolution*. Chicago: Rand McNally, 1975.

Birket-Smith, Kaj, *The Paths of Culture: A General Ethnology*, trans. Karin Fennow. Madison and Milwaukee: University of Wisconsin Press, 1965.

*———, *Primitive Man and His Ways*. Cleveland, Ohio: World, 1960, 1961.

Bohannon, Paul, *Africa and Africans*. Garden City, N.Y.: Doubleday/Natural History Press, 1964.

———, and John Middleton, *Marriage, Family and Residence*. Garden City, N.Y.: Doubleday/Natural History Press, 1968.

Bordes, François, *The Old Stone Age*. New York: McGraw-Hill/ World University Library, 1970.

Borun, Minda, Molly McLaughlin, Gina Oboler, Norma Perchonock and Lorraine Sexton, *Women's Liberation: An Anthropological View*. Pittsburgh: KNOW, Inc., 1971.

*Boserup, Ester, *The Conditions of Agricultural Growth*. Chicago: Aldine, 1965.

**———, *Woman's Role in Economic Development*. New York: St. Martin's Press, 1970.

Boston Women's Health Book Collective, *Our Bodies, Ourselves*. New York: Simon and Schuster, 1973.

Brace, C. Loring, *The Stages of Human Evolution*. Englewood Cliffs, N.J.: Prentice-Hall, 1967.

Briffault, Robert, *The Mothers*, 3 vols. New York: Macmillan, 1927.

**Brownmiller, Susan, *Against Our Will: Men, Women, and Rape*. New York: Simon and Schuster, 1975.

Buettner-Janusch, John, *Origins of Man*. New York: Wiley, 1966.

Bullough, Vern L., *The Subordinate Sex*. Urbana: University of Illinois Press, 1973.

Calverton, V. F., and S. D. Schmalhousen (eds.), *Sex in Civilization*. New York: Macaulay, 1929.

Cambridge Ancient History, Vol. I, Part 1: *Prolegomena and Prehistory*, and Part 2: *Early History of the Middle East*;

Vol. II, Part 1: *History of the Middle East and the Aegean Region, c. 1800–1380 B.C.* London: Cambridge University Press, 1970, 1971, 1973.

Campbell, Joseph, *The Masks of God*, 4 vols. New York: Viking, 1968, 1970, 1971. Editions used: Vol. I, *Primitive Mythology*, 1970 (Compass); Vol. II, *Oriental Mythology*, 1968; Vol. III, *Occidental Mythology*, 1971 (Compass); Vol. IV, *Creative Mythology*, 1968.

Chance, Michael R. A., and Clifford Jolly, *Social Groups of Monkeys, Apes and Men*. New York: Dutton, 1970.

Chiera, Edward, *They Wrote on Clay: The Babylonian Tablets Speak Today*, ed. George G. Cameron. Chicago: University of Chicago Press/Phoenix, 1938, 1962.

Childe, V. Gordon, *New Light on the Most Ancient East*. New York: Praeger, 1953.

Chomsky, Noam, *Language and Mind*. New York: Harcourt, Brace & World, 1968.

———, *Problems of Knowledge and Freedom*. New York: Random House/Vintage, 1971.

Clark, Grahame, *The Stone Age Hunters*. New York: McGraw-Hill, 1967, 1970.

———, and Stuart Piggott, *Prehistoric Societies*. Harmondsworth, Middlesex, Eng.: Penguin, 1970.

Clark, J. Desmond, *The Prehistory of Africa*. New York: Praeger, 1970.

Clark, W. E. LeGros, *History of the Primates*. Chicago: University of Chicago Press/Phoenix, 1964.

Cohen, Ronald, and John Middleton (eds.), *Comparative Political Systems*. Garden City, N.Y.: Doubleday/Natural History Press, 1967.

Contenau, Georges, *Everyday Life in Babylon and Assyria*. London: Edward Arnold, 1954.

Crawley, Ernest, *The Mystic Rose: A Study of Primitive Marriage and of Primitive Thought in Its Bearing on Marriage*, revised and enlarged by Theodore Besterman. New York: Meridian, 1960.

Darwin, Charles, *The Descent of Man*. New York: Appleton, 1927.

———, *The Origin of Species*. New York: New American Library/Mentor, 1958.

Davis, Elizabeth Gould, *The First Sex*. New York: Putnam, 1971.

Day, Clarence, *This Simian World*. New York: Knopf, 1921.

Delaney, Janice, Mary Jane Lupton, and Emily Toth, *The Curse: A Cultural History of Menstruation*. New York: Dutton, 1976.

DeVore, Irven (ed.), *Primate Behavior: Field Studies of Monkeys and Apes*. New York: Holt, Rinehart and Winston, 1965.

*Diamond, Stanley, *In Search of the Primitive*. New Brunswick, N.J.: Transaction Books, 1974.

Dimbleby, G. W., *Plants and Archeology*. London: John Baker, 1967.

Diner, Helen, *Mothers and Amazons: The First Feminine History of Culture*, ed. and trans. John Philip Lundin. New York: Julian Press, 1965.

Dobzhansky, Theodosius, *Genetics of the Evolutionary Process*. New York: Columbia University Press, 1970.

——, *Mankind Evolving*. New York: Bantam/Matrix, 1970.

*Douglas, Mary, and Phyllis M. Kaberry (eds.), *Man in Africa*. Garden City, N.Y.: Doubleday/Anchor, 1971.

Du Bois, Cora, *The People of Alor*. Cambridge, Mass.: Harvard University Press, 1969.

**Engels, Frederick, *The Origin of the Family, Private Property and the State*, ed. and with an introduction by Eleanor Burke Leacock. New York: International, 1972.

Erikson, Erik H., *Gandhi's Truth: On the Origins of Militant Nonviolence*. New York: Norton, 1969.

Feldman, David M., *Birth Control in Jewish Law*. New York: New York University Press, 1968.

Fernea, Elizabeth Warnock, *Guests of the Sheik: An Ethnography of an Iraqi Village*. Garden City, N.Y.: Doubleday/Anchor, 1969.

Finley, M. I., *The Ancient Economy*. New York: Viking Press, 1973.

——, *Aspects of Antiquity*. New York: Viking Press, 1968.

——, *The Use and Abuse of History*. New York: Viking Press, 1975.

—— (ed.), *Slavery in Classical Antiquity*. Cambridge: Heffer and New York: Barnes and Noble, 1968.

Firestone, Shulamith, *The Dialectic of Sex*. New York: Bantam, 1972.

Firth, Raymond, *Tikopia Ritual and Belief*. Boston: Beacon Press, 1968.

——, *We, the Tikopia: Kinship in Primitive Polynesia*. Boston:

Beacon Press, 1970.

Ford, C. S., and F. A. Beach, *Patterns of Sexual Behavior*. New York: Harper, 1949.

*Forde, C. Daryll, *Habitat, Economy and Society: A Geographical Introduction to Ethnology*. New York: Dutton, 1963.

Fox, Robin, *Kinship and Marriage*. Harmondsworth, Middlesex, Eng.: Penguin/Pelican, 1967.

Francoeur, Robert T., *Utopian Motherhood: New Trends in Human Reproduction*. South Brunswick, N.J., and New York: Barnes/Perpetua, 1973.

Frankfort, Henri, *The Birth of Civilization in the Near East*. Garden City, N.Y.: Doubleday/Anchor, n.d.

*——, Mrs. H. A. Frankfort, John A. Wilson, Thorkild Jacobsen, *Before Philosophy: The Intellectual Adventure of Ancient Man*. Baltimore: Penguin, 1968.

Frazer, Sir James George, *The Golden Bough: A Study in Magic and Religion* (1890). Abr. ed. New York: Macmillan Paperbacks, 1960.

Freud, Sigmund, *The Basic Writings of Sigmund Freud*, trans. and ed. A. A. Brill. New York: Modern Library, 1938.

*Fried, Morton H., *The Evolution of Political Society*. New York: Random House, 1967.

—— (ed.), *Explorations in Anthropology: Readings in Culture, Man, and Nature*. New York: Crowell, 1973.

Friedan, Betty, *The Feminine Mystique*. New York: Dell, 1975.

Gibbs, James L., Jr. (ed.), *Peoples of Africa*. New York: Holt, Rinehart and Winston, 1965.

**Gimbutas, Marija, *The Gods and Goddesses of Old Europe 7000–3500 BC Myths, Legends and Cult Images*. Berkeley and Los Angeles, University of California Press, 1974.

Glob, P. V., *The Bog People: Iron-Age Man Preserved*. New York: Ballantine, 1971.

**Goodale, Jane C., *Tiwi Wives: A Study of the Women of Melville Island, North Australia*. Seattle: University of Washington Press, 1971.

Goodall, Jane (Jane van Lawick-Goodall), *In the Shadow of Man*. Boston: Houghton Mifflin, 1971.

—— (Baroness Jane van Lawick-Goodall), *My Friends the Wild Chimpanzees*. Washington, D.C.: National Geographic Society, 1967.

Gornick, Vivian, and Barbara Moran (eds.), *Woman in Sexist Society*. New York: Basic, 1971.

Grant, Douglas, *The Fortunate Slave: An Illustration of African Slavery in the Early Eighteenth Century*. London: Oxford University Press, 1968.

Graves, Robert, *The Greek Myths*, 2 vols. Baltimore: Penguin, 1955.

——, *The White Goddess: A Historical Grammar of Poetic Myth*. New York: Random House/Vintage, 1960.

Hahn, Emily, *On the Side of the Apes*. New York: Crowell, 1971.

Harding, Thomas G., and Ben J. Wallace (eds.), *Cultures of the Pacific*. New York: Macmillan/Free Press, 1970.

**Harlan, Jack R., *Crops and Man*. Madison, Wis.: American Society of Agronomy, Crop Science Society of America, 1975.

Harrison, Jane Ellen, *Prolegomena to the Study of Greek Religion* (1903). New York: Meridian, 1957.

Hawkes, Jacquetta, *The Dawn of the Gods*. New York: Random House, 1968.

——, *The First Great Civilizations: Life in Mesopotamia, the Indus Valley, and Egypt*. New York: Knopf, 1973.

——, *Man on Earth*. New York: Random House, 1955.

——, and Sir Charles Leonard Woolley, *Prehistory and the Beginnings of Civilization*. New York: Harper & Row, 1962.

Hays, H. R., *The Dangerous Sex: The Myth of Feminine Evil*. New York: Pocket Books, 1972.

Hebraic Literature: Translations from the Talmud, Midrashim and Kabbala, ed. Maurice H. Harris. New York: M. Walter Dunne, 1901.

*Heiser, Charles B., Jr., *Seed to Civilization: The Story of Man's Food*. San Francisco: Freeman, 1970.

Henriques, Fernando, *Stews and Strumpets*. London: MacGibbon and Kee, 1961.

*Herodotus, *The Histories*, trans. Aubrey de Sélincourt, revised edition. Harmondsworth, Middlesex, Eng.: Penguin, 1972.

**Herschberger, Ruth, *Adam's Rib*. New York: Pellegrini & Cudahy, 1948.

*Himes, Norman E., *Medical History of Contraception*. New York: Schocken, 1970.

Hite, Shere, *The Hite Report: A Nationwide Study of Female Sexuality*. New York: Macmillan, 1976.

Hogbin, Ian, *The Island of Menstruating Men: Religion in Wogeo, New Guinea*. Scranton, Pa.: Chandler, 1970.

Hole, Frank, Kent V. Flannery, and James A. Neely, *Prehistory and Human Ecology of the Deh Luran Plain*. Museum of Anthropology, Memoir No. I, University of Michigan. Ann Arbor, Mich., 1969.

Horney, Karen, *Feminine Psychology*, ed. Harold Kelman. New York: Norton, 1973.

——, *The Neurotic Personality of Our Time* (1937). New York: Norton, 1964.

Iglitzin, Lynne B., and Ruth Ross (eds.), *Women in the World: A Comparative Study*. Santa Barbara, Cal.: Clio Press, 1976.

*Isaac, Erich, *Geography of Domestication*. Englewood Cliffs, N.J.: Prentice-Hall, 1971.

*Jacobsen, Thorkild, *Toward the Image of Tammuz and Other Essays on Mesopotamian History and Culture*. Cambridge, Mass.: Harvard University Press, 1970.

*——, *The Treasures of Darkness: A History of Mesopotamian Religion*. New Haven: Yale University Press, 1976.

Jay, Phyllis C. (ed.), *Primates: Studies in Adaptation and Variability*. New York: Holt, Rinehart & Winston, 1968.

Jeanniere, Abel, *Anthropology of Sex*. New York: Harper & Row, 1967.

*Jolly, Alison, *The Evolution of Primate Behavior*. New York: Macmillan, 1972.

Josephus, *The Jewish War*, trans. G. A. Williamson. Baltimore: Penguin, 1960.

*Kaberry, Phyllis M., *Aboriginal Woman: Sacred and Profane*. London: Routledge, 1939.

Kapelrud, Arvid, *The Violent Goddess*. Oslo: Scandinavian University Books, 1969.

Kenyon, Kathleen, *Archaeology in the Holy Land*. New York: Praeger, 1970.

Kramer, Samuel Noah, *History Begins at Sumer* (original title *From the Tablets of Sumer*, issued in 1956). Garden City, N.Y.: Doubleday/Anchor, 1959.

——, *The Sacred Marriage Rite*. Bloomington: Indiana University Press, 1969.

——, *Sumerian Mythology*. New York: Harper & Bros., 1961. (Philadelphia: American Philosophical Society, Memoir No. XXI, 1944).

——, *The Sumerians: Their History, Culture, and Character.* Chicago: University of Chicago Press, 1963.

—— (ed.), *Mythologies of the Ancient World.* Garden City, N.Y.: Doubleday/Anchor, 1961.

Kraus, Bertram S., *The Basis of Human Evolution.* New York: Harper & Row, 1964.

Kropotkin, Peter, *Mutual Aid.* New York: Knopf, 1918.

Kurtén, Björn, *Not from the Apes: A Study of Man's Origins and Evolution.* New York: Random House/Vintage, 1972.

*Lancaster, Jane B., *Primate Behavior and the Emergence of Human Culture.* New York: Holt, Rinehart and Winston, 1975.

Landes, Ruth, *The City of Women.* New York: Macmillan, 1947.

——, *The Ojibwa Woman.* New York: Norton, 1971.

*Leacock, Eleanor Burke, and Nancy Oestreich Lurie (eds.), *North American Indians in Historical Perspective.* New York: Random House, 1971.

**Lee, Richard B., and Irven DeVore (eds.), *Kalahari Hunter-Gatherers: Studies of the !Kung San and Their Neighbors.* Cambridge, Mass.: Harvard University Press, 1976.

**——, *Man the Hunter.* Chicago: Aldine, 1968.

Lévi-Strauss, Claude, *The Elementary Structures of Kinship*, rev. ed. Boston: Beacon, 1969.

——, *The Savage Mind.* Chicago: University of Chicago Press, 1970.

——, *Totemism*, trans. Rodney Needham. Boston: Beacon Press, 1963.

——, *A World on the Wane (Tristes Tropiques)*, trans. John Russell. New York: Criterion, 1961.

Levy, G. Rachel, *Religious Conceptions of the Stone Age and Their Influence upon European Thought* (originally published 1948 under title *Gate of Horn*). New York: Harper Torchbooks, 1963.

*Lewis, Helen Block, *Psychic War in Men and Women.* New York: New York University Press, 1976.

Lorenz, Konrad, *On Aggression.* New York: Bantam/Matrix, 1970.

——, *King Solomon's Ring* (1952). New York: Crowell/Apollo, 1961.

Malinowski, Bronislaw, *Argonauts of the Western Pacific* (1922). New York: Dutton, 1961.

——, *Magic, Science and Religion and Other Essays.* Garden City, N.Y.: Doubleday/Anchor, 1954.

——, *The Sexual Life of Savages in North-Western Melanesia* (1929). New York: Harcourt, Brace & World/Harvest, n.d.

Marcus, Steven, *The Other Victorians: A Study of Sexuality and Pornography in Mid-Nineteenth-Century England.* New York: Basic, 1966.

**Marshack, Alexander, *The Roots of Civilization.* New York: McGraw-Hill, 1972.

Marshall, Donald S., and Robert C. Suggs (eds.), *Human Sexual Behavior: Variations in the Ethnographic Spectrum.* Englewood Cliffs, N.J.: Prentice-Hall/Prism, 1972.

Mead, Margaret, *Coming of Age in Samoa* (1928). New American Library/Mentor, 1949.

——, *Growing Up in New Guinea* (1930). New York: Dell, 1968.

——, *Male and Female.* New York: Morrow, 1949.

**——, *Sex and Temperament in Three Primitive Societies* (1935). New York: Dell/Laurel, 1971.

*—— (ed.), *Cooperation and Competition Among Primitive Peoples.* Boston: Beacon Press, 1961.

Mellaart, James, *Çatal Hüyük.* New York: McGraw-Hill, 1967.

——, *Earliest Civilizations of the Near East.* New York: McGraw-Hill, 1971.

*——, *Excavations at Hacilar*, 2 vols. Edinburgh: Edinburgh University Press, 1970.

**Miller, Casey, and Kate Swift, *Words and Women.* Garden City, N.Y.: Doubleday/Anchor Press, 1976.

**Miller, Jean Baker (ed.), *Psychoanalysis and Women.* Baltimore: Penguin, 1973.

Mitchell, Juliet, *Woman's Estate.* New York: Pantheon, 1971.

Money, John, and Anke A. Ehrhardt, *Man and Woman, Boy and Girl.* Baltimore: Johns Hopkins University Press, 1972.

Montagu, M. F. Ashley (ed.), *Man and Aggression.* New York: Oxford Paperback, 1971.

Morris, Desmond, *The Naked Ape.* New York: McGraw-Hill, 1967.

—— (ed.), *Primate Ethology*, Chicago: Aldine, 1967.

Murray, Henry A. (ed.), *Myth and Mythmaking.* Boston: Beacon Press, 1968.

Myrdal, Jan, *Report from a Chinese Village*, trans. Maurice
    Michael. New York: Random House/Pantheon, 1965.
Neumann, Erich, *The Great Mother: An Analysis of the Arche-
    type*, trans. Ralph Manheim. Princeton: Princeton Univer-
    sity Press/Bollingen Series, 1972.
——, *The Origins and History of Consciousness*, trans. R. F. C.
    Hull. Princeton: Princeton University Press/Bollingen Series,
    1970.
Newman, Lucile F., *Birth Control: An Anthropological View*,
    Addison-Wesley Module 27. Reading, Mass.: Addison-
    Wesley, 1972.
*Noonan, John T., Jr., *Contraception: A History of Its Treatment
    by the Catholic Theologians and Canonists*. Cambridge,
    Mass.: Harvard University Press/Belknap Press, 1965.
Oakley, Kenneth P., *Man the Tool-maker*. Chicago: University of
    Chicago Press/Phoenix, 1964.
*Oppenheim, A. Leo, *Ancient Mesopotamia: Portrait of a Dead
    Civilization*. Chicago: University of Chicago Press, 1972.
Patai, R., *The Hebrew Goddess*. New York: Ktav, 1967.
Pfeiffer, John E., *The Emergence of Man*, rev. and enl. ed. New
    York: Harper & Row, 1972.
Piers, Maria, *Infanticide*. New York: Norton, 1978.
Piggott, Stuart, *Ancient Europe from the Beginnings of Agricul-
    ture to Classical Antiquity*. Chicago: Aldine, 1965.
*Pilbeam, David R., *The Ascent of Man*. New York: Macmillan,
    1972.
——, *The Evolution of Man*. London: Thames and Hudson,
    1970.
Plato, *The Symposium*, trans. Walter Hamilton. Harmondsworth,
    Middlesex, Eng.: Penguin, 1974.
Plutarch, *Lives of the Noble Greeks*, trans. and ed. Edmund
    Fuller. New York: Dell, 1959.
Polanyi, Karl, *Primitive, Archaic and Modern Economies*. New
    York: Doubleday/Anchor, 1968.
——, Conrad M. Arensberg, and Harry W. Pearson, *Trade and
    Market in the Early Empires*. Glencoe, Ill.: Free Press, 1957.
**Pomeroy, Sarah B., *Goddesses, Whores, Wives, and Slaves*. New
    York: Schocken, 1975, 1976.
Powdermaker, Hortense, *Life in Lesu: The Study of a Melanesian
    Society in New Ireland*. New York: Norton, 1971.
Pritchard, James B. (ed.), *Ancient Near Eastern Texts Relating to*

the Old Testament with Supplement. 3rd ed. Princeton: Princeton University Press, 1969.

Raphael, Dana (ed.), *Being Female: Reproduction, Power, and Change.* The Hague: Mouton, 1975 (distr. in U.S. by Aldine, Chicago).

Rawson, Philip, *Primitive Erotic Art.* New York: Putnam, 1973.

Reed, Evelyn, *Problems of Women's Liberation.* New York: Merit, 1969.

*———, *Sexism and Science.* New York: Pathfinder, 1978.

———, *Woman's Evolution from Matriarchal Clan to Patriarchal Family.* New York: Pathfinder, 1975.

Reich, Wilhelm, *The Discovery of the Orgone:* Vol. 1, *The Function of the Orgasm* (1942, 1948), trans. Theodore P. Wolfe. New York: Farrar, Straus and Cudahy/Noonday, 1961.

———, *The Invasion of Compulsory Sex-Morality* (1931, 1934, 1951). New York: Farrar, Straus and Giroux, 1971.

———, *Sex-Pol: Essays, 1929–1934,* ed. Lee Baxandall; trans. Anna Bostock, Tom DuBose, and Lee Baxandall. New York: Random House/Vintage, 1972.

———, *The Sexual Revolution,* 4th ed., rev., trans. Theodore P. Wolfe. New York: Farrar, Straus and Giroux, 1970.

*Reid, John Phillip, *A Law of Blood: The Primitive Law of the Cherokee Nation.* New York: New York University Press, 1970.

**Reiter, Rayna R. (ed.), *Toward an Anthropology of Women.* New York: Monthly Review Press, 1975.

Renfrew, Colin, *Before Civilization.* London: Cape, 1973.

———, *The Emergence of Civilization.* London: Methuen, 1972.

Reynolds, Vernon, *The Apes: The Gorilla, Orang-utan, Chimpanzee, and Gibbon.* New York: Dutton, 1967.

———, *Budongo: An African Forest and Its Chimpanzees.* Garden City, N.Y.: Doubleday/Natural History Press, 1965.

**Rich, Adrienne, *Of Woman Born: Motherhood as Experience and Institution.* New York: Norton, 1976.

Rogers, Katherine M., *The Troublesome Helpmate: A History of Misogyny in Literature.* Seattle: University of Washington Press, 1966.

*Rohrlich-Leavitt, Ruby, *Peaceable Primates and Gentle People: Anthropological Approaches to Women's Studies.* New York: Harper and Row (Harper Studies in Language and Literature), 1975.

—— (ed.), *Women Cross-Culturally: Change and Challenge.*
The Hague: Mouton Publishers, 1975 (distr. in U.S. by
Aldine, Chicago).

Rosaldo, Michelle, and Louise Lamphere (eds.), *Women, Culture
and Society.* Stanford, Cal.: Stanford University Press, 1974.

Rougemont, Denis de, *Love in the Western World.* New York:
Harcourt, Brace, 1940.

Ruether, Rosemary Radford (ed.), *Religion and Sexism: Images
of Woman in the Jewish and Christian Traditions.* New
York: Simon and Schuster, 1974.

Ruitenbeek, Hendrik M. (ed.), *Psychoanalysis and Female Sexuality.* New Haven: College & University Press, 1966.

Russell, Bertrand, *A History of Western Philosophy.* New York:
Simon and Schuster, 1945.

Sabloff, Jeremy A., and C. C. Lamberg-Karlovsky (eds.), *The Rise
and Fall of Civilizations.* Menlo Park, Cal.: Cummings, 1974.

Saggs, H. W. F., *Everyday Life in Babylonia and Assyria.* New
York: Putnam, 1965.

——, *The Greatness That Was Babylon.* London: Sidgwick and
Jackson, 1969.

Schaller, George, *The Mountain Gorilla.* Chicago: University of
Chicago Press, 1963.

*Schlegel, Alice, *Male Dominance and Female Autonomy.* New
Haven: HRAF Press, 1972.

Schneider, David, and Kathleen Gough (eds.), *Matrilineal Kinship.* Berkeley: University of California Press, 1961.

Sévigné, Marie de Rabutin Chantal, Marquise de, *Letters from
Madame la Marquise de Sévigné,* sel. and trans. Violet Ham-
mersley. New York: Harcourt, Brace, 1956.

Sherfey, Mary Jane, *The Nature and Evolution of Female Sexuality.* New York: Random House, 1972.

Shneour, Elie, *The Malnourished Mind.* New York: Doubleday/
Anchor, 1976.

Singer, Irving, *The Goals of Human Sexuality.* New York: Norton,
1973.

*Smith, C. U. M., *The Brain: Toward an Understanding.* New
York: Putnam, 1970.

Southwick, Charles H. (ed.), *Animal Aggression.* New York: Van
Nostrand-Reinhold, 1971.

—— (ed.), *Primate Social Behavior.* Princeton: Van Nostrand,
1963.

Stuard, Susan Mosher (ed.), *Women in Medieval Society*. Philadelphia: University of Pennsylvania Press, 1976.

Suetonius, *The Twelve Caesars*, trans. Robert Graves. Baltimore: Penguin, 1957.

Tacitus, *The Agricola and the Germania*, trans. H. Mattingly, rev. S. A. Handford. Harmondsworth, Middlesex, Eng.: Penguin, 1970.

Thomas, Elizabeth Marshall, *The Harmless People*. New York: Random House/Vintage, 1959, 1972.

Thompson, Clara M., *On Women* (1964), ed. Maurice R. Green. New York: New American Library/Mentor, 1971.

Thomson, George, *Studies in Ancient Greek Society*, Vol. I: *The Prehistoric Aegean*. London: Lawrence and Wishart, 1949.

Tiger, Lionel, and Robin Fox, *The Imperial Animal*. New York: Holt, Rinehart and Winston, 1971.

Tringham, Ruth, *Hunters, Fishers, and Farmers of Eastern Europe, 6000–3000 B.C.*, London: Hutchinson, 1971.

Turnbull, Colin M., *The Forest People: A Study of the Pygmies of the Congo*. New York: Simon and Schuster, 1961.

———, *Man in Africa*. Garden City, N.Y.: Doubleday/Anchor, 1976.

Ucko, Peter J., *Anthropomorphic Figurines of Predynastic Egypt and Neolithic Crete with Comparative Material from the Prehistoric Near East and Mainland Greece*. Royal Anthropological Institute Occasional Paper No. 24. London: Szmidla, 1968.

*———, and G. W. Dimbleby (eds.), *The Domestication and Exploitation of Plants and Animals*. Chicago: Aldine, 1969.

*———, and Andrée Rosenfeld, *Palaeolithic Cave Art*. New York: McGraw-Hill/World University Library, 1967.

*———, Ruth Tringham, and G. W. Dimbleby (eds.), *Man, Settlement and Urbanism*. Cambridge, Mass.: Schenkman, 1972.

Van Lawick-Goodall, Jane, *In the Shadow of Man*. Boston: Houghton Mifflin, 1971.

Vermaseren, Maarten J., *Cybele and Attis: The Myth and the Cult*. London: Thames and Hudson, 1977.

War: The Anthropology of Armed Conflict and Aggression. Supplement Based on Plenary Session in Washington at 66th Annual Meeting of American Anthropological Association. New York: Museum of Natural History, 1967.

Weideger, Paula, *Menstruation and Menopause*. New York: Knopf, 1976.

Wilson, Edmund, *To the Finland Station*. New York: Farrar, Straus and Giroux, 1973.

Wollstonecraft, Mary, *The Rights of Woman* (1792), and John Stuart Mill, *The Subjection of Women* (1869). Everyman's Library, No. 825. New York: Dutton, 1955.

PAPERS AND PERIODICALS

*Abramova, Z. A., "Palaeolithic Art in the U.S.S.R.," *Arctic Anthropology*, Vol. IV (1967), No. 2, pp. 1–179.

*Angel, J. Lawrence, "Early Neolithic Skeletons from Çatal Hüyük: Demography and Pathology," *Anatolian Studies*, Vol. 21 (1971), pp. 80–95.

Barash, David P., "Sociobiology of Rape in Mallards: Responses of the Mated Male," *Science*, Vol. 197 (August 1977), pp. 788–89.

Barker-Benfield, Ben, "The Spermatic Economy: A Nineteenth-Century View of Sexuality," *Feminist Studies*, Vol. 1, No. 1 (Summer 1972), pp. 45–74.

Binford, Sally R., "A Structural Comparison of Disposal of the Dead in the Mousterian and the Upper Paleolithic," *Southwestern Journal of Anthropology*, Vol. 24, No. 2 (Summer 1968), pp. 139–54.

——, "Apes and Original Sin," *Human Behavior*, Vol. 1, No. 6 (November–December 1972), pp. 65–71.

——, "Early Upper Pleistocene Adaptations in the Levant," *American Anthropologist*, Vol. 70, No. 4 (August 1968), pp. 707–17.

——, "Late Middle Paleolithic Adaptations and Their Possible Consequences," *BioScience*, Vol. 20, No. 5 (March 1, 1970), pp. 280–83.

——, "The Significance of Variability: A Minority Report," in *The Origin of Homo Sapiens*. Paris: Unesco (Ecology and Conservation 3), 1971.

——, and Lewis R. Binford, "Stone Tools and Human Behavior," *Scientific American*, Vol. 220, No. 4 (April 1969), pp. 70–72, 77–82.

Birdsall, Nancy, "Women and Population Studies," *Signs*, Vol. I, No. 3, Part I (Spring 1976), pp. 699–712.

*Bryant, Vaughn M., Jr., and Glenna Williams-Dean, "The Coprolites of Man," *Scientific American,* Vol. 232, No. 1 (January 1975), pp. 100–10.

Chevalier-Skolnikoff, Suzanne, "Male-Female, Female-Female, and Male-Male Sexual Behavior in the Stumptail Monkey," *Archives of Sexual Behavior,* Vol. 3, No. 2 (March 1974), pp. 95–117.

Dworkin, Andrea, "Pornography: The New Terrorism," *The Body Politic,* No. 45 (August 1978), pp. 12–14.

El-Wailly, Faisal, and Behnam Abu es-Soof, "The Excavations at Tell Es-Sawwan: First Preliminary Report (1964)," *Sumer,* Vol. 21 (1965), pp. 17–32.

Eaton, G. Gray, "The Social Order of Japanese Macaques," *Scientific American,* Vol. 235, No. 4 (October 1976), pp. 97–107.

Fayerweather, Mary, "Women of the Medieval Towns: The Interaction of Familial and Economic Roles in the Late Middle Ages," unpublished paper.

Fisher, Elizabeth, "Hustlers All: A Speculation," *APHRA,* Vol. 2, No. 2 (Spring 1971), pp. 2–14.

Fossey, Dian, "More Years with Mountain Gorillas," *National Geographic,* Vol. 140, No. 4 (October 1971), pp. 574–85.

Fried, Morton H., "On the Evolution of Social Stratification and the State," in S. Diamond (ed.), *Culture in History* (New York: Columbia University, 1960).

Fritz, Leah, "Is Pornography Gynocidal Propaganda?" *Review of Law and Social Change,* in press.

Gardner, Howard, "The Loss of Language," *Human Nature,* Vol. 1, No. 3 (March 1978), pp. 76–84.

Gelb, I. J., "The Ancient Mesopotamian Ration System," *Journal of Near Eastern Studies,* Vol. 24 (July 1965), pp. 230–43.

*Griffin, Susan, "Rape: The All-American Crime," *Ramparts,* Vol. 10, No. 3 (September 1971), pp. 26–35.

Hage, Dorothy, "There's Glory for You," *APHRA,* Vol. 3, No. 3 (Summer 1972), pp. 2–14.

Harlan, Jack R., "The Plants and Animals That Nourish Man," *Scientific American,* Vol. 235, No. 3 (September 1976), pp. 88–97.

Harold, Ellen, "More Thinking About Feminism," *APHRA,* Vol. 3, No. 3 (Summer 1972), pp. 56–71.

——, "Thinking About Feminism," *APHRA,* Vol. 2, No. 3 (Summer 1971), pp. 14–24.

Harrell-Bond, Barbara, "The Influence of the Family Caseworker on the Structure of the Family: The Sierra Leone Case," *Social Research*, Summer 1977, pp. 193–215.

Helbaek, Hans, "First Impressions of the Çatal Hüyük Plant Husbandry," *Anatolian Studies*, Vol. 14 (1964), pp. 121–23.

Herman, Judith, and Lisa Hirschman, "Father-Daughter Incest," *Signs*, Vol. 2, No. 4 (Summer 1977), pp. 735–56.

Holloway, Ralph L., Jr., "Australopithecine Endocasts, Brain Evolution in the Hominoidae, and a Model of Hominid Evolution," Ch. 8 in *The Functional and Evolutionary Biology of Primates*, ed. Russell Tuttle (Chicago: Aldine, 1972).

———, "Culture: A Human Domain," *Current Anthropology*, Vol. 10, No. 4 (October 1969), pp. 395–412.

———, "New Australopithecine Endocast, SK 1585, from Swartkrans, South Africa," *American Journal of Physical Anthropology*, Vol. 37, No. 2 (September 1972), pp. 173–86.

Hughes, Diane, "Domestic Ideals and Social Behavior: Evidence from Medieval Genoa," in Charles E. Rosenberg (ed.), *The Family in History* (Philadelphia: The University of Pennsylvania Press, Inc., 1975).

Isaac, Erich, "On the Domestication of Cattle," *Science*, Vol. 137 (1962), pp. 195–204.

Isaac, Glynn, "The Food-Sharing Behavior of Protohuman Hominids," *Scientific American*, Vol. 238, No. 4 (April 1978), pp. 90–108.

———, and Garniss Curtis, "Acheulian Tools," *Nature*, Vol. 249, No. 5458 (June 14, 1974), pp. 624–27.

Jolly, Clifford J., "The Seed-Eaters: A New Model of Hominid Differentiation Based on a Baboon Analogy," *Man*, Vol. 5, No. 5 (1970), pp. 3–25.

Jacobsen, Thomas W., "17,000 Years of Greek Prehistory," *Scientific American*, Vol. 234, No. 6 (June 1976), pp. 76–87.

*Kolata, Gina Bari, "Primate Behavior: Sex and the Dominant Male," *Science*, Vol. 191, No. 4222 (January 9, 1976), pp. 55–58.

Lancaster, Jane B., "Carrying and Sharing in Human Evolution," *Human Nature*, Vol. 1, No. 2 (February 1978), pp. 82–89.

Leacock, Eleanor, "The Changing Family and Lévi-Strauss, or Whatever Happened to Fathers?" *Social Research*, Summer 1977, pp. 235–59.

——, "Women, Social Evolution, and Errors, Crude and Subtle." Unpublished paper.

*Lee, Richard Borshay, "Male-Female Residence Arrangements and Political Power in Human Hunter-Gatherers," *Archives of Sexual Behavior*, Vol. III, No. 2 (March 1974), pp. 167–73.

Levine, Seymour, "Sex Differences in the Brain," *Scientific American*, Vol. 214, No. 20 (April 1966), pp. 84–90.

Leakey, Louis, and Robert Ardrey, "Man the Killer, a Dialogue," *Psychology Today*, Vol. 6, No. 4 (1972), pp. 73–85.

Lore, Richard, and Kevin Flannelly, "Rat Societies," *Scientific American*, Vol. 236, No. 5 (May 1977), pp. 106–16.

Mellaart, James, "A Neolithic City in Turkey," *Scientific American*, Vol. 210, No. 27 (April 1964), pp. 94–104.

——, "Excavations at Çatal Hüyük, 1962," *Anatolian Studies*, Vol. 13 (1963), pp. 43–103.

——, "Excavations at Çatal Hüyük, 1963," *Anatolian Studies*, Vol. 14 (1964), pp. 39–119.

——, "Excavations at Çatal Hüyük, 1965," *Anatolian Studies*, Vol. 16 (1966), pp. 165–91.

Money, John, and Anke A. Ehrhardt, "Gender Dimorphic Behavior and Fetal Sex Hormones," *Recent Progress in Hormone Research*, Vol. 28 (1972), pp. 735–63.

Monter, E. William, "Women in the Economy of Calvinist Geneva, 1580–1780." Unpublished paper.

Moss, Cynthia, "A New Image for Hyenas," *Smithsonian*, Vol. 6, No. 4 (June 1975), pp. 38–45. Later published in Cynthia Moss, *Portraits in the Wild: Behavior Studies of East African Mammals* (Boston: Houghton Mifflin Co., 1975).

Newton, Esther, and Paula Webster, "Matriarchy: As Women See It," *APHRA*, Vol. 4, No. 3 (Summer 1973), pp. 6–22.

Newton, Niles, and Charlotte Modahl, "Pregnancy: The Closest Human Relationship," *Human Nature*, Vol. 1, No. 3 (March 1978), pp. 40–49.

——, and Michael Newton, "Psychological Aspects of Lactation," *New England Journal of Medicine*, Vol. 277, No. 22 (November 30, 1967), pp. 1179–86.

*Oates, Joan, "Goddesses of Choga Mami," *The Illustrated London News*, April 19, 1969, pp. 28–30.

*——, "New Perspectives from Iraq," *The Illustrated London News*, April 5, 1969, pp. 30–33.

Pagels, Elaine H., "What Became of God the Mother? Conflict-
    ing Images of God in Early Christianity," *Signs*, Vol. 2, No. 2
    (Winter 1976), pp. 293–303.
———, "When Did Man Make God in His Image? A Case Study
    in Religion and Politics," paper presented at the Scholar and
    the Feminist III Conference, Barnard College Women's
    Center, Columbia University, New York, April 10, 1976.
Pilbeam, David, "An Idea We Could Live Without—The Naked
    Ape," *Discovery*, Vol. 7, No. 2 (Spring 1972), pp. 63–70.
    Later published in D. Hunter and P. Whitten (eds.), *An-
    thropology: Contemporary Perspectives* (Boston: Little,
    Brown, 1975).
———, "Rearranging Our Family Tree," *Human Nature*, Vol. 1,
    No. 6 (June 1978), pp. 38–45.
Rakoff, Vivian M., "The Family: An Ethological Imperative,"
    Social Research, Summer 1977, pp. 206–34.
Revelle, Roger, "The Resources Available for Agriculture," *Sci-
    entific American*, Vol. 235, No. 3 (September 1976), pp.
    164–78.
Rohrlich-Leavitt, Ruby, "Women and the Origin of the State of
    Sumer," revision of paper presented at the annual meeting
    of the American Anthropological Association, Washington,
    D.C., November 1976.
———, "Women in Transition: Crete and Sumer," in Bridenthal
    and Koonz (eds.), *Becoming Visible: Women in European
    History*. Boston: Houghton Mifflin Co., 1977.
Rossi, Alice S., "The Biosocial Side of Parenthood," *Human Na-
    ture*, Vol. 1, No. 6 (June 1978), pp. 72–79.
———, "Maternalism, Sexuality and the New Feminism," in Joseph
    Zubin and John Money (eds.), *Contemporary Sexual Behav-
    ior*. Baltimore: Johns Hopkins University Press, 1973.
Scott, Joan, and Louise Tilly, "Woman's Work and the Family
    in Nineteenth-Century Europe," in Charles E. Rosenberg
    (ed.), *The Family in History*. Philadelphia: The University
    of Pennsylvania Press, Inc., 1975.
Sidel, Victor W., and Ruth Sidel, "The Delivery of Medical Care
    in China," *Scientific American*, Vol. 230, No. 4 (April 1974),
    pp. 19–27.
Silver, Catherine Bodard, "Salon, Foyer, Bureau: Women and the
    Professions in France," *American Journal of Sociology*, Vol.
    78, No. 4 (January 1973).

Simons, Elwyn L., "Ramapithecus," *Scientific American*, Vol. 236, No. 5 (May 1977), pp. 28–35.

Smith, Cyril J., "History and Rape Laws," *International Bar Journal*, May 1975, pp. 33–40.

Snitow, Ann, and Ellen Harold, "Her Daughter Was Her Muse," *APHRA*, Vol. 2, No. 4 (Fall 1971), pp. 40–52.

Stewart, Abigail J., and David G. Winter, "The Nature and Causes of Female Suppression," *Signs*, Vol. 2, No. 3 (Spring 1977), pp. 531–53.

Stone, Lawrence, "The Rise of the Nuclear Family in Early Modern England," in Charles E. Rosenberg (ed.), *The Family in History*. Philadelphia: The University of Pennsylvania Press, Inc., 1975.

**Tanner, Nancy, and Adrienne Zihlman, "Women in Evolution," *Signs*, Vol. 1, No. 3, Part I (Spring 1976), pp. 585–608.

Teleki, Geza, "The Omnivorous Chimpanzee," *Scientific American*, Vol. 228, No. 1 (January 1973), pp. 32–42.

Walkowitz, Judith, "Notes on the History of Victorian Prostitution," *Feminist Studies*, Vol. 1, No. 1 (Summer 1972), pp. 105–14.

Index

About the Author

ELIZABETH FISHER is one of the pioneers of the current feminist movement. In 1969 she founded the first feminist literary magazine, *APHRA*. Her articles have appeared in the *New York Times*, the *Nation*, the New York *Post*, and other newspapers and magazines, and she has written and translated fiction and drama. She was visiting professor at the Women's Writer's Center at Cazenovia College, Cazenovia, N.Y., and has taught Women's Studies at New York University.

Catalog

If you are interested in a list of fine Paperback
books, covering a wide range of subjects
and interests, send your name and address,
requesting your free catalog, to:

McGraw-Hill Paperbacks
1221 Avenue of Americas
New York, N.Y. 10020